D1539974

EDITED BY THE COMMITTEE CELEBRATING
PROFESSOR T. H. TSIEN'S CENTENARY BIRTHDAY

James Cheng, Theodore Foss, Cho-yun Hsu
Leo Ou-fan Lee, Ming-sun Poon, Yuan Zhou
and Tai-loi Ma, Chief Editor

Collected Writings on Chinese Culture

TSUEN-HSUIN TSIEN

The Chinese University Press

Collected Writings on Chinese Culture
   by Tsuen-Hsuin Tsien

© The Chinese University of Hong Kong 2011

Grateful acknowledgment is made to the following presses for permission
to reprint material from previous editions for the sections on *Ancient
Documents and Artifacts* and *Paper, Ink, and Printing*:

from *Biographical Dictionary of Republican China* edited by Howard L. Boorman,
Copyright © 1971 and *Dictionary of Ming Biographies* edited by Carrington Goodrich,
Copyright © 1976. By permission of Columbia University Press.

from *Science & Civilisation in China* by Tsuen-Hsuin Tsien, series edited by Joseph
Needham, Copyright © 1985. By permission of Cambridge University Press.

from *Written on Bamboo and Silk: The Beginnings of Chinese Books & Inscriptions* by
Tsuen-Hsuin Tsien, Copyright © 2004. By permission of Chicago University Press.

ISBN 978-962-996-422-1

The Chinese University Press
The Chinese University of Hong Kong
Sha Tin, N.T., Hong Kong
Fax: +852 2603 6692
     +852 2603 7355
E-mail: cup@cuhk.edu.hk
Web-site: www.chineseupress.com

Printed in Hong Kong

CONTENTS

T. H. TSIEN WITH FAMILY AFTER RECEIVING HIS PH.D. (1957)
(*left to right*): Mary Tsien Dunkel (Daughter), Tsuen-Hsuin Tsien,
Wen-ching Hsu (Wife), Gloria and Ginger Tsien (Daughters)

Edward L. Shaughnessy
Chairman, Department of East Asian Languages and Civilizations
The University of Chicago

Professor Tsuen-Hsuin Tsien formally retired from his positions as professor in the Department of Far Eastern Languages and Civilizations and curator of the Far Eastern Library of the University of Chicago in 1978. In that same year, half a continent away, I entered graduate school. I soon came to know the name and the work of Professor Tsien, first through reading his then already classic *Written on Bamboo and Silk: The Beginnings of Chinese Books and Inscriptions* (Chicago: University of Chicago Press, 1962), and then through using his *China: An Annotated Bibliography of Bibliographies* (Boston: G. K. Hall, 1978). A young man still in my mid-twenties, I never imagined that I would someday meet and come to know Professor Tsien, much less that I would have the honor to contribute this preface to a collection of his English-language articles.

I arrived at the University of Chicago in the autumn of 1985, and almost immediately met Professor Tsien, or T.H., as most of his friends call him. Even though his still more monumental volume, *Paper and Printing,* for Joseph Needham's *Science and Civilisation in China* had just been published, Professor Tsien was still a daily presence at the library, the contents of which he knew like the back of his hand. Not only had he cataloged the core of the collection by himself, he seemed to have read each volume. Questions to him brought forth more information than I could possibly assimilate at the time. But that did not stop me from continuing to seek his help and advice.

As we moved into the 1990s, new responsibilities in the University kept me away from the library more than I would have wished, but I still managed to see T.H. on important occasions. Some of these occasions were happy, such as a memorable dinner party to celebrate his eightieth birthday; others were less so, such as the memorial services for Herrlee

Creel and then, shortly thereafter, for his wife, Lorraine Creel. Professor Creel had been instrumental in bringing T.H. to the University of Chicago shortly after the end of the Second World War; he thereafter served as his teacher, his colleague, and his good friend. It was also when I came to the University that I met Professor Creel for the first time. He too had been retired for a number of years and lived quite a distance from the university, visiting the library only infrequently. Nevertheless, because of our shared interests in the cultural history of ancient China, we made time on each of his visits for long chats. Unlike T.H., Professor Creel was no longer keeping up with new developments in the field; instead, he enjoyed reminiscing about his time in China in the 1930s and his early years at the University. I know that he regarded with great pride his role in establishing the University's East Asian library, and I know too that of all the persons he had been associated with during his sixty years at the University, his fondest feelings and greatest respect were for T. H. Tsien. At the memorial service for Professor Creel, who passed away in 1994, Professor Tsien spoke very movingly about their long relationship; it was clear that the respect these two great scholars felt for each other was completely reciprocal.

Although I was two generations junior to both Professors Tsien and Creel, I was able to benefit to some extent from their relationship, and at least in some small measure to reunite them. Towards the end of his life, Professor Creel donated to the University a number of artifacts that he had collected during his time in China in the 1930s, especially in the course of his visits to Anyang, where the Institute of History and Philology of Academia Sinica was conducting archaeological excavations. Included among these artifacts was a collection of about forty inscribed oracle bones, most of which had only been seen by a select group of students and friends. When these oracle bones arrived at the University's Smart Gallery of Art (now the Smart Museum of Art), I had the privilege, together with my own student and colleague Cai Fangpei, of presenting them to the scholarly world, first in a small catalog published by the Smart Gallery (*Ritual and Reverence: Chinese Art at the University of Chicago* [Chicago: Smart Gallery of Art, 1989]), and then shortly thereafter in a Chinese version in honor of Professor Tsien's eightieth birthday ("Zhijiage daxue suocang Shangdai jiagu" 芝加哥大學所藏商代甲骨 [Shang dynasty oracle bones in the collection of the University of Chicago], in *Zhongguo tushu wenshi lunji* 中國圖書文史論集 [*Collected Essays on Chinese Bibiliography, Literature and History*], ed. Ma Tai-loi 馬泰來 [Taipei: Zhengzhong shuju, 1991], 197–207; [Beijing: Xiandai chubanshe, 1992], 231–243). It is a continuing honor for me to be able to escort visitors to the Smart Museum and to examine these oracle bones with them. For Chinese visitors, I invariably give them a copy of the article published in the volume dedicated to T.H.

Sometime around 1995, Anthony Yu, Carl Darling Buck Professor in the Humanities and then my successor as chair of the Department of East Asian Languages and Civilizations, asked me if I might help Professor Tsien with a revised second edition of his book *Written on Bamboo and Silk*. Of course, I could not say no. Together with another student of mine, Peng Ke, we collated the revisions that Professor Tsien had introduced into the various Chinese-language editions of his book, translated them, and interpolated them at the appropriate points in the English-language text. At Professor Tsien's express request, I then set about writing an Afterword to the book that surveyed Western-language contributions to the study of early Chinese paleography over the forty years since his book had first been published. This second edition was finally published by the University of Chicago Press in 2004.

Even though Professor Tsien was already in his nineties, still he oversaw much of the copyediting, which was a formidable task indeed for such a complicated book. What is more, shortly after its publication, he arranged to have this new edition translated into Chinese and published in China. When I protested that my own Afterword, filled with citations of Western scholarship, was essentially untranslatable, he enlisted a former student of the University of Chicago, Chester Wang 王正義, to undertake the translation, and quickly had it published in both mainland China and also Taiwan ("1960 nian yilai Zhongguo guwenzixue de fazhan" 1960 年以來中國古文字學的發展, *Wenxian* 文獻 2005:4–2006:1; *Zhongguo tushuguan xuehui huibao* 中國圖書館學會會報 Bulletin of the Library Association of China, 74, June 2005, 51–68).

This last feature brings me to the final point that I wish to make about Tsuen-Hsuin Tsien's remarkable career, and the focus of the present volume of his essays. Beginning with his packing of the rare book collection of China's National Library in 1941 and shipping it to the United States for safekeeping during the war with Japan, Professor Tsien has strived ceaselessly to connect China and the West. It goes without saying that his efforts to develop the East Asian collection of the University of Chicago Library into one of the truly great research libraries in the world was undertaken in this spirit. So too was his training of an entire generation of Chinese librarians in the United States, now including the heads of the Harvard-Yenching Library and Princeton University's Gest Library, as well as senior members in the Library of Congress.

This concern for East-West exchange is also to be seen throughout his published scholarship, including much of that included in the present volume, beginning with his 1954 article, "Western Impact on China through Translation" (*Far Eastern Quarterly*, 14.3 [May 1954], through his biographies of many of his colleagues and friends. I think it is also this concern that has driven him not only to translate his Chinese writings into English, but just as important, to translate his English writings into Chinese. As I noted previously, *Written on Bamboo and Silk* has been translated and published (and re-published) throughout the Chinese world (Hong Kong, 1975; Beijing, 1981; Taipei, 1987; Shanghai, 2002), as well as being translated into Japanese in 1980 and Korean in 1991. Likewise, his contribution to *Science and Civilisation in China* has also been translated into Chinese, Japanese, and Korean and is routinely cited in studies there of the history of printing in China. It is thus altogether fitting that he has been honored both in his adopted city of Chicago (being elected as a member of The Chicago Senior Citizen Hall of Fame in 1987, and in 1996 being awarded a Distinguished Alumni Award from the University of Chicago) and also by his alma mater Nanjing University, which in 2007 named its new library of the Advanced Institute of Humanities and Social Sciences for him.

In comparison to such truly prestigious awards, any praise from me for Tsuen-Hsuin Tsien would surely be superfluous. Let me just say that it has been an honor and privilege for me to know and work with T.H. for almost twenty-five years. I look forward to celebrating more birthdays with him, and to further scholarship and awards.

Anthony C. Yu
Carl Darling Buck Distinguished Service
Professor Emeritus In Humanities
The University of Chicago

I knew Dr. T. H. Tsien when he was still active as both the Curator of the East Asian Library at the University of Chicago and concurrently a professor in our Department of East Asian Languages and Civilizations. However, my first acquaintance with him happened some forty years ago.

I began my doctoral work at the University of Chicago in the fall of 1963. My field had nothing to do with Chinese Studies, so I had little cause to visit the East Asian library, which was then housed in a building eventually renovated to serve as the undergraduate Harper Library. Nonetheless, the desire to keep up my reading of classical Chinese poetry, as well as other historical material unrelated to my formal schoolwork, led me to be a frequent visitor to the shelved riches of the library. Lacking, however, any rudimentary training in Western sinological scholarship, I hadn't the faintest clue how to search for a particular volume embedded in the many sets of traditional encyclopedic collectanea or how to distinguish the Harvard-Yenching call numbers from those specified by the Library of Congress. It was at one such moment of confusion that I had the great fortune of catching the attention of a gentle, courteous, and soft-spoken scholar of infinite patience. To my unending barrage of ill-informed or ignorant questions on the content of the collections and the methods of their use, he was never less than clear and meticulous in his explanations. When he discovered that I was enrolled in a different academic unit and unable (at least at that time) to attend his acclaimed course on "Chinese Bibliography"—required of all Ph.D. students in that department—he one day provided me with the entire course pack, including a detailed syllabus and voluminous pages documenting crucial reference works in both Chinese and Japanese histories. This precious gift, the first of numerous tokens of his generosity—which came in the form of books, essays, and occasional pieces in two languages over the next four decades—quickly converted me into a grateful student keen to learn from his ever productive pen.

The miscellaneous publications (originally in two languages) gathered in this volume are eloquent testimony to his amazing and wide-ranging productivity. They include enlightening studies of the distinctive instruments and materials for writing in China's historical culture, the early invention of apparatus and technology for the rapid and large-scale dissemination of written materials, the history, method, and experience of East Asian librarianship in a Western context, and Tsien's personal reminiscences of such enduring masters of sinology as Tung Tso-pin, Herrlee Creel, and Joseph Needham. This volume provides a rich and illuminating context for a greater appreciation of Dr. Tsien's eminent stature and numerous achievements.

Many scholars of China and of the history of science in Europe, America, and Asia have long regarded Tsien as "the Dean of East Asian scholar-librarians in the United States." His first book, *Written on Bamboo and Silk: The Beginnings of Chinese Books and Inscriptions*, published in 1962 by The University of Chicago Press (revised edition 2004), has gone through several printings, and it remains the standard work on this subject four decades after its initial publication. Though unavoidably dated in sections now, his *China: An Annotated Bibliography of Bibliographies* (1978) also remains an indispensable reference work. *Paper and Printing* (1985; revised third printing 1987), the much longer masterpiece complementary to his first book, was commissioned by Joseph Needham for his own monumental series on *Science and Civilisation in China*, a series now comprising some thirty large tomes in seven volumes of multiple parts that Cambridge University Press regards as its most important publication in its three hundred plus year history, second only to the printing of the English Bible in various versions. In this series, Tsien's volume enjoys the unique honor of being the first tome published as a single work without Joseph Needham's byline as author.

Paper and Printing has received the most glowing notice from both experts and the educated public, for it succeeds in detailing for the reader in concise and elegant prose the best current knowledge of these two important inventions that have had an enormous, indeed revolutionary, impact on world civilization. While other volumes in the series—though equally erudite and significant—struggle to break even, Dr. Tsien's volume has become a best seller—a feat tantamount to having one volume of the *Encyclopedia Britannica* attain such status! Not surprisingly, a Chinese translation was published in Shanghai in 1990, another version was released in Taiwan in 1995, and a new version in Guilin in 2004.

Dr. Tsien's contribution to The University of Chicago and to both the United States and China is not confined to his primary areas of scholarship, although his major books and scores of learned articles (written in both English and Chinese) would have been coveted items on any scholar's bibliography. Even prior to his schooling in the U.S., Tsien already had rendered significant service to the larger world. A distinguished librarian in his native China before arriving at Chicago in 1947, he was recruited by Professor Herrlee Creel to come to the Chicago campus to help build the fledgling East Asian collection, after Creel learned of Tsien's pivotal role in the shipping of 30,000 volumes of Chinese rare books from Shanghai to the Library of Congress for safekeeping shortly before Pearl Harbor. Appointed Curator of Chicago's then Far Eastern Library in 1949, Tsien spent the next three decades building it into one of the pre-eminent East Asian collections in the entire U.S.

Teaching in both the Graduate Library School and the Department of East Asian Languages and Civilizations, he helped trained many of today's senior librarians and sinologists in North America and elsewhere, including the current curators of the Harvard-Yenching Library and Princeton's Gest Library. When Chicago alums who had anything to do with East Asian Studies return to campus, the person most frequently sought out again and again is T. H. Tsien. In 1969, he directed the first Summer Institute for Far Eastern Librarianship sponsored by the U.S. Office of Education. In 1966–1968, he was elected chair of the Association for Asian Studies' Committee on East Asian Libraries, and from the same learned society he received its Distinguished Service Award in 1978, the year of his retirement.

Retirement, of course, did not mean the cessation of his scholastic labor and the diffusion of hard-won knowledge. Free from curatorial and teaching chores, Tsien proceeded to garner successive grants from the National Science Foundation, the National Endowment for the Humanities, the East Asian History of Science Trust, and Chicago's Center for East Asian

Studies. These awards both betokened his scholarly stature and recognition and provided the needed assistance to harvest the fruits of his labor, culminating in the Cambridge volume before he moved on to his other writings. Astonishingly, thirty years after his formal retirement, his publications continue to educate this and future generations. In 1994, he was appointed by China to the Advisory Board for the compilation of the Sequel to the *Siku Quanshu*, an honor reserved for only three scholars outside the mainland. Most people would be proud to claim the accomplishments of just one of Dr. Tsien's three careers. As a librarian, educator, and scholar, he is virtually peerless.

Those acquainted with the history of China realize that the subjects receiving Dr. Tsien's sustained and astute investigation are also highly prized artifacts. The persons entrusted with their custodial care have been similarly honored. After all, the legendary Li Er (Laozi) was reputed to have been a Zhou royal archivist, and subsequent individuals firmly linked to history and charged to oversee imperial libraries and collections were often the most learned officials. T. H. Tsien might not have been engaged in lengthy service to any single government of the modern state, but he stands securely in a grand tradition of the erudite dedicated to the knowledge and preservation of the book. I join Professor Edward Shaughnessy and others in wishing him continual good health, and in the hope that we shall celebrate his hundredth birthday and beyond while commemorating anew his lasting gifts to all students of Chinese civilization.

This collection includes selected articles on Chinese documents, paper, ink-making, printing, cultural interchange, libraries, and biographies, which were Professor T. H. Tsien's primary fields of interest over his past sixty years in the United States, primarily at the University of Chicago. A majority of these articles were written in English, with a few originally in Chinese and translated into English for inclusion in this collection. Companion volumes in Chinese, including *Huigu ji* 回顧集 (*Looking Back*) and two other titles will also be published in celebration of the author's centenary birthday.

As Professor Tsien points out in the opening chapter of this volume, the continuity, productivity, and popularity of Chinese documents rank among the major landmarks in world history, and the Chinese characters used some three thousand years ago are still in use today in China and across all of Asia. At the close of the fifteenth century A.D., China had produced more books by title and volume than all other nations combined. Paper and printing, the universal media of communication invented by the Chinese, contributed incalculably to world civilizations long before their adoption in the West centuries later. The introduction of these modes of communication ultimately made possible the production and broad circulation of multiple copies of the modern book.

This volume also details the history of cultural interactions between China and the West, including the study of various languages, translations, book exchanges, and the foundation of libraries in the West that now contain millions of Chinese-language materials. These cultural exchanges have contributed tremendously to the mutual understanding of languages and cultures, which only continues to grow in importance in today's society.

The biographies and personalities of distinguished scholars contribute to a deeper understanding in many fields of interest between China and the West. Included is also a summary of the author's memoir of his time in China as well as many years of academic activities in the United

States. Some background information about the author as appended to this volume will provide a better understanding of the writings in this collection.

We wish to offer many thanks to those who have supported the publication of this volume, especially to Professors Edward Shaughnessy and Anthony Yu for their contribution to the prefaces, to Director Gan Qi of the Chinese University Press, and its former director Dr. Steven Luk, for their help in the publication of this volume, to Mr. Wai-keung Tse, Ms. Yongxi Wu, Ms. Ellen McGill, and Mr. Christopher Mattison for editing this book. Finally, we would like to expresss our appreciation to many others who contributed to the appearance of this book and to Professor Alexander and Mary Tsien Dunkel for editing sections of the articles in this volume.

Editorial Committee
James Cheng, Theodore Foss, Cho-yun Hsu,
Leo Ou-fan Lee, Ming-sun Poon, Yuan Zhou,
and Tai-loi Ma, Chief Editor

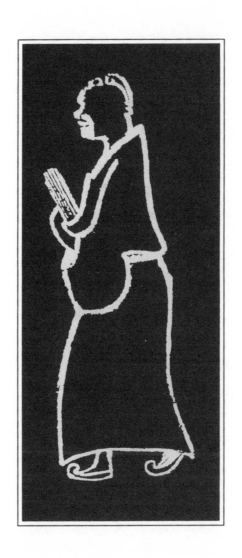

1 THE LEGACY OF EARLY CHINESE RECORDS

The history of Chinese books and other written records should command our attention for countless reasons. It is generally acknowledged that the Chinese are credited with the invention of paper, which remains the most popular material for writing, and for developing block printing, a method of bookmaking still in use today. Paper was invented in China before the Christian era, block printing early in the eighth century, and movable type four hundred years before Gutenberg.[1] Even before these advances, the Chinese made distinctive contributions to the development of human records. Unusual materials, such as bamboo and silk, were used exclusively by the Chinese for writing. Other materials, such as bone, bronze, and stone, also used by the ancient peoples of various civilizations, were inscribed by the Chinese much more extensively and with greater refinement.[2] The use of the brush-pen and lampblack ink as the basic vehicle for committing thoughts to writing can be traced back to remote antiquity in China. The brush has not only influenced the style and arrangement of Chinese writing but also contributed to making calligraphy, along with painting, an outstanding branch of Chinese art. Chinese ink is particularly known for its permanence and brightness, and as Dr. Laufer said: "For centuries it was employed by artists of Europe under the misnomer 'India ink' and is still unrivaled."[3]

From early times, the Chinese made attempts at the mechanical duplication of writing. The use of stamping seals cut in relief for obtaining copies of inscriptions from molds or matrices started in China as early as a millennium before the Christian era. The later use of large wooden seals, containing more than one hundred characters, also indicates efforts to make copies other than writing by hand. As soon as paper and ink were perfected, a technique was developed for taking impressions from stone inscriptions and using paper pounces to multiply designs and figures. The combination of these media and techniques made possible the duplication of writing on a much larger scale and paved the way for the invention of printing.

Continuity, Popularity, and Productivity

Chinese records are also distinguished for their unique continuity as the carrier of an old and ingenious civilization that bound the Chinese people together as the world's largest homogeneous cultural group. The continuous use of Chinese writing as a living medium of communication has maintained Chinese ideas and aspirations and perpetuates the memory of successes and failures in a long tradition that has been carried forward from generation to generation. The origins of numerous aspects of modern life and institutions can be traced back to ancient times. Even books printed by modern techniques sometimes preserve the narrow vertical columns on a printed page that are believed to have been derived from the old system of bamboo and wooden tablets. This unbroken tradition of Chinese civilization is due largely to the uninterrupted use of early literature in fundamental education, and also to the assiduous study of the books preserved from antiquity, which was for many centuries the primary way of achieving prominence in society.

Another characteristic of Chinese writing is its popularity and universality, as it was not used exclusively by the Chinese; many other peoples in East Asia, though they spoke different languages, used Chinese characters as part of their writing systems. Books written in Chinese and produced in China were introduced to many of her immediate neighbors as they first came into contact with the Chinese civilization. In some of these countries, especially Indo-China, Korea, Japan, and Liuqiu (or Okinawa), Chinese was the language of books and writing for a long time. Still constituting part of some of these languages even today, Chinese characters are used by the largest number of people in the world.[4]

The production of books and documents in China was outstanding both in terms of quantity and quality, and Chinese classical literature ranks among the greatest of all written traditions. Moreover, China has an extremely rich and detailed historical record. From 722 B.C. of the Spring and Autumn period until now, the Chinese have maintained their annals almost every year. Also of note is that the number of words in the *Thirteen Classics* is several times that of the *Old Testament*, which is of the same genre and period. In terms of volume, at the close of the fifteenth century A.D. China probably had produced more books than all other nations combined.[5] Even the nascent stages of Chinese books were extremely varied in subject matter, as can be seen from the range of titles in ancient bibliographies.

Because of the increasing varieties of books, an elaborate classification system in seven divisions and a number of sub-divisions was introduced as early as the first century B.C. This marked the first step toward the systematic classification of literature. A modified fourfold scheme constructed in the third century A.D., which later evolved into the categories of classics, philosophy, history, and belles-lettres during the fifth century A.D., has been used by Chinese bibliographers ever since. The four divisions might have influenced Francis Bacon's (1561–1626) triadic system of history, poetry, and philosophy, which is the basis of modern Western classification. His scheme is quite similar to that of the Chinese, except for the category of classics, which is unique to China. Bacon further subdivided philosophy into divinity, nature, and humanity, which are exactly the same as the ancient Chinese classification of knowledge into *tian* 天, *di* 地, and *ren* 人, or Heaven, Earth, and Human. This triadic division, which derived from the *Book of Changes*, had been used for grouping all literary passages in Chinese classified encyclopedias since the sixth century or even earlier. As Bacon was very much interested in Chinese culture and mentioned many Chinese inventions in his works, it is likely that he was influenced by Chinese thought and classification.[6]

The splendid achievements of Chinese civilization were originally written on bamboo and silk and have continuously been transmitted to our times over the millennia. Not only do modern Chinese writings and certain book formats derive from these materials, but the basis of thought and daily life of the Chinese people and others are influenced by the titles produced on bamboo and silk. The continuity, popularity, and productivity of early Chinese records reflect the splendid state of communication, scholarship, and literary history of ancient China, which constitute the unique basis of Chinese civilization.

Types of Ancient Writing Materials

Early Chinese documents and books were recorded on a variety of materials. Some of them were hard and durable, others soft and perishable. The writings preserved on hard surfaces, including bones, shells, metal, stone, jade, pottery, and clay are generally referred to as inscriptions; while those on perishable materials, such as bamboo, wood, silk, and paper are generally considered "books." Although bamboo and wood have hard surfaces, they are perishable.

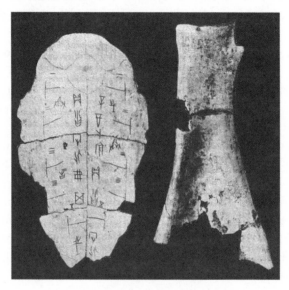

SHELL AND BONE INSCRIPTIONS

Apparently two major groups of materials first were used for different forms of communication. Perishable materials, which were more convenient and sometimes less expensive, were used extensively for government documents, historical records, literary compositions, personal correspondence, and other writings of daily use. Permanent materials, which were hard and durable, were reserved for commemorative or other inscriptions of more lasting value. The former were intended primarily for horizontal communication among contemporaries and the latter for vertical communication across generations. The ancient Chinese seem to have preferred hard and permanent materials not only to communicate with the spirits or their ancestors but also to record messages for their sons and grandsons in posterity.

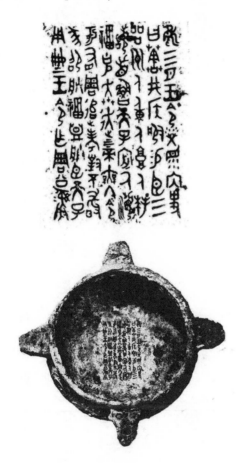

BRONZE INSCRIPTIONS, ELEVENTH CENTURY B.C.

The demarcation between inscription and book, however, cannot be arbitrarily defined as being that between hard and soft or permanent and perishable, for monumental and commemorative records were sometimes kept on soft and perishable materials and literary writings or books were inscribed on hard and durable surfaces.

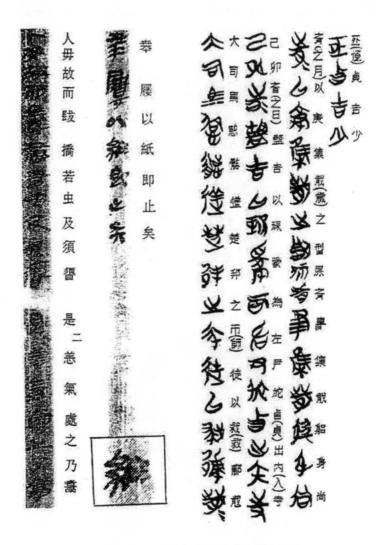

BAMBOO DOCUMENTS, THIRD CENTURY B.C.

Transmission of Ancient Literature

The written records surviving from ancient times consist of two different types of materials: archeological and literary. Archeological materials have generally been unearthed from ruins or found in hidden places, where they were originally made or preserved. The perishable materials have been discovered in various sites in or outside of China, where the weather or underground conditions were suitable for their preservation.

The literary materials, which preserve a greater number of the ancient texts, have generally been transmitted through transcription and mechanical reproduction, although their contents could have been retold from memory by oral tradition if the originals had been destroyed. The processes of transmission include inscribing on permanent materials, transcription by handwriting, reproduction by inked squeezes or various methods of printing, and preservation in quotations from earlier sources. About 150 works, or one-fourth of the total number of books which are known to have existed in the first century A.D., have been transmitted by these processes. Even when the text has been lost, the descriptions of books are sometimes recorded in historical bibliographies.

These texts have been handed down through repeated destructions and restorations, revisions and reproductions, which sometimes results in corruptions and interpolations in the original texts, through intentional changes or unintentional errors. Archeological materials, if genuine, preserve the exact original or earlier manuscript, while literary materials are less accurate but generally include more complete texts than the former.

Dates of Inscriptions

The earliest known writings in China today are records of divination preserved on bones and shells, dating from the thirteenth century B.C. Inscriptions made during this period are also found on bronze, stone, jade, and pottery, but these are generally limited to a few characters. The use of bones and shells for writing lasted for about three centuries, and was gradually discontinued in the late eleventh century B.C. after the fall of the Shang and the early years of the Zhou dynasty.

Bronze inscriptions were then developed as permanent records of political, social, and ceremonial affairs. They remained in use for over a millennium until sometime in the second or third century A.D. Since that time, stone has been extensively used not only for monumental inscriptions but also for the preservation of canonical texts of Confucian, Buddhist, and Daoist literatures. It is the only permanent material that has been used continuously for inscriptions. Clay inscriptions, including those on pottery vessels, bricks, tiles, and sealing clay, flourished from the fifth or fourth century B.C. until the early fourth century A.D. They record primarily the names of persons and places, official titles, and good-luck sayings.

Development of the Chinese Book

Inscriptions cast, engraved, or impressed on permanent materials are hardly to be considered "books." The direct ancestry of the Chinese book begins with strips and tablets made of bamboo or wood. These were bound together by two or more lines of cords and used in a manner similar to a modern paged book. The length of the tablets was determined by the nature of the content, and the width was invariably narrow, bearing most often one vertical column of characters. Although no specimen of such books before the fifth or fourth century B.C. survives today, early literature records that the age of their flourishing was no later than that of bones and bronzes.

Silk was made in China as early as Neolithic times, but no evidence has yet been found that it was used for writing until sometime in the seventh or sixth century B.C. Because bamboo was too bulky and silk too expensive to be wholly practical as a popular medium of communication, *zhi* 紙 (paper), composed of sheets of refuse fibers, was invented before the Christian era and used for writing books and documents in the first or early second century A.D. Since that time paper has been the most convenient and popular material for writing. Paper books appeared first in the form of rolls, then of folded leaves, which gradually evolved into wrapped and stitched volumes.

STONE INSCRIPTIONS OF CONFUCIAN CLASSICS
Engraved on both sides, A.D. 178–85

The old-fashioned materials, however, were not supplanted imme-diately by paper, but replaced gradually after its introduction. Bamboo and wood as writing materials survived for some three centuries, and silk for five hundred years more, in competition with paper after the new material was adopted for writing. Tradition oftentimes favors estab-lished systems and practices that are more familiar to individuals and that sometimes have certain advantages over the new developments.

Methods of Writing and Duplication

Various methods and tools were employed for producing early Chinese records. Certain hard and durable materials, such as bone and stone, were incised or engraved by means of a metal stylus or knife, while the perish-able and soft materials—such as bamboo, wood, silk, and paper—were written on with a brush-pen and lampblack ink. Although the brush was sometimes used to write on hard and solid materials, such inscriptions are occasional and exceptional. Styluses made of bamboo, wood, horn, or metal are said to have been used in ancient times, but the date of their existence is uncertain. Ink was used in China as early as the Neolithic era. Lampblack ink in solid form was mixed with water in an ink slab, and such pigments as turquoise and cinnabar were also used very early. Whether lacquer was ever employed for writing is doubtful, but it could have been an ingredient for inkmaking. The book knife is believed to have been used as an eraser to remove mistakes in writing from the surface of bamboo or wooden tablets and not for inscribing on them.

Handwriting by brush-pen or stylus was, however, not the only method for making Chinese records before the use of printing. Mechanical devices were sometimes employed for their production and duplication. Inscriptions on bronzes were generally cast from molds and those on clay were either made by molds or impressed with a stamp. Seals, which were either cast from metal or cut in stone or jade, were impressed on soft and sticky clay and later on silk and paper to make duplicate inscriptions.

The most interesting technique for the duplication of writing before the invention of block printing was the process of taking inked impressions from stone or other inscriptions by rubbing or squeezing paper over their surfaces. It is known to have been practiced no later than the early part of the sixth century A.D. This method is in principle quite similar to that of printing, although the material on which the engravings are made and the result obtained from the surfaces are sometimes different. This technique, nevertheless, has been considered as the forerunner of the multiple production of early writings and eventually led to the invention of printing.

Styles of Chinese Writing

The surviving records tell the story of the evolution of Chinese writing by which the texts of different periods have been presented. Although the general principles of the Chinese written language have remained unchanged, the variations in number, shape, and position of writing strokes has resulted in the formation of different styles.

These styles are sometimes named for the materials on which the characters are inscribed, such as the "shell-and-bone" and "bronze" scripts, or the forms or functions for which the script was used, such as the "seal," "clerical," "running," "model," and "rapid" styles. Almost all of the styles were introduced before the fourth century A.D., when the "model" style was standardized as the book script, which is still the most commonly used form of writing today.

In general, the writing style has evolved from complex to simple construction, from irregular to stabilized forms, from formal to free lines, and from slow to rapid execution. Its evolution is parallel to the successive changes of materials, tools, and other vehicles of writing and to the increasing frequency of communication, which demands a simpler and quicker medium for the expression of thought in writing.

Growth of Vocabulary

The evolution of Chinese writing is also reflected in the increasing number of characters contained in the vocabulary and the methods used for multiplying them. The bone inscriptions contain about 5,000 characters, and bronze inscriptions are known to have made use of around 3,500. These figures, however, do not represent the entire vocabulary used in Shang and Zhou literature, because it is based merely on the inscriptions so far discovered. These numbers are limited to the recording of certain particular matters on specific occasions. We know more definitely, however, that over 9,000 characters were used around A.D. 100, when the first Chinese etymological dictionary was compiled. This figure doubled at the end of the fifth century, tripled around A.D. 1000, and has increased to more than five times as many characters today. The method used for the multiplication of characters is primarily based on the principles of phonetic combination and borrowing. The bone inscriptions contain mostly pictograms and ideograms but only a few phonograms. This last category increased to a much greater proportion in the later vocabularies.

Order of Chinese Writing

No matter what kind of material was used or what form of records was produced, Chinese characters have always been written and read from top to bottom with the columns following from right to left. Even though the order of reading and writing has recently been changed to horizontal, the vertical arrangement is still preferred by many.

Why are Chinese characters written and read vertically and the lines moved from right to left? This has never been explained in literature or history. It is believed that the predominantly downward strokes of brush writing are the result of the materials and tools of writing, as well as specific physical and psychological factors. The grain of bamboo and wood, and the narrow strips that allow only a single line of characters on the surface, likely influenced such movement. When one holds the narrow tablet straight with a left hand, it is generally easier to write with a soft brush with the right hand in a downward sequence. The tradition of a right-handed scribe, who would lay the strips to his right in order as he finished them, could have resulted in a right-to-left arrangement of the columns. The Chinese ideographs, such as those for the human body, animals, and artificial objects, mostly face upright and to the left.

There is no reason to suppose that the vertical arrangement of writing is inconvenient or inefficient in reading. On the contrary, recent research indicates that "vertical reading was found to be faster than horizontal reading by all investigators," as reported by a UNESCO study.[7] Psychologists have suggested that the manner in which the eyes open, the range of one's vision, and the peculiar structure of Chinese characters are possible reasons why vertical movement is preferable to the Chinese. Undoubtedly, the bamboo strips and soft brush were determinative factors in this tradition.

Social and Intellectual Development

The development of early Chinese documents and books was influenced by various social, political, economic, and intellectual forces. The religious beliefs of the ancient people encouraged the use of writing to communicate with the spirits. Divination, prayer, and sacrifice were all recorded in writing. Nevertheless, they reflect to a large extent the actual life of their times. Frequent communication among the feudal states and within the government structure increased the production of official and diplomatic documents and archives. Since the literate class before the time of Confucius consisted primarily of aristocrats, their leisure and wealth undoubtedly granted them such privileges as reading and writing.

With the social and intellectual changes that took place after the time of Confucius, private writers and book collectors rose rapidly through the popularization of education. The triumph of Confucianism in government in the second century B.C. resulted in the restoration of early literature, after repeated destructions by waves of censorship and war. The centralized Imperial Library was established for the preservation— and library techniques were introduced for the control—of the increasing numbers of books. Since this time, a majority of the texts have been collated and edited by Confucian scholars.

With the spread of Buddhism in the third or fourth century A.D., a large amount of religious literature was imported; for the first time, foreign books were extensively translated, and alien thought introduced to Chinese scholarship and subsequently integrated into Chinese life. Daoist works also flourished alongside the increasing output of Buddhist writings. Although their quantity cannot compare with that of Confucian and Buddhist canons, they represent a major school of Chinese thought and embody material that contains the development of early scientific methods.

The increasing demand for more religious literature stimulated the development of printing. This new application, however, did not alter the nature of the book's format, content, quality, or even the quantity of creative writing. It merely increased the number of copies by facilitating duplication of the writing, so that communication through books became simpler and more widespread. Nevertheless, quantity did not necessarily improve the quality or depth of the material. Even today, mass media have yet to produce a book that can compare with the originality or creativeness in style and language of the *Shiji* 史記 (*Records of the Grand Historian*). This masterpiece was written on hundreds of thousands of bamboo tablets by Sima Qian 司馬遷 (145–186 B.C.) more than a thousand years ago, and it has been followed by every successive dynastic history. One must also take into account the inherent conservatism of human nature, as printing did not become popular until some three hundred years after its introduction in the seventh or early eighth century. Commemorative writings have always been inscribed on permanent materials, and manuscripts continue to be more treasured than printed editions.

Notes

1. Carter, *The Invention of Printing in China and Its Spread Westward*, 2d ed. rev., 41, 212. Tsien, *Paper and Printing*, 3d rev., 38, 149, 201.

2. Diringer, *The Hand-Produced Book*, 23–52, 79–112.

3. Wiborg, *Printing Ink: A History with a Treatise on Modern Methods of Manufacture and Use*, 2.

4. See *Cambridge Factfinders*, 3d ed., 456–457.

5. Cf. Latourette, *The Chinese: Their History and Culture*, 3d ed., ix, 770. He apparently followed what was suggested by Herbert Giles and W. T. Swingle that more pages existed in China as late as 1700 or 1800. My estimate is that more than 50,000 titles or over half a million *juan* (volumes) produced before the late Ming period are known to have been registered in Chinese bibliographies and other sources. Europe produced more books after printing came to be widely used at the end of the fifteenth century.

6. Bacon referred in his works to the principles and application of Chinese characters many times, as well as to Chinese inventions such as paper, porcelain, and gun powder. See Tsien, "A History of Bibliographical Classification in China," 308.

7. Gray, *The Teaching of Reading and Writing: An International Survey*, 50.

2 WRITTEN ON BAMBOO AND SILK

The use of various writing materials in China was intermingled but can generally be divided into three successive stages: (1) bamboo from earliest times and wood around the Christian era to the third or fourth century A.D.; (2) silk from the sixth or fifth century B.C. to the fifth or sixth century A.D.; and (3) paper roughly from the first century to the present time. However, a few examples suggest that bamboo and wood were carried over to a later date and that silk was introduced even earlier. Thus the uses of bamboo and silk overlapped by more than 1,000 years, those of silk and paper by 500 years, and those of bamboo and paper by about 300 years.

Ancient Chinese records engraved on bone and stone, cast on bronze, or impressed on pottery and clay can hardly be considered "books."[1] The direct ancestry of the Chinese book is believed to have been tablets made of bamboo or wood that were connected by a string and used like a modern, paged book. Bamboo and wood were the most popular materials for writing before paper was introduced, and they were most likely used for a longer period of time in Chinese history than any other writing medium. Even after paper was adopted as the primary writing material in the second century A.D., bamboo and wood still were used for some three centuries in competition with the new material. Their popularity was undoubtedly due to tradition, that they were native to China (as papyrus was to Egypt or palm-leaves to India), and that they were both abundant in supply and inexpensive.

The origin of bamboo or wood as a medium for writing in China remains unknown, but the practice is evidently quite ancient. Although no books made of bamboo or wood before the Warring States period (468–221 B.C.) are extant today, ancient inscriptions and literary records indicate that they were probably the earliest form of Chinese books. The character *ce* 冊 (books), which represents a bundle of tablets bound with two lines of cords, was already used in connection with sacrifice in the bone inscriptions of the Shang dynasty.[2] This same character and the related word *dian* 典 (used for documents or archives) depicts a book placed respectfully on a table. These characters are found more frequently in bronze inscriptions of the Zhou dynasty and usually referred to official documents in which literary passages were written by scribes at the order of the king.[3] The system of conveying orders by means of written tablets was handed down to the Han and used as late as the fifth century A.D.[4]

A considerable amount of Zhou literature describes the extensive use of bamboo and wooden tablets for written orders, records of sacrifice, and official documents. In the *Book of Poetry*, for example, a poem of the early Zhou dynasty describes the return from an expedition of soldiers who wished that they could have come back earlier but who were "in awe of the orders in the [bamboo] tablets."[5] The *Book of Documents* records that two years after the conquest of the Shang dynasty, or 1048 B.C., King Wu fell ill. The Duke of Zhou prayed for the king, and "the Grand Historiographer by his order wrote his prayer on tablets."[6] When the Zhou king conquered the Shang, he referred to a purportedly historical precedent, declaring that "the ancestors of the Shang had *ce* 冊 (books) and *dian* 典 (documents) showing how the Shang superseded the Xia dynasty."[7] This statement implies that bamboo and wooden tablets were used as official documents as early as the beginning of the Shang dynasty.

Although bamboo and wood are often mentioned together to refer to ancient writing materials, it is believed that only bamboo was used in the earliest period of Chinese history. Wood was used later than bamboo or only as a substitute for bamboo. Bamboo strips came into existence before wooden tablets, which were used for specific purposes, such as map boards, and probably began to serve as substitutes for bamboo around the turn of the Christian era in the Han dynasty.

Recent archeological discoveries of ancient documents have confirmed the assumption that the old-fashioned materials were only gradually replaced by new ones, and that the later the sites, the fewer the remains of the older materials. In the central part of China, where ancient writings prior to and around the Christian era were found, documents were exclusively made of bamboo, wood, or silk. In Dunhuang, Juyan, and other parts of the northwest, where documents of the period from the first century B.C. to the second century A.D. were discovered,

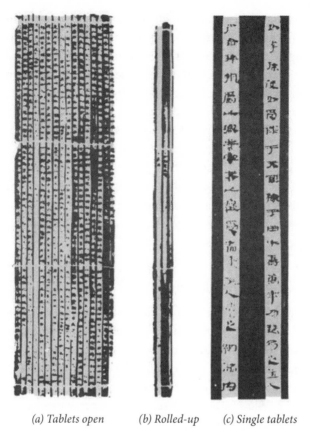

(a) Tablets open   (b) Rolled-up   (c) Single tablets

BAMBOO TABLETS, FIRST CENTURY B.C.

paper is extremely scarce. But at the Loulan site, where documents of the third to fourth century A.D. were found, the number of paper documents amounts to about twenty percent of the number of documents on wood.[8] At the Turfan site, most of the documents from the fifth century A.D. were written on paper.[9] The increased proportion of paper indicates greater accessibility to the new material, especially since such locations as Loulan and Turfan were extremely distant from the locations where paper was being produced in China proper. During the initial stages, when paper was first being introduced for writing, the supply of new materials was probably limited or would have been too expensive for general use.

The records of the dynastic bibliographies also illustrate the changing trends in the use of various kinds of materials. The later the record, the more apparent is the decrease in the number of *pian* 篇, a term for bamboo or wooden tablets, and the increase in *juan* 卷, a term generally used for silk or paper rolls. In the bibliographical section of the *Han shu* 漢書 *History of the Han Dynasty* (206 B.C.–A.D. 24), about three-fourths of the books then extant are listed as *pian* and only one-fourth as *juan*. The ratio, however, was about equal in the Later or Eastern Han (25–220), and rolls were more numerous than tablets in the period of the Three Kingdoms (221–280). In the Jin dynasty (265–419) and after, when paper was extensively employed as a popular writing material, books of bamboo and wooden tablets generally disappeared from the records, evidently supplanted by paper rolls.[10]

Preparation of Bamboo and Wood for Writing

Bamboo is a rapid-growing plant usually found in tropical and subtropical regions. In most parts of China, except the extreme northern regions, bamboo was extensively cultivated. Ancient records mention that bamboo formerly grew as far north as the states of Wei, Jin, Qin, and Qi, which correspond to the modern provinces of Henan, Shanxi, Shaanxi, and Shandong along the Yellow River.[11] It is likely that changes in weather patterns or deforestation drove the plant much farther south, though it is still found in some parts of the region. Because of its lightweight and smooth surface, in comparison with other hard materials, bamboo was chosen as the principal medium for writing before paper was extensively adopted.

Preparing bamboo tablets for writing was more complicated than preparing wood. Writing was not done on the outer cuticle of the bamboo stem but under the surface after the green skin was scraped off, although sometimes the inner side of the stem was also used for writing. The stem was first cut into cylinders of a specific length, which were then split into tablets of a defined width. The raw tablets, however, were not ready for writing until they had been treated and cured, the process of which was called *shaqing* 殺青 (killing the green). After the external covering of green skin was scraped off, the tablets were dried over a fire to prevent quick decaying.

There is juice in fresh bamboo that leads to decay and insect infestation, so it is necessary to first dry the bamboo tablets over a fire.[12]

Old tablets could be used again after the writing on the surface was removed. This process was called *xueyi* 削衣 (removing surfaces) and the removed surface was called *shi* 柿. When mistakes were made, the error could be erased by scraping the surface with a knife. Tablets then could be used again in a process analogous to the production of vellum palimpsests.

Size and Form of Ancient Tablets

Ancient documents on bamboo and wood generally differed in terms of their format and use. Bamboo tablets came in long and narrow strips of various lengths, were written in a single line of characters, and were then bound together with silk cords or leather thongs to form a volume. Although wooden tablets were also made in long and narrow strips, they were sometimes square or rectangular in shape. These wooden boards formed a distinct unit, and they were not usually strung together. According to literary records, wooden tablets were primarily used for official documents, ordinances, short messages, and personal correspondence, whereas literary writings and books of considerable length were generally done on bamboo.

There were standard sizes for bamboo and wooden tablets used in ancient times. The standard varied according to the relative importance of the documents. The size of bamboo tablets for literary writing was fixed at two feet four inches, one foot two inches, and eight inches. The system was to use longer tablets for writing more significant literature and shorter tablets for books of lesser importance. The standard lengths of the wooden tablets used during the Han dynasty varied from five inches to two feet. The great mass of wooden tablets discovered in Dunhuang, Juyan, and elsewhere measured, in most cases, 23 or 24 cm, which is equivalent to about one foot in Han times. The standard size for wooden stationery was fixed at one foot. The modern term *chidu* 尺牘 (one-foot tablet), or "letter," originated from this system. The shortest tablets, five inches long, served as identification tickets for travel through the guarded passes.

The width of the tablets, unlike their length, has not been specifically defined in the literature. There is one note in the dynastic history that the tablets discovered in A.D. 479 were "several tenths of one inch wide."[13] The tablets discovered by Stein and recorded by Chavannes in *Les documents chinois* range from 8 mm to 46 mm wide, with the majority being 10 mm. The inventory list discovered at Juyan was reported to be 13 mm wide for each tablet. Those bamboo tablets recently discovered at Changsha are reported to be 12 mm wide in one group and 6 mm in another. In most cases the width of the tablets was not more than 2 cm, but wooden boards for official documents sometimes had a much wider surface and could accommodate up to five or more lines of characters.

Columns and Styles of Writing

The number of columns and characters in each tablet also varied. Characters were usually written on one side in one column, but in some cases they were written on both sides or in two or more columns. According to Zheng Xuan 鄭玄 (127–200), each tablet for the *Book of Documents* includes thirty characters.[14] It is assumed that tablets for other classics, including the *Spring and Autumn Annals*, which were all two feet four inches long, must have included the same number of characters. The *Zuo zhuan* 左傳, which is the commentary on the *Annals*, had eight characters in each.[15] The *Zuo zhuan* must have been written on tablets of eight inches, as it was less important than the text of the *Annals*. The bibliographical section of the *History of the Han Dynasty* noted that on some of the missing tablets of the *Book of Documents* there were twenty-five characters, and on others, twenty-two.[16]

Among the discoveries from Dunhuang, the beginner's lexicon was written with one paragraph containing sixty-three characters on each tablet. One tablet in the form of a prism was written on three sides with twenty-one characters in each column, and another tablet had two columns of thirty-two and thirty-one characters, respectively. The bamboo tablets discovered at Changsha have from two to twenty-one characters on each tablet of similar length. The long tablets discovered at Wuwei contain as many as sixty to eighty characters on each tablet.[17] From the literary and archeological evidence, it seems correct to assume that no definite number of characters was set in each column of a tablet, but that it depended upon the size of the characters and the length of the tablet.

Different styles of writing were used in the preparation of ancient tablets, depending not only upon the period when they were produced but also upon the relative importance of the documents. Although the *kai* or model style has been popularly used since the late third century, some official appointments of the sixth century were still written in the seal style.[18] The tradition of using conventional forms in writing important documents persisted for a long time. It seems that the six classics of the Han dynasty were all written in the popular clerical style. From the writings on ancient tablets discovered so far, it can be seen that the texts of the Chu state are all in the seal style, while those of the Qin are mainly in the clerical style. Although texts from the Han are in both seal and clerical styles, the clerical style predominates. These differences represent the general development of ancient styles of writing.

In the middle of the first century B.C., a new style of writing was developed, known as *zhang cao* 章草, which is actually a free version of the clerical style derived from the rapid execution of the strokes. This is the first step toward the development of the *xing* 行 (running style) in the second century A.D. and the later *cao* 草 (rapid style) in the fourth century A.D.

Units and Types of Ancient Documents

Ancient book forms vary according to the different materials used, the sizes and shapes of tablets, and the forms of binding. Ancient terms used to signify books, however, were not consistent in their application to different forms. This has resulted in confusion as the terms were sometimes used interchangeably in ancient literature.

There are some distinctions between tablets made of bamboo and those of wood. Generally, those terms referring to tablets of bamboo bear a radical *zhu* 竹 for bamboo, and those of wood a *mu* 木 for wood or *pian* 篇 for a strip. A single tablet made of bamboo was called *jian* 簡; it was generally written with one line of characters and read vertically from top to bottom. When more characters were required, they were written on several tablets bound with cords to form a unit called *ce* 冊. When a document of a certain length formed a literary unit such as a chapter, it was called *pian*. While *ce* referred to a smaller physical unit of a document, *pian* was used as a larger unit which might include several *ce*.

There were other kinds of documents made of bamboo and used for particular purposes. For example, the *fu* 符, which means to trust, is divided into two halves to be fitted in exact agreement. It was made of bamboo of six inches in the Han dynasty. The tally called *qian* 籤 was used as calculating rods for the higher forms of mathematics. When oracle verses were written on the rods, they were used for drawing lots in divination. Another short tablet called *hu* 笏, made of bamboo or other materials, was used as a medium of official communication between subordinates and the emperor. It was slightly tapered at the end with short messages written on it for presentation to the emperor. They were usually held in front of the presenter's chest at the audience with the emperor.

Wooden tablets were used primarily as official documents and not intended for longer writings of literary compositions. A *fang* 方 was a square board carrying a passage of not more than one hundred characters written in five to nine lines, primarily for official registers or other documents. It was similar in use but different in shape or size from a *ban* 版, which was a rectangular board with a smooth and wide polished surface, and from a *die* 牒, a thin and short board, or from a *du* 牘, a narrow board about one foot long primarily for official documents or private correspondence. These different kinds of wooden boards were all prepared from a raw wooden cylinder three feet long. They were generally used separately; but when a number were fastened together, they were called *zha* 札, a term equivalent to *ce* for bamboo tablets. All of these characters and terms are still used in modern vocabulary for different purposes.

Systems of Binding and Sealing

The individual tablet, corresponding to a folio, constituted the basic unit of an ancient book. The complete text of a literary composition was usually composed of a series of tablets, bound together with cords to keep them in proper order. Tablets were bound in different ways. Some were bound after the writing was done, while others were bound before. In

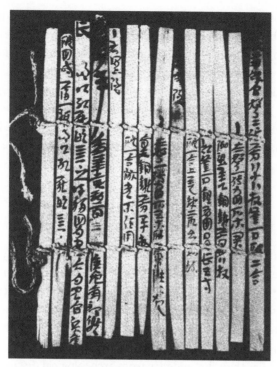

BOUND TABLETS FOUND IN JUYAN, FIRST CENTURY, A.D.

addition, the way the cord was bound varies. One binding technique was the roll form, where tablets were connected with a cord. Another was the accordion form in which the tablets were placed face to face in a *ce*, from which the modern volume is derived. The binding cords were made of silk, hemp, or leather. Traces of cords impressed on ancient tablets indicate that the direction of wrapping might be horizontal, vertical, or in the form of a cross, but was generally horizontal.

For sealing documents, a separate piece of wood called a "sealing board" was bound with cords over the face of the documents. Clay was spread over the cords and impressed with a seal which became an official signature of the sender of the document. The receiver's name and a brief description of the contents of the document were usually written on the outside of the sealing board. The place for the seal impression was a square cut into the sealing board, known as "sealing teeth," to hold the clay.

The sealing board, however, could be applied to only one document. When a number of documents were dispatched, they were sealed in a bag made of cloth or silk in different colors to indicate the methods of delivery—red and white for urgent messages, green for imperial edicts, and black for ordinary documents. A square bag with seamless ends, it opened in the center for the documents. The two ends of the bag were folded to cover the seam in the middle, and then wrapped with cords and impressed with the seal on clay. The methods of dispatch were usually indicated on the board. Messages were passed from one station to another, carried by couriers or, for urgent business, delivered by special messengers on horseback.

Date of Using Silk for Writing

Early literature indicates that the use of silk for writing originated no later than the sixth or seventh century B.C. and continued even after the third or fourth century A.D. The silk documents from Changsha give indisputable evidence for the use of silk as a writing material during the Warring States period. Although no actual silk documents before this time are extant today, records in ancient literature indicate that writing on silk was earlier than the evidence from archeological discoveries. One early literary reference to writing on silk comes from the *Confucian Analects,* that materials made of silk were used for writing as early as the time of Confucius (551–479 B.C.). The philosopher Mo Di 墨翟 (ca. 480–390 B.C.), wrote that the "ancient sage-kings . . . recorded them on bamboo and silk."[19] Han Fei Zi 韓非子 (d. 233 B.C.) also noted that "the ancient kings left principles of government on bamboo and silk."[20] One reference does indicate the name of the ancestor of the seventh century B.C.

Although writing on silk was mentioned in pre-Qin literature, its use seems to have been limited to important and sacred documents. From the time of the Han dynasty, however, it evidently became very common and popular. Not only does the Han bibliography, compiled in the first century A.D., record books written on silk rolls, but much of Han literature frequently mentions this fact. It is evident that silk was employed because it was much easier to carry than tablets. For this reason, silk became a common material for correspondence.

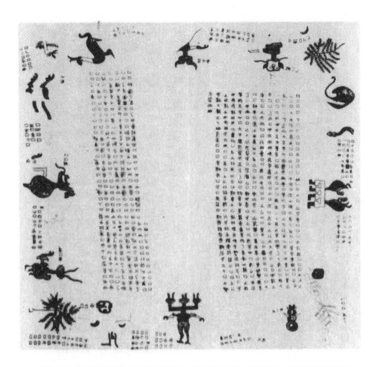

SILK DOCUMENT FROM THE CHU STATE, THIRD CENTURY B.C.

Silk was used as a writing material in the Qin dynasty (265–419) even though paper was already popular. As late as the Tang dynasty (618–906), silk probably was still being used for writing. Although silk is used for painting today, its use for writing evidently decreased after the third or fourth century. When Emperor Wu 武 (r. 420–422) of the Song dynasty came into power, he collected all the documents and books that could be found to be preserved in the Imperial Library; but he could only muster four thousand *juan*, "written on blue paper and decorated with red rollers."[21]

Discoveries of Silk Documents

Remnants of silk materials bearing short and long inscriptions have been discovered in many sites in China as well as in some parts of Central Asia. They provide not only knowledge about the different kinds of materials and methods of weaving but also evidence that actual writings were

Laotze from Mawangdui
WESTERN HAN, FIRST CENTURY B.C.   *Personal letter from Dunhuang*
EASTERN HAN, FIRST CENTURY A.D.

made with brush-pen and ink on silk fabrics. Since the turn of the twentieth century, archeologists have found fragments of silk in Eastern Turkestan along the "Silk Road." In 1901 Sven Hedin found silk fragments of various colors at Loulan, but no writings on any of them. During Aurel Stein's second expedition in 1908, he discovered at Dunhuang two well-preserved letters on silk belonging to the first half of the first century A.D., when paper was not yet popularly used for writing.[22]

These scattered discoveries prove that silk fabrics were used for writing but were not yet in book form. The most important discovery of silk books came from the Former or Western Han (206 B.C.–8 A.D.) tomb at Mawangdui, Changsha in 1973. More than ten books were uncovered, dating back to the second century B.C. or earlier, with more than 130,000 characters written in small seal and clerical style in black ink on silk fabric. This discovery has not only supplied much information that is important for textual criticism but also provided actual examples of books in complete form from ancient China.[23] Besides these silk books, the most interesting finds in the same tomb are three maps on silk, dating from before 168 B.C.

A large number of other objects associated with the Chu culture have been discovered at various sites in central China since the 1930s. The Chu culture was not entirely Han Chinese in origin but came increasingly under Chinese influence and was finally absorbed by the metropolitan northern culture. Among the ancient relics that have come to light from Changsha are numerous silk documents and pictures, which represent the oldest specimens of brush writing and painting on silk extant today.

One silk document on divination discovered between 1936–1937 is a piece of silk, 30 cm wide and 39 cm high, written with brush-pen and black ink in the archaic style and surrounded by a border of strange, colored drawings accompanied by brief writings.[24] The main text of this document consists of two paragraphs, one of eight lines and the other of thirteen, with a total of about 600 remaining characters. Each paragraph is upside down in relation to the other. The pictures in red, blue, and brown surround the text on four sides and are associated with brief writings in some 170 characters. Including characters now missing, this document is said to contain over 900 characters.[25] The readable parts of the text include the names of Chu ancestors, passages in Chu dialects, and terms for the four seasons, five plants, five elements, and five directions, which are identical with those included in other ancient literature and contemporary inscriptions. All evidence indicates that this document belonged to the Chu state of the Warring States period.

Format of Silk Books

Silk is characterized by softness, light weight, durability, and absorbency. As a writing material, it has many advantages over bamboo or wood. Being much lighter and less bulky, silk is easier to keep and carry. Its filaments have great tensile strength. It is insoluble but swells slightly in water and can be preserved longer than bamboo and wood. Having greater power of absorption, the silk surface takes up fluid ink much more easily than that of bamboo, and its whiteness makes a brighter background. All these qualities made it the best material for writing before the use of paper.

According to ancient literature, a great variety of materials was made of silk fiber, and there were more than sixty names for different textiles.[26] Only a few, however, could be used for writing. The names of different silk textiles are usually defined in ancient literature by approximate synonyms, which do not tell specifically what the quality is. In general, such technical details as fineness, coarseness, thinness, closeness of weave, and whiteness of the textile have been the basis for the names of the plain fabric.

Silk books must have been in the form of rolls, as indicated by the character *juan* 卷 used in ancient literature. However, the silk documents discovered in the Chu tomb at Changsha were folded eight times and kept in a lacquer box. The silk books of Mawangdui were found in two forms: those written on a whole piece of silk were folded in rectangles, while those written on half pieces were rolled on a bamboo or wooden stick. All the books were stored in a lacquer box.[27]

The length of a silk scroll depended upon the length of the text, and the silk could be cut accordingly. The standard length of plain silk was forty feet, so the book could be extended up to that length without a seam. A silk book of the second century A.D. is described as having been written on "white silk ruled with red columns and wrapped in blue silk with the title written in red."[28] Silk scrolls could have been preserved in wrappers or covers to avoid damage in handling or transporting. Other particulars of a silk roll can be observed from a paper roll. Since the term *zhi* 紙 for paper and *juan* 卷 for roll are both inherited from silk or silk rolls, we can assume that the systems of both silk and paper rolls were analogous.

Specialized Uses of Silk Documents

The earliest known literary references to the use of silk as a writing material date from about the sixth century B.C. These references testify not only to the use of silk for writing but also frequently describe the peculiar nature of its use. The term *zhu bo* 竹帛 for bamboo and silk to indicate a written document has been in wide use only since the Warring States period. Since silk had a wider surface and was comparatively expensive, it was used only when bamboo and wood did not suit the specific purposes.

Silk was usually employed as a material for final editions of books, while bamboo tablets were sometimes used for drafts. Although bamboo was also used for final editions, it was especially useful for preliminary texts because changes in writing could be made on it easily. It was also less costly than the absorbent silk. This applied, however, only to certain categories of books which were considered important enough to be carefully collated and copied for permanent preservation.

Silk was particularly used for illustrations, appended to books of bamboo tablets. As recorded in the Han bibliography, 790 *pian* of military works were written on tablets, but 43 *juan* were on silk for appended illustrations.[29] Ancient maps generally were drawn on silk because its surface was much wider than the wooden boards that had been used. Among the famous ancient maps, a general topographical drawing of the Empire in eleven rolls has been considered by a Tang writer as the rarest item among the ancient collections of famous paintings.[30] The discovery in Mawangdui of the three silk maps of the Warring States period folded in a lacquer box has provided actual examples of ancient cartography on silk fabric.

Silk appears to have been used for inscriptions for sacrifice to spirits and ancestor worship. In the earlier period, silk also was used primarily by kings and royal houses to record their sayings for posterity. Like those sage-kings mentioned by ancient philosophers, they employed silk along with bamboo for permanent records. Silk was also used for permanent records of exceptional honors awarded to great statesmen and brilliant heroes of military achievements in the government. Such commemorative inscriptions were generally engraved on metal vessels or stone tablets but sometimes were also written on bamboo and silk.

Notes

1.   The word "book" has been variously defined. *Webster's* says it is "a collection of tablets, as of wood, ivory, or paper, strung or bound together." *Encyclopedia Britannica* emphasizes its literary aspect: "book is the name for any literary production of some bulk." *Columbia Encyclopedia* comes to the conclusion that "the inscription cannot be considered a book even under the widest definition."
2.   Sun Haibo, *Jiaguwen bian* 2/27–28, 5/3; Jin Xiangheng, *Xu jiaguwen bian*, 2/34–35; Creel, *Studies in Early Chinese Culture*, 38.

3. Hiraoka Takeo, "Chikusatsu to Shina kodai no kiroku." Tōhō gakuho. XIII (1943), 171–73.

4. *Sui Shu*, 9/3b, 12a.

5. Legge, *She King*, 264.

6. Legge, *Shoo King*, 353.

7. Legge, *She King*, 264.

8. Stein, *Serindia*, 2:674.

9. Huang Wenbi, *Tulufan kaogu ji*, 2.

10. Cf. dynastic bibliographies in *Ershiwu shi, bubian*.

11. Cf. Legge, *She King*, 91, 195, 303, etc.; *Ch'un ts'ew with Tso Chuen*, 281.

12. Ying Shao, *Fengsu tongyi*, 88.

13. Xiao Zixian, *Nan Qi shu*, 21/2a.

14. *Yili zhushu*, 24/3b.

15. Ibid.

16. Ban Gu, *Han shu*, 30/5a.

17. *Kaogu*, 1960: 5, 11.

18. *Sui shu*, 9/3a.

19. Mei Yi-pao, *Motse*, 167.

20. *Hanfeizi*, 8/6b.

21. Wei Zheng, *Sui shu*, 32/4b.

22. Stein, *Serindia*, 2:726–763; Chavannes, *Les documents chinois*, nos. 398, 398A, 503.

23. For discovery of silk books, see *Wenwu*, no. 7 (1974): 39–48, 40–45; no. 2 (1975): 35–48; no. 3 (1984): 1–8; for textual problems of individual books, see "Chan Kuo Ts'e," "I ching," "Lao tzu tao te ching," etc. in *Early Chinese Texts*. For silk maps, see *Mawangdui Han mu boshu gu ditu*; cf. old maps on wood, p. 104 and on paper, p. 147 in this book.

24. The document was obtained by Cai Jixiang, who reproduced the text and drawings in color by hand copying, publishing it about 1946. It was later reproduced by Jiang Xuanyi, Rao Zongyi, Chen Pan, Dong Zuobin, and Noel Barnard. The various versions have slight differences. Other discussions include research by An Zhimin and Chen Gongrou, Shang Chengzuo, Rao Zongyi, Yan Yiping, Zeng Xiantong, Shang Zhitan, and Li Xueqin.

25. Barnard, *The Ch'u Silk Manuscript—Translation and Commentary*, 4.

26. Wang Shiduo, "Shi bo," 1/23a–25b.

27. Shang Chengzuo, *Changsha guwu wenjianji*, 46a; Kaogu, no. 1 (1975): 47–61.

28. Fan Ye, *Hou Han shu*, 60b/24a.

29. Ban Gu, *Han shu*, 30/41a.

30. The map "Hetu kuodixiang tu" is recorded in Zhang Yanyuan's, *Lidai minghua ji*, 3/27a-32a.

Among the few surviving pre-Qin documents, the *Zhanguo ce* 戰國策, or *Strategies of Warring States,* is perhaps the only work which deals with all the states of the Zhanguo period. It includes stories of warfare and political manipulation and concerns the personalities of that period, which marked a major transition from ancient times to a new era in Chinese history. As with the term *Chunqiu* 春秋, so with the term *Zhanguo*; the title of a text came to be used to denote an historical period (variously taken to refer to 481 or 403 to 221 B.C.). The unique style and content of the book set a precedent by explaining the strategies of power politics through diplomatic argumentation. The clever methods of persuasion with their vivid characterizations, wit, and humor impart a literary merit that is considerably more significant than its historical value.

ZHANGUO CE   LIU XIANG

The *Zhanguo ce* is concerned with the use of intrigue to secure advantage in a manner that runs contrary to the principles of Confucian morality. Because of its subject matter, the book has not received the same degree of respect as other ancient Chinese editions. Almost all Confucian scholars, including Liu Xiang 劉向 (79–8 B.C.), the original compiler, have attacked its historical implications.

In his preface to the work, Liu Xiang condemned the Zhanguo rulers for "renouncing courteousness but honoring warfare, and for rejecting benevolence and justice, using improper means for the sole end of achieving power." Other scholars, while disapproving of the moral implications of the book, were nevertheless attracted to its refined rhetoric and vigorous literary style. The opinion of Lu Longqi 陸隴其 (1630–1693) that the book "is almost like poison in delicious food" represents the traditional attitude towards the *Zhanguo ce*; i.e., that of appreciating it as literature while condemning it as history.

Sources of the Work

Opinions vary as to the meaning of the title and the origin and nature of the book. Some scholars interpret the word *ce* to mean "schemes," "intrigues," or "plots"; others believe that it should be taken to refer to the bamboo or wooden tablets used in writing, and thus to mean "documents." Liu Xiang, who gave the work this title, stated his view clearly. He wrote that "the book contains material used by the diplomats of the Warring States to advise those states that employed them by contriving plans and plots for their use; it is therefore proper to call the book *Zhanguo ce*." There is thus good reason to follow Liu Xiang's original intention and to interpret the title as meaning "Plots of warring states." Some renderings of the title use the term "intrigues" or "stratagems."

Controversy has also arisen as to the nature and style of this writing, and as to whether it should be regarded as history or fiction. Most standard histories and bibliographies list the work in the class of *zashi* 雜史; the *Standard History of the Song Dynasty* (*Song shi* 宋史 ch.205, 5203) and other bibliographies place it within the category of *zongheng jia* 縱橫家.

Liu Xiang wrote of the confused fragments of records that he had found in the Han Imperial Library, in addition to eight incomplete *pian* 篇 that concerned various states. He had arranged such material in rough chronological order for those states and supplemented it with other writings that had not been set out in any sequence; and after eliminating material that was found to be duplicated, he made a total of thirty-three *pian*.

From Liu Xiang's reference to named documents that were present in the archive (i.e., *Guoce* 國策, *Guoshi* 國事, *Duanchang* 短長, *Shiyu* 事語, *Changshu* 長書, and *Xiushu* 脩書), it is apparent that at least six different sources of the same nature and scope were used in the compilation of the *Zhanguo ce*. Although none of these documents exist today, they can be classified into three distinct categories on the basis of their titles.

(a) Regional records of various states, including the *Guoce* (state documents) and *Guoshi* (state affairs). Because these two titles begin with the word *guo*, the documents must have been arranged in order according to the states that were concerned, as is the case with the *Guoyu* 國語. This is evidently the material to which Liu Xiang referred as the eight *pian* arranged for the various states. The received text of the *Zhanguo ce* includes sections on the royal house of Zhou 周; the seven major states of Qin 秦, Qi 齊, Chu 楚, Zhao 趙, Wei 魏, Han 韓, and Yan 燕; and the three minor states of Song 宋, Wei 衛, and Zhongshan 中山. Thus, the eight *pian* that Liu Xiang mentions specifically seem to have concerned the Zhou and the seven major states, with the latter three occupying only a small portion of the material. These documents were probably not official histories of the states, which are known to have been written in the form of annals and to have been destroyed under the Qin; the *Guoce* and the *Guoshi* were more likely additional records arranged by state that dealt with state affairs.

Throughout the entire text, each paragraph, whether short or long, usually represents an independent incident that is unconnected with those that precede and follow. Some of these stories relate to authenticated historical facts and were probably drawn from state documents. For example, the initial passage that concerns the Qin records that Wei Yang 衛鞅 (better known as Shang Yang 商鞅) left Wei for Qin, there to put his reforms into practice for eight years before dying under violent circumstances, after the death of Duke Xiao 孝. This paragraph includes information which is similar to that included in *Shiji* 史記 (*Records of the Grand Historian*) ch. 68. Other stories, such as those about the physician Bian Que 扁鵲, Wangsun Gu 王孫賈, and Zhi Bo 知伯, or about political relations among the six states, can be confirmed in the *Shiji* or other historical documents.

(b) Anecdotes, such as those in the item which Liu Xiang identified as *Shiyu* (topical discourses). This was probably a collection of historical romances of various states, written in the form of discourses and arranged by topic. The term *yu* is seen in the title *Guoyu*, which is a collection of anecdotes from the Chunqiu period arranged by state. The *Shiyu* must have consisted of the same type of material for the Zhanguo period, as is exemplified in the story of Su Qin 蘇秦 (380–284), and his change of loyalties from an alliance that was pro-Qin to anti-Qin. The Confucian tradition strongly disapproved of the moral implications of the story, but for literary merit it has been considered the best of the historical romances. The vivid, if greatly exaggerated presentation might have been derived from anecdotes transmitted by storytellers, which then gradually became popular legends. Because these stories were written mostly in the form of highly imaginative discourses, there is reason to believe that this kind of narration was probably based on the anecdotes or *Shiyu* described previously.

(c) Material concerning the theories and practices of the diplomats, including the *Duanchang*, *Changshu*, and *Xiushu*, which were probably arranged by types of argument. The term *duanchang* (short and long, wrong and right, loss and gain, or defects and merits) seems to refer to the presentation of contradictory arguments from each of two sides. It was apparently the practice of some diplomats to present their case by exaggerating one point and belittling another or to please a person by praising (*chang*) him to his face while decrying (*duan*) others behind their backs.

Some scholars have thought that the term *duanchang* refers to the use of pieces of bamboo or wooden stationery of differing lengths for the composition of one and the same document. In fact, no examples of such a usage have arisen. Even if documents had been made up of long and short tablets, there is no reason to suppose that the term should refer particularly to diplomatic writings.

The items named *Changshu* and *Xiushu* may have set forth only one aspect of a plot, or they may have included a longer version of an argument. The *Zhanguo ce* is especially rich in such augmentation of the plans and plots of various diplomats; less common are stories, anecdotes, or fables; those passages that can be considered historical records are rather few and far between. It is clear that the *Zhanguo ce* is a work of a composite nature, drawing on materials from different sources; it cannot therefore be classified arbitrarily within a single category of either history or fiction.

Dating and Authorship

The dating of the events narrated in the *Zhanguo ce* is generally in agreement with the statement in Liu Xiang's preface that the book covers a period of 245 years, from the end of the Chunqiu until the rise of the Chu 楚 and Han 漢. The rise of the Chu as a contender for imperial power is dated to 209 B.C.; 245 years earlier brings the date to 454 B.C. All the incidents included in the book fall within this period, except for one which concerns Duke Ling 靈 of Wei 衛, who reigned from 534 to 493 B.C. According to some scholars, this passage was inserted as a quotation, in connection with the preceding and following paragraphs, rather than as a separate incident from the Chunqiu period. Most of the book deals with the middle part of the Zhanguo period; only a few incidents are from an earlier date, such as the stories about Zhi Bo, whose fief was divided by Zhao, Wei, and Han in 453 B.C.

The latest events that are described in the book date from around 221 B.C. (e.g., the unsuccessful attempt to assassinate the king of Qin in 227 B.C.; the second attempt to do so, after he had become emperor, in 221 B.C.). As there is a gap of about 200 years between the latest of the events mentioned and the compilation of the *Zhanguo ce* at the end of the first century B.C., it is possible that some material written during the Former (or Western) Han (202 B.C.–8 A.D.) has been included.

The question of authorship of the book has long come into question with some scholars ascribing this to Liu Xiang since the Tang dynasty. The bibliography of the *Jiu Tangshu* 舊唐書 (ch. 46, 1993–94) includes the note that the book was written (*zuan* 撰) by Liu Xiang; the bibliography of the *Xin Tangshu* 新唐書 (ch. 58, 1463) names the item as Liu Xiang's *Zhanguo ce*. Gu Guanqi 顧廣圻 (1776–1835) even wrote that "the *Zhanguo ce* derives from Liu Xiang's own school, and it is therefore not hard to understand why it is different from the writings of Han Fei 韓非, Sima Qian 司馬遷 and other schools." Because it is clearly stated in the preface that the book was collated and compiled by Liu Xiang from various early sources then extant, it seems evident that Liu Xiang was the compiler and not the author of the work.

Some scholars (e.g., Luo Genze 羅根澤) have suggested that the *Zhanguo ce* is the same as the lost work entitled *Jun yong* 雋永, which was written by Kuai Tong 蒯通 (ca. 236–196 B.C.). This argument is based on the statement in the *Shiji* that Kuai Tong was an expert in diplomatic theory and discussed the intrigues of the warring states in eighty-one headings (*shou* 首). This theory rests on the arbitrary association of the term *Jun yong* (delicious and lasting) with the terms *changshu* and *xiushu*, and it is assumed that Liu Xiang must have taken thirty-three *pian* from the eighty-one *shou* of the *Jun yong* with which to make the *Zhanguo ce*. Liu Xiang, however, does not mention *Jun yong* in his sources, and there is no evidence with which to support this view.

All attributions of the *Zhanguo ce* to a single author have been based on the mistaken assumption that the book originally existed as a complete work; and they have ignored Liu Xiang's statement in his preface that the book was a collection based on various sources that existed during the Zhanguo period. With his reorganization of the original materials that were then in the imperial archives, the new title *Zhanguo ce*, which was assigned by Liu Xiang, naturally replaced the previous titles of *Guoce* or *Guoshi*; for this reason, the original titles were no longer used, and they were not recorded in the bibliography that is now contained in the *Han shu*. Other works, however, which were listed in that bibliography do not feature as items from which the compiler of the *Zhanguo ce* drew. There is little doubt that this work is an anthology of existing materials written by unknown authors of the Zhanguo period.

Transmission of the Text and Early Commentaries

The *Zhanguo ce* was compiled by Liu Xiang between 26 and 8 B.C., at a time when a whole variety of documents in the imperial archives were being examined by the commission that he led. The text was first annotated by Gao You 高誘 (ca. 168–112), also known as the commentator of the *Huainanzi* 淮南子. Gao You's annotation is entered in the bibliography of the *Sui shu* 隋書 (ch. 33, 959) as an item of twenty-one *juan*, and the same list includes an entry for the *Zhanguo ce* compiled by Liu Xiang, in thirty-two *juan*. The lists in both the *Jiu Tangshu* and the *Xin Tangshu* include entries both for Gao You's annotation and for Liu Xiang's text, each of thirty-two *juan*. By Song times it had become customary to include both text and commentary together as one item. *The Bibliography of the Song Dynasty* (ch. 205, 5203) carries an entry for Gao You's *Zhanguo ce*, in thirty-three *juan*; a copy of thirty-three *juan*, with Gao You's notes, was entered in Fujiwara Sukeyo's catalogue.

During the Song period, parts of the text, together with Gao You's annotation, gradually disappeared. According to the *Chongwen zongmu* 崇文總目 (compiled 1034–1042), twelve *pian* of the text (nos. 2–10 and 31–33) and twelve *pian* of the annotation (nos. 1, 5, and 11–20) were missing from the copy kept in the Imperial Library. Some time later, when a number of scholars began to work on the recovery of the book, the most important contribution was made by Zeng Gong 曾鞏 (1019–1083), who had been working on the collation of ancient documents as editor in the Historical Commission between 1060 and 1067. By searching for all copies that were then available in private collections, he was able to examine twenty-one *pian* (nos. 1 and 11–30) of the original text and ten *pian* (nos. 2–4, 6–10, and 32–33) of the annotation; and by reconstructing two *pian* (nos. 5 and 31) he was able to recover a text with a total of thirty-three *pian*. It is clear that Zeng Gong's version is not identical with Liu Xiang's original text, particularly in respect of *pian* nos. 5 and 31; nevertheless, Zeng's text, which was collated and revised three times, has been considered the authoritative version; all later editions have been based upon it.

Almost contemporary with Zeng Gong, a private scholar named Wang Jue 王覺 was also working on the collation of this book in about 1064–67, but his edition does not survive. When Sun Pu 孫朴 (ca. 1050–1093) was appointed in 1086 editor in the Imperial Library, he made further collations of the text, with corrections of some 550 words. This text was termed the *Huangben* 黃本 and was copied for the Imperial Library in 1093.

During the Southern Song, two scholars were working on the book almost simultaneously, but independently, and their collations have become the direct progenitors of the various editions that are available today. Yao Hong 姚宏 (ca. 1100–1146) made some 480 corrections to the book on the basis of Zeng Gong's work and other editions; his preface, dated 1146, was copied by his brother Yao Kuan 姚寬 (1104–1161) in 1100.

A second popular commentary was made by Bao Biao 鮑彪 (1106–1149). In this edition, which carries a preface dated 1147 and a revision of 1149, the complete text is rearranged into ten *juan* according to the states,

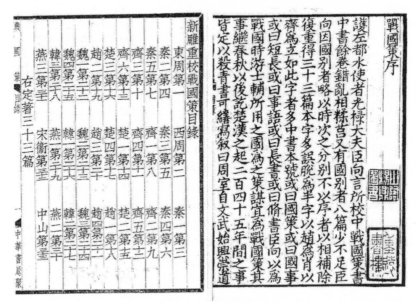

ZHANGUO CE EDITIONS
Contents of a 33-pian edition   *Preface of a 10-juan edition*

and then in chronological order. Although Bao did not follow the traditional practice of preserving the original text and order, some of his corrections and judgments show outstanding ability and scholarship and have served to settle a great many disputes.

During the Yuan dynasty, Wu Shidao 吳師道 (1283–1344) wrote what was the most highly critical study of the *Zhanguo ce*, which was based on Bao Biao's edition but also used the commentaries of Yao Hong. This work was completed in 1325, with a postscript dated 1333. First printed in 1355, the work was praised by the editors of the *Siku* 四庫 project as being the best commentary ever made on the study of this work since ancient times.

No important studies were contributed by Ming scholars, except for the many reprints with additional notes that were based on the Bao Wu edition. These included those by Wang Tingxiang 王廷相 (1522), Ge Zi 葛鼐 (1523), Gong Lei 龔雷 (1528), Du Shi 杜詩 (1552), Zhang Wenguan 張文燦 (1587) and Li Kejia 李克家; there was also a three-color edition, made by the well-known printer Min Qiji 閔齊伋 in 1619. During the Qing period, the last edition was reprinted by Kong Guangsen 孔廣森 (ca. 1780) and Li

Xiling 李錫齡 (ca. 1850). Later it was included in several *congshu* 叢書 (collectanea) of the nineteenth and early twentieth centuries. This edition has been popular in Japan, forming the basis of most of the Japanese reprints and translations.

Perhaps for political reasons, Yao Hong's version did not become popular until the middle of the eighteenth century, when Lu Jianzeng 盧見曾 (1690–1768) found and reproduced a Song printing (1156). Another Song printing with Yao Hong's commentary was re-engraved in facsimile in 1803 by Huang Pilie 黃丕烈 (1763–1825), who followed the copy in his own library exactly, adding his own critical notes as a supplement in three *juan*. This edition is prized for its rarity, its faithful reproduction, and the careful notes that are appended. It has subsequently been collated or emended by several scholars. This edition was used for the *Sibubeiyao* 四部備要 series in 1927. Bao Biao's edition, as transmitted with Wu Shidao's commentary, was popular throughout the Ming and early Qing periods, when Yao Hong's edition was unknown. It was first included in the *Sibucongkan* 四部叢刊 series in 1921.

These two rival editions, one by Yao Hong in thirty-three *pian* arranged by states and the other by Bao Biao with Wu Shidao's revisions rearranged in chronological sequence, in ten *juan*, have thus become the most influential and popular texts and commentaries on the *Zhanguo ce*.

Newly Discovered Zhanguo Manuscript Documents

The manuscript documents discovered at Mawangdui in 1973 included texts which are related to the *Zhanguo ce* and which have been variously termed *bieben* 別本, *bo shu*, 帛書 and *Zhanguo zonghengjia shu* 戰國縱橫家書. These manuscripts carry twenty-seven items of text in which 11,000 out of a total of some 17,000 characters survive; about sixty percent of the material does not appear in the received text of the *Zhanguo ce*. The new texts include correspondence, dialogues, and argumentation of the diplomatic school, and the content is similar in nature and style to that of the *Zhanguo ce*; but the material is not arranged according to the states or in chronological sequence. As certain misplaced passages of length equal to that of individual wooden strips can be clearly identified, the text is

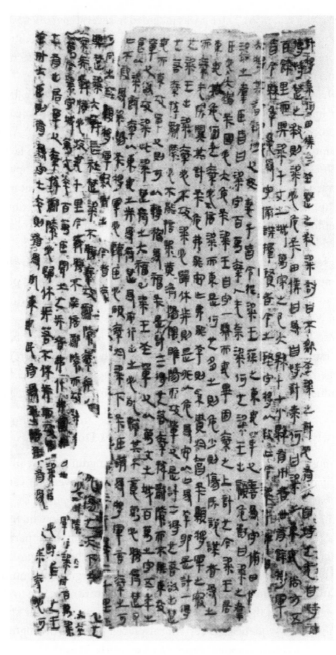

NEWLY DISCOVERED ZHANGUO DOCUMENT

believed to have been copied, on silk, from one that had been written on wooden or bamboo strips.

Nine items of this material (nos. 15–16 and 18–24) have counterparts in the received text of the *Zhanguo ce* and the *Shiji*, and two items (nos. 4 and 5) are in part identical with sections of the *Zhanguo ce*. The other sixteen items are not found in any other extant literature. The material may be divided into three groups, according to content and layout:

(a) Items 1 to 14 are all stories that relate to three members of the Su 蘇 family and two other persons. The coherence of the contents and the uniform style in which certain characters are written indicate that all these items derive from a single source.

(b) The contents of items 15 to 19 are unrelated to one another. However, there is a note at the end of each item giving the number of characters therein, and at the end of the group the total number is given as 2,870. This figure matches up with the sum of the figures given at the end of each of the five items, thus confirming that they were taken from a single source.

(c) Items 20 to 17 are unrelated in content; no numbering of characters is given, and they appear to have been taken from other sources.

The events recorded in these documents all relate to the middle and late parts of the Zhanguo period. The stories in items 1 to 14 concern events which can be dated to about 300–286 B.C.; those in items 15 to 27 concern events in 353 to 235 B.C. Twenty-four of these items concern the period 307 to 221 B.C., and 10 of these concentrate on 289 to 283 B.C.

The newly discovered texts represent a different source of information, which is perhaps older than the sources on which Liu Xiang based his work, and there is nothing to show that their text was seen by Sima Tan 司馬談 (d. ca. 110 B.C.) or Sima Qian 司馬遷 (145–86 B.C.). In addition, the new material is of considerable importance for the textual criticism of the received text of the *Zhanguo ce* and for the study of China's history during the Zhanguo period. The chronology of the later part of that period has been based primarily on the historical events related in the *Zhushu jinian* 竹書紀年, which end at 299 B.C., and in the *Shiji*, and there is thus a gap of 78 years between 299 B.C. and the unification of 221 B.C. The newly found documents, which mostly concern events dating to the later part of the Zhanguo period, are especially useful for the reconstruction of the chronology of that time.

For transcriptions and critical studies, see the following under 6 (d):

(i) Mawangdui Hanmu boshu zhengli xiaozu (ed.), *Mawangdui Hanmu boshu Zhanguo zonghengjia shu*; Peking: Wenwu, 1976; text of the twenty-seven items transcribed in abbreviated characters (previously published in *Wenwu* 1975.4, 14–26), followed by articles by Tang Lan, Yang Kuan, and Ma Yong (for earlier versions of the latter two items, see *Wenwu* 1975.2, 26–34, and *Wenwu* 1975.4, 21–40).

(ii) Mawangdui Hanmu boshu zhengli xiaozu (ed.), *Changsha Mawangdui Hanmu boshu.* (3); Peking: Wenwu, 1978; facsimiles and annotated transcriptions.

(iii) Zeng Ming, "Guanyu boshu 'Zhanguo ce' zhong Su Qin shuxin ruogan niandai wenti di shangque"; *Wenwu* 1975:8, 23–30.

(iv) Kudo Motoo, Maotai shutsudo "Sengoku juoka sho" to "Shiki"; *Chūgoku seishi no kisoteki kenkyū*; Tokyo: Waseda daigaku. 1984, 1–26.

Principal Editions

(a) *Zhanguo ce zhu*, 33 *pian*, annotated by Gao You and with commentary by Yao Hong; collated by Lu Jianzeng; in *Yayutang congshu* and *Jifu congshu*.

(b) *Zhanguo ce zhu*, 33 *pian*: text of a Song edition, collated by Huang Pilie, with critical notes in three *juan*; facsimile blockprint in *Shiliju Huangshi congshu* (1803); recut by Hubei congwen shuju (1869); typeset reprint in *Sibubeiyao* (1927) and *Congshu ji-cheng* (punctuated, 1936).

(c) *Zhanguo ce jiao zhu*; ten *juan*, with commentary by Bao Biao and Wu Shidao; in *Xiyinxuan congshu* (1846); facsimile reprint of 1355–65 ed. in *Sibu congkan* (1922).

(d) *Zhanguo ce*, 3 vols., Shanghai: Guji chubanshe, 1978; punctuated text (unabbreviated characters), based on Yao Hong's text, with variant readings and collected annotation from other editions; followed by (i) a chronology of the *Zhanguo ce* by Yu Chang from a manuscript in the Shanghai Library; (ii) index of names mentioned in the text; and (iii) transcription of texts from Mawangdui.

Selected Studies

(a) Zhang Qi (1764–1833), *Zhanguo ce shidi*, two *juan*; in *Guangya shuju congshu* (1900); reprinted in *Congshu jicheng* (1936).

(b) Zhong Fengnian, *Guoce kanyan*; Beiping: Harvard-Yenching Institute, 1936.

(c) Qi Sihe, "Zhanguo ce zhuzuo shihdai kao"; *Yanjing xuebao*, 34 (1948), 257–78.

(d) Crump, J.I. Jr, "The Chan-kuo ts'e and its fiction"; *ToungPao*, XLVIII (1960), 305–75.

(e) Zheng Liangshu, *Zhanguo ce yanjiu*; Singapore: Youlian, 1972; also Taibei: Xuesheng shudian, 1975.

(f) Zhu Zugeng, *Zhanguo ce jizhu huikao*; 3 vols.; Yangzhou: Jiangsu guji, 1985.

(g) He Jianzhang, *Zhanguo ce zhushi*; 4 vols.; Beijing: Zhonghua; 1990.

(h) Feng Zuomin, *Baihua Zhanguo ce*; 3 vols., Taibei: Xingguang, 1979.

(i) Meng Qingxiang, *Zhanguo ce yizhu*; Harbin: Heilongjiang: Ren min, 1986.

Translations

In English:

(a) Crump, J. I., Jr., *Intrigues: Studies of the Chan-kuo ts'e*. Ann Arbor, Michigan: University of Michigan Press, 1964; contains fifty selected items with a critical analysis of the content, treated as fiction; reviewed by T. H. Tsien, *JAS* 24 (1965), 328–329.

(b) Crump, J. I., Jr., *Chan-kuo ts'e*; Oxford: Clarendon Press, 1970; a complete translation of the text.

In Japanese:

(1) *Kanbun taikei*; no. 19, 1915, edited by Yokota Koretaka and Yasui Kotarō (Mamoru); new edition with commentaries by Nagasawa Kikuya and index, 1958.

(2) *Kanseki kokujikai zensho*; nos. 38–40, 1917, edited by Makino Kenjiro (Sōshū).

(3) *Kokuyaku kanbun taisei*; no. 12, 1920, edited by Uno Tetsuto.

(4) *Kanbun sōsho*, 1927, edited by Nakamura Kyoshiro.

(5) *Shinshaku kanbun taikei*; nos. 47–49, 1977, 1981, edited by Hayashi Hideichi.

(6) *Tōyō bunko*; nos. 64, 74, 86, 1966–67, edited by Tsuneishi Shigeru.

(7) *Chūgoku no shiso*; no. 2; 1964, edited by Moriya Hiroshi.

(8) *Chūgoku koten bungaku taikei*; no. 7, 1972, edited by Tsuneishi Shigeru.

(9) *Chūgoku koten shinsho*, 1968–69, edited by Sawada Masahiro.

Index

(a) *Zhanguo ce tongjian*; Beijing; Centre franco-chinois, 1948.

(b) *Sengokusaku koyū meishi sakuin*; compiled under the direction of Shigezawa Toshio; Kyōto: Kyōto daigaku bungakubu tetsugaku shi kenkyūshitsu, 1960; based on Yao Hong's edition.

(c) Fidler, Sharon J., with J. I. Crump, Jr, *Index to the Chan-kuo ts'e*; Ann Arbor, Michigan: University of Michigan, 1973.

(d) *A Concordance to the Zhanguo ce*, ed. D.C. Lau and Chen Fangzheng; *ICS* series, Hong Kong: Commercial Press, 1992.

Published in Early Chinese Texts: A Bibliographical Guide,
ed. by Michael Loewe, Berkeley, 1993.

4   SEALING CLAYS OF HAN CHINA

The East Asian Collection of the University of Chicago Library includes eleven seal inscriptions impressed on ten pieces of clay that date from just before or the beginning of the Christian era. The collection was acquired from a collector in Paris during my trip to Europe in 1968. The pieces were displayed at the Exhibition of Far Eastern Library Resources in the Rare Book Department of the University Library in 1973. These artifacts have attracted great attention among scholars and visitors because they are the oldest documents in the University of Chicago Library and remain extremely rare among library and museum collections in the U.S.

Documents in ancient China were written on bamboo and wooden tablets before paper was extensively used in the third century A.D. For certification of authenticity and confidentiality of official documents, they were bound with string and impressed with a seal on a piece of sticky clay attached to the documents during transportation. For a large quantity of tablets, they could also be put in a bag folded on both ends with an opening at the center, which was sealed with a board and impressed with a clay seal in a similar manner. When the tablets decayed, the sealing clays survived underground.

Clay seals were first discovered in 1822 in Sichuan and then in Shaanxi, Henan, Shandong, and elsewhere. A few thousand pieces of these are kept in public and private collections in China, and only a small number can be found in Western countries. Because they bear official titles and place names, many of which are not recorded in the historical literature, the inscriptions are valuable for the study of historical geography and government agencies, as well as being vital documentary evidence of ancient China.

The eleven inscriptions and illustrations found on these clays at the University of Chicago Library are listed and appended to this chapter. In the following section the clays are deciphered and verified in correspondence with the chapters on *Dili zhi* 地理志 (Geography) and *Baiguan gongqing biao* 百官公卿表 (Administrative Offices) of the *Han shu* 漢書 (*History of the Han Dynasty*):

1. (a) *Heyang cheng yin* 郃陽丞印 (Assistant Prefect of Heyang seal) and (b) *Dushui cheng yin* 都水丞印 (Assistant Director of Water seal) Two seals impressed on one piece of clay were used on documents presented jointly by two concerned offices. Heyang (modern Heyang, Shaanxi) on the northern bank of the Heyang River was one of thirteen satellite cities of the capital in the Han dynasty. *Dushui* was an office in charge of hydraulic affairs, together with such departments as foundries, mining, forestry, and fruit plantations. It is extremely rare to find two seals on one piece of clay.

2. *Guangsiling yin* 廣祀令印 (Prefect of the Office of Court Ceremonies seal) From the Qin and throughout the Han dynasty, the chief official in charge of state sacrifices was called *fengchang* 奉常, *taichang* 太常, or *taisiling* 太祀令; but the title on this clay seal is not found in the official *History of the Han Dynasty*. With its inscriptions in mirror image and carved in intaglio—unlike other pieces with positive but reverse inscriptions—this clay seal is perhaps a matrix for casting metal seals and is also quite rare.

3. *Chu Chengxiang yin* 楚丞相印 (Prime Minister of the Chu State seal) The office of *chengxiang* was established by the first Emperor of the Han for feudal lords, but it was abolished by Emperor Jing 景 in 152 B.C., after the suppression of a rebellion by seven of these lords, including the Lord of Chu. Based on this information, the piece should date from before the middle of the second century B.C., prior to the abolition of this office.

4. *Neishi* 內史 (Administrator of the Capital) This administrative office in the capital, equivalent to the modern-day post of mayor, was established in the Zhou dynasty, but its duties were divided into two offices, Left and Right, under Emperor Jing in 155 B.C. Because this piece has only two characters and does not mention Left or Right, it must date from before the middle of the second century.

5. *Changxin zhanshi* 長信詹事 (Superintendent of the Changxin Palace) The Queen Mother lived in this palace. Because the office in charge of the Changxin Palace was renamed *Changxin shaofu* 長信少府 in 144 B.C., this clay must date from before the name change in the middle of the second century B.C.

6. *Jushi cheng yin* 居室丞印 (Assistant for the Convict Barracks seal) The name of this office, which was charged with handling prisoners, was altered to Baogong 保宮 in 104 B.C. during the reign of Emperor Wu 武. Thus, this must date from before the early second century B.C.

7. *Ruyin cheng yin* 女(汝)陰丞印 (Assistant Prefect of the Ruyin District seal) Ruying is located on the north bank of the Ruyin River in Fuyang 阜阳, Anhui Province.

8. *Wufang cheng yin* 吳房丞印 (Assistant to the Chancellor of Wufang State seal) Wufang was the site where the brother of the King of the Wu Kingdom was enfeoffed by the Chu State. The ancient site of Wufang is located in modern Suiping 遂平, Henan Province.

9. *Changyi hou yin* 昌邑侯印 (Captain of the Changyi State seal) This district was established in the Qin dynasty and was referred to as Shanyang 山陽 under the Han. It became the Kingdom of Changyi in 97 B.C. Therefore, this piece must date from after that year when its statehood was established. The ancient site of Changyi is located forty miles northwest of modern Jinxiang 金鄉, Shandong province.

10. *Yandao juyuan* 嚴道橘園 (Orange Plantation of the Yandao District) *Yandao juyuan* was an administrative office in charge of orange-growing operations from which tribute was sent to the imperial court, as recorded in the chapter on Geography in the *History of the Han Dynasty*. Yandao, modern Rongjing 榮經 in Sichuan Province, has long been famous for growing oranges.

The inscriptions described from the Chicago collection represent the names of six geographical locations (nos. 1a, 3, 7, 8, 9, 10), eight central and local administrative offices (nos. 1b, 2–10), and three specific locations, including the imperial palace (no. 5), prison barracks (no. 6), and orange plantation (no. 10). Four of these date to the Former or Western Han (206 B.C.–8 A.D.) and others belong to either the Former or to the Later or Eastern Han (25–220). Except for three (nos. 1a, 6, 10), which are also found in collections in China, all the other inscriptions do not appear in any published catalogues or reproductions. Especially rare is the example with two seals impressed jointly on a single piece (no. 1a-b), as well as the artifact with negative inscriptions carved in intaglio (no. 2), which is likely to be a matrix for casting seals.

Ancient Clay Inscriptions in the University of Chicago Library

1. (a) *Heyang cheng yin*   (b) *Dushui cheng yin*

2. *Guangsiling yin*

3. *Chu Chengxiang yin*

4. *Neishi*

5. *Changxin zhanshi*

6. *Jushi cheng yin*

7. *Ruyin cheng yin*

8. *Wufang cheng yin*

9. *Changyi hou yin*

10. *Yandao juyuan*

5   IMPLEMENTS AND TOOLS FOR WRITING

Chinese writing as a distinct form of art has been developed through the use and improvement of various tools and implements since ancient times. Paper, brush, ink, and ink slab, the "four treasures of a scholar's studio," have been the basic implements for committing thoughts to writing. How early these four items became a standard set is uncertain. When one starts to write, these implements are naturally used together. Brush, ink, ink slab, rubbing stone, and blank wood tablets were discovered in a bamboo box in a tomb of the Former or Western Han period (206 B.C.–8 A.D.) at Fenghuangshan in Jiangling, Hubei, and similar implements were found at other sites.[1] Together they constitute a precise set of writing tools that date from long before paper was used for writing. It is recorded that under the Later Han dynasty, brush and ink were given to high officials every month, and in the Qin these four articles were used at court when princes were crowned.[2] Some of these articles were elaborately designed and luxuriously decorated so that their usefulness and artistic designs greatly inspired both scholars and artists.

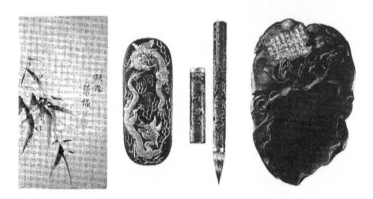

FOUR TREASURES OF A SCHOLAR'S STUDIO

Origin of the Writing Brush

For many centuries the Chinese have attributed the invention of paper to Cai Lun 蔡倫 in the second century A.D. and the writing brush to Meng Tian 蒙恬 in the third century B.C. The use of paper during Cai Lun's time is well documented in contemporary literature, but the association of the brush with Meng Tian is not as clear. According to the *Shuowen jiezi* (*Dictionary of Characters*), compiled in the early second century, the brush was called *yu* in Chu, *bulu* in Wu, *fu* in Yan, and *bi* in Qin.[3] These characters probably indicate different pronunciations of the same term in southern, eastern, northern, and western China respectively, as dialectic variants of a basic form *bluet*.[4] They might have meant the same implement but of varying form and material.

Not only is the evidence of Meng Tian's invention insufficient, but literary and archeological testimony indicates that the brush had been used long before his time. The earliest lexicon, the *Erya* 爾雅, defines *bulu* as writing brush.[5] The *Records of Ceremonial* mentions that "a scribe should carry with him his *bi*, 'writing brush,' and a scholar the recorded words."[6] The *Zhanguo ce* 戰國策 (*Strategies of Warring States*) contains a story about the queen dowager of Qi, who, about to die in 249 B.C., said to her son, King Jian 建: "Bring the brush and tablets to write down my words."[7] Not only do recent archeological discoveries show that characters were written on bamboo and silk with a brush, but actual writing brushes made of bamboo holders and animal hair were found at various sites of the Warring States period in Hunan, Hubei, and elsewhere.

The use of the brush in the early Zhou and Shang dynasties has been inferred by scholars because characters inscribed on Shang and Zhou bronzes resemble brush-written patterns.[8] The oracle inscriptions of the Shang dynasty appear to have been written with a brush on the surface and then carved into the bone. Several pieces of ox bone, dated roughly to 1300–1000 B.C., bear inscriptions which were not engraved but made by hair brush and ink.[9] The character *yu* for a writing brush in the bone or bronze inscriptions of the Shang dynasty clearly depicts a hand holding a brush either with hair full of ink or with spread-out dried hairs.[10]

Some archeologists have even carried the account of the use of brushes back to prehistoric times when fine designs on painted pottery discovered at Neolithic sites in Yangshao, Henan, were drawn with a brush.[11] This need not have been the same brush made of rabbit hair with a bamboo holder that was used later, but it must have been a bunch of animal hair tied to a holder and used for writing or drawing with black fluid or other pigments. Brush writing, therefore, must be considered as a traditional method developed long before our knowledge of ancient writings begins.

Forms of the Brush-Pen

The writing brush usually includes three main parts: holder, hair, and sheath. The holder was generally a bamboo tube, but it was not uncommon to use a wooden rod. The body of the brush was made of rabbit, deer, or goat hairs, which were tied with silk or hemp string at one end, covered with lacquer to stiffen it, and inserted into the end of the holder. In order to protect the delicate hair, a sheath was used to cover the whole implement. The total length of the brush was about one foot according to the measure of that era. In a poem on the writing brush, the scholar Cai Yong 蔡邕 (132–192) noted: "Cutting a bamboo to make a [brush] holder; Tied with silk string, covered with lacquer."[12] The philosopher Wang Chong 王充 (ca. 27–100) reported that "the person with wisdom and ability could better serve in the court by his tongue of three inches and his writing brush of one foot."[13] Since the foot of the Han period was equivalent to about 23 cm, the size of the brush as recorded in early literature is in general agreement with modern archeological discoveries.

Many early brushes belonging to the Warring States, Qin, and Han periods have been discovered at various sites in Hunan, Hubei, Henan, Shandong, and Gansu since the 1920s. One of the earliest samples from the Warring States period was found in Changsha, Hunan, in 1954. It has a bamboo holder 21 cm long, with a sheath 23.5 cm, and the hair is said to be rabbit.[14] Three brushes were excavated from a Qin tomb dated to 217 B.C. at Shuihudi in Yunmeng, Hubei, in 1975. The holders are made of bamboo, 20.9–21.5 cm long and 0.4 cm in diameter, with a worn-out tip of hair 2.5 cm long. The sheath is a longer tube with two sides at the center hollowed out and decorated with bones at both ends of the tube. Another brush was found in a corked bamboo tube from a Chu tomb dated 292 B.C. at

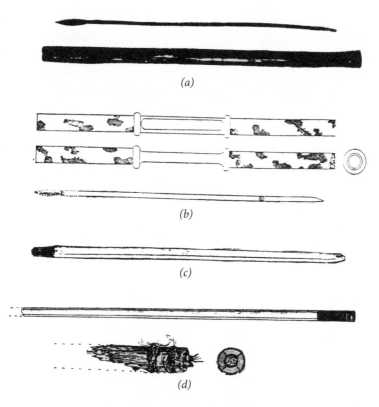

EARLY WRITING BRUSHES
(a), (b) Writing brush sets with bamboo holder, hair, and bamboo sheath
(c) Writing brush with split wooden holder and hair
(d) Fragment of wooden holder and a hair tip

Baoshan in 1986. It is 22.3 cm long with a bamboo holder. In the same year, two brushes and one sheath were discovered in a Qin tomb at Fangmatan in Tianshui, Gansu. The sheath has two combined tubes and can actually accommodate both brushes. The top of the holder is pointed, while the lower end is hollowed out in order to hold the hair.[15]

The Han brushes are similar in form to those of the earlier periods. One dated to 167 B.C. found at Fenghuangshan in Jiangling, Hubei, in 1975, is 24.9 cm long with the sheath hollowed out in the center and decorated with a colored painting. Another Former Han brush was discovered at

Yinqueshan in Linyi, Shandong, in 1978 with a bamboo sheath, on which eight holes are cut, perhaps for the brush tip to dry after the holder was put into it. Some of the brushes bear the name of maker on their holders.[16]

However, some special brush holders were made of wood instead of bamboo in the northwestern regions. A writing brush of the Han dynasty, found by Folke Bergman in 1927 at Mu-durbeljin near Juyan, is made of four vertical pieces of wood that are fastened into a rod with two hanks of hemp string. Thus the hair can be inserted into the end of the tubular rod and changed when necessary, like the pen point used in a modern penholder. The total length of this brush is 23.2 cm, including the hair outside of the holder.[17]

The discoveries of these writing brushes have provided full data on the shape, size, and material of this implement of writing, which is quite similar to what is used today. The inner portion of the brush was made of rabbit or deer hair and the outer portion of goat hair, as a stiff center covered with soft hair is most suitable for writing. Wang Ying 王穎 (ca. A.D. 300) wrote: "Why is rabbit hair necessary in making the brush? Deer hair is also sharp and durable."[18]

The size of the hair point depends upon its use in writing different sizes of characters. The one from Baoshan measures 3.5 cm, the one from Changsha, 2.5 cm, another from Xuanquan, 2.2 cm, and that from Juyan, 1.4 cm with the tip worn short. Several hair nibs lacking the holder were found in Juyan, Korea, and elsewhere. The one discovered in the tomb of Wang Guang 王光 at Lelang, Korea, measures 2.9 cm long, and one end of it is tied with a string.[19] The string was usually stiffened with black lacquer as an adhesive and so arranged that a fine point was available for writing. Fu Xuan 傅玄 of the third century A.D. noted that the hair was "tied with white hemp and fixed with black lacquer."[20] This is the traditional method of making the writing brush even today.

While the brush has been a widely accepted implement of writing for many centuries in China, some scholars believe that a kind of stylus made of bamboo, wood, or other materials must also have been employed. The sharpened bamboo or wooden stylus is traditionally considered to have been the pioneer instrument used for writing before the Qin dynasty.[21] Zhao Xigu 趙希鵠 of the thirteenth century (ca. 1231) wrote: "In very ancient times, writing was done with a bamboo stylus dipped in lacquer."[22] The noted Tang poet Bai Juyi 白居易 (772–846) also mentioned that "the Khotan people used wood for writing pens."[23] During the expedition of Aurel Stein in 1900–1901, some reed and wooden pens, perhaps of the third century A.D. or later, were found at the Niya site near Khotan. The wooden pens are merely thin twigs sharpened at one end and, in some cases, split up from the tip a short distance. Their length ranges from 15 to 23.5 cm; some have a knob made of horn at one end, and are fitted with a polished conical top which is intended to serve as a burnisher.[24] It is also reported that a wood stylus 24 cm long was found in Nara, Japan, and a kind of stylus called *juebi* 角筆, or horn pen, was used in China during Tang and Song times.[25] From both literary and archaeological evidence, it is believed that styluses made of bamboo, wood, reed, animal bone, ivory, and horn have been used for writing throughout a wide range of Chinese history.

Writing Fluid and Pigments

Where a brush was employed for writing, there must have been some kind of fluid or pigments to with which to write.[26] Hence, the phrase "brush and ink" has been used in Chinese literature to refer both to the basic implement and the vehicle of writing. The date of the first manufacture of true ink in China is unknown, but traditionally its invention was ascribed to a famous calligrapher and inkmaker named Wei Dan 韋誕 (179–253). Many scholars believe that, before this time, writings were inscribed on bamboo or wood by means of a pointed stylus dipped in black varnish.[27] The arbitrary dating of the use of ink to the third century A.D. is apparently speculation and runs contrary to both early literature and later archeological discoveries.

Wei Dan is described in Chinese records as one of the earliest known inkmakers. He refused the ink bestowed on him by the emperor, preferring to use ink of his own making in order to produce better calligraphy.[28] Xiao Ziliang 蕭子良, prince of the Southern Qi dynasty (479–501), commented that the ink made by Wei Dan was so black that "every drop was like lacquer."[29] Before this time, literary records indicate that ink was offered to the Han court at the beginning of the second century as tribute from various countries.[30] On certain important occasions, ink was bestowed on princes, high officials, and scholars by the favor of the emperor.[31] Even before the Han dynasty, the use of ink was common.

Mencius (372–289 B.C.) speaks of a carpenter's "string and ink"; ink was apparently used for writing in his time.[32] The earliest form of the character for ink, *mo* 墨, was used in Western Zhou bronze inscriptions, and apparently refers to a punishment of blackening or tattooing rather than to use of a writing fluid. The *Zhuangzi* 莊子 mentions that when Prince Yuan 元 of Song desired to have a picture painted, all the scribes of the court stood up "licking their writing brushes and mixing their ink."[33] Zhou She 周捨 (fifth century B.C.) of the Qin state said to his master: "I wish I could be your critical subordinate, handling tablets with brush and ink and watching after you to record whatever faults you may have."[34] The *Guanzi* 管子, a collected work attributed to Guan Zhong 管仲 (d. 645 B.C.) but probably written at a later date, records that Duke Huan 桓 of Qi (r. 685–643 B.C.), in regard to the improvement of his administration, "asked the officials to record his orders on a wooden board with ink and brush."[35] All of these records show that ink was used in the Spring and Autumn period.

While no reference to the use of black ink is found in literary records of the early Zhou dynasty, archeological evidence indicates that some form of writing fluid, black and red, was used as early as the Neolithic age and Shang dynasty. Red and black patterns and symbols are found on the painted pottery excavated at Banpo in Xi'an, Shaanxi.[36] A potsherd of about the same period bears the character *si* 祀 "to sacrifice," also written with black ink.[37] And on the oracle bones of the Shang dynasty, red and black inscriptions have also been found.[38] Chemical microanalysis of the specimens of oracle bone inscriptions indicates that the black is a carbon mixture of the nature of ink and that the red pigment is cinnabar.[39]

The use of red pigments for writing was also not rare. They seem to have been applied on the more important official documents. The *Da Dai liji* 大戴禮記, written about 100 B.C., states that when King Wu 武 (twelfth century B.C.) ascended the throne, he asked about the ways of the past administration. Master Lü Shang 呂尚 replied: "They were preserved in documents written with cinnabar."[40] A king of the state of Yue (ca. fifth century B.C.) is said to have kept the official documents written with cinnabar as a state treasure.[41] In 550 B.C., Fan Xuanzi 範宣子 had a slave whose name was entered on the documents written with cinnabar.[42] Many jade and stone tablets, dating to the early Warring States period and excavated in the 1930s–1980s, also are inscribed in red ink.

Although other pigments were used in writing or drawing, as evidenced by the drawings on the silk document discovered at Changsha, red ink was most common. The ink was generally made of cinnabar and vermilion. Cinnabar is a natural product, known as *dansha* 丹砂 or *zhusha* 朱砂 in literature; and it was studied by the early alchemists as a medicine for longevity. Vermilion was produced from the mineral cinnabar by powdering and water flotation. It was also prepared by the direct combination of mercury and sulfur.

Soot was used for the preparation of black ink probably at a very early period since it was naturally produced by fires. When fire was controlled, lampblack, a finer soot, could be collected.

Lampblack was obtained by burning certain kinds of woods or liquid, including pine, tung oil, petroleum, and probably lacquer. The use of tung came rather late; it seems not to have been used until the tenth century when Li Tinggui 李廷珪, a famous inkmaker, is believed to have used tung oil exclusively.[43] Soot made by burning crude petroleum was used in the eleventh century by Shen Kuo 沈括, who said that this soot was even darker than that made of pine.[44]

Pinewood was probably the most popular material for obtaining lampblack, and pine soot is still the best material for making black or "India ink" today. It is certain that before the end of the second century A.D., pinewood was already being used. This is testified to by the famous writer Cao Zhi 曹植 (192–224), whose poem opens with the line: "Ink is made from the soot of blue pine."[45]

Lacquer and Mineral Ink

Many Chinese and Western scholars have believed that the development of Chinese ink follows the order of lacquer, minerals, and lampblack. They contended that, according to the principle of evolution, natural products must have been used first and manufactured products later.

Thus Chavannes thought that Chinese writing was first done with lacquer and later with ink.[46] Laufer added that under the Han dynasty, ink was prepared from mineral products and from the third century A.D. onward was made from vegetable matter.[47] Carter also believed that lacquer was known in classical times.[48]

These theories by various noted sinologists were undoubtedly influenced by some medieval or late Chinese sources. A thirteenth-century author, Zhao Xigu, wrote: "In very ancient times writings were made with a bamboo stylus dipped in lacquer; in mid-ancient times with a liquid obtained by rubbing a piece of stone ink, and not until the Wei and Qin dynasties (221–419) were ink balls made by mixing the soot of lacquer and pinewood."[49] Many later scholars have inherited this theory that lacquer was first used for writing. Wuqiu Yan 吾丘衍 of the fourteenth century stated: "No brush and ink existed in antiquity; writings were made on bamboo tablets with a bamboo stylus dipped in lacquer."[50] Tao Zongyi 陶宗儀 of the fourteenth century and Jiang Shaoshu 江紹書 of the eighteenth century have made similar statements that lacquer, stone ink, and lampblack are the order of development of Chinese ink.[51]

Whether lacquer was ever used as a writing fluid is doubtful. There is no archeological evidence that any writings were ever made with lacquer. On the contrary, writings on bones, bamboo, and silk, as discovered from time to time, were all made with lampblack ink or vermilion. In early literature, a few references to lacquer writing are found, all written in or after the fifth century A.D. Fan Ye 范曄 (398–445) said that "Du Lin 杜林 (d. A.D. 47) had found at Xizhou one roll of the old text of the *Book of Documents*, written with lacquer."[52] He further mentioned the corruptions and controversies among the academic circles during the second century A.D. and that "scholars even privately bribed with gold to change the lacquer writings of the official text of the classics so as to be in conformity with their own versions."[53]

Another reference to lacquer writing was made by Fang Xuanling 房玄齡 (578–648), who described that bamboo tablets of the third century B.C., discovered in A.D. 280, were "written with lacquer in the tadpole style."[54] These tablets, however, were recorded as "written in black ink"[55] by Xun Xu 荀旭, who was an eyewitness to the discovery and edited the documents in the Imperial Library. Furthermore, ink is defined in the *Shuowen jiezi* as "something used for writing," but there is no mention of such use in the definition under the character *qi* 漆 for "lacquer."

The dubious nature of the evidence has led some modern scholars to the opinion that lacquer was probably never used as a writing material. One suggested that the term *qishu* 漆書, "lacquer writing," merely meant that the color of ink is as black as that of lacquer.[56] Another thought that since manufactured ink was popular in the Later Han dynasty, lacquer, being a natural product, would not still be used for writing.[57] Others considered that lacquer had no advantages over ink but had, on the contrary, decided disadvantages. It is difficult to write with after being mixed, and it dries slowly on the surface of bamboo or wood. As soon as silk and paper were available for writing, the brush proved most useful, and it is impossible to write in lacquer with a brush.[58]

The use of lacquer in writing, however, can only be possible in two situations. First, as a natural product obtained easily from the sap of the lacquer tree, it might have been used for writing on certain smooth surfaces for decorative purpose as evidenced by recent discoveries. But it was certainly not a major medium such as lampblack. Nor, judging from existing evidence, was it the original form of Chinese ink, as many scholars have believed. Secondly, the term "lacquer writing" could mean the use of soot manufactured by burning the sap of the lacquer tree, as is mentioned by many writers from the thirteenth century onward. Zhao Xigu and Tao Zongyi both wrote that "since the Wei and Qin dynasties, ink balls were made by mixing the smoke of lacquer and the soot of pinewood."[59] Some early recipes mention the use of dried lacquer as one of many ingredients to be mixed with pine soot in order to increase the brightness of the color.[60] In any case, lacquer could have been used as a minor substance in inkmaking, but there is no evidence that it was ever used as a fluid for regular writing.

Ink was probably also prepared from mineral substances as well as from lampblack. Many records, especially those written in the Qin dynasty, mention the use of *shimo* 石墨, or "stone ink." They generally relate the discovery of black minerals in the mountains located in present Guangdong, Hubei, Henan, Jiangxi, and other locations. Gu Wei

顧微 of the fourth century reported the stone ink of Huaihua (in modern Guangdong) as "fine and good for writing."[61] Sheng Hongzhi 盛弘之 of the fifth century mentioned a black mountain in Zhuyang (in modern Hubei), "where rocks are all dark as ink."[62] Li Daoyuan 酈道元 in the sixth century said that Xin'an and Ye (in modern Henan) all produced stone ink which could be used for writing.[63] Other sources mention similar black minerals in Lushan in modern Jiangxi.[64] Modern scholars believe that the so-called stone ink was either coal, graphite, or petroleum.[65] Since coal could not have produced an ink by rubbing on the palette, the so-called stone ink was probably graphite, which is a soft native carbon used for manufacturing "lead" pencils today. The locations in modern China where graphite is produced correspond closely to those described in the early literature.[66]

Materials and Forms of Ink Slabs

Chinese ink was probably made in solid form from very early times. In order to obtain a liquid for writing, the solid ink was rubbed with water on a palette. How early the ink slab was used in China is unknown, but as there were black and red pigments in the Shang dynasty, there might have been some kind of palette for mixing the fluid. We have, however, no literature concerning the ink slab earlier than the Han, nor any surviving ink slab before the Qin period. Certain statements concerning the use of the ink slab made by later scholars are mostly speculation, based upon insufficient evidence.[67] The earliest reliable information about the ink slab comes from the lexicon *Shuowen jiezi*, written about A.D. 100, which defines the *yan* 硯, or inkslab, as "a polished stone."[68] The *Shiming* 釋名 (ca. A.D. 200) says that "*yan* means rubbing."[69] It seems certain that the Chinese ink slab of the Han period was made of stone and used for grinding ink.

The earliest ink slab to survive was found in the Qin tomb in Shuihudi, Hubei, in 1975. It is made of cobblestone, oblong but irregular in shape, 6.8–7 cm long, 5.3–6 cm wide, and 2 cm thick. A rubber made of the same material was also found there with remnants of ink on it. Many other ink slabs of the Han and later period have also been discovered in recent years. A round stone ink slab and a stone rubber of the Former Han

INK SLAB MADE OF COBBLESTONE WITH A STONE RUBBER

dynasty were excavated in Fufeng, Shaanxi, in 1980. The ink slab is 4.7 cm thick and 23 cm in diameter, and its working surface is as glossy as a mirror. The rubber, light green in color and semi-circular in shape, stands on it. Two stone ink slabs made of cobblestone and stone rubbers of the Han period were also discovered at Zhangjiashan in Jiangling, Hubei. A rectangular stone ink slab of the Former Han period was excavated from a tomb in Tongshan, Jiangsu, in 1984. It is blue-black in color, 10 cm long, 4.5 cm wide, and 0.4 cm thick, with ink still on the slab. Another stone ink slab with a lacquer box was discovered in a tomb of the Han period at Yinqueshan, and its design is extremely well executed.[70]

The selection of stone for making the ink slab was a special art. Its quality, color, sound, texture, and markings were especially considered by both the makers and the users.[71] It is easy to grind and produce ink on a fine stone, but a coarse one that is too absorbent dries the ink too quickly. Ink slabs were of oblong, round, or other shapes, with wooden or lacquer fittings. The surface of the palette usually included a water cavity at the end away from the user and an oval ink grinding area at the center of the stone. Elaborate decorations or designs were sometimes made.

Besides stone, bricks and tiles were also common materials for making ink slabs. The bricks from the Han ruins of the Bronze Bird Terrace built by Cao Cao 曹操 in A.D. 210 have been especially prized for their quality of not absorbing ink. An oblong ink slab made of this brick is still preserved in the Palace Museum.[72] A round ink slab made of a Han palace tile with an inscription has also survived.[73] They were not, however, used for writing but made in the Han dynasty. Ink slabs dating to the Han period have been excavated in Anhui, Jiangsu, Henan, Gansu, Hunan, Hubei, Shandong, and Shanxi in recent years. They are often decorated with birds and animals, especially snakes, frogs, and turtles, and occasionally with landscapes.[74]

In 1934, a complete ink slab set with accompanying case was discovered in a Han tomb in Korea dating from the second or third century A.D. It consists of two parts, an ink slab and a rubbing piece, and a desk-shaped case or stand. The slab is an oblong slate; the rubber is a semicircular, knob-like wooden piece. The two are placed on a black lacquered wooden board. The desk-shaped case has a drawer which is partitioned into six sections, large and small, for keeping liquid ink. On the surface of the case there are two pairs of bronze tubes for holding writing brushes.[75] Besides this complete set, some detached or independent ink slabs and rubbers have been found in other tombs in Lelang, Korea, and also in China.

Besides stone, some special ink slabs were occasionally made of such unusual materials as jade, crystal, silver, iron, bronze, shells, and perhaps bamboo and wood. The *Xijing zaji* 西京雜記 says that the emperor used a jade ink slab because the water on it would not freeze.[76] The crystal ink slab was not used for grinding ink but for preserving the fluid prepared on other ink slabs. The ink slab made of iron from Khotan was said to have been bestowed by the Emperor Wu (r. 265–290) upon the scholar Zhang Hua 張華 (232–300) when his writing of the *Bowu zhi* 博物志 was completed.[77] Bronze ink slabs with three legs and a cover are mentioned among the discoveries in a tomb of unknown date during the Song dynasty.[78]

The tripod ink slab was probably the form generally used in the Han dynasty, as shown on the mural from Wangdu. A poem on an ink slab made by Fan Qin 繁欽 in the Later Han is quoted as saying: "Balanced with three legs comparable to a tripod of Xia bronze, symbolizing the mutual help of the constellations."[79] Fu Xuan 傅玄 (217–278) wrote: "Wood is prized for its softness; stone is good for its smoothness and hardness."[80] Here the wood mentioned by the writer was probably for making the cases or fittings, as it absorbs ink quickly and does not seem to be a good material for ink slabs. There are many literary records concerning ink slabs made of silver, shells, and other materials,[81] but their use was probably at a later date.

Book Knife as Eraser

The book knife was an important tool for preparing bamboo and wood for writing and for deleting and correcting writings on the tablets. Pieces of bamboo and wood must have been sliced and cut into narrow tablets of specific length, and their surface was then smoothed ready for writing with brush and ink. When mistakes were made, the surface would be scraped off for correction and rewriting. When an old tablet was used over again, the used surface had to be removed in order to obtain a new one. For many of these processes a sharp tool was used, either an ordinary knife called *dao* 刀 or *xue* 削, or a specially designed "book knife" known as *shudao* 書刀.[82]

There has been some confusion about the different kinds of cutting tools in connection with their use in writing. For example, the Song imperial catalogue of antique objects includes a short knife called the *daobi* 刀筆, or knife pen, which was described as being carried by people in the Han dynasty for deleting writings from tablets.[83] Ruan Yuan 阮元 (1764–1849), a Qing scholar, named a short cutting knife the *xue*, which was described as being similar to the *shudao*.[84] Another scholar even confused the *daobi* with the *qijue* 奇劂, a crooked burin for engraving on stone and other hard materials, and with the *huodao* 貨刀, or knife money.[85] Actually all of these were different objects with different names, forms, and uses.

The words *dao* (knife) and *bi* (brush) were often used together as a designation for a scribe or an official who was of low rank but powerful in terms of law enforcement. Sima Qian 司馬遷 (145–186 B.C.) noted that Xiao He 蕭何 (d. 193 B.C.), the prime minister of the Former Han dynasty, was formerly a *daobi li* 刀筆吏, a knife pen official, of the Qin.[86] Ban Gu 班固 (32–92) said that the *dao* and *bi*, basket and chest (for holding tablets), are common things employed by ordinary officials.[87] Many writers since the Tang dynasty have mistakenly believed that these two were one object used for engraving writings on tablets. Jia Gongyan 賈公彥 (fl. 650) noted, "In ancient times when paper and brush were not used, the book knife was employed for engraving characters; and in the Han period, even when paper and brush were accessible, it was still used as a matter of tradition."[88] Modern scholars have concluded that the *dao* was a knife for deleting and

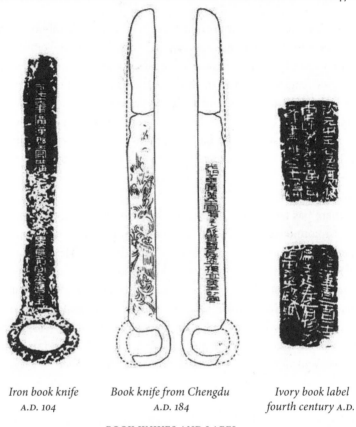

Iron book knife
A.D. 104

Book knife from Chengdu
A.D. 184

Ivory book label
fourth century A.D.

BOOK KNIVES AND LABEL

the *bi* was a brush for writing.[89] Since erasing was always necessary, the knife was probably an indispensable tool that accompanied the "four treasures of a scholar's studio" before paper was used for writing.[90]

Many literary references indicate that the *xue*, or cutter, also was used for erasing writings from the tablets. Sima Qian writes that Confucius "used the *bi*, brush, when it was proper to write and the *xue* when it was proper to delete."[91] The *Zuo zhuan* 左傳 also mentions that in 546 B.C., when Zuo Si 左思 of the Song state asked for a reward, the duke offered him sixty towns, but Zuo rejected the offer by scratching (*xue*) the statement off the tablet and throwing it back.[92] On other occasions, the *xue* is mentioned as having been used for cutting oranges, melons, or wooden instruments.[93] It is apparent that both *dao* and *xue* were common knives for cutting not only tablets but other objects.

According to literature, the *dao* was a longer and wider knife with a straight blade attached to a ring-shaped end, while the *xue* was a shorter and narrower knife with a curved blade attached to a solid handle.[94] The *Kaogong ji* 考工记, a chapter on manufacture in the *Rituals of Zhou*, states that metal artisans manufactured the *xue*, one foot long and one inch wide, with a curved blade bending 60 degrees. It is further described as being made of an alloy with "two parts of tin in every five parts of copper."[95] This would produce a sharper and more elastic blade than other kinds of metal.

The earliest reference to associate the *xue* with the *shudao*, book knife, comes from Zheng Xuan 鄭玄 (127–200), who interpreted the *xue* as "the *shudao* of today."[96] Zheng did not elaborate upon its use, but his contemporary Liu Xi 劉熙 defined the term *shudao* in his lexicon as "a knife provided for deleting when writing was made on the bamboo and wooden tablets."[97] The *Dongguan Han ji* 東觀漢記, an official history of A.D. 25–180, mentions that the *shudao* was granted together with gold and other rare provisions to a prefect of Chenliu by the emperor.[98] Ru Chun 如淳 of the third century said: "The *shudao* with the design of a golden horse is now used for bestowing on officials. The design consists of horses inlaid with gold on the ring."[99] The so-called "golden-horse book knife" is further described in a poem by Li You 李尤 (ca. 60–140), who wrote:

> It is skillfully smelted and tempered,
> Finished with a design of a golden horse;
> Polished and carved with yellow lines,
> And inscribed with the manufacturer's name.[100]

These descriptions are confirmed by recent discoveries and other specimens surviving in private collections. All these specimens are made of iron and bear inscriptions on one side and fine designs on the other. Both sides are decorated with gold inlaid in the blade and the ring handle. The designs consist of birds and animals. One specimen discovered in 1957 in a mountain tomb in Tianhuishan, Chengdu, Sichuan, bears a picture of a flying phoenix in the center followed by two small ones. Others bear designs of flying horses with wings.

The inscription tells the date and place of manufacture, name of object, and of the manufacturer. Specimen (a) in the former collection of Luo Zhenyu 羅振玉 (1866–1940) bears a long inscription of twenty-eight characters in one line on the blade. It reads "Made in the sixteenth year of Yongyuan 永元 (A.D. 104) by Feng Wu 馮武, an official charged with the manufacture of book knives at Guanghan prefecture (modern Guanghan, near Chengdu, Sichuan)."[101] Specimen (b) discovered in Sichuan bears an inscription which reads: "Made in the seventh year of Guanghe 光和 (A.D. 184) by an official in charge of manufacturing at Guanghan,"[102] followed by some good-will sayings similar to those in mirror inscriptions of the Later Han period. The mention of Guanghan as the place of manufacture in all the inscriptions agrees with the record in the dynastic history, which describes Sichuan as the place where book knives were made in the Former Han dynasty.

The recent discovery in Chengdu, Sichuan, confirms the fact that it was still the center of book knife manufacturing during the Later Han period.

Notes

1. For stationeries discovered in Fenghuangshan, Jiangling, see *Wenwu* 1976:10, 31–34; at the site of Xuanquan, see *Wenwu* 2000:5, 15; for recent discoveries of various writing implements, see Lily Kecskes, "Jinnianlai kaogu faxian de gudai shuxie gongju," *Tushu wenshi lunji* (Taibei, 1991), 91–99; (Beijing, 1992), 119–132.

2. *Taiping yulan*, 605/2b, 4b, 6a–b, 8b.

3. Ding Fubao, *Shuowen jiezi gulin*, 1271b, 1273a.

4. Pelliot, "Les bronze de la collection Eumorfopoulos," 375–378.

5. *Erya zhushu*, 5/17a.

6. Cf. Legge, *Li ki*, I, 91.

7. *Zhanguo ce*, 13/7a.

8. Yetts, *George Eumorfopoulos Collection Catalogue*, 1:15–17.

9. Dong Zuobin, "Jiaguwen duandai yanjiu li," 1:417–418.

10. Yetts, op. cit., 16; Creel, *Studies in Early Chinese Culture*, 43.

11. Liang Siyong, "Xiaotun Longshan yu Yangshao," *Qingzhu Cai Yuanpei xiansheng liushiwu sui lunwenji*, 2:555–568.

12. Cai Yong, *Cai Zhonglang ji*, 3/3b.

13. Wang Chong, *Lun Heng*, 13/4b.

14. For discovery of a brush in Changsha, see *Wenwu cankao ziliao*, 1954:12, 8.

15. For Qin brushes from Shuihudi, see *Yunmeng Shuihudi Qin mu*, 26. fig. 19, plate 10.1; from Baoshan, see *Wenwu* 1988:5, 9–10; from Fangmatan, see *Wenwu* 1989:12.

16. For Han brushes from Fenghuangshan, see *Wenwu* 1976:10, 31–35; *Zhongguo kaogu xuebao* 1993:4, 494–495; from Linyi, see *Wenwu* 1984:11, 41–58; from Wuwei, see *Wenwu* 1972:12, 9–21; and from Xuanquan, see *Wenwu* 2000:5, 12–15, fig. 14.

17. Ma Heng, "Ji Han Juyan bi," *Guoxue jikan*, III:1 (1932), 67–72.

18. Xu Jian, *Chuxue ji*, 21/27a.

19. Oba Tsunekichi and Kayamoto Kamejirō, *Rakurō Ō Kō bo*, 49.

20. Fu Xuan, *Fu Chungu ji*, 3/4b.

21. Chavannes, "Les livres chinois avant l'invention du papier," 70; Li Shuhua, "Zhi wei faming yiqian Zhongguo wenzi liuchuan gongju," *Dalu zazhi*, no. 9 (1954), 170.

22. Zhao Xigu, *Dongtian qinglu*, quoted in *Gezhi jingyuan*, 37/20a.

23. Bai Juyi and Kong Zhuan, *Bai Kong liutie*, 14/30a; Ouyang Xiu, *Xin Tang shu*, 221a–223a.

24. Stein, *Ancient Khotan*, 1:398, 403; plate cv.

25. Wan Jinli, *Wenfang sibao jinping jianshang yu jiazhi* (Beijing, 1994), 14.

26. For the history and appreciation of Chinese ink, see Tsien, *Paper and Printing*, 234–252; Lily Kecskes, "Chinese Ink and Inkmaking," *Printing History* 8:1 (1986), 3–12.

27. Chavannes, op. cit., 66; Laufer, op. cit., 11.

28. Lu You, *Mo shi*, 1/1a–b.

29. *Gezhi jingyuan*, 37/21a.

30. *Hou Han shu*, 10a/19b.

31. *Taiping yulan*, 605/4b.

32. Legge, *The Life and Works of Mencius*, 474.

33. *Zhuangzi*, 7/36.

34. Han Ying, *Han shi waizhuan*, 7/6a–b.

35. *Guanzi*, 9/1b.

36. *Xi'an Banpo* (Beijing, 1963), 156.

37. Creel, *Studies in Early Chinese Culture*, 45.

38. Dong Zuobin, "Jiaguwen duandai yanjiu li," op. cit., I, 417–418.

39. Britton, "Oracle-Bone Color Pigments," *HJAS*, II (1937), 1–3.

40. *Da Dai liji*, 6/1a.

41. Quoted in *Taiping yulan*, 707/3a.

42. Legge, *Ch'un Ts'ew with the Tso Chuen*, 501.

43. Wang Chi-chen, "Notes on Chinese Ink," *Metropolitan Museum Studies*, III (1930–31), 115.

44. Shen Kuo, *Mengxi bitan*, 24/1a–b.

45. Ding Yan, *Cao ji quanping*, 58.

46. Chavannes, op. cit., 66.

47. Laufer, op. cit., 11, 13.

48. Carter, op. cit., (1925), 24; (rev. ed., 1955), 32, 35, note 1.

49. *Gezhi jingyuan*, 37/20a.

50. Wuqiu Yan, *Xue gu bian*, in *Shuofu* (1927 ed.), 91/la.

51. Tao Zongyi, *Chuogeng lu*, 29/11; Jiang Shaoshu, *Yunshizhai bitan*, first ser. 2/22–23.

52. *Hou Han shu*, 57/8a.

53. Ibid., 108/21b, 109a/3a.

54. *Jin shu*, 51/25b.

55. *Mutianzi zhuan*, preface, 3a.

56. Wang Guowei, "Jiandu jianshu kao," 8a, in *Haining Wang Jing'an xiansheng yishu*, v. 26.

57. Ma Heng, "Zhongguo shuji zhidu bianqian zhi yanjiu," *Tushuguanxue jikan*, 205–206

58. Wang Chi-chen, op. cit., 119.

59. *Gezhi jingyuan*, 37/20a.

60. Ibid., 37/25a.

61. *Taiping yulan*, 605/5b.

62. Ibid., 605/5a.

63. Li Daoyuan, *Shuijing zhu*, 10/9a; 15/9a.

64. *Gezhi jingyuan*, 37/29b–30a.

65. Laufer, op. cit., 13; Wang Chi-chen, op. cit., 124.

66. Cihai says that *shimo*, or graphite, is produced in Jiangxi, Hunan, Guangdong, Jiangsu, and Anhui.

67. See passages quoted in *Taiping yulan*, 605/6a; *Gezhi jingyuan*, 38/1–2.

68. Ding Fubao, *Shuowen jiezi gulin*, 4207b.

69. Liu Xi, *Shiming*, 6–45a.

70. For discoveries of ink slabs in Shuihudi, see *Shuihudi Qin mu*, 26; in Fufeng, *Zhongyuan wenwu* 1985:1, 10–13; in Jiangling, *Wenwu* 1985:1, 1–8; in Tongshan, *Wenwu ziliao congkan* 1977:1; and in Linyi, *Wenwu* 1984:11, 59–61.

71. Cf. van Gulik, *Mi Fu on Ink-stones*, 22–23.

72. *Gugong zhoukan*, no. 339 (1934), 4.

73. *Hebei diyi bowuyuan banyuekan*, no. 35 (1933), 1.

74. Ferguson, *Lidai zhulu jijin mu*, 1111, lists seven items dating from the Han period as having been recorded and reproduced in various works.

75. Koizumi and Hamada, *Rakurō saikyōzuka*, 45–46.

76. *Xijing zaji*, 1/1b.

77. *Taiping yulan*, 605/6a.

78. Van Gulik, *Mi Fu on Ink-stones*, 54.

79. Su Yijian, *Wenfang sipu*, 3/6a–b.

80. Ibid., 3/6a.

81. *Gezhi jingyuan*, 38/20a–21b.

82. For a detailed study of the "book knife," see Tsien, "Handai shudao kao," *Guoli zhongyang yanjiuyuan lishi yuyan yanjiusuo jikan*, Extra Volume, no. 4 (1961), 997–1008, translated by John H. Winkelman, "A Study of the Book Knives in Han China," *Chinese Culture*, 21:1 (March, 1971), 87–101.

83. Wang Fu, *Xuanhe bogu tulu*, 27/40.

84. Ruan Yuan, *Jiguzhai zhongding yiqi kuanzhi*, 8/22b.

85. Ma Ang, *Huobu wenzi kao*, 4/24b–25b.

86. *Shi ji*, 53/6a.

87. *Han shu*, 48/17a.

88. *Zhouli zhushu*, 40/10a–b.

89. Including Chavannes, Wang Guowei, Ma Heng, Wang Zhongmin, and Li Shuhua; see discussions in Tsien, op. cit., 1004.

90. Tsien, *Zhongguo shuji zhimo ji yinshuashi lunwenji* (Hong Kong, 1992), 43–56.

91. *Shiji*, 47/26b.

92. Legge, *Ch'un Ts'ew with the Tso Chuen*, 531.

93. See quotations from *Yanzi chunqiu*, *Zhouli*, *Li ji*, *Zhuangzi*, *Xunzi*, *Mozi*, and discussions in Tsien, op. cit., 999.

94. Sun Yirang, *Zhouli zhengyi*, 78/2b.

95. *Zhouli zhushu*, 40/10a.

96. Ibid.

97. Liu Xi, *Shi ming*, 7/52b.

98. Quoted in *Taiping yulan*, 345/3a.

99. *Han shu*, 89/3a.

100. Quoted in *Taiping yulan*, 103/46; but the author of the poem is mistakenly given as Li Yuan. According to the *Hou Han shu*, 110a/14b, Li You, a noted scholar, was a native of Guanghan, where fine book knives are known to have been manufactured.

101. Luo Zhenyu, *Zhensongtang jigu yiwen*, 15/11a–12a; Huang Jun, *Hengzhai jijin shixiaolu*, II, 6–7.

102. *Kaogu xuebao*, 1958:1, 101, Plate XII: 4.

6   RAW MATERIALS FOR PAPERMAKING

The discovery that fibers can be formed into a thin sheet on a screen is the key to the invention of paper. According to studies of existing specimens and documentary evidence, the first Chinese papermakers utilized almost every type of plant known to the modern paper industry that produces the best fibers and also is known for being the most economical.

Hemp is the earliest material known to have been used for papermaking in China prior to the Christian era, followed by paper mulberry in the early second century A.D. Rattan was especially popular for making the finest papers in southeast China for almost a millennium—from the third to about the twelfth century—until the supply of the raw material was exhausted. Bamboo then gradually replaced both rattan and hemp as the chief material for papermaking in the latter part of the eighth century. Rice and wheat straw, the bark of sandalwood and different species of trees, stalks of hibiscus, seaweed, and various other plants were also used in making specialty papers. Whether cotton and silk have ever been used remains controversial. Raw cotton is needed for textiles and is not economical, and pure silk is said to be technically unfeasible for papermaking. It was most likely the floss silk from the waste of silk cocoons that was used for making specialty papers. Apparently, the raw plant fibers were not used by European papermakers until the eighteenth century, when Western papers began to be fabricated from raw hemp, straw, wood, and other materials as the supply of linen and cotton rags became insufficient. It was not until the early part of the nineteenth century that wood pulp was widely used as the primary raw material in papermaking.

The most important process in papermaking is the forming of felted fibers into a thin sheet on a mat or screen from a water suspension. The manufacture of paper in China is generally believed to have originated from pounding and stirring rags in water, after which the wadded fibers were collected on a mat.[1] It is likely that an accidental placing of fibers from rags on a mat with water draining away suggested the idea of making a thin sheet of paper. It is believed that paper was first made of reused materials, the supply of which was limited. When the materials expanded to include such fresh vegetable fibers as those of raw hemp and tree bark, the large-scale production of paper from an unlimited supply of fibers became possible.

Almost all plants produce fibers, but only those rich in cellulose, abundant in supply, easy to treat, and cheap in cost are most suitable. Especially ideal are those plants containing higher yields of long cellulose and that are lower in binding substances that must be eliminated in the process of maceration. These materials include the bast plants, such as hemp, jute, flax, ramie, and rattan; tree bark of mulberry and paper mulberry; grasses such as bamboo, reeds, and stalks of rice and wheat; and such fibers as cotton. Hemp and cotton are probably the best options, because they produce the highest yields of pure fibers, but as they are needed primarily for the textile industry, paper mulberry and bamboo became the chief raw materials for papermaking in China.

Chronologically speaking, hemp was probably the earliest material used for papermaking from the Former or Western Han (206 B.C.–8 A.D.), followed by paper mulberry from the Later or Eastern Han (25–220), rattan from the Jin (265–420), bamboo from the middle of the Tang (618–906), and straw probably from before the Song dynasty (960–1280). Except for hemp, which was no longer used in large quantity after the Tang, and rattan, the supply of which was exhausted by the early Song, these materials are still in use today. The use of raw fibers for papermaking varied a great deal according to the local production of the materials. Su Yijian 蘇易簡 (957–995), author of the first treatise on paper, wrote that hemp was used in Sichuan, bamboo in Jiangsu and Zhejiang, mulberry bark in the north, rattan in Shanxi, and seaweed by the people in the south seas. Paper made of wheat stalks and rice straw by the people of Zhejiang was brittle and thin; and that of wheat stalks mixed with rattan from Youquan was the best.[2] This seems to be true even in much earlier and later times. The following section details some of the most common raw materials known to have been used in China. The nature and preparation of the fibers and the origin and extent of their use are carefully traced to document the long history of Chinese hand papermaking throughout the centuries.

Hemp, Jute, Flax, and Ramie

The plants which yield the richest and strongest bast fibers were the earliest materials used in Chinese papermaking. The major varieties of the bast-yielding group are hemp (*Cannabis salioa*), known in Chinese as *dama* 大麻, jute (*Corchorus capsularis*) or *huangma* 黃麻, flax (*Linum perenne*), *yama* 亞麻, and ramie or China grass (*Boehmeria nivea*), *zhuma* 苧麻. They were grown in all parts of China, especially in the northern and western regions. Chinese documents refer to all of these varieties as *ma*, which has generally been rendered as hemp. This was probably the earliest fiber plant used for clothing in China before the extensive use of cotton fibers for textiles in the Ming dynasty. Ramie or China grass is a

HEMP AND ITS FIBERS

perennial plant. Song Yingxing 宋應星 (ca. 1600–1660) described two varieties of ramie, green and yellow. Their stems could be cut two or three times each year; from these fibers were obtained material for making summer clothing, curtains, and mosquito nets.[3] Most of the ancient papers were made of either reused materials or raw fibers from the bast plants.

The oldest paper of the Former Han period discovered in Northwest China is said to have been made of hemp fibers. The specimens found in Ba Qiao, Shanxi, in 1957, and dated no later than the period of Wudi (r. 140–87 B.C.) are probably made of rags or other used materials of hemp, as some remnants and impressions of textiles are visible on the surface.[4] The fragments found in Lopnor in 1934 and dated to the first century B.C. are reported to have been made of similar material.[5] Hemp was also one of the raw materials used by Cai Lun 蔡倫 (fl. 75–121), as mentioned in the dynastic history, and other materials such as the rags and fish nets used by him might also have been made of hemp.[6] Those papers from the third to the eighth centuries found in Chinese Turkestan consist of, besides mulberry bark, chiefly raw and fabricated fibers of hemp, flax, and China grass.[7] The manuscripts found in Dunhuang, dating from the fourth to the tenth century, were made chiefly of hemp, jute, and China grass.[8] Some thirty-two documents in the Beijing collection, dated 265–960, are reported to have been made mostly of hemp.[9]

Hemp paper, which is described as pliable but tough, fine, and waterproof, was especially popular for use in calligraphy, bookmaking, and official documents in the Tang dynasty. It was produced largely in Sichuan in different sizes and colors, and it was especially chosen by the imperial court for writing decrees, daily instructions and orders, and other official documents.[10] Every month the court provided scholars in the Academy of Assembled Worthies (*Jixian Shuyuan* 集賢書院) five thousand sheets of hemp paper made in Sichuan.[11] In the Kaiyuan period (713–42), all the books in the imperial collections in the two capitals were written on hemp paper made in Yizhou (modern Sichuan).[12] No specific mention of hemp is found after the Tang dynasty. It is assumed that hemp has not been the chief material for papermaking since that time. The proof of hemp being the first material used in papermaking was the discovery of a sheet of fibers drained on a mat. The fibers were derived from rags made primarily of hemp. Hemp was also used for papermaking in Europe before the early nineteenth century, when wood pulp was commercialized. Even today, many high-quality papers are still made of hemp. Being more in demand as a material for textile, ropes, and other uses, however, it was gradually replaced by rattan and bamboo after the Tang dynasty.

Rattan

The climbing rattan (*Calamus rotang*) is known to have been used for making paper in certain regions of China, especially in the southeastern part corresponding to modern Zhejiang and Jiangxi, where paper made of this plant was popular for almost a thousand years. Rattan paper is said to have also been made in Sichuan, but its production was apparently limited in comparison with that from the southeast. The origin of the use of rattan for papermaking can be traced back to the third century at Shanxi (modern Shengxian, Zhejiang), where rattan plants were said to have

spread over hundreds of miles on the mountains along the Shanxi river. The old paper made of rattan from Shanxi has been called Shanteng 剡藤, or "rattan paper of Shanxi." Fan Ning 范寧 (339–401), a native of Henan and an official who served in the capital, recorded that locally made paper could not be used for official documents and that rattan and bark paper was used instead.[13]

Rattan paper became most popular in the Tang dynasty, and the area of its production was greatly extended beyond Shanxi to many neighboring districts in Zhejiang and Jiangxi. During the first part of the eighth century, it was recorded in official gazetteers and other documents that paper was an item of local tribute from some eleven districts, including Hangzhou, Chuzhou, Wuzhou (all in modern Zhejiang), and Xinzhou (in modern Jiangxi), from where only rattan paper was sent.[14] Some of the districts are said to have sent as many as six thousand sheets of rattan paper at one time. A special variety of rattan paper made in Youquan 由拳, a village of Hangzhou, known as "Youquan paper," was especially popular.

Rattan paper—described as smooth, durable, with fine texture, and in different colors—was selected for documents, bookmaking, calligraphy, and other uses. The administrative codes of the Tang dynasty specified that the white rattan paper be used for decrees on bestowing, requisition, and punishment; blue for sacrificial messages at the Daoist temple Taiqinggong; and yellow for imperial instructions and orders.[15] Many manuscripts from Dunhuang are written on rattan paper dyed yellow. The famous calligrapher Mi Fu 米芾 (1051–1107) said: "The back of the rattan paper from Taizhou can be written on, since it is smooth and hairless. It is the best in the world and can never be matched."[16] It was also used for making bags to preserve tea leaves after roasting, because its firm texture prevented the loss of flavor.[17]

Because the rattan plant grew naturally in a limited area and its growth was slow as compared with that of hemp, which can be harvested in one year, or of paper mulberry, in three years, the supply of rattan was gradually exhausted. Many writers lamented the extermination of the plant through excessive cutting without cultivation. A Tang scholar-official, Shu Yuanyu 舒元輿 (d. 835), satirized people who frequently wrote millions of useless words, which easily killed the growth of rattan.[18] The gradual exhaustion of rattan in Shanxi shifted the center of production of rattan paper from the western to the eastern part of Zhejiang in the Song dynasty. The rattan paper made in Tiantai, known as *taiteng* 台藤, became popular in the Song, while that of Youquan continued to be popular. There were several reasons for the gradual decline of the use of rattan in papermaking after the Song. One was the depletion of the material, and another was the growing use of bamboo, which replaced rattan and hemp as the chief raw material for papermaking after the middle of the Tang dynasty.

Paper Mulberry and Mulberry

The earliest reference to the use of tree bark for papermaking is found in the biography of Cai Lun in the *Hou Han shu* 後漢書 *History of the Later Han Dynasty*. It does not specify the kind of tree bark, but Dong Ba 董巴 of the early third century wrote that "The Eastern Capital (Loyang) has the paper of Marquis Cai, which was the paper made by Cai Lun; that made of used hemp is called hemp paper; that of tree bark *guzhi* 穀紙 (paper mulberry paper); and that of used nets net paper."[19] *Gu* 穀 or paper mulberry (*Broussonetia papyrifera*) is a shrub which grows naturally in many parts of China, especially in the north. It became domesticated by farmers who cultivated the tree as one of their subsidiary crops because a large supply of its bark was needed for papermaking. The *gu, chu* 楮, and *gou* 構 (also pronounced *gu*) all belong to the same mulberry family but are different species. The three names have been confused because the shapes of the three kinds of leaves and also the pronunciation of the three names are very similar.

The earliest literature to describe the methods of planting and harvesting the shrub and the treatment of its bark is included in a work on agriculture and farming by Jia Sixie 賈思勰 (fl. 543–559), a magistrate of Gaoyang district in modern Shandong. The chapter on planting paper mulberry reads:

PAPER MULBERRY AND ITS FIBERS

The *gu* (paper mulberry) should be planted in very good ground along the streams in a valley. In the autumn, when the fruits of the paper mulberry are ripe, collect them abundantly, wash, clean, and dry in the sun. Till the ground thoroughly. In the second month, after the soil is plowed, sow seeds of the tree mixed with those of flax, and smooth the ground with labor. In the autumn and winter, the flax should not be cut in order to keep the paper mulberry warm. [If this is not done, the tree will die in most cases.] In the first month of the next year, cut the trunks close to the ground and burn them. Thus the trees will grow taller than a man after one year. [If not burnt, it grows lean, although long but slow.] The tree can be cut for use after three years. [If cut in less than three years, the skin will be too thin and not suitable for use.]

The method of cutting: The best time for cutting is in the twelfth month, or the next best, the fourth month [If cut at other times, the paper mulberry usually withers and dies.] In the first month of every year, burn the ground with fire. [The dry leaves on the ground will be enough for burning. If not burnt, it will not grow luxuriantly.] In the middle of the second month, select and weed out the weak ones. [Weeding is to enrich the trees and to preserve enough strength and moisture in the ground.] Those transplanted should also be planted in the second month and cut every three years [If not cut by three years, there will be loss of money and no profit.]

If the trees are sold on the ground, labor is saved, but the profit will be less; selling the bark after boiling and peeling is more laborious but profitable. [The wood is useful as fuel.] If the bark can be used for making the paper by itself, the profit will be even higher. Those who plant 30 *mou* 畝 can harvest 10 *mou* every year, thus the field can be rotated every three years and make an annual income equal to one hundred *pi* 匹[20] of silk.[21]

This passage points out that the major purpose of planting the paper mulberry was to produce raw material for papermaking and that the process of boiling and peeling the tree bark was the first step in making paper. It was a highly profitable agricultural practice to combine planting the tree and manufacturing the paper as a handicraft by farmers.

The use of paper mulberry bark for papermaking might have originated from the craft of making *tapa*, a beaten bark cloth that was very popular throughout the Pacific.[22] The name *tapa* is very close to the Chinese terms for bark cloth: *dabu* 答布 or *tabu* 榻（搨）布, which may mean a cloth made by beating,[23] or *gubu* 穀布, a cloth made of paper mulberry. This kind of bark cloth appears often in early Chinese literature as a local product of the non-Chinese tribes in the south and southwest regions. As this was made primarily for clothing rather than for writing, it has been called cloth instead of paper, although the process of making it by beating is closer to papermaking than it is to the spinning and weaving of cloth. It is also suggested that the Chinese invention of the art of papermaking could have been influenced by the bark cloth culture that existed in China before the manufacture of paper through a process of felting.[24]

Paper mulberry bark is known to have been used to make hats, called *chuguan* 楮冠, during the time of Confucius.[25] Many paper articles such as garments, armor, bed sheets, curtains, and screens, popular in the Tang and Song dynasties, might have been made of the flexible and durable paper mulberry bark. It was the chief material of the paper money known as *chuchao* 楮鈔 and for windows, book covers, and other uses. Paper mulberry bark paper was commonly used for writing in the Qin and Tang dynasties. Many manuscripts found in Dunhuang and Turfan are reported to have been made of *chu* bark.[26]

Whether mulberry bark was used for papermaking in China has been controversial. Commenting on Marco Polo's observation that Chinese paper money was made of "the bark of certain trees, in fact of the mulberry tree,"[27] Bretschneider replied: "He seems to be mistaken, paper in China is not made from mulberry trees, but from the *Broussonetia papyrifera*."[28] To prove that bark of the mulberry tree, as well as that of paper mulberry, was used as a material for paper, Laufer cited a number of authorities and concluded: "Marco Polo is perfectly correct: not only did the Chinese actually manufacture paper from the bark of the mulberry tree (*Morus alba*), but also it was this paper which was preferred for the making of paper money."[29]

Chinese sources testify that the mulberry tree was and is still used for papermaking. Su Yijian noted that paper was made from the bark of the mulberry tree (*sangpi* 桑皮) by the people in the north.[30] *The History of the Ming Dynasty* also specifies that paper money was "made of mulberry fiber (*sangrang* 桑穰) in rectangular sheets, one foot long and six inches wide, the material being of a greenish color."[31] The levy of some two million catties of mulberry bark for the manufacture of paper money in 1644, apparently because of inflation, almost provoked the peasants into rebellion.[32] Song Yingxing noted that "mulberry fiber paper (*sangrang zhi* 桑穰紙), made from the bark of mulberry trees, is extremely thick and smooth; that produced in east Zhejiang it is vital to the silk producers in the lower Yangtze region for repositories for silkworm eggs."[33] Even today, the mulberry is described as "produced in all provinces of China and its bark is a very good material for papermaking."[34]

Bamboo

This plant was extensively cultivated in China, except for the extreme northern part of the country. It was grown as far north as the provinces along the Yellow River, but was driven much farther south by the change of weather or deforestation. It is now abundantly grown in the Yangtze valley and the provinces to the south, especially Jiangsu, Zhejiang, Fujian, and Guangdong. Because of its long fibers, rapid growth, and low cost, it has been a major source of raw fibers for papermaking since the middle of the Tang dynasty.[35]

The earliest reference to the use of bamboo for making paper is found in a book by the Tang historian Li Zhao 李肇 (fl. 806–820), who wrote that "bamboo paper (*zhu zhi* 竹紙) was made in Shaozhou (in modern Guangdong)."[36] His contemporary Duan Gonglu 段公路 (fl. 850) also mentioned the use of "bamboo-membrane paper," which was said to have been produced in Wuzhou in modern Zhejiang.[37] Because the first use of the material must have been earlier than the recorded date, it is assumed that bamboo was first used in papermaking not later than the middle of the Tang, or the second half of the eighth century. It was apparently devel-

BAMBOO AND ITS FIBERS

oped as a substitute for hemp, which was a chief material for textiles, and for rattan, which was nearly exhausted by the end of the Tang dynasty.

The use of bamboo probably originated in Guangdong, where the plant grew abundantly in the warm and humid climate. The method had spread to Zhejiang and Jiangsu by the Song dynasty, but the technique of making bamboo paper seems to have been still in the initial stages of experimentation and the product not then perfected. Su Yijian wrote that paper was made of young shoots of bamboo in the Jiangsu and Zhejiang areas in his time. When this paper was used in confidential correspondence, no one would try to open the letter (during delivery), as it would break upon touching and would not hold together again.[38] The great poet Su Shi 蘇軾 (1032–1101) said, "Modern people use bamboo for making paper, which was not done in ancient times."[39] Another Sung author, Zhou Mi 周密 (1232–1298), said that the use of bamboo paper began in the Shunxi period (1174–1189).[40] This suggests that bamboo paper was unknown in his locality until the second part of the twelfth century. A local gazetteer of Guiji (in modern Zhejiang), compiled in 1201, records: "The name of rattan paper of Shanxi came the earliest, seaweed paper next, and bamboo paper has become popular throughout the country only recently."[41]

From the literary records, it can be concluded that bamboo paper was invented in the latter part of the eighth century and not yet perfected in the tenth century, but the product from Shanxi, with many different varieties and colors, became popular especially with artists toward the end of the twelfth or beginning of the thirteenth century. It is still not clear, however, how bamboo paper was developed during the long period between its initiation in the eighth and its perfection in the twelfth century. But the description in the gazetteer suggests that the methods of preparing bamboo fibers were apparently borrowed from those used in the long experience with rattan.

A detailed account of the use of bamboo for papermaking is included in a seventeenth-century work on Chinese technology by Song Yingxing, who devoted a long chapter to papermaking with bamboo and paper mulberry bark. Of bamboo paper, he recorded:

> The making of bamboo paper is a craft of the south, especially popular in Fujian province. After the bamboo shoots have started to grow, the topography of the mountain area should be surveyed. The best material for papermaking is the shoots that are about to put forth branches and leaves. During the season of mangzhong 芒種 (about the sixth day of the sixth month), the bamboo on the mountains, with new branches that are about to emerge, are cut into pieces from five to seven feet long. A pool is dug right there in the mountain and filled with water in which the bamboo stems are soaked. Water is constantly led into it by means of bamboo pipes to prevent the pool from drying up.
>
> After soaking for more than one hundred days, the bamboo is carefully pounded and washed to remove the coarse husk and green bark. The inner fibers of the bamboo, with a hemp-like appearance, are mixed with high-grade lime in a thick fluid and put into a pot to be boiled over a fire for eight days and nights . . . After the fire has been put out for one day, the bamboo fibers are taken from the cask and thoroughly washed in a pool with clean water . . . When the fibers have been washed clean, they are soaked in a solution of wood ashes and put again into a pot, pressed to flatten the top, and covered with about an inch of rice straw ashes . . . After some ten days of treatment, the bamboo pulp naturally becomes odorous and decayed. It is then taken out to be pounded in a mortar until it has the appearance of clay or dough, and the pulp is then poured into a vat for use.[42]

Song Yingxing continues to describe the steps of collecting the bamboo pulp on the screen-mold, removing and pressing the sheets to release the water, and finally drying the paper on a heated wall. This method must have continued in use, as about two centuries later the process of making bamboo paper was described by a scholar, Yang Zhongxi 楊鍾羲 (1865–1940), whose eyewitness account is similar to that of Song, except that he mentions that from the cutting of the shoots to the drying by heat the material changes hands seventy-two times before it becomes paper. In his account he recalls a proverb in the paper trade: "A sheet of paper does not come easy; it takes seventy-two steps to make."[43] The process of making bamboo paper by hand continues to be more or less the same in modern times.[44]

Other Materials

Besides the major materials discussed above, many other plants were used. Most common among these were the stalks of rice and wheat. The process of making straw paper (*caozhi* 草紙) was much simpler than that for other materials. Since these fibers are tender, less time was required for beating in preparation. Su Yijian noted that straw of wheat and rice was used in Zhejiang and that it produced the best paper when mixed with rattan.[45] Song Yingxing mentioned the mixing of rice stalks with bamboo fibers to make wrapping paper,[46] and Dard Hunter recorded that the straw first receives a preliminary pounding and then, after saturation in a lime solution, is buried in a trench. When properly disintegrated, the straw is removed and placed in porous cloth bags, which in turn are suspended in a running stream so that the fibers may be cleansed of all particles of lime.[47] Straw is still one of the most commonly used raw materials for making paper for wrapping, burning, and sanitary purposes.

Sandalwood bark (*Dalbergia hupeana*), known in Chinese as *tanpi* 檀皮, was the major material for making the famous *xuanzhi* 宣紙 for painting and calligraphy. It is a hard wood, primarily grown in the Xuancheng area in Anhui, and is said to have been discovered as a raw material for paper by accident in the Later Han dynasty. A legend of the present-day Jinxian area, where *xuanzhi* was made, relates that Kong Dan 孔丹, a sup-

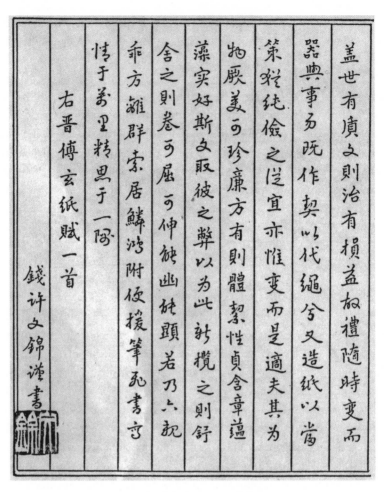

EARLIEST POEM ON PAPER

Poem by Fu Xian, 239–293 (Calligraphy by Wen-ching H. Tsien);
an English translation was presented to the Needham Institute, England

posed disciple of Cai Lun, found the bark of a tan tree which had turned rotten and white after being soaked in a stream, and such fibers have since been used for making a white paper.[48]

Another fiber often mentioned as a raw material for papermaking is the bark of the hibiscus (*Hibiscus mulabilis*), known in Chinese as *furongpi* 芙蓉皮. It is generally believed that the famous stationery designed by the courtesan Xue Tao 薛涛 (768–831) of Sichuan was made of hibiscus bark. Song Yingxing said that "the bark of the hibiscus is cooked to a pulp, and aqueous extract of powdered hibiscus flower petals is added. This process was probably first devised by Xue Tao and has been known by that name down to the present day. This paper is famous for its beauty, not for the quality of its material."[49]

The use of seaweed for making "intricate filament paper" (celizhi 侧理紙) appears frequently in early Chinese literature. Wang Jia 王嘉 of the fourth century wrote: "When Zhang Hua 張華 (232–300) presented his work Bowuzhi 博物志 to the emperor, he was granted ten thousand pieces of zhili paper, which was sent as tribute from Nan Yue 南越 (modern Vietnam). The Chinese pronounced zhi 紙 as zhili 陟貍 by mistake. Since the people in the south used seaweed (haidai 海帶) in the making of paper with intricate and crooked lines, it was so called."[50] Many other authors from the fourth century continued to make reference to the use of seaweed in papermaking.[51] Su Yijian noted that paper was made from tai 苔 in the south.[52] It is uncertain, however, whether seaweed was the chief raw material or merely an ingredient to be mixed with other fibrous materials for papermaking. Since seaweed contains long, strong, viscous filaments, it is possible that this material was used for making paper or for sizing, and thus the intricate hairy filaments appeared on the surface of the paper as a decorative pattern.

Although cotton produces the best fiber of all, it has not been used as a major material for paper because of its importance in the textile industry. A certain variety called cotton paper (mianzhi 棉紙) was not actually made of cotton but of paper mulberry. Song Yingxing wrote: "Torn lengthwise, the strong, hard-sized bark paper will show ragged edges resembling cotton fibers, hence it is called 'cotton paper.'"[53] Cotton stems have been used for papermaking, but "cotton paper" is certainly not made from raw cotton.

Whether silk has ever been used as a raw material for papermaking is uncertain. Mention of the use of silk fibers is based primarily upon philological speculation without sufficient evidence. It was thought that since the character zhi 紙 for paper bears the silk radical at its left, the zhi before Cai Lun's time must have been made of silk fiber.[54] It is true that silk cloth was

CHINESE PAPERMAKING

(a) Cutting and soaking bamboo twigs   (b) Cooking inner mass of bamboo in a pot
(c) Dipping the mold and lifting pulp from the vat   (d) Pressing moist paper sheets
to release water   (e, f) Drying paper sheets on a heated wall

written on before the invention of paper. The word *zhi* is thought to be derived from one for silk, but the material for *zhi* was not necessarily made of
silk fibers. Technically, as many experts have said, silk fibers do not possess

the colloid properties which contribute so essentially to the entanglement and binding of plant fibers.[55] At present, no actual paper made of pure silk fibers is known to exist, nor is their use documented in literature.

It is possible, however, that silk fibers have been used in a mixture with other fibers, or that floss silk from silk cocoons has been used. Several references have been made to the use of silk cocoon paper (*canjianzhi* 蠶繭紙). One reference from the early eighth century states that the famous calligrapher Wang Xizhi 王羲之 (321–379) used silk cocoon paper in writing.[56] The Jinsu 金粟 paper made in Suzhou in 1068–1094 for copying the *Tripitaka* was said also to have been made of silk cocoons.[57] Song Yingxing remarked that the entangled or broken cocoons cannot be reeled into ordinary silk, but are made into a wadding known as "pot-bottom silk," used for quilting garments and bedding.[58] It is likely that silk waste or floss silk was used to make silk paper, since cocoons contain a gum which would serve to bind fibers and which is removed when pure silk is reeled.

The use of fresh plant fibers as raw material was apparently unknown to European papermakers when the craft of papermaking was introduced to Europe in the middle of the twelfth century. For over five hundred years after the introduction, all paper of occidental origin was made from linen and cotton rags or a mixture of these second-hand fibers. Ever since the beginning of the eighteenth century, as rags gradually became less plentiful and no longer an economical material, European scientists have been looking for other materials to meet the increasing need of the paper industry.[59] A great variety of vegetation, including hemp, bark, wood, straw, vines, moss, and grain husks, was tested and examined, even though such materials had already been in use in China for many centuries. Finally, wood pulp was widely adopted and has become, since the beginning of the nineteenth century, the chief raw material of the modern paper industry. Because of the limitations of forest resources in China, where most wood must be used in construction, this material was little utilized for paper. Even today, use of other materials other than wood is encouraged.[60]

Published in the Journal of the American Oriental Society, *v. 93, no. 4 (October–December, 1973)*

Notes

1. See the commentaries of Duan Yucai (1735–1805) on the definition of paper as "a mat of refuse fibers," given by Xu Shen about A.D. 100, in Ding Fubao, *Shuowen jiezi gulin* (Shanghai, 1930), 5902. This theory was further expounded by Lao Gan, "Lun Zhongguo zaozhishu zhi yuanshi," *Bulletin of the Institute of History and Philology, Academia Sinica*, 19 (1948), 489–498; see also Tsuen-hsuin Tsien, *Written on Bamboo and Silk* (Chicago, 1962), 133.

2. *Wenfang sipu (CSJC)*, 53.

3. *Tiangong kaiwu (GXJB)*, 39; cf. trans. E-tu Zen Sun and Shiou-chuan Sun, *T'ien-kung k'ai-wu: Chinese Technology in the Seventeenth Century* (University Park, PA, 1966), 63.

4. A 1957 report states that this paper was made of material similar to silk fiber, but a microscopic study of the paper in 1964 by the Institute of Papermaking in Beijing shows that jute (*Corchorus capsularis*) is included in the specimens; and a subsequent note in an article of 1966 says that jute should be corrected to hemp (*Cannabis sativa*); see *Wenwu cankao ziliao*, 1957:7, 78–79, 81; Pan Jixing (1), "Shijieshang zuizaodi zhiwu xianwei zhi," *Wenwu*, 1964:11, 48–49; and Pan Jixing (2), "Dunhuang shishi xiejingzhi yanjiu," *Wenwu*, 1966:3, 47.

5. Huang Wenbi, *Lobuzuoer kaoguji* (Beijing, 1948), 168; pl. 23, fig. 25.

6. *Hou Han shu (YWYSG)*, 108–115a-b; Tsien, op. cit., 136.

7. Cf. A. F. R. Hoernle, "Who Was the Inventor of Rag Paper?" *Journal of the Royal Asiatic Society* (1903), 665ff; Thomas F. Carter, *The Invention of Printing in China and Its Spread Westward*, rev. ed. by L. C. Goodrich (New York, 1955), 6–7.

8. See the analytical study of Dunhuang papers by Robert H. Clapperton, in *Paper: An Historical Account of Its Making by Hand* (Oxford, 1934), 18.

9. Pan Jixing (2), *op. cit*, 40–41.

10. *Da Tang liudian* (1836), 9/66a.

11. *Xin Tang shu (YWYSG)*, 57/2b.

12. *Jiu Tang shu (YWYSG)*, 47/46b.

13. Quoted in *Beitang shuchao* (1888), 104/5b.

14. See *Yuanhe junxianzhi (CSJC)*, 26/681–94; 28/743–63.

15. *Hanlin zhi (BCXH)*, 3a; cf. Wang Ming, "Sui Tang shidai di zaozhi," *Kaogu xuebao*, no. 11 (1956), 123.

16. *Shu shi (CSJC)*, 20.

17. *Chajing (BCXH)*, 2/3a.

18. See his essay: "The lament of the old rattan of Shanqi" in *Quan Tang wen* (1818), 727/20a–21b.

19. A quotation from *Yufu zhi (TPYL)*, 605/72a.

20. One *pi* equals 40 feet, according to the *Shuowen* and *Wei shu pi (YWYSG)*, 110, 4b.

21. *Qimin yaoshu (CSJC)*, 92–93; cf. new commentaries and punctuation by Shi Shenghan, *Qimin yaoshu jinshi* (Beijing, 1957–1958). The passages in brackets are in smaller characters in the text, apparently indicating explanation by the author or an early commentator.

22. See Dard Hunter, *Papermaking: The History and Technique of an Ancient Craft*, rev. ed. (New York, 1957), 27–47.

23. The word *ta* with the wood radical is also sometimes printed with the hand radical, meaning "to beat"; see Ling Shun-sheng, "Bark Cloth Culture and the Invention of Paper-making in Ancient China," *Bulletin of the Institute of Ethnology Academia Sinica*, 11 (1961), 2–5, 29–31.

24. Ibid., 21–26, 40–43.

25. *Hanshi waizhuan* (*CSJC*), 4.

26. Wang Ming, op. cit., 120.

27. Henry Yule, *The Book of Ser Marco Polo*, (London, 1903), 3rd ed. rev., I, 423.

28. E. V. E. Bretschneider, *History of European Botanical Discoveries in China* (Leipzig, 1935), I, 4.

29. Berthold Laufer, *Sino-Iranica* (Chicago, 1919), 560–563, cites among others S. Julien, Ahmed Sibab Eddin, Aurel Stein, J. Weisner, and some Chinese works to prove that "good Marco Polo is cleared, and his veracity and exactness have been established again."

30. *Wenfang sipu* (*CSJC*), 53.

31. *Ming shi* (*YWYSG*), 81/1.

32. *Ni Wenzhengong nianpu* (*CSJC*), 60; *Rizitu* (*CSJC*), 4/103.

33. *Tiangong kaiwu* (*GXJB*), 219; cf. tr. Sun, op. cit., 230; Laufer, op. cit., 561, n.1-2, quotes S. Julien that "according to the notions of the Chinese, everything made from hemp, like cord and weavings, is banished from the establishments where silkworms are reared"; and adds, "There seems to be a sympathetic relation between the silkworm feeding on the leaves of mulberry and the mulberry paper on which the cocoons of the females are placed."

34. Yu Chenghong and Li Yun, *Zhongguo zaozhi yong zhiwu xianwei tupu* (Beijing, 1955), 37, PL XXXIV.

35. A theory that bamboo paper existed in the Qin dynasty (265–420) is generally considered invalid. It is based on a statement, in *Dongtian qinglu* by Zhao Xigu (fl. 1225–1264), that "genuine" specimens of the work of the famous calligraphers Wang Xizhi and his son Wang Xianzhi were written on bamboo paper with vertical screen-marks, made in Guiji of modern Zhejiang. But the same author mentions later in the same work that these "genuine" specimens from the two Wangs were no longer extant in his time. Thus the specimens must actually have been imitations made later.

36. *Tang guoshi bu* (*JDMS*), 3/18b.

37. *Beihu lu* (*HBXZYS*), 3/7b.

38. *Wenfang sipu* (*CSJC*), 56.

39. *Dongpo zhilin* (*CSJC*), 43.

40. *Guixin zashi* (*JDMS*), 1st series, 35b.

41. *Jiatai Kuaiji zhi* (1926), 17/42a.

42. *Tiangong kaiwu* (*GXJB*), 217–219; cf. trans. Sun, op. cit., 224–227.

43. *Xueqiao shihua: xuji* (1917), 5/39a–40b.

44. See description in Dard Hunter, op. cit., 214–217; Luo Ji, *Zhulei zaozhi xue* (1935); Zhejiang Shengzhengfu, *Zhejiang zhi zhiye* (Hangzhou, 1930), 240–258.

45. *Wenfang sipu (CSJC)*, 53.

46. *Tiangong kaiwu (GXJB)*, 219; cf. trans. Sun, op. cit., 230.

47. Dard Hunter, *Chinese Ceremonial Paper* (Mountain House, 1937), 16.

48. Hong Guang and Huang Tianyou, *Zhongguo zaozhi fazhan shilue* (Beijing, 1957), 22.

49. *Tiangong kaiwu (GXJB)*, 219; cf. trans. Sun, op. cit., 231.

50. *Shiyi ji (HWCS)*, 9, 7b; also quoted in *TPYL*, 605/7b.

51. See statements by Tao Hongjing (451–536), Su Qing (seventh century), and others in *Wenfang sipu (CSJC)*, 54; also E. V. E. Bretschneider. *Botanicon Sinicum: Notes on Chinese Botany from Native and Western Sources* (London, 1882–95), pt. 3, 369–370.

52. *Wenfang sipu (CSJC)*, 53.

53. *Tiangong kaiwu (GXJB)*, 219; cf. trans. Sun, op. cit., 230.

54. Édouard Chavannes, "Les livres chinois avant l'invention du papier," *Journal Asiatique* (1905), 12; Carter, op. cit., 4; Lao Gan, op. cit., 489–491.

55. Armin Renker, in *Papier und Druck im Fernen Osten* (Mainz, 1936), 9, doubted the feasibility of using silk fiber for papermaking, and Henri Alibaux, President of the Chambre Sindicale du Papier de Lyon, in "L'Invention du papier," *Gutenberg-Jahrbuch* (1939), 24, agreed with Renker.

56. He Yanzhi (fl. 713–742), *Lanting ji (ZBZZ,* series 10), 3/9a; a later scholar commented: "The so called 'silk cocoon paper' is actually silk cloth," see Chen You (fl. 1190–1219), *Fuxuan yelu (ZBZZ,* series 26), 1/4a.

57. Zhang Yanchang, *Jinsujian shuo (CSJC)*, 1–17.

58. *Tiangong kaiwu (CSJC)*, 33–34; cf. Sun, op. cit., 48.

59. Hunter, op. cit., 312–340.

60. Yu Chenghong and Li Yun, op. cit., 1.

7   USES OF PAPER AND PAPER PRODUCTS

Paper has always been a cheap and convenient substitute for more expensive materials or for more clumsy objects that have other uses. It is also sometimes suitable in instances where other materials will not serve. Paper was apparently not invented for writing, but as time went on writing on paper developed into a distinct branch of art. For both calligraphy and painting, paper turned out to be the best medium for artistic expression. Paper made further progress when it became available in a wide range of colors and delicate designs for stationery and decorative purposes. Being cheap and light, it has been a medium of exchange, or a substitute material for personal furnishings, household articles, and recreational objects. Paper has also been chosen for the craft of making replicas or models of treasured objects for ceremonial and festive occasions. Today, paper and paper products have hundreds of uses in the areas of communication, business, industry, as well as in households. Many of these can be traced back several centuries when paper was used extensively in China, as it is elsewhere in the world today.

Generally speaking, paper was most likely used for wrapping objects from the moment of its invention in the Former or Western Han (206 B.C.–8 A.D.); for writing from the Later Han; for cutting into designs, making stationery, fans, and umbrellas from the third or fourth century; for clothing, furnishings, visiting cards, kites, lanterns, napkins, and toilet purposes no later than the fifth or sixth century; for family ceremonies in the seventh; for state sacrifices and making replicas of real objects from the eighth; and for playing cards and in lieu of metal as a medium of exchange from the ninth century. In other words, all of these uses for the graphic and decorative arts, for commercial and ceremonial occasions, and for household and recreational purposes, existed in China long before paper was known to the West.

The evolution of papermaking is reflected in the increasing varieties of and names for paper, which have various origins. Some of the names denote the raw materials from which the paper was made; others refer to places where it was manufactured; and still others are the names of designers or the studios that the product has made famous. Papers are also named for the methods of treatment, such as sizing, coating, dyeing, or treating with spices; for their appearance or size; and the use for which a variety is specifically made.

Paper for Graphic Arts and Stationery

Paper was used early on as a substitute for bamboo and silk as a writing material from the Later Han. It is recorded that paper was used together with brush and ink at the court in A.D. 76. Some two dozen characters were found on a paper remnant from Juyan dated around A.D. 110, and samples from the late second century A.D. discovered in Handanpo, Gansu, contained several characters. Numerous paper documents discovered in Chinese Turkestan bear dates from the third century A.D. onwards, while a custodian of the Imperial Library of the Qin dynasty wrote that the bamboo books discovered in the tomb in A.D. 280 were copied on paper and stored in three imperial collections. The increased use of paper for books is also reflected in the records of earlier historical bibliographies. From such evidence, it can be concluded that paper was adopted for writing from the first century A.D., but not extensively used for books and documents until the late second or third century.

The earliest extant copy of a complete book on paper is the *Piyujing* 譬喻經 *sutra* written in A.D. 256. The most common papers used in the Tang dynasty were made from hemp, paper mulberry, and rattan. Those from Dunhuang are well sized and other papers that were used for copying *sutras* were made heavy by loading or coating and treated with an insecticidal liquid. This same type of paper has continued to be manufactured throughout the centuries, and it is still used today by calligraphers and for labels on books and scrolls.

From the Song dynasty on, papermaking evolved with the popularity of printing. The raw materials were primarily bamboo and paper mulberry, with an occasional admixture of rice stalks and miscellaneous other substances. In the Yuan and Ming dynasties, fine bamboo was made into an especially heavy and sturdy paper primarily for official documents. The high-

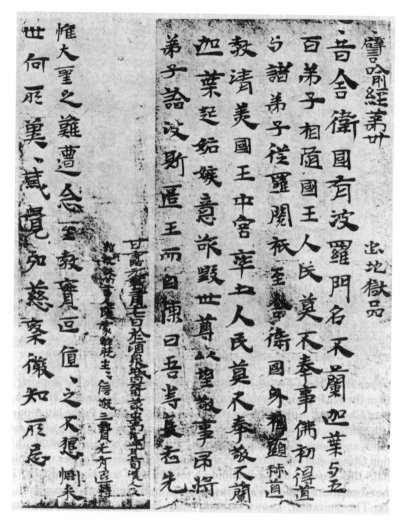

PIYUJIN SUTRA, A.D. 256

est quality was a white, sturdy cotton paper that was made of paper mulberry; next was a soft, heavy stationery paper; then a less expensive book paper, and the lowest quality paper from bamboo, which was short, narrow, dark, brittle, and cheap. The extraordinary paper made in Kaihua, Zhejiang, was selected by the Qing court for the printing of the Palace editions.

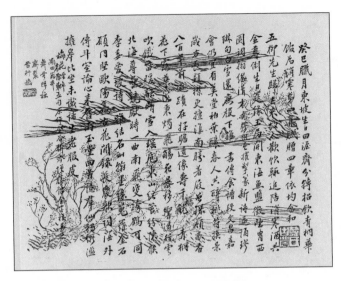

STATIONERY WITH DESIGN

The most popular paper for artistic use has continued to be the fine, soft white paper known as *xuanzhi* 宣紙, made in Xuanzhou (modern Xuancheng, Anhui). This paper was first mentioned in Tang documents as an article of tribute. Many other kinds were made of bamboo or straw, and used for wrapping, burning, or handicrafts such as making umbrellas; only those of pure bark are suitable for calligraphy and painting. These high-grade papers are soft, absorbent, smooth, strong, and elastic, suitable for books, documents, stationery, rubbings, and especially for calligraphy and painting.

For many centuries, paper has been designed with a variety of patterns, plain or colored, for writing letters, poems, and commercial documents. These papers were sometimes dyed a single color, printed with multi-colored paintings, embossed in patterns, or sprinkled with gold or silver dust in order to make them as elegant and aesthetically pleasing as possible.

According to early records, stationery papers in multiple colors made in the Tang dynasty were called by such elaborate names as pine flower, golden sand, rosy clouds, or dragon and phoenix. However, the most famous notepaper was designed by Xue Tao 薛濤 (768–831), a courtesan well-versed in poetry. This paper was made of hibiscus bark mixed with powdered hibiscus flower petals to increase its luster.[1]

The earliest stationery to contain multi-colored pictures was probably developed in the tenth century, when papers with beautifully colored designs embossed with watermarks, and even marbled papers, were being developed. Western scholars have set the origin of watermarks in Europe at A.D. 1282, and of marbled paper at 1550 as "a Persian invention," but the literary record as well as extant specimens show that the Chinese were making similar papers at least three to five hundred years earlier.[2]

A close relationship between the manufacture of writing papers and the art of color prints developed in the late Ming dynasty. The most famous example is the manual of ornamental letter papers designed at the Ten Bamboo Studio, published about 1645.[3] The manual included various designs printed in multiple colors or blind embossed from wood blocks. Designs can be found in earlier examples with similar but simpler details, which shows that both the techniques and artistic schemes were influenced by earlier works. Besides letters, ornamental stationery was also used for commercial papers.

A piece of paper used to present a visitor's name when calling was known as *ming ci* 名刺 (name card) or *bai tie* 拜貼 (visiting card). This custom was derived from use in the Han dynasty of a strip of wood, which was replaced by paper probably in the fifth or sixth century A.D. The paper card, about two to three inches wide, was originally white, and was later replaced by red cards in the Tang. It became customary for visitors to write their business on the card when calling on high officials in their offices or private residences. An endorsement was made on the back of the card before they were allowed entrance. In the middle of the Ming dynasty, the visiting card was enlarged, with the name written in large characters for Hanlin scholars, who were privileged to use a red card, while common people used white.

Paper as a Medium of Exchange

The use of paper to represent money most likely originated in the early ninth century A.D., when the ever increasing needs of business and government transactions encouraged the institution of *feiqian* 飛錢 (flying money) as a convenient way to obviate carrying heavy metal coins.[4] Provincial merchants who sold their commodities in the capital could deposit their proceeds at an office and receive a certificate for cash in the designated provinces. This institution was originally a private arrangement by the merchants but was taken over by the government in A.D. 812 as a way of forwarding local taxes and revenues to the capital. Because the flying money was primarily a draft, it is generally considered a credit medium rather than true money.[5]

The system gradually evolved into a true paper currency in the early eleventh century, when private houses were authorized by the government to issue notes called *jiaozi* 交子 (exchange media). Later on, new notes called *qianyin* 錢引 (money vouchers) and *huizi* 會子 (check media) were issued and printed with six blocks of elaborate designs in various colors. Increased government expenditure caused inflation because of the unlimited issue of paper notes beyond the original quota and period of circulation.

The paper notes issued in 1167–1179 were described as being printed in color on specially made paper with very elaborate patterns. There were characters to indicate the installment number of the issue, the year issued, the time limit for circulation, and the ceiling for the amount to be issued during the period. Patterned seals were stamped in blue, red, and black on both sides of the paper.[6] Paper for printing the notes was at first acquired from private paper mills, but as the need grew and counterfeiting increased, the government established its own factories for manufacturing special paper for the notes. The material used was paper mulberry bark, silk, or other fibers and ingredients that were combined in such a way as to make imitation difficult. The Chengdu factory, established in 1068, was reported to have employed sixty-one papermakers and thirty-one additional workers in 1194,[7] but because the shipment of Sichuan paper to Hangzhou was inconvenient, a government factory was established in 1168, in which some 1220 workers were employed. The printing was done at the Treasury, called the *Huiziku* 會子庫, where 204 workers were employed.[8] Both wood blocks and copper plates were used.[9] The complexity of the designs with additional signatures and seals printed or stamped on specially made paper, plus heavy penalties for counterfeiting, likely discouraged such a crime, though counterfeiting cases continued to occur.

PAPER MONEY, ELEVENTH CENTURY

In the north, the Qin Tartars also used paper money called *jiaochao* 交鈔 (exchange notes) first issued in 1153. They had large and small bills in various denominations and spoiled notes could be exchanged for new ones with a charge for the printing cost. At first, the circulation rules were carefully observed, but towards the end of the twelfth and early in the thirteenth century, excessive military expenditures caused inflation, and the value of the depreciated notes dropped to as little as one percent of their original value.

After the Mongol conquest of China, the Yuan dynasty issued several forms of paper money. The *sichao* 絲鈔 (silk note) that was first issued in 1260 was backed by silk yarn as a reserve, which unified the currency system of China. Old notes issued earlier were exchanged for this new note, which not only circulated universally within the empire but also spread to other parts of the world. It reached the Uighur regions in 1280 and Persia in 1294 and was introduced to many other nations over the following centuries. Paper currency arrived in Korea in 1296 and was circulated there in 1332. The Japanese first issued the paper notes for copper in 1334, and the Vietnamese printed paper money in 1396, but the use of bank notes did not occur in western countries until the later part of the seventeenth century.[10] It is likely that certain European systems of banking and accounting, as well as vouchers for deposited money, were also influenced by Chinese examples obtained by merchants and travelers to China.[11]

The Mongols certainly used paper money effectively and circulated it on a vast scale in a broad area, but its name and issuance changed frequently within a short period. The Ming government, on the other hand, operated less effectively but issued only one kind of note during the entire dynasty. A memorial by a Ming official in 1643 enumerated its many advantages. It could be manufactured at a low cost, circulated widely, carried with ease, and kept in concealment; it was not liable to suffer impurity like silver, did not need weighing whenever it was used in transactions, could not be clipped, was not exposed to thieves' rapacity, and, finally, saved metals for other uses.

Manchu rulers preferred to use hard money and did not issue any paper currency on a large scale, except as an emergency measure. However, printed paper documents for commercial transactions were frequent, and in 1853, the military cost of suppressing the Taiping rebellion resulted in the government issue of paper. As these were not convertible, their value dropped rapidly, and the notes ceased to be used after a brief period of time. It was not until the later part of the nineteenth century that a Chinese bank issued a new form of bank note, which was inspired primarily by the West.

Ceremonial Uses of Paper

Paper has played a significant role in many Chinese ceremonies and fes-
tivities in connection with ancestor worship, folk religion, and, to some
extent, the cult of scholarship. Ordinary or specialty papers were cut, folded, or decorated to represent various objects to be used or burned on such
occasions as family ceremonies and state sacrifices. This symbolic use of
paper served as an economical substitute for real but expensive objects.
The objects most commonly substituted for were money, garments, utensils, vehicles, servants, livestock, and buildings; they were used at funerals,
festivals, and in ancestor worship. Effigies of paper were used and burned
as a symbol of offerings to the spirits in the other world.[12]

The original ceremonial use of paper was probably as a substitute for
metallic coins at a burial. Rich deposits of treasures, as well as human and
animal sacrifices, were buried with the dead, though by the time of the
Han dynasty, metal coins were placed in tombs as a substitute for the valuable treasures and living beings. Later, for economical or other reasons,
among them the discouragement of grave robberies, paper imitations for
money and real objects were used.

The paper spirit money consisted of imitations either of metal coins
or of real paper money, but the latter had different sets of inscriptions and
patterns to distinguish it from counterfeit money. Coins were usually represented by a sheet of plain paper with coin designs cut in, or a small sheet
of paper coated with tinfoil, folded in the form of silver or gold ingots. The
custom of burning paper money seems to have begun with imitations of
metal money; at a later date, when real paper money was in circulation,
imitation paper money was used along with imitation coins for offerings.

The burning of paper money was formally introduced to the imperial
sacrifice in A.D. 738.[13] The adoption of this practice for state sacrifices was
a subject of controversy among many officials and scholars at the time and
thereafter. Some of them condemned it as absurd, while others were in
favor of the use of paper money as a substitute for actual silver and copper coins. This not only made the tombs less attractive to grave robbers,
but also kept the actual money in circulation. Paper clothing was also offered to the spirits in lieu of silk or other textile materials. Even though

the intention of the offerings was questioned by scholars, the use of paper replicas for funeral objects has continued even today.

Paper printed or painted with colorful images of folk gods or national heroes has played a prominent part in many Chinese households and shops. The pictures of these gods—which might be hung or pasted on the walls or doors of a house—were used primarily for worship or for protection from evil spirits. Included among them were images of the gods of the kitchen, doors, and gates, which were among the five household spirits to be worshipped.[14] The picture of the kitchen god was hung on a kitchen wall and was sacrificed to with confectionery and paper money on the twenty-third day of the twelfth month each year. After the sacrifice, the picture was burnt to send the god to heaven. Then, on New Year's Eve, he was invited back, and a new picture was put up.[15]

The most common household pictures represented the gate gods. These were pasted on both sides of the double gate at the house's entrance. The figures represent military generals, the god of longevity, wealth, and sometimes three gods standing together for happiness, prosperity, and longevity.

Many other gods or national heroes were worshipped in shops or handicraft factories in honor of their contribution to the profession. Thus, the drinking poet Li Bo became the saint of wine shops; the legendary butcher Zhang Fei was worshipped in meat shops; the hero of the Three Kingdoms, Guan Yu, the god of war, warded off calamities, and was the most popular tutelary god in many houses. Cai Lun, the supposed inventor of paper, who has become the patron saint of the profession of papermaking, has been worshipped continually by papermakers and others.

While the worship of gods drawn on paper was primarily instituted under Buddhist influence, the Daoists multiplied their potent charms with messages of good luck, written or painted on paper smeared with cinnabar to invoke protection. Sometimes large charm seals were used to impress the message on clay and later on paper with red ink to indicate authority. It seems that paper was also used by Daoists as a symbol of their magic power.

Confucians also paid respect to paper on which characters had been written. As Confucian scholars enjoyed high prestige in society, what they wrote represented the sacred words of sages, worthy of respect and preservation; thus every scrap of paper bearing written or printed characters was to be revered. In order to dispose of the written characters reverently, brick furnaces were built at street corners or in temple courtyards where scraps of written paper could be collected and placed for burning. The ashes were kept in jars and finally deposited in a river.

Paper Clothing and Furnishings

Paper has also been used for various kinds of garments, bed furnishings, and household articles in place of woven fabric. Early Chinese records reveal the existence of a material made of bark, which might have some affinity with *tapa*.

There are in Han literature several references to the use of paper mulberry for hats and headdress. In the Later Han, it was fashionable for men to wear headbands made of paper mulberry bark in red or other colors.[16] During the Tang and Song dynasties, paper mulberry hats were worn by Daoist priests and were fashionable among scholars and poets. Several hats of stiff paper covered with plain black silk were found in a Tang tomb in modern Xinjiang.[17] Another hat, a paper belt, and a paper shoe dated A.D. 418—made of hemp fiber, yellowish and thick with a textile pattern— were among the objects discovered at Turfan.[18] Paper was also widely used as lining in cloth shoes.

The most common paper apparel of bark and dyed grass seeds included paper clothing used as early as the Han dynasty. Because the bark cloth was a local product, the non-Chinese tribes who lived in the south and southwest regions presented it to the court as tribute. It was made of the bark of paper mulberry and was used by people for clothing. It was very durable and fine,[19] and it was worn throughout all the seasons by the poor as well as by Buddhist and Daoist priests.[20] The material was boiled with walnut and frankincense or other liquids. When cooked and ready to be dried, it was rolled up on a stick and then pressed into wrinkles to give it elasticity, which prevented it from being easily torn.

Personal outfits and household articles were also made of paper and paper furnishings, including screens, curtains, bed-nets, blankets, and mattresses, which were frequently mentioned in Tang and Song poems.

A defensive covering made of paper, known as *zhijia* 紙甲 or *zhikai*

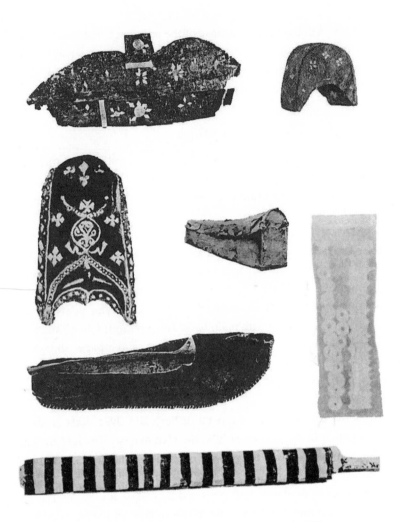

PAPER ARTICLES FROM THE TANG DYNASTY

紙鎧, was used to protect the body and arms in battle. It was light, convenient, and especially suitable for foot soldiers in the north, where the terrain prevented the use of the heavy armor normally worn by soldiers on horseback or on ships.

For the protection of arms and hands, a paper arm-and-hand cover called *zhibeishou* 紙背手 was also created. Each pair of these coverings used four layers of cloth of a specific length on both outer and inner sides, plus a certain amount of cotton, cocoon paper, and silk thread. The paper armor was similar to the iron armor made in the north, but was flexible and convenient, light and ingenious. An entire sleeve was generally made thicker in the upper section and thinner in the lower, with a thin segment in the middle to facilitate movement of the elbow joint.[21]

Wallpaper and Household Use of Paper

It is generally believed that wallpaper was first brought from China to Europe by French missionaries in the sixteenth century, then later from Canton by Dutch, English, and French traders, and that it began to be imitated in Europe in the seventeenth century.[22] Certainly the colorful papers from China with hand-painted designs of flowers and birds, landscapes, and scenes of domestic life were especially fashionable in Europe from the seventeenth to the nineteenth century. It was introduced to America in 1735 and manufactured there some fifty years later. Before the use around the middle of the nineteenth century of machinery for printing wallpaper, it was all made according to Chinese methods in small sheets with unit designs printed successively either by stencils or by woodblocks to give a continuous pattern.

The earliest mention of Chinese wallpaper was a 1693 reference in England to Queen Mary's Chinese and Indian cabinets, screens, and hangings, the last of which is believed to refer to Chinese painted papers.[23] Then, in about 1772, John Macky described the palace of Wanstead as "finely adorned with China paper [showing] the figures of men, women, birds and flowers the liveliest [the author] ever saw come from that country." Some of these papers were so accurately drawn that "a man need go no further to study the Chinese than the Chinese paper. Some of the plants which are common in China and Java as bamboo, are better figured there than in its best botanical authors that I have seen."[24] Even in this century, the Chinese hand-painted wallpapers are still considered the most excellent and beautiful of all, and a leading British architect has said: "No experience could be more delightful than to waken in a bedroom hung with 'painted paper of Pekin'."[25]

No information has been found on how early wallpaper was used in Chinese houses. Most room partitions in Chinese buildings were wooden panels or plastered walls, and colored designs were sometimes painted directly on the walls or ceilings.[26] Wallpaper must have been used in China in the sixteenth or seventeenth century, as indicated by Chinese works which state that paper covering on walls was vulgar and disliked by people of good taste.

The paper screen used as a movable partition in the room has been an important item for interior decoration in Chinese houses since Tang times. There were two major forms of such screens, folding and stiff, both of which were originally made of wooden board and sometimes painted on lacquered surfaces. When paper grew in popularity, the wooden panels were replaced with paper and decorated with calligraphy and painting.

It has been common to use white paper in lieu of glass for windows and doors in Chinese houses ranging from imperial palaces to peasant homes. Windows were designed with lattices on which paper was pasted to admit a softened sunlight.[27] Living room doors were similarly designed with lattice on the upper section and solid panels below. Gauze was also used, though later thin but strong paper in large sheets took its place. This was generally made of paper mulberry bark mixed with bamboo and sometimes rice stalks, the strong and hard-sized bark paper being difficult to tear cross-wise.

A pair of sheets of red paper inscribed with good-luck characters or a poetic couplet is pasted on the double doors of Chinese houses on the eve of a new year. The origin of the custom is unknown, but it probably derived from the use of peachwood tablets, which were placed on doors as charms against evils in Han or earlier times. Since the Tang, they have been replaced by red paper.

An early kind of quasi-paper is mentioned in the official history as having been used to wrap poisonous medicine in the second century B.C.[28] Because paper was soft and cheap, it was natural to use it for wrapping objects. In the Tang dynasty, paper made of rattan was folded and sewn into square bags to preserve the flavor of tea leaves. At this time, tea was served from baskets made of rushes which held tea cups with paper napkins folded into squares,[29] and a set of several tens of paper cups in different sizes

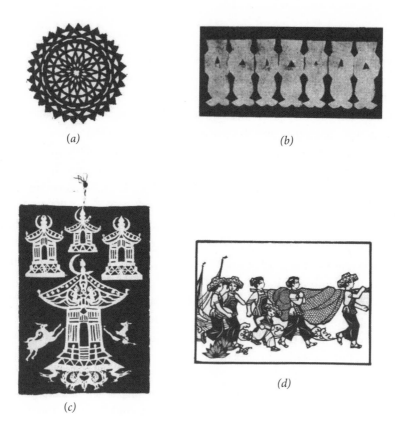

PAPER CUTS
(a) Geometric design, sixth century   (b) Human figures, seventh century
(c) Shrine from Dunhuang, ninth century   (d) Modern paper cut

and colors with delicate designs is said to have been seen in the possession of a family of Hangzhou.[30] Gift money for bestowing upon officials by the imperial court was wrapped in paper envelopes.[31]

Although Chinese sources are generally silent about the use of paper for cleaning the body after elimination, one reference dated as early as the sixth century A.D. refers to the prohibition of paper with characters being used for such purposes. Toilet paper was made from rice straw, the fibers of which were tender and required less time and labor to process; it thus cost less than any other kind of paper, and great quantities of such paper were needed for daily use, as well as for the imperial court.

Papercraft and Recreational Use of Paper

Paper has great potential as a creative material for recreational purposes. It may be cut into designs to be pasted on windows, doors, lamps, and other surfaces, and on clothing and shoes in place of embroidery. It can also be folded into flat or three-dimensional forms for art or entertainment; and making flowers by folding, cutting, and pasting is a popular amusement. Because of its lightness, paper is also especially suitable for making kites. Numerous articles for popular use were originally made of far more expensive materials such as silk, leather, horn, or ivory, but later these were replaced with paper. Sturdy paper for papier-mâché was also substituted for many more expensive materials for games, toys, and other objects for entertainment. Paper was used in China for some of these purposes as early as the third or fourth century A.D., and for all of them by the sixth or seventh century A.D.

Cutting paper into various designs with scissors and knives, as festival decorations or on other occasions, is a Chinese folk art with a history of many centuries. It probably derives from the custom of cutting out human figures, flowers, or landscapes in silk at the spring festival. The subjects of paper cutting included scenes from farm life: tilling land, weaving, fishing, or tending cattle; symbols of good luck or blessings; legendary stories and theatrical figures; and flowers and plants, birds and animals. The design might be one independent picture, a symmetrical pair, or multiple sets of from four to as many as twenty-four. If used in corners, a set of four triangular designs was usually made; and for a ceiling a multiple design round in shape. Unlike paintings, the composition of papercuts was generally symmetrical and well balanced, with intricate designs covering an entire space, and with a strong local flavor.

The process of cutting paper involved several steps. A master design was first cut and fastened over a piece of white paper on a wooden board. The paper was then moistened with water and blackened with smoke, and when the master design was removed, a white design appeared on the paper against a black background. A pile of sheets of white paper was then laid under the design, and fastened with paper thread at the corners and the center before cutting. For symmetrical designs the paper was folded and cut with scissors to duplicate the design, but only a few sheets can be cut in this way at a time. Independent designs were usually cut with a knife through as many as sixty or seventy sheets of paper at once. Lines could be cut out to make a positive impression, or left between cuts to make a negative impression, simple lines being cut with an ordinary blade, but delicate ones with a specially sharp, small, round knife. The inside lines were cut first and then the outside lines. After cutting was completed, the paper could be dyed with colors mixed with white wine or arsenic, with as many as forty sheets being colored at a time. Multiple colors were applied separately, a fresh color being added when the previous one had dried. For the decoration of houses, red or multiple colors were usually used for auspicious occasions and blue for mourning.[32]

A flat piece of paper can be folded into various shapes and forms such as figurines, animals, flowers, garments, furniture, buildings, and numerous other objects. Paper folding is probably one of the most interesting folk arts. It helps train nimble fingers, cultivates a sense of balance and symmetry, and can be used to provide visual illustrations to explain modern physics and geometry.[33] Indeed, many mathematicians have demonstrated their scientific interest in paper folding, especially in dealing with three-dimensional problems and the geometric construction of regular polygons and spheres.[34]

Paper folding probably flourished in China for many centuries before it spread worldwide. Its origin was not later than early in the Tang dynasty,[35] for several artificial flowers of folded and cut paper have been found in Dunhuang, which demonstrate highly sophisticated paper-craft techniques.[36] Today, paper folding is one of the most popular crafts and pastimes for teaching children in classrooms, and among adults throughout the world; it is especially popular in Japan, Europe, and America, with extensive literature in different languages.[37]

Flying paper kites was a pastime enjoyed by children in spring and autumn. It was said that when their kites flew in the sky, children lifted their heads, opened their mouths, and breathed deeply, which was good for their health, and the ninth day of the ninth month of each year, or the 'double ninth' festival, was especially devoted to this form of amusement. The paper kite, consisting of a light bamboo frame covered with sturdy

CALLIGRAPHY AND PAINTING ON FOLDED FANS, MING AND QING DYNASTY

paper, and with a string attached, was made in the forms of butterflies, men, birds, or other animals, often in many colors. Kites were, perhaps, originally made of light wood or silk before paper became common, and how early paper was used for making them is unknown. However, a story about sending a message to a rescue mission by flying a paper kite in ca. A.D. 549 indicates that it must have been earlier than this date.[38]

Other Chinese literary sources frequently tell of the use of kites for measuring distances, testing the wind, lifting men, signaling, and communicating for military purposes. The earliest known reference to their use for amusement or pleasure tells of someone in a palace in the tenth century A.D. fastening a bamboo whistle to a kite so that it made a musical sound in the wind. The term for the Aeolian harp was derived from this. Kite flying diffused very early to all other nations of East and Southeast Asia, especially Korea, Japan, Indo-China, and Malaysia, and was sometimes associated with religious practices. It was introduced to Europe as a Chinese contrivance at the end of the sixteenth century A.D.

Lanterns in China generally consisted of wooden or bamboo frames covered with a variety of such translucent materials as horn, silk, or skin, but those of paper are said to have been especially elegant and skillfully made. They were lit with candles and were hung indoors or outdoors as decorations, or carried as aids for walking at night. Especially interesting was the massive display of lanterns at the annual lantern festival around the fifteenth of the new moon each year, a festival which was not instituted until the Tang dynasty, although poems about lanterns were written in China as early as the sixth century A.D.[39]

Fans were frequently used in daily life as a shield against dust and the sun; they were first made of feathers but later of silk, bamboo, ivory, bone, sandalwood, and palm leaves. It is believed that paper fans first appeared in the third or fourth century. Later, silk was banned for economic reasons, and the use of paper increased. Circular fans of paper were popular in the Song dynasty. The folding fan made of durable paper with various kinds of frames and designs was perhaps introduced to China from Japan via Korea in the eleventh century A.D. Small sheets of a special kind of strong, hard-sized bark paper were used in the Ming dynasty for the manufacture of oiled-paper fans. These fans usually bore no artistic decoration and were used by the common people in summer.

The same kind of oiled paper was also used for the manufacture of umbrellas in the Ming dynasty. The origin of umbrellas derived from the use of chariot covers. For protection against rain, a piece of silk was spread above the chariot. The use of paper umbrellas is believed to have been introduced in the late fourth or early fifth century A.D. Red and yellow

PAPER TIGER

umbrellas were used by the emperor, and blue by commoners.[40] It was decreed in A.D. 1368 that silk umbrellas were reserved for the imperial family, while oiled-paper umbrellas for rain were allowed to the common people. They were not only used for protection from sun or rain but also taken on ceremonial occasions. Umbrellas were carried in official processions;[41] and "umbrellas of ten thousand names" were presented to honored officials, inscribed with the donors' names.

Paper flags must have been used early on, as several flags were found in Tang tombs in Xinjiang. One was made of paper manuscripts pasted together, painted with horizontal stripes of black and white, and pasted on one side to a stick.[42]

Playing cards made of paper, written or printed with designs, probably existed no later than the ninth century A.D., when the relatives of a princess are said to have played the *Yezixi* 葉子戲 (leaf game).[43] These playing cards were described in a Ming work as being about one inch wide, two inches high, and several tenths of a finger thick. The Ming document enumerated the numerous advantages of playing cards, as they were convenient to carry, stimulated thinking, could be played by a group of four without annoying conversation, and without the difficulties which accompanied playing chess or meditation. The game could be played under almost any conditions without restriction of time, place, weather, or the qualification of partners.[44]

Many other items made of paper for household, recreation, and entertainment purposes were occasionally recorded in art and literature.[45] Such articles as paper chessmen, paper flutes, shadow puppets, fireworks and firecrackers, and numerous kinds of toys such as paper tigers were some of the most notable.

Notes

1. *Tiangong kaiwu* (*Guoxue jiben congshu*), 219; cf. tr. Sun & Sun (1), 231.

2. Cf. Labarre, Dictionary of Paper and Paper-making Terms, 260; Hunter, *Paper-making*, 474, 479.

3. The preface of the manual is dated A.D. 1644, but one orchid design, in *juan* 2, bears the date A.D. 1645. The work was reprinted in facsimile by the Peking Society of Woodcuts in 1935; see also below, 283ff.

4. Sources are silent about the material for the "flying money," but it is believed that it must have been made of paper since imitation money of paper for spirit offerings was already used in the eighth century A.D., and the word *fei* (*flying*) implies a light material such as paper.

5. Yang Liansheng, *Money and Credit in China*, 51–52; Sogabe Shizuo, *Shihei hattatsu shi*, 6–7; Peng Xinwei, *Zhongguo huobi shi*, 280.

6. Ten samples given in a Yuan work on money are illustrated in *Shu Zhongguang ji*, ch. 67, 18a–23b.

7. *Shu Zhong Guang Ji*, ch. 67, 14b.

8. *Xianchun Lin'ann zhi* (1830 ed.), ch. 9, 7b–8a; *Meng lianglu* (*Congshu jicheng*), 77.

9. See *Wenxian tongkao* (*Shi dong*), ch. 100, 3.

10. Paper money was first issued in Sweden in 1661; America, 1690; France, 1720; Russia, 1768; England, 1797; and Germany, 1806.

11.   Max Weber said that the accounting system (*Verrechungswesen*) of the old Hamburg Bank was based on a Chinese model, and Robert Eisler noted that the old Swedish system of banking and money deposit vouchers followed the Chinese system; see Yang Liansheng, *op. cit.*, 65.

12.   For ceremonial use of paper, see Hunter, *Chinese Ceremonial Paper*, 1–79, 203–217.

13.   Cf. *Jiu Tang Shu* (*Ershisi shi* [*Tongwen shuju*, 1886]), ch. 130, 1a; a similar story is found in *Xin Tang Shu* (*Ershisi shi* [*Tongwen shuju*, 1886]), ch. 109, 13a, and *Zizhi Tongjian* (1956 ed.), 683.

14.   The five tutelary gods of the house are those of the kitchen, gates, doors, center of the room or impluvium, and well; see Bodde, *Annual Customs and Festivals in Peking*, 4.

15.   Bodde, *op.cit.*, 98.

16.   See *Hou Han shu* (*Ershisi shi* [*Tongwen Shuju*, 1886]), ch. 71, 32a; ch. 73, 7a.

17.   See Stein, *Innermost Asia*, IV, pl. XCIII.

18.   See Pan Jixing "Xinjiang chutu guzhi yanjiu," 54; *Zhongguo zaozhi jishu shigao*, 135.

19.   See quotations in *Bencao gangmu* (Beijing, 1975), ch. 36, 78–79.

20.   See poems quoted in Xiong Zhengwen (1), 34–35.

21.   *Wubei zhi*, ch. 105, 19a–b.

22.   For Chinese wallpapers in Europe, see Ackerman *Wall Paper: Its History, Design and Use*, 11–20; Entwisle *The Book of Wallpaper*, 43–48; Sanborn *Old Time Wall Papers*, 14–29; for a chronological development of the art, see Entwisle *A Literary History of Wall Paper*, 11ff.

23.   Cf. Entwisle *The Book of Wallpaper*, 21, 43–44.

24.   See Entwisle *A Literary History of Wall Paper*, 13, 23, 49.

25.   See Sitwell *British Architects and Craftsmen*, 196.

26.   See quotations on wall paintings in *Gujin tushu jicheng* (Taibei, 1964), ch. 98, 56; also, painting on ceilings and walls in a Ming house of a Wu family was recently recovered in Huizhou (modern Xiuning, Anhui); cf. Zhang Zhongyi, *Huizhou Mingdai zhuzhai*, 32, figs. 75–80.

27.   The use of lattices in windows in Chinese architecture has a long history, and some of these attached to old wooden buildings have survived from the Ming dynasty. For a brief history and designs of Chinese lattice, see D. S. Dye *A Grammar of Chinese Lattice*.

28.   *Qian Han shu* (*Ershi sishi* [*Tongwen Shuju*, 1884]), ch. 97b, 13a.

29.   *Chajing* (*Xue jin tao Yyan*), ch. 2, 1b.

30.   See *Shi Hongbao* (1), 125.

31.   *Tongsu bian* (reprint, 1979), 513.

32.   Cf. A Ying, *Minjian chuanghua*, 1–9.

33.   Shen *Introducing Chinese Paper-folding*, 7–8. Dr. Shen, an expert in paper folding, has provided much information on its worldwide popularity.

34.   Row (1) is completely devoted to the use of folding in geometry; see also Cooper

Union Museum, *Plane Geometry and Fancy Figures: An Exhibition of the Art and Technique of Paper Folding* (New York, 1959), introduction by Edward Kallop.

35. Vacca "Della piegatura della carta applicata alla Geometria," 43, says that the *zhe zhi* is mentioned in a poem by Tu Fu, but the original reference has been found to be a mistake. One poem by Du Fu does mention "paper cutting" (*jian zhi*) but not "paper folding" (*zhe zhi*), see 124ff. above.

36. Stein, *Serindia*, 11, 967; iv, pl. XCII.

37. Some 200 entries are included in Legman, "Bibliography of Paperfolding," 3–8.

38. *Gaiyu congkao* (1790 ed.), ch. 40, 25a.

39. *Gaiyu congkao* (1790 ed.), ch. 31, 19a–b.

40. See *Sancai tuhui* (1609 ed.), ch. 12, 22a–b.

41. See *Gujin shiwu kao* (*Congshu jicheng*), 140.

42. See Stein, *Serindia*, iv, pl. XCIII.

43. *Yexi yuanqi* (*Congmu Wang shi yishu*), 1a.

44. Quoted in *Yexi yuanqi*, 19a–b.

45. *Shu yuan zaji (Congshu jicheng)*, (CSJC) vol. 2, 140; *Min xiaoji (Congshu jicheng)*, 26–27; Shi Hongbao, *Min zaji*, 123; Deng Zhicheng, *Gudong suoji; xuji; sanji*, ch. 1, 132a–b.

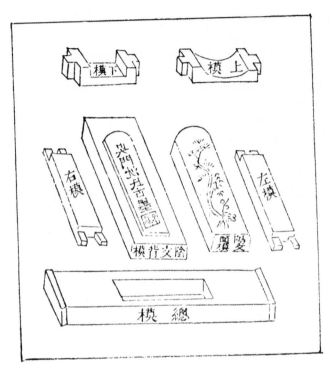

SIX-PIECE INKMAKING MOLD SET

8   DEVELOPMENT OF INKMAKING

Chinese ink has undergone a long process of development, commencing perhaps as early as three millennia ago. Ink has played a vital role, together with paper and printing, in the progress of Chinese civilization. The prominence of ink in Chinese culture is evident not only in its extensive use in writing but also as an object of art and a subject of scholarship.

The earliest samples of Chinese ink are to be found in traces of writings and drawings in black or color on bone, stone, clay, bamboo, wood, silk, and paper documents dating from the fourteenth century B.C. to the fourth century A.D. A few specimens of solid ink dating from the third century B.C. to the third or fourth century A.D. have recently been discovered, and a number of artifacts from later times still survive.

From the Han until the Song dynasty, most ink appears to have been made from a combination of pine soot, glue, and miscellaneous additives. Lacquer might have been used to write short inscriptions on hard-surfaced objects prior to this time, but it was not used for general writing. "Stone ink," possibly a form of graphite, was also in use at this time, probably to a much more limited extent. From the Song period on, lampblack made out of animal, vegetable, or mineral oils was often substituted for pine soot, but the pigments, binding agents, and additives remained much the same in spite of the passage of time, though their proportions tended to vary with individual inkmakers.

Ink was probably first decorated with designs and calligraphy after it came to be manufactured in a prismatic shape with flat surfaces, a development which may have occurred before the Tang dynasty. Such decoration of ink evolved into an elaborate enterprise, and large sets of inksticks, decorated with associated designs, were produced for a collector's market. Eventually, connoisseurs of ink in China attached as much importance to the decoration of the ink as to its writing qualities.

Role of Ink in Chinese Culture

Writing in China was something more than just a functional means of recording. From at least as early as the Han dynasty, calligraphy was considered a major art form, and eventually all objects associated with it came to share in the general aesthetic of writing and were themselves elevated to the status of art. Consequently, paper, ink, the writing brush, and the ink stone—the basic equipment used in writing known as the "four treasures of a scholar's studio"—were collected by connoisseurs as *objets d'art*, as well as being used in the production of works of art. In addition to its use in writing, ink was also employed in painting, printing, as a cosmetic, and even in medicine.

Chinese ink is generally kept in a solid form until shortly before use when a small amount is converted into a liquid by grinding the ink on an ink stone moistened by water. The solid form was conducive to lengthy preservation because it was not subject to evaporation. This also facilitated the development of ink as an artistic medium, as designs could easily be incorporated in the molds used for forming the solid ink or applied directly to the surface. Permanence and luster are other important qualities of Chinese ink, and these are clearly apparent in extant documents and paintings that are more than a thousand years old.

Pigmentation and Composition of Chinese Ink

From the thirteenth century A.D., scholars have suggested that Chinese ink was first made from lacquer, then minerals, and finally pine soot and lampblack. There has been controversy among modern scholars, however, about whether Chinese ink was ever made from lacquer.

From recent discoveries it seems entirely possible that hard, non-absorbent surfaces might have necessitated the use of a more adhesive ink than was used eventually on silk and paper, and that lacquer could have suited this requirement. The text of a collection of bamboo tabled documents, discovered in one of the previously mentioned Qin and Han graves found at Shuihudi, indicates that lacquer and cinnabar were used in writing the names of official units on the surfaces of government tools, armor, and weapons when these did not lend themselves to incising. These tablets also cite regulations for lacquer orchards and testing the quality of lacquer. The references indicate that lacquer was used at an early date for writing on certain kinds of materials such as metals, which do not absorb watery ink. But it seems certain that lacquer was not a major vehicle for writing, as there is no archaeological evidence that it was used on more conventional hard-surfaced writing media, such as bamboo or wooden tablets. However, lacquer was possibly present as a minor ingredient in some inks.

Silk was used as a writing medium at least as early as the fifth century B.C., and silk documents, dating from the Warring States through to the Han period, have been found at many sites in China and Central Asia. Paper was also used for writing beginning in the Later or Eastern Han (25–220) dynasty. Specimens of writing with black ink from the second century A.D. have been found at Juyan, Dunhuang, Loulan, and other sites, but because the ink on these early silk and paper documents has never been chemically analyzed, it is difficult to speculate on its exact composition.

Pine soot, traditionally the favorite pigment in ink, was used in ink manufacture in the time of Wei Dan 韋誕 (179–253). An ink-making formula in a fifth-century work that is attributed to him calls for the use of fine and pure soot, pounded and strained to remove any adhering vegetable substance. Recent studies carried out with a scanning electron microscope have shown that the sizes of carbon particles found in fourteenth-century Chinese ink made from pine soot are remarkably small and uniform, superior in these respects to a sample of modern ink also made with soot.

Although pine soot probably remained the most popular pigment used in making ink, it was soon rivaled from the Song dynasty onwards by lampblack made from combustion, in lamps with wicks, of animal, vegetable, and mineral oils such as fish oil, rapeseed oil, bean oil, hemp oil, sesame oil, tung oil, and petroleum. In Ming times, it is said that nine-tenths of all ink was made from pine soot and one-tenth from oil lampblack.

Another type of ink mentioned in early Chinese sources is "stone ink," or *shi mo* 石墨. This appears to have been a mineral substance of some sort that was either used as found or prepared by grinding. It was possibly a form of coal, petroleum, or graphite, for the discovery sites specified in early records are all located in areas where graphite is currently produced.

Pine soot and lampblack consist principally of carbon, which, in its free state, does not combine readily with other materials. Consequently, the use of carbon in ink necessitates the use of an agent that will bind the carbon pigment to the writing surface. Binding agents also play another role in Chinese ink in holding the carbon particles together in a solid form.

The binding agents used in Chinese ink were traditionally glues made from a variety of animal remains, including raw hides or leather, muscles, bones, shells, horns, fish skin, fish scales, and fish maw. The quality of the water used also was important. After one of these substances was boiled, the resulting hot viscous fluid was strained through a silk gauze or cotton filter to remove lumps, and then allowed to condense into solid form until needed for use. The solid glue was then dissolved with solvents before use in inkmaking.

In addition to the essential pigments and binding agents, other materials were often added to improve consistency, color, and aroma. Miscellaneous additives were sometimes used, such as egg whites, garbage, raw lacquer sap, soaptree pods, and croton seeds to improve consistency; cinnabar, purple herb, madder root, yellow reed, black beans, copper vitriol, gall nuts, curled pine, walnut, peony rind, pig and carp galls, pearls, tonka beans, pomegranate skins, and vermilion to improve color and gloss; and cloves, sandalwood, sweet pine, camphor, and musk to improve scent.

Technical Processes of Inkmaking

It seems likely that inkmaking formulae were usually kept secret to guard against competition; consequently, the formulae that were recorded and survive to the present day perhaps represent only a very small fraction of those actually used. Although the ingredients used in making any ink are generally not that numerous, the exact composition, preparation, and quality of each ingredient were subject to considerable variation. According to early works on inkmaking, the steps involved consist of gathering soot or lampblack, straining and then mixing with pre-dissolved glue and miscellaneous additives, kneading, pounding, steaming, molding, covering with ashes, drying, waxing, storing, and testing.

No details about the manufacture of pine soot in those early days are available today. One later writer notes that lampblack was obtained by burning the resin, and others the wood, of the pine tree.[1] Although an old recipe for the preparation of the ink exists, there is no mention of the source from which lampblack was obtained. The old recipe is included in the *Qimin yaoshu* 齊民要術, a work on agriculture and manufacture written by Jia Sixie 賈思勰 in the fifth century A.D. The section called "Method of Mixing Ink" reads:

> Fine and pure soot is to be pounded and strained in a jar through a sieve of thin silk. This process is to free the soot of any adhering vegetable substance so that it becomes like fine sand or dust. It is very light in weight, and great care should be taken to prevent it from being scattered around by not exposing it to the air after straining. To make one catty of ink, five ounces of the best glue must be dissolved in the juice of the bark of the *cen* tree, which is called *fanji* wood in the southern part of the Yangtze valley. The juice of this bark is green in color; it dissolves the glue and improves the color of the ink.
>
> Add five egg whites, one ounce of cinnabar, and the same amount of musk, after they have been separately treated and well strained. All these ingredients are mixed in an iron mortar; a paste, preferably dry rather than damp, is obtained after pounding thirty thousand times, or pounding more for a better quality.
>
> The best time for mixing ink is before the second and after the ninth month in a year. It will decay and produce a bad odor if the weather is too warm, or will be hard to dry and melt if too cold, which causes breakage when exposed to air. The weight of each piece of ink cake should not exceed two or three ounces. The secret of an ink is as described; to keep the pieces small rather than large.[2]

Although this recipe was first described in this fifth-century work, its author is believed to have been the famous inkmaker Wei Dan 韋誕 (179–253), previously mentioned as the supposed inventor of Chinese ink. His name is not mentioned in this recipe but does appear in the preceding section on the making of the brush. The same recipe as quoted in the *Taiping yulan*

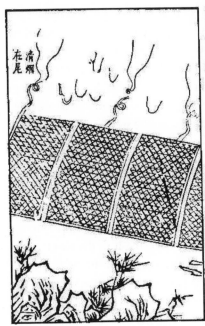

INKMAKING WITH PINE SOOT

太平御覽, an encyclopedia compiled in A.D. 983, mentions Wei Dan as its author. It seems certain that this recipe must have been experimented with for many years before it was perfected in the second or third century A.D. It was still renowned at the end of the fifth century, and later methods are believed to have been copied or improved from this formula without significant differences.

Glue was also of importance in making lampblack ink. It serves the purpose of uniting the fine particles of carbon and permanently fixing the ink on paper. Glue was usually manufactured from deer horn, cowhide, fish skin, or the waste of leather. The materials were soaked in water to soften them and then boiled with water and filtered through silk gauze or a cotton filter to obtain a clear liquid. The proportion of glue and lampblack for preparing a solid ink cake was probably kept a closely guarded secret by inkmakers. It is mentioned in later literature as an equal weight of lampblack and glue, although this varied by maker.[3] In order to increase

INKMAKING WITH LAMPBLACK, EIGHTEENTH CENTURY

the intensity of the black color, other ingredients such as cinnabar were mixed into the paste. As disinfectants for preservation and for maintaining the permanent color of the ink, the bark of *cen* 岑 wood, the skin of the pomegranate, blue vitriol, and similar materials were used. To camouflage the unpleasant odor of the glue, perfumes such as musk, camphor, or patchouli were sometimes added.

The form of the pre-Qin ink is not known today, but it was probably made in solid form from an early time, as the *Zhuangzi* notes that ink was mixed before using. Recent archaeological discoveries support this point. A conical black ink cake of the Warring States period found at Shuihudi in Yunmeng, Hubei in 1975 is 2.1 cm in diameter, and the remnant is still 1.2 cm high. Five cylindrical ink cakes of the Later Han period discovered at Liujiaqu in Shanxian, Henan in 1965, were made of pine soot from molds. Another ink cake of the Qin period, unearthed at Laohushan in Nanjing in 1958, is 6 cm long and 2.5 cm wide. Scientific analysis shows that its composition of carbon is close to that of modern ink. These archaeological data help us to understand the general shape and composition of ancient ink.[4]

Under the Han and Qin dynasties, the unit of ink was described as *wan* 丸 and *mei* 枚. One Han source records that "one large and one small *mei* of Yumei ink [made of pine from Yumei mountain] were given each month to the high officials in the court."[5] Zhang Chang of the Qin dynasty writes that "four *wan* of fragrant ink were bestowed upon a prince when he was first crowned."[6] No one seems to understand clearly what the *wan* and *mei* looked like. Laufer explained the *wan* as "pills, pellets, and balls . . . to be easily swallowed."[7] Apparently, *wan* is round in shape, while *mei* is a flat unit.

Although ink was later used as a kind of medicine, it is doubtful that such balls were originally made for "swallowing." A mural painting discovered in 1953 in a Han tomb at Wangdu in Western Hebei shows a scribe sitting on a low couch and before him is a round ink slab with a conical piece of ink in the middle. A water container is shown at the right side of the ink. This picture seems to indicate clearly the so-called *wan*.[8] In 1973, an ink cake and ink slab were excavated from a tomb of the Former or Western Han (206 B.C.–8 A.D.) at Bicun in Hunyuan, Shanxi. The ink cake is semi-cylindrical in shape and placed with an ink slab in a wooden box.[9] This discovery provides material evidence for the conical piece in the Wangdu painting.

(a)

(b)

(a) Ancient piece of solid ink with a hole at one end
(b) Section of a mural painting showing a set
of writing implements for a scribe

During the first expedition to Chinese Turkestan in 1900–1901, Stein reported that he found in the Endere ruins at Khotan "a cylindrical piece of hard Chinese ink drilled for a string at one end."[10] It was 2.3 cm long with a diameter of about 1 cm. On another trip he also found a prismatic piece of ink that perhaps comes from the Tang dynasty.[11] It seems to be the case that ink has been made in the form of round or flat cakes since the Han dynasty. Later on, ink was made into different shapes, decorated with designs and calligraphy, and colored with gold and other pigments in order to suit artistic taste.

The qualities sought in Chinese ink are often reflected in remarks made concerning the ink of other noted inkmakers.

Although Chinese ink was generally produced in a solid form, some liquid ink was also made. Special liquid inks were also made for commercial applications such as printing. Printing ink was first prepared as a paste made of coarse soot and mixed with glue and wine, and then preserved in jars for three or four summers, for its bad odor to disappear; printing with freshly prepared ink was easily smeared.

The best ink for printing in red was a mixture of vermilion and red lead boiled in water with the mucilaginous root of a plant. Next best was the liquid obtained from boiling the red-stem amaranth, but this easily turns purple and does not give as fresh a color as the vermilion and red lead mixture. Blue ink was made from indigo. And Prussian blue is not suitable for printing, as the color runs when the paper is wet.

Invisible ink was already known to the Chinese perhaps no later than the twelfth century. A story from the time says a man was deprived of his title because he had spread a scandal about a high military general of the Song dynasty, but during his banishment he met a magician who could write invisible characters with liquid on paper. When it was treated with water, the characters disappeared. So for fun the man's son wrote the characters and applied water to test the technique. The magician then went away, intending to show the paper to the government, and was only prevented by being bribed with a great deal of money. The process might be magic, as the characters were written with chemicals, perhaps alum, on paper; they appeared when treated with some kind of solution.

Ink was also commonly used in medicine as early as the tenth century A.D. Ink made from fine pine soot, roasted, ground, and mixed with water, vinegar, and other ingredients such as turnip, onion, foxglove juice, bile, wine, and dried ginger, was used as a cure for bleeding after childbirth, dysentery, ulcers and sores, nose bleeds, swelling, and eye irritations, among other disorders. The ink mixture was taken either orally or applied externally. Ink made of lampblack from other materials such as oil, petroleum, or straw was not used for medical purposes.

Art and Connoisseurship of Chinese Ink

Prismatic shapes, of course, feature flat surfaces. The development of such ink surfaces could have been due to their capacity for facilitating design, which became increasingly prevalent as ink was transformed from a simple object of utility to an *objet d'art*. The earliest known decorative elements used on ink surfaces, dating from the Tang period, consisted of propitious animals, such as the dragon and the carp, as well as calligraphy. During the Ming and Qing periods, many ink sticks were decorated with a pictorial design on one side and calligraphy on the other. The pictorial designs, often symbolic in nature, included dragons, lions, carp, deer, pine trees, cranes, tortoises, gourds, plum flowers, pomegranates,

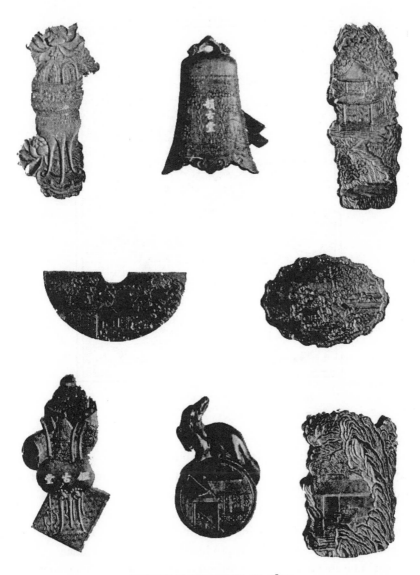

PICTORIAL INK CAKES, CA. 1800

bamboo shoots, landscapes, scenes from everyday life, inventions, religious personages and symbols. The inscriptions, which are sometimes gilded, include details of the manufacture, explanations of the pictorial

INK DESIGN WITH BIBLICAL STORY, 1606

design on the reverse side, moralizations, religious sayings, auspicious phrases, poems, and examples of calligraphy. Ink was also made in a variety of special shapes, often in imitation of different artistic objects such as jade pendants, bronze mirrors, and knife-shaped coins.

The various shapes and designs of the ink stick were conditioned by the construction and engraving of the mold, which was made of either copper or wood. Copper molds produced sharp and clear images of the design but were hard to engrave. Wood was easier to carve but sometimes showed its grain on the surface of the ink. The designs into which the ink paste was pressed were cut intaglio into the mold, resulting in their appearance in relief on the surface of the ink stick.

Decorated sets of ink sticks were also quite popular in the Qing period and are still sold today. Usually a set was organized around a common theme, such as different types of animal, the eight trigrams, views of the imperial palace, or landscapes of scenic splendors. Each set was usually encased in a specially made ornate box that could be opened to show off its contents to best advantage. The largest set of inkcakes ever made in China was perhaps a group of sixty-four pieces entitled "Pictorial Inks Commemorating the Gardens" made by imperial order of the Jiaqing emperor (r. 1796–1821).

Ink was probably collected in China almost as soon as it was noticed that two different specimens could differ widely in quality, but extant records do not reveal much about the art of collecting before the tenth century, in the southern Tang and Song periods. The imperial collections of the Ming and Qing dynasties featured numerous inks which still survive.

Many catalogues of ink collections have been published since the late sixteenth century by inkmakers, ink dealers, and ink collectors, primarily for appreciation and connoisseurship of the artistic aspects of ink tablets. The earliest and most influential examples are two collections of ink designs reproduced by woodcuts. One titled *Fangshi mopu* 方氏墨譜 by Fang Yulu 方于魯 (fl. 1580), containing more than 380 illustrations, arranged by the form and subject matter of the designs under six categories, as well as a number of laudatory essays, was published in A.D. 1588. Eighteen years later, his professional competitor Cheng Dayue 程大約 (fl. 1541–1616) published another collection entitled *Cheng shi moyuan* 程氏墨苑, which contains some 500 designs printed in color together with essays, poems, eulogies, and testimonials from his friends. The two works are similar in nature and content and many of their designs are even identical, but the latter surpassed the former not only in the number of illustrations it provided but also in artistic excellence; furthermore it included some special features such as the Western alphabets and biblical pictures copied from European engravings given to Cheng by Matteo Ricci (1552–1610) in 1606. It is perhaps the first Chinese book that includes illustrations of an occidental origin.

Another type of ink catalogue, produced by ink dealers, includes among other things the prices at which the items featured were apparently offered for sale. A third category of ink catalogues is represented by those of private collections. They manually list the names of inkmakers, ink titles, designs, dates of manufacture, forms, number of pieces, and weights, all of them standard items described in such catalogues.

Notes

1. Jiang Shaoshu, *Yunshizhai bitan*, 2/21a.
2. Jia Sixie, *Qimin yaoshu*, 9/28; Shi Shenghan, op. cit., 722.
3. *Gezhi jingyuan*, 37/26–27.
4. For ink from Shuihudi, see *Wenwu* 1976:9, 51–61; also *Yunmeng Shuihudi Qin mu* (Beijing, 1981), 26; for discoveries in Liujiagu, see *Zhongguo kaogu xuebao* 1965:1, 160, Plate 26:12–13; and in Laohushan, see *Kaogu* 1959:6, 295.
5. Quoted in *Taiping yulan*, 605/4b.
6. Ibid.
7. Wiborg, *Printing Ink*, 22–23.
8. *Wangdu Hanmu biehua*, 13–14; Plates 16, 17.
9. *Wenwu* 1980:6, 42–46, fig. 7.
10. Stein, *Ancient Khotan*, I, 438, 442; Plate CV.
11. Stein, *Serindia*, I, 316.

9 TECHNIQUES OF WOODBLOCK PRINTING

Unlike papermaking and inkmaking, the technical procedures of Chinese woodblock printing have scarcely been documented in Chinese literature. Nothing has been written on how woodblocks were prepared, engraved, and used for printing in early times, nor on how many copies were printed from each block at one time or throughout its life. Movable types, on the other hand, have been described at length, but none or only very few of them survive for examination, and thus certain technical questions cannot be fully answered. Details of the materials, tools, and methods can only be deduced from an interpretation of related terms, by examination of printed editions, and from the oral testimony of the few surviving craftsmen. The following account of the techniques and procedures of Chinese traditional printing is based primarily on scattered information available and on interviews with woodblock cutters at their workshops during my trip to China in 1979.[1]

Materials and Tools for Block Printing

The basic materials for Chinese printing included wood, ink, and paper, while clay and metals were also used for making movable types. Printing blocks were normally cut from the wood of pear (*li* 梨, *Pyrus sinensis*), jujube (*zao* 棗, *Zizyphus vulgaris*), and catalpa (*zi* 梓, *Lindera tsu-mu*) trees. Boxwood (*huangyang* 黃楊, *Buxus sempervirens*), gingko (*yinxing* 銀杏, *Gingko biloba*), Chinese honey locust (*baitao* 白桃, *Gleditsia sinensis*), and other species of tree are also used today. These deciduous woods are chosen because they have a smooth and even texture with various degrees of hardness for different purposes; also, they are abundant and inexpensive, as well as suitable for carving in any direction. Boxwood is the softest and pear has a medium hard surface, so both have been used for carving text. Jujube is harder and gingko is absorbent, while catalpa and honey locust are very hard woods, useful for cutting delicate lines such as on pictures for illustration. The wood of coniferous trees, while soft and straight grained, is impregnated with resin that would affect the evenness of the ink coating and thus is unsuitable for printing blocks.

Two methods have been used for cutting wood into blocks for engraving—with the grain and cross grain. For best results in carving and inking, Chinese carvers usually choose the former method, preferring blocks with a straight and close grain. This not only makes possible a larger area for the text but also avoids using the heart of the wood. Also to be avoided in choosing blocks are knots and spots in the wood, which would interfere with both carving and printing. After the blocks have been cut, they are usually soaked in water for about a month before use, but if needed immediately, they can be boiled instead. Then they are left to dry in a shaded place before being planed on both sides. Vegetable oil can be spread over the block surface, which is then polished with the stems of a polishing grass (jicao 棘草). The size of a block depends upon that of the sheet to be printed. Normally it is rectangular, averaging twelve inches wide, eight inches high, and one-half inch thick. Both sides are usually carved to enable the printing of two pages, or one leaf, on each side.

Woodblock engraving requires a set of sharp-edged tools of different shapes for various purposes in cutting and carving.[2] The cutting knife (kezidao 刻字刀) is a steel graver with a sharp blade and is the most important tool for cutting the main lines along the edges of the inked areas. A double-edged chisel (zan 鏨) is then applied to cut away surfaces of the block not covered with ink. A gouge (zao 鑿) scoops out the space from the surface, sometimes leaving a groove in the columns. A pick with two sharp ends (liangtoumang 兩頭忙) is used for detail work too fine for other tools.

Besides the woodblock, ink and paper are the other important elements for printing.[3] Chinese ink is generally kept in a solid form until shortly before use, when a small amount is converted into a liquid by grinding the ink on an ink stone moistened with water. Ink in liquid form was specially prepared for printing where the volume of ink needed made grinding of the solid ink impractical. Printing ink was first prepared as a paste made of coarse soot taken from the far end of a smoke chamber and mixed with glue and wine, and then preserved in jars or vats for later use. It had to be kept for three or four summers to enable the foul odor to disappear, and the longer the period of preservation, the better it became. When needed, water was added to the paste, and it was mixed thoroughly and strained through a sieve made of hair from horse tails.

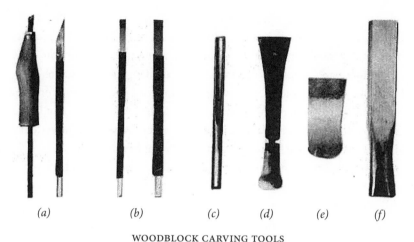

WOODBLOCK CARVING TOOLS
(a) Cutting knives (b) Double-edged chisels (c) Gouge with semi-circular edge
(d) Flat-edge chisel (e) Scraper (f) Wood mallet

Sample printing from blocks was usually made in red or blue, and final copies almost always in black. Certain books for special occasions were also printed in red and blue colors. The best red ink for printing was a mixture of vermilion and red lead boiled in water with the mucilaginous root of a plant called *baiji* (白芨 *Bletilla straiata*); next best was the liquid obtained from boiling the red-stem amaranth (*xiancai* 莧菜, *Amaranthus tricolor*), but this easily turns purple and does not give as fresh a color as the vermilion and red lead mixture. Blue ink was made from indigo (*dian* 澱 or *mulan* 木蘭, *Indigofera tinctoria)*, a Chinese native blue dye with a permanent color. Prussian blue is not suitable for printing, as the color runs when the paper is wet.

A great variety of paper was used for books and printing throughout the centuries. A close examination of the extant Song, Yuan, Ming, and Qing editions shows that the paper used is mostly made of bamboo and paper mulberry, with an occasional mixture of rice stalks and other raw materials. The most popular among the many high quality papers remains the *Xuanzhi* 宣紙, a soft, white, and fine paper made from the bark of the *tan* tree (檀 *Pteroceltis tartarinowii*) and straw in Xuancheng, Anhui, which is primarily used for art works. In the Song dynasty, papers popular for book printing included *beichao zhi* 卑鈔紙, a lustrous white paper made from a creeping plant in Fuzhou, Jiangxi; *Puqi zhi* 蒲圻紙, a medium heavy paper made in Puqi, Hubei; *Guangdu zhi* 廣都紙, a product of the paper mulberry from Guangdu, Sichuan; and *Youquan zhi* 由拳紙, a rattan paper made in Youquan village of Hangzhou, Zhejiang. Also, a specially treated, golden yellow paper, known as *jiao zhi* 椒紙, or pepper paper, made in Jianyang, Fujian, is said to have been dyed in a liquid prepared from the seeds of the pepper tree, which contains an insecticidal substance with a spice flavor that can last several hundred years.

Generally speaking, papers for books and printing came in two colors, white and yellow. The *mian zhi* 棉紙 (cotton paper) and *liansi* 連四 (fourfold) are white, sturdy, and of higher quality; they are actually made of paper mulberry or bleached bamboo fibers and not from raw cotton. The *zhu zhi* 竹紙, *shu zhi* 書紙, and *maobian zhi* 毛邊紙 are yellowish papers made of unbleached bamboo fibers and are generally used for commercial printing. In the Ming dynasty, a heavy and sturdy paper called *gongdu zhi* 公牘紙 (documents paper) was made of fine bamboo for official documents only, but its back was sometimes used for printing books. In the Qing dynasty, a paper of extraordinary quality made in Kaihua, Zhejiang, called *Kaihua zhi* 開化紙, was especially selected by the Qing court for printing the *dianben* 殿本, or palace editions, at the Imperial Printing Office or Wuying dian 武英殿.

Engraving, Printing, and Multicolor Process

The procedures for block printing can be summarized in ten successive steps: (1) preparation of the woodblocks, (2) transcription of the text, (3) proofreading of the transcription, (4) transferring the text to the blocks, (5) cutting the blocks, (6) chiseling the blanks, (7) polishing the blocks, (8) sample printing, (9) final proof, and (10) printing.[4] In the preparation for engraving, the manuscript is transcribed onto thin sheets of paper by a calligrapher. For this work, a blank sheet is ruled into columns and spaces with a centerline in each column used as a guide for writing the characters within each space in a balanced arrangement. This sheet, known as a *huage* 花格 (variegated space), is waxed lightly and smoothed with a stone burnisher to make the surface easier to write on with a brush.

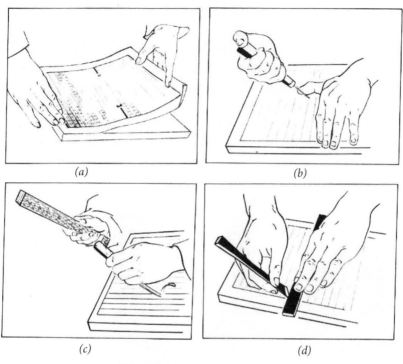

WOODBLOCK CUTTING PROCESS
(a) Transferring text to woodblock   (b) Starting cut
(c) Chiseling blanks   (d) Cutting lines

The transcript is then placed, written side down, on a block over which a thin layer of rice paste has been evenly spread. The back of the paper is rubbed with a flat palm-fiber brush so that a clear impression of the inked area is transferred to the block. When the paper has dried, its upper layer is rubbed away with fingertips and brush to expose a fine mirror image of the characters or designs remaining on the block, as if they had been inscribed directly on it. The block is then ready for carving.

The general practice of engraving is to leave all black lines in the mirror image in relief. A cut is first made narrowly bordering each character; this process is called *fadao* 發刀, or starting cut. The knife is held like a dagger in the right hand and is usually drawn toward, and not pushed away from, the cutter. This ensures that a close cut is made along the very edge of the black line. All the vertical lines are cut first, in one direction, and then the block is turned around for cutting of the horizontal or slanting strokes as well as the dots. When this has been done, the blank space between the outer and inner lines is cut away in a step known as *tiaodao* 挑刀, or close cut, leaving the characters with a relief of about one-eighth inch. The gouge with a semi-circular edge is used to cut away all the blank surfaces, known as *dakong* 打空 or chiseling blanks. A wooden hammer, *paizi* 拍子, is used to strike lightly on the tools to aid in clearing away the remnants of wood. The black lines of the columns and edges of the block

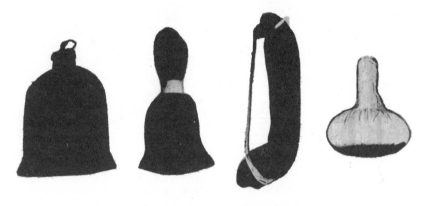

PRINTING BRUSHES AND ACCESSORIES
(from left to right) Flat palm-fiber brush, Round brush for inking,
Long pad for taking impressions, Stuffed pad for inked rubbing

are carefully trimmed with a small straight-edged knife to make all the lines sharp and clear; this process is called *laxian* 拉線, or cutting lines. Finally, the four edges of the block are sawed off and smoothed with a plane and its surface is cleaned of any remaining wood refuse or paper tissue and washed.

After the preparation is complete, the block is then held firmly on a table, with paper, ink, brushes, and other accessories placed close at hand. The printer takes a round inking brush (*yuanmushua* 圓木刷) made of horsehair, dips it into the water-based ink, and applies it to the raised surface of the block. A sheet of paper is immediately laid over the inked block and a long, narrow rubbing pad (*changshua* 長刷 or *bazi* 把子) is brushed lightly over the back of the paper. A positive image of the characters or illustrations is transferred to the paper, which is peeled off the block and laid aside to dry. The process is repeated until the required number of copies is obtained. It is said that a skilled printer could print as many as 1,500 to 2,000 double-page sheets in a day.[5] Fifteen thousand prints can be taken from the original cutting of one block and another 10,000 after slight touching up. The blocks can be stored and used again and again when additional copies are needed.

Four proofreadings are normally required in the engraving and printing processes: the first when the transcript is written, the second after corrections have been made on the sheets, the third when the first sample sheets are printed from the blocks, and the fourth after any repairs are carried out on the block. When a mistake is discovered or a line is chipped off, a block can be repaired. If the error is minor, the area can be excised with one edge of the chisel (*dingzao* 釘鑿) by making a notch into which a wedge-shaped piece of wood is hammered. If a large area is involved, a suitable piece of wood is inlaid. In either case, the new surface is smoothed and carved as if it were the original.

Chinese multicolor woodblock printing, known as *taoban* (套版, set of blocks) or *douban* (餖版 assembled blocks), is produced by a set of separate blocks, each of which is registered with water-based ink in different colors to be printed on the paper in succession. The number of blocks in a set varies from a few to several dozen or more, depending upon the variety of colors and tones printed. This polychrome process was used for printing text with punctuation and commentaries, cartographic works, paper money, book illustrations, ornamental letter-papers, New Year pictures, and works of painting, calligraphy, and decorative arts.

Color prints from woodblocks require considerable skill and expertise to master the various steps in designing, engraving, registering, and printing. The first step is to study and analyze the colors used in the original. Separate outline copies of each basic color are traced on thin transparent paper, which is then transferred to the surface of the woodblock as described above. The lines and colored areas require the exactness of the original work, which is always kept beside the carver and the printer.

The paper used for Chinese color prints is usually *Xuanzhi*, and the inks are the same water colors, most of which are earth pigments mixed with peach-tree resin or hide glue and water. These are mixed as they were for the originals, so they produce the exact colors after drying. The work-table is made of two wooden boards placed to leave a slit between them. On the left side the engraved block is fixed to the table with brushes and inks close at hand. On the right side, sheets of paper are firmly held together under a clamp. When the block is inked, the printer must see that no color runs beyond its proper boundaries. A sheet of paper is then laid upon the inked block and softly brushed over. Different pressure is applied to different parts of the block, depending upon the expression and texture needed for each stroke. Sometimes certain colors have to be printed first and dried before others are applied, and sometimes later printing must be done while the earlier colors are still wet. Gradation is achieved by applying varying degrees of color from light to dark repeatedly from the same block, either by causing the ink to run on the block with a special brush, or by wiping away the ink at the desired place.[6] In this way an exact copy is produced and sometimes cannot be distinguished from the original.

Movable Type Printing

Movable type printing was invented as an alternative to the cumbersome process of block printing. For economy and efficiency, experiments were made from time to time with the use of movable type, even though it was not entirely satisfactory for printing Chinese. It is well known that movable type made of earthenware was first used by Bi Sheng 畢昇 (ca. 990–1051) in the middle of the eleventh century. Movable wood type by Wang Zhen 王 禎 (fl. 1290–1333) towards the end of the thirteenth century, and movable type of bronze by Hua Sui 華燧 (1439–1513), An Guo 安國 (1481–1534), and many others at the end of the fifteenth and early sixteenth century. Various materials were used in the Qing, especially for printing in the imperial palace in the eighteenth century. Since all these processes are well described elsewhere,[7] the focus will be on some of the technical problems involved, and why movable type was not particularly popular in Chinese printing.

The material for the "bronze" movable type was, in all probability,

MOVABLE TYPE PRINTING AT THE IMPERIAL PRINTING OFFICE
(a) Making type blanks   (b) Carving type
(c) Making sorting trays   (d) Setting type

an alloy because pure copper is too soft to be serviceable, and it must be combined with tin or lead to increase its hardness, as was done in the manufacture of bronze weapons and vessels. A question that remains unanswered is whether earlier metal movable type in China was cast from molds or engraved individually. There are no surviving specimens for examination, nor any existing detailed records to answer this question. But examination of Ming and Qing imprints of bronze types reveal that they are markedly irregular in the shaping of characters.[8] Even on the same leaf, the strokes of the same character are not uniform, as if they were individually carved and not cast from matrices.

However, to exploit fully the advantages of movable type printing, casting seems to be the logical method, as it is much harder to cut in bronze than in wood and each set of type for composition includes tens or hundreds of thousands of characters; to cut them individually by hand would go against the principle of economy that dictated the use of movable type. Things do not always happen according to principle, however, and for reasons unknown, the engraving of individual type might have been a necessity.

Until the advent of modern typography, woodblock printing had always been the principal vehicle of Chinese printing and movable type but a sideline. The obvious reason is, of course, the nature of written Chinese, which includes thousands of ideographs that are needed in any extensive writing. Since several types are needed for each character, and for the more common ones twenty or more, a set of at least 200,000 Chinese characters is not unusual. This can be contrasted with an alphabetic language, which consists of no more than a hundred different symbols. So the need for such a large amount of type in an ideographic language reduced the practicability of movable type.

Another factor has been the time and labor required in assembling the type and, after use, its distribution for future use. Thus movable type printing is desirable only for large-quantity production, because only then is the average time for each copy reduced to a practical and economic level. Block printing and movable type printing therefore serve different needs: the former, recurrent demands for small quantities over relatively long periods; the latter, large quantities at one printing. Printers in old

China made tens of copies at a time and stored the printing blocks for later use. Thus they avoided the accumulation of printed books in stock and the tying up of capital. As far as capital is concerned, movable type printing requires a tremendous initial investment for making the vast number of types and compares very unfavorably with the small cost of woodblocks and the labor of engraving them.

Furthermore, scholars required that the printed page be free of textual errors and that the calligraphy be artistic. Movable type did not always fulfill these requirements, while printing from woodblocks made possible a great variety of typographical effects and lent a distinction and individuality to the printed page. From a technical point of view, the production of a hundred movable types was much more difficult than engraving a printed block with a hundred characters; grouping the types into retrievable order posed another problem. The collective effect of all these factors therefore produced a situation unfavorable for the development of movable type printing in the very culture where it was invented.

Signs, Formats, and Binding

Chinese books in the traditional style have always been printed on one side of the paper. Each leaf of the paper is folded double at the center of the sheet, making a double-leaf page. The printed portion of the leaf, which is the actual size of the block, is called *banmian* 版面 (block face) and the center fold *banxin* 版心 (heart of the block). At the center of the leaf there is a vertical rectangle called *xiangbi* 象鼻 (elephant trunk), a light or heavy line used to mark the center for folding, and *yuwei* 魚尾 (fish tail), a pair of sharp-angled spots at the upper and lower parts of the center used to indicate the level for folding. A running title, leaf number, and sometimes the number and heading of the chapter—or the number of characters on the leaf and the name of the carver—may be given in a narrow column at the fold. A square sign with the chapter number occasionally appears in some of the Song editions on the upper left side of the margin, called *shu'er* 書耳 (book ear), serving as a thumb index for the book, especially in the butterfly binding.[9]

The upper margin of the leaf called *shumei* 書眉 (book eyebrow) or

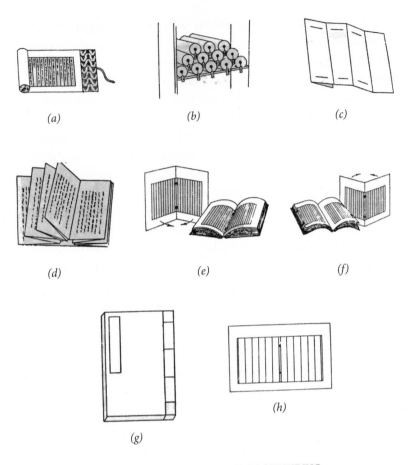

VARIOUS TYPES OF CHINESE BOOKBINDING
(a) Roll   (b) Rolls with identification labels   (c) Sutra
(d) Whirlwind   (e) Butterfly   (f) Wrapped-back
(g) Thread-stitched   (h) Double-leap with printed columns

tiantou 天頭 (heavenly head), is usually wider than the lower margin, *di-jiao* 地腳 (earthly foot). The page on each side of the leaf is ruled into columns and spaces (*hangge* 行格) with border lines (*jie* 界) to divide the individual columns and marginal lines (*bianlan* 邊欄), single or double, on four sides. The characters of the text are usually arranged in one vertical line within a column, and notes or commentaries in smaller characters in two lines. Each page may contain from five to ten columns, with from ten to thirty characters in each column. This basic format of the printed sheet and some of the bibliographical terms used for referring to the traditional format of the Chinese book have been continued into modern times.

The most important part of the book is certainly the text, which is normally printed in different styles of *kaishu* 楷書 (model script). Since books printed in different periods and in various locations show some variation of calligraphic styles, this has become one of the special features not only for judging a book's artistic qualities but also for dating printed editions.[10] Generally speaking, the Northern Song editions follow closely the style of Yan Zhenqing 顏真卿 (709–785), whose strokes are muscularly rigid and broad with thick and heavy lines; those of the Southern Song in the Hangzhou area imitate the style of Ouyang Xun 歐陽詢 (557–641), which is more slender and elegant with balanced and even lines, while those in Fujian and Sichuan are inclined to be a mixture of Yan and Liu Gongquan 柳公權 (778–865), whose calligraphy shows a compromise between the former two.

The early Yuan editions continued the Southern Song tradition of the Yan-Liu style but later shifted to that of the contemporary calligrapher Zhao Mengfu 趙孟頫 (1254–1322), whose style is particularly soft, feminine, and charming. The earlier Ming editions continued the Song and Yuan tradition of the Zhao and Ouyang styles, but from the middle of the sixteenth century, the style gradually changed to *jiang ti zi* 匠體字 (craftman script, or so-called *Song ti zi* 宋體字 (Song style), which is more rigid and square in construction with heavy lines for vertical strokes, lighter lines for horizontal strokes, and a heavy tail at the end of the strokes. This stereotyped form has been followed by printers ever since, and the modern metal type has adopted this style for all printed matter.

Chinese books on paper were kept first in the roll form (*juanzi* 卷子), with the end attached to a wooden roller and the beginning to a piece of silk or extra paper as an extension for protection of the text and a ribbon to fasten the roll. The tips of the roller were sometimes decorated with precious materials like gold, porcelain, ivory, coral, or horn. The color of ribbon denoted the genre of literature. Up until the ninth century, when printing began to be mentioned in literature, long continuous sheets of paper were folded into accordion pleat-like leaves, known as *jingzhe zhuang* 經折裝 (sutra binding), which made different parts of the text more immediately accessible than had been possible with rolls. When the first and last pages were connected, it was called *xuanfeng zhuang* 旋風裝 (whirlwind binding), which enabled the reader to turn from the last page directly back to the first for continuous reading. The frequent use of the books wore the sheets out along the folded line, and this resulted in the creation of the *hudie zhuang* 蝴蝶裝 (butterfly binding), which folded the printed leaves down the center and gathered them into a pile with a stiff paper cover pasted against the spine for protection. When the book was opened, the leaves suggested the wings of a butterfly.

Some time in the thirteenth or fourteenth century, during the Yuan dynasty, the format changed to the *baobei zhuang* 包背裝 (wrapped-back binding), the leaves of which were pasted into the spine and the folded centers brought to the mouth of the book. Paper twists were used to pass through the holes pierced near the spine of the fascicle to prevent the pasted spine from breaking away from the cover. When the wrapped-back binding separated, silk or cotton thread was stab-stitched at the spine to reinforce the twists. This process, known as *xian zhuang* 線裝 (stitched binding), was the most common method used until today. The printed sheets were folded singly and gathered into a fascicle rather than into signatures. With the fascicle aligned, the flyleaf and sometimes the inner leaf of the double-leaved cover paper was attached to the book with paper twists. Four holes for the thread were normally pierced along the spine, and the thread was then passed into them and over the top, bottom, and side edges until the thread returned to the first hole where it was then tied. The procedure was quick and simple and the format handy and durable compared with earlier bindings. It has been continued for books of traditional style in modern times.[11]

A number of fascicles of the book could be placed together in a detached case (*han* 函 or *tao* 套) made of wood or paperboard covered with textiles in various designs, which covered four or sometimes six sides of the fascicles. The paperboard was covered by linen, brocade, or some other fabric with paste to make a case, one side of which was locked with two sharp-edged clips (*qian* 籤) made of ivory or bone. Wooden chests made to hold books were fashioned from wood like *jiansi* cedar that was decay-resistant and insect-repellent. Sometimes pressing boards (*jiaban* 夾板) were used for tightening the fascicles together by cloth straps.[12]

Unlike its counterpart in the West, the stitched-bound Chinese book could be separated from its protective case. It therefore was much lighter and free from the strains that had to be sustained by Western books hanging by a cumbersome mechanism of tapes, thread, and mull to their heavy protective covers. Moreover, the compactness of the Western book, together with its heavy paper, increased the strain on its covers considerably. By sacrificing compactness and permanent union to its protective shields, the Chinese book, with its simple and easily repaired binding and its leaves printed on one side, was superior to books bound in the Western style in its ability to remain in a good state after repeated use.

Notes

1.   The writer is grateful to Mr. Gu Tinglong, Director of the Shanghai Library, for his information and for arranging the interviews in September, 1979, with the staff of the Shanghai Shuhuashe and Duoyunxuan in Shanghai, where block books and color prints are still made. My thanks go also to the staff of Rongbaozhai in Beijing, where discussions were held and a set of tools and blocks was presented to me as a gift.

2.   A list of Chinese printing and engraving tools sent to the First International Library Exhibition at Rome, 1929, is given in the *Bulletin of the Library Association of China*, IV:5 (April, 1929), 12–23.

3.   For a study of Chinese inkmaking, see Herbert Franke, *Kulturgeschichtliches über die chinesische Tusche*. Munchen: Verlag der Bayerischen Akademie der Wissenschaften, 1962; Lily Kesckes. "A Study of Chinese Ink-making: Historical, Technical and Aesthetic." Unpublished Master's Thesis, University of Chicago, 1981; Tsuen-hsuin Tsien, *Written on Bamboo and Silk: the Beginnings of Chinese Books and Inscriptions*. Chicago: University of Chicago Press, 1962, 164–174; rev. ed., 2004, 182–193. The kinds of paper for writing and printing are discussed in Tsien, "Raw Materials for Old Papermaking in China," *Journal of the American Oriental Society*, 93 (1973), 510ff.; Tsien, "Chinese Paper for Graphic and Decorative Arts," *Journal of the Institute of Chinese Studies of the Chinese University of Hong Kong*, 9 (1978), 87ff. In Chinese with English abstract.

4.   Cf. Lu Qian, *Shulin bihua* (1947).

5.   Matteo Ricci reported 1,500 sheets per day; see L. J. Gallagher (tr.), *China in the*

Sixteenth Century: The Journal of Matteo Ricci, 1583–1610 (New York, 1953), 21. Other sources reported 2,000 or even 6,000 to 8,000 per ten-hour day.

6. The above account is primarily based on my observations at the workshops of Rongbaozhai in Beijing and Duoyunxuan in Shanghai and also on descriptions in Jan Tschichold, *Chinese Colour Prints from the Ten Bamboo Studio*. Trans. by Katherine Watson. London: Lund Humphries, 1972, 41–44.

7. See Thomas F. Carter, *The Invention of Printing in China and Its Spread Westward*. Rev. ed. by L. Carrington Goodrich. New York: Ronald Press, 1955, 212–213; Richard C. Rudolph, "Chinese Movable Type Printing in the 18th Century," *Silver Jubilee Volume of the Zinbunkagaku Kenkyūsyo, Kyoto University* (1954), 317–35, and *A Chinese Printing Manual, 1776*. Los Angeles: Ward Ritchie Press, 1954; Tsien, "Bronze Movable Type Printing of Ming China: Problems of Its Origin and Technology," in *Collected Essays in Honor of the 70th Birthday of Dr. Chiang Fu-ts'ung* (Taipei, 1968), 129–144, in Chinese with English abstract: and his articles on An Guo and Hua Sui in Goodrich and Fang, *Dictionary of Ming Biography*, 9P 12, 64 7–49; and articles on movable types of the Yuan, Ming, and Qing by Zhang Xiumin in *Tushuguan* (1961:4, 1962:1) and *Wenwu* (1961:3, 1962:1).

8. The Korean bronze movable types were all cast from matrices, yet the shapes of their characters are often irregular and strokes not uniform, showing this problem was not particular to Chinese bronze movable types.

9. See discussion of the terms in Ye Dehui, *Shulin qinghua*, (reprint, 1961), 27–28; and translation of Chinese terminology of the books and bibliography in Tsien, "Terminology of the Chinese Book and Bibliography." Chicago: Graduate Library School, University of Chicago, 1969, 1–18.

10. See discussion in Poon Ming-sun, "Books and Printing in Sung China, 960–1279." Unpublished Doctoral Dissertation, University of Chicago, 1979.

11. See detailed description in Ove K. Nordstrand, "Chinese Double-leaved Books and Their Restoration," *Libri*, 17 (1967), 104-130, 106ff.

12. See discussion and illustrations in Edward Martinique. "The Binding and Preservation of Chinese Double-leaved Books," *Library Quarterly*, 43 (1973), 227–236, and *Chinese Traditional Bookbinding: A Study of Its Evolution and Techniques*. San Francisco: Chinese Materials Center, 1983.

Published in Chinese Rare Books in American Collections.
New York: China Institute in America, 1984; updated 2008.

Grateful acknowledgment is due to the National Science Foundation and the National Endowment for the Humanities for their support of the project for the study of Paper and Printing in Chinese Civilization, *of which this article is a part.*

CHINESE INVENTION OF
PAPER AND PRINTING

Paper was invented in China before the Christian era, adopted for writing at the beginning of the first century A.D., and manufactured with new and fresh fibers from the early second century. Paper began to cross China's borders in all directions not long after it became widely used there in the third century. Woodblock printing was first employed by the Chinese around A.D. 700, and movable type in the middle of the eleventh century. Even the indelible lampblack ink, which has been manufactured in the West under the misnomer "India ink," can be traced back to antiquity in Chinese civilization. It was the early introduction of these elements that made possible the mass production and wide distribution of written records. The Chinese have contributed most to the beginnings and development of the materials and techniques for the modern paged book, printed with black ink on white paper.

Paper was introduced to Europe through the Arab world in the ninth century and manufactured there in the twelfth century. Woodblock printing appeared there in the fourteenth century, and typography in the middle of the fifteenth. Thus, paper had been used in China at least a thousand years before it was known in Europe; woodblock printing six hundred years; and movable type four hundred years.[1] Although techniques were considerably altered and improved after their appearance in the West, the basic concepts of papermaking and printing germinated in China.

The prerequisites for a useful invention include both the physical and mental readiness for the event. In addition to the creative mind and popular demand, the availability of proper materials and the existence of basic techniques are essential. Since all the required materials and facilities for the invention of papermaking and printing were available in the West as well as in China, several questions naturally arise. Why did the combination of these prerequisites lead to the invention in one culture and not in the other? What were the factors responsible for such development? What elements or background forces made it possible for these two great inventions to appear early in Chinese culture but only after a considerable lag in the West?

Basic Elements for Papermaking

The three basic elements for the manufacture of paper are fibers, a mold, and water. The use of water, an inexpensive agent, contributed to the swelling and binding of the fibers and also to the increase of the mechanical strength of the paper. Water was readily available everywhere, but only pure and clear water was ideal for making paper pulp. Muddy or polluted rivers were not suitable situations for paper mills, which were usually located upstream or near springs. Rags of hemp or linen existed as early as the weaving of textiles. It was common to use water and textiles together, but the processes of turning rags into separate fibers through maceration and of using a mold to sustain the fibers while allowing the water to drain away were the key factors in the invention of papermaking.

The literature frequently testifies to the washing, pounding, or stirring of rags in water by women many centuries before the Christian era.[2] The treatment of refuse silk, the re-use of old fibers in quilted clothes, and the washing of rags of hemp and linen required such constant activities with fabrics in water. It is very likely that an accidental drying of refuse fibers on a mat suggested the idea of making a thin sheet of paper.

The first mold was probably no more than a square of coarsely woven cloth held within a four-sided frame, onto which the macerated fibers were poured.[3] The woven material retained the fibers in a moist sheet while allowing the water to drain through the interstices. No molds from this time survives, but the definition of paper in the old lexicon compiled about A.D. 100 by Xu Shen 許慎 throws some light on the form and material of the early mold. The *Shuowen jiezi* 說文解字 defines paper as "a mat of refuse fibres."[4] The key word *shan* 苫 (mat), which includes the radical for grass in the earlier texts,[5] means a kind of cloth for a covering, made of woven rushes, according to the early commentators.[6] It is possible that this early mat used in Han times was made of some type of grass, or possibly of ramie, woven into a cloth to support the macerated

(a)

(b)

(c)

TRADITIONAL PAPERMAKING IN CHINA

(a) Cutting, stamping, and washing the raw material
(b) Cooking, pounding, and mixing the fibers
(c) Dipping and lifting the mold; drying and sorting sheets

fibers and to allow the water to escape through its mesh. This form of primitive mold and the method of pouring the macerated fibers upon it can still be found in modern times in South China, Tibet, Thailand, and certain other locations in South and Southeast Asia.[7]

Actually, the invention of papermaking was a gradual process rather than a single event. An important advance in this process was the introduction of new and fresh raw materials for unlimited production. At this point, the availability of adequate material and the demand for a better writing medium were equally significant. The earlier materials of papermaking were all worn-out or secondhand items such as rags of clothing and fishing nets, the supply of which was limited. As demand increased, these materials were insufficient to meet the need, and new and fresh fibers were searched for and adopted. We are told that all the paper specimens from the Former or Western Han (206 B.C.–8 A.D.) discovered in recent years in the northwestern provinces of China were made of used hemp fibers and bear no writing.[8] As paper was improved and began to be used for writing, perhaps from the beginning of the first century A.D., great demand must have developed at this time. Early Chinese papermakers selected such fresh raw materials as the paper mulberry, which produced the best fibers and was most economical in terms of cost.

The paper mulberry is native to China and has been cultivated extensively in temperate and tropical zones throughout the world. The bark of paper mulberry, soaked in water and beaten into a thin sheet, known as *tapa* or bark cloth, has been used for clothing and occasionally for drawing or writing in the Pacific Islands, Central America, and elsewhere.[9] The bark cloth mentioned in early Chinese literature may have some affiliation with *tapa*.[10] Apparently, the inner bark of the paper mulberry could be prepared in different ways and used for different purposes. The invention of papermaking from tree bark attributed to Cai Lun 蔡倫 in the early second century was possibly influenced by his acquaintance with this material.[11] Cai Lun was a native of Leiyang in modern Hunan province. where the paper mulberry is said to have been grown, traded, and used for making bark cloth by beating or making bark paper after maceration.[12] Since the maceration process for turning rags into pulp was already known in China, it is very likely that the people in South China were the first to convert paper mulberry bark into a pulp for papermaking. The paper mulberry was apparently not used in Europe, where its cultivation seems to have been unknown.[13]

The popular demand for a better writing material was another important factor toward the invention and use of paper in China. It was a much cheaper and more ideal writing medium than the expensive silk and the clumsy bamboo or wood. In Europe, paper did not hold many advantages over papyrus or parchment. Papyrus was plentiful, inexpensive, and perhaps as light and convenient as paper. Parchment, although more expensive, had a smoother surface and was much more durable than paper. In the early days, paper was not much cheaper than parchment,[14] in contrast to silk, and no more portable than papyrus, in contrast to bamboo and wood. Because of its fragility, paper was even banned for official documents in Europe.[15] It was not a welcome commodity when first introduced to Europe from the Arab world, as Europeans were distrustful of anything from that hostile land during and after the Crusades, and its use was attacked by clergymen such as the abbot of Cluny.[16] Not until the spread of printing in Europe did a great demand for paper arise, although it had been in use for manuscripts and household records before then. The situation in China was different, as paper established its supremacy as a popular medium for writing even before it was officially adopted by the court in the early second century A.D.

Technical Prerequisites for the Invention of Printing

The basic materials needed for block printing include wood, ink, and paper. The same kinds of wood from pear, box, or other deciduous trees were used for woodblocks for printing in both China and the West. Lampblack ink was probably discovered very early, since soot was naturally produced and collected when fire was controlled. Some inscriptions on oracle bones were written with black ink or illuminated with a carbon mixture of the nature of ink.[17] The early symbols and signs appearing on painted pottery found in Banpo, Shanxi, indicate the use of red and black pigments as early as the Neolithic period.[18] Traditionally,

Chinese ink has always been made in solid form. Pure, clean soot was mixed with animal glue, with other ingredients added for preservation, increased brightness, and permanence of color. Water was added when the ink was used in writing or printing.

A similar ink of lampblack mixed with an aqueous solution of vegetable gum was used by Egyptian scribes as early as 1300 B.C. and its use spread to Western Asia by 1100 B.C. The Greeks made an ink of soot from burnt ivory or dried wine-lees, which consisted of the same basic ingredients of lampblack and gum and the same solid form as the Chinese ink.[19]

Of the three basic necessities for printing, paper was perhaps the most important. Without a soft and absorbent medium, it would have been impossible for printing to develop. The early use of paper by the Chinese certainly contributed to the early invention of printing in China. The late introduction of paper to Europe had a significant effect on the slow development of printing in the West. This is especially evident in that paper was not in great demand in Europe until after the spread of typography toward the second half of the fifteenth century.

However, paper was certainly not the only essential prerequisite for this invention, for printing did not appear in China until paper had been used for writing for at least six or seven hundred years, and four centuries passed after the arrival of paper in Europe before printing took place. Printing developed quite naturally from such techniques as making and using seals and stamps, engraving on stone and metals, and taking inked rubbings from stone and other inscriptions. Religious and secular demand for great numbers of copies called for some mechanical means to replace hand copying.

Seals inscribed in reverse from which the correct inscription was obtained by stamping on clay, and later on paper, embody the technique closest to that which eventually led to the invention of printing. The use of seals began in antiquity in both Chinese and Western civilizations. In China, seals cast in bronze with designs and inscriptions in relief survive from the Shang dynasty. Other seals made of metals or carved on stone, jade, ivory, horn, earthenware, and wood have continued in use.[20] They are characterized in general by a flat, square, or oblong surface, bearing inscriptions in relief or intaglio of personal names or official titles, always in reverse. They have been used to indicate ownership, authenticate documents, and establish authority.

The use of seals in Western culture began and flourished in Mesopotamia and Egypt, perhaps even before the invention of writing.[21] These seals were made of stone, ivory, shell, or metals. There were two principal types of Western seals, cylinders and stamps. The cylindrical type was used in Mesopotamia and in areas under Babylonian influence. Their designs, primarily of deities, heroes, animals, celestial bodies, instruments, and emblems, were impressed by rolling the cylinder over a flat surface of clay, mortar, cement, or wax to indicate ownership, authentication, or authority.[22] The stamp seals have a variety of shapes. The backs of those used in Egypt were in the form of a scarab beetle, a sacred symbol of resurrection and immortality. Their bases are flat and engraved with designs or inscriptions of mottoes, personal names, and titles of officials.[23] These had strong religious overtones as well as practical functions. Both the cylindrical and the stamp forms of seals were also used in Asia Minor, Syria, and Palestine. Their use was discontinued after the fall of the Western Roman Empire but revived in the second half of the eighth century. Since then round or oval seals engraved with designs and legends have been employed in the West until modern times.

Generally speaking, the seals developed in Chinese and Western cultures bear certain similarities and differences. They were both made of the same kinds of materials, impressed originally on the same kinds of surfaces, and used primarily for the same purposes. But there were also major differences, which perhaps led to the development of seals in different directions. Chinese seals were mostly made in a square or rectangular shape with a flat base, inscribed with characters in reverse, and in later times were used to stamp on paper. These characteristics are very close to those of block printing. Although the surfaces and inscriptions of most seals are small and limited, some wooden seals were as large as printing blocks and were inscribed with texts of more than one hundred characters.[24]

The seals of the West, on the other hand, were cylindrical or scaraboid, round or oval, and inscribed primarily with pictures and only occasionally with writing. The cylindrical seals used to roll over clay had no potential to develop into a printing surface. While the scaraboid seals were flat-based, their primarily religious nature was predominant over their functional aspects as a tool for multiplication.[25] Furthermore, seal inscriptions were always in relief, and impressions continue even today to be made on such stiff materials as wax rather than on flexible mediums such as paper or parchment. These different usages discouraged the development of the idea of printing from seals in the West.

Seals as symbols of authority and authenticity were similar to inscriptions on coins. The circulation and acceptance of metal money depended upon official sponsorship and approval, which was usually indicated by marking on the coins their value, place of minting, and sometimes the official symbol of approval. These numismatic inscriptions were made either by casting in a mold or by stamping or punching on the face of the coins. From very early times, Chinese coins in spade, knife, plate, and circular shapes were cast from molds.[26] Coins in the West were first inscribed by stamping and later by casting. The casting technique was subsequently borrowed by bookbinders, who cast separate metal characters for stamping on bindings. This craft was eventually adapted by printers to cast metal type and thus was the forerunner of typography in the West.[27]

The technique of engraving on stone tablets is similar to that of carving on wood blocks, and taking inked squeezes or rubbings from stone inscriptions is very similar to the process of block printing. Inscribing on stone was well developed very early in both China and the West. Chinese inscriptions on stone survive from the Chou dynasty. Subsequently, stone became the most popular medium for commemorative writings and for the preservation and standardization of the canonical texts.[28] Stone was also used, in addition to clay tablets, for writing by the Mesopotamians, for tomb inscriptions by the Egyptians, and for monuments by the Romans and other peoples throughout the world,[29] but their inscriptions were not as extensive and refined as those in China. Stone inscriptions in the West never compared in scale with those in China, where hundreds of thousands of characters of Buddhist, Daoist, and Confucian texts were copied on stone throughout many centuries.[30] Stone was used in the West

INK RUBBING FROM A STONE CARVING

more as an artistic material than, as it was in China, for writing. These differences in the nature, scope, and content of stone inscriptions caused them to develop in divergent directions in China and the West.

Taking inked squeezes or rubbings from stone inscription is similar to printing in principle and purpose, but different in process and end product.[31] Both result in the duplication on a sheet of paper of an engraved object, but their varying methods result in different kinds of reproductions.[32] The technique of taking inked rubbings from stone, and eventually from all kinds of hard surfaces in China, can be traced back to the sixth century A.D. The technique seems not to have been used in the West until perhaps the nineteenth century, when antiquarians and artists began to experiment with the use of a crayon-like agent in tracing designs from memorial brasses, tombstones, brick walls, carved wood, and sewer-plates. The duplication was far less sophisticated than that of the inked squeezes in China. It was a combination of the techniques of carving seals with a mirror image in relief and of making duplications by inking and rubbing on a sheet of paper that resulted in the methods of block printing. The long Chinese tradition of using seal impressions, carving stone inscriptions, and taking rubbings from hard surfaces certainly contributed to the techniques of printing.

Social and Cultural Influences on Printing

Besides the materials and techniques which were necessary for the invention, specific social and cultural factors had a great effect on the application or rejection of printing. Since printing is a mechanical extension of writing, the nature of a given system of writing is one of the most important factors affecting the development of printing. Chinese writing was from the very beginning characterized by an ideographic script, which is basically composed of numerous separate strokes of different shapes.[33] Because each character has a definite and distinct form, the writing of characters tends to be elevated to an art and thus is more complicated and time-consuming than alphabetical writing, especially when a special style is sought for a formal and respected text.

On the other hand, Western writing, ever since the Phoenicians

WOODEN MOVABLE TYPE PRINTING, THIRTEENTH CENTURY
*Typesetting with characters at right; on the left, brushing the back
of paper from the type frames*

developed the rudiments of an alphabet, has evolved into a system of symbols representing sounds. Its components of written forms are merely substitutes for their spoken counterparts, and they have tended to evolve into simple signs composed of continuous lines.[34] Copying in an alphabetical language is easier than in an ideographic script. It is likely that the slower and more complicated process of copying Chinese resulted in a greater demand for mechanical aid in duplication in China than in the West. It is also rather natural that movable type was more acceptable for an alphabetic language, while block printing was more suitable to the Chinese writing system.

Chinese culture embodied an extensive writing or bookish tradition that is characterized by productivity, continuity, and universality. It is unique among ancient civilizations in the volume of its output, in the length of its period of coverage, and in its uninterrupted and widespread application to intellectual transmission. From very early times, documents were systematically produced and archives carefully kept by professional recorders. Written words were revered and books were assiduously studied in order to achieve prominence in society. These factors had contributed to the production of more written and printed pages before the end of the fifteenth century than had been produced by all other nations put together.[35] Although this bookish tradition may not have been the only factor to contribute to the first use of printing, the need for standardized texts of Confucian classics and for more copies of textbooks, reference works, examination aids, and other scholarly literature in conjunction with the civil service examinations did promote the application of printing on a broader scope and to a higher degree of perfection.[36]

Hand copying of text was time-consuming and expensive. The cost ratio between a hand-copied manuscript and a printed edition was about ten to one when printing was begun in Tang times.[37] During the later part of the Tang, the charge for a professional copyist was about 1,000 pieces of cash per juan (of about 5,000 to 10,000 characters). This was the cost of copying the Buddhist sutras found in Dunhuang, on which the charges are sometimes given.[38] The price was similar for other copied manuscripts such as the rhymed dictionary copied by a woman calligrapher of the early ninth century.[39] The cost of a printed edition at this time was about one tenth that of a written copy.[40] This ratio between hand copying and printing remained constant without much change in later times, in spite of the fluctuating prices.[41]

In the long history of the development of printing, the earliest appearances of printing in many areas of the world were associated with the world's great religions. Religious zeal to spread sacred scriptures to all believers created a demand for a ready means of reduplication. Buddhism even teaches that the mass production of its sutras is a way to receive blessings from the Buddha. The Buddha is said to have remarked, "Whoever wishes to gain power from the dharani (charms) must write out seventy-seven copies and place them in pagodas. . . . The dharani is spoken by the ninety-nine thousand koti[42] of Buddhas, and he who repeats it with all his heart shall have his sins forgiven.[43] The enthusiasm of the Buddhist devotees for producing a great multitude of sacred texts was highly influential in the birth of printing in China, which occurred during the high tide of Buddhism in the early Tang. This relationship is emphasized by the discoveries of the earliest Buddhist printed texts, *dharani*, in pagodas in both Japan and Korea.[44]

In the West, there was not as strong a demand for multiple copies as in China. Hand copying by slave scribes could produce more than were needed in the Roman Empire.[45] In the Middle Ages the reading public was very small, and the copyist tradition was carried on in monasteries and churches. Demand for books could be met with hand copies made by scribes, and there were no incentives to produce them in large quantity. Not until the Renaissance and the Reformation did the demand for the Bible and other reading materials significantly increase.

Another factor influencing the relatively slow development of printing in Europe might have been the growth of various kinds of craft unions and guilds. These were first organized in Greece and Rome to facilitate the sharing of common interests of skilled men, but they eventually gained political influence and took on the role of protectors of the professional skills and livelihood of their members in the Middle Ages. These guilds naturally became very exclusive memberships. For instance, block printers such as those who engraved and printed cards and religious images belonged to the company of painters or artists, which represented such craftsmen as scribes, illuminators, sculptors, stonecutters, glassmakers, and wood engravers; typographers were not admitted as members of that society.[46] As late as 1470, guilds of scribes and illuminators in France still forbade the multiplication of religious images other than by hand.[47] The power of the guilds to restrict membership in crafts in the Middle Ages likely had a negative impact on the early development of printing in Europe.

In summation, the use of printing in China was due to the early invention of paper, the similar uses of seals and rubbing for duplication, the greater need for mechanical aid in duplicating texts written in a complex ideographic script, the standardization of Confucian texts used for the civil service examinations, and finally the demand for large quantities of copies of Buddhist scriptures which could not be met by hand copying. In the West, paper was not introduced until a rather late date, seals were not used as duplicating devices, rubbing was not known until the nineteenth century, printers were restricted by craft unions or guilds, and the relative simplicity of the alphabetic script lessened the need for a mechanical duplication aid. The materials and techniques requisite for the invention of printing either were not developed, or did not lead in the direction of the printing process.

Furthermore, there was no such incentive or demand for a great number of copies as developed in connection with Buddhism; the needs that did exist could be met by hand copying. Until all these factors changed in the middle of the fifteenth century, the threshold for the invention of printing was not reached in Western society.

Notes

1. There is no dispute that paper was invented in China and spread to the West step by step overland across Eurasia; material evidence exists. How printing was introduced to Europe is not so clear. The close resemblance of the early block books of Europe to those of China and other evidence suggest that European block printers followed Chinese models. Although many book historians believe that European typography was an independent invention, emphasizing the technical differences between Chinese and European printing, circumstantial evidence based on cultural considerations is strong for Chinese influence. For details, see Thomas F. Carter, *The Invention of Printing in China and Its Spread Westward*, revised by L. Carrington Goodrich (New York: Ronald Press. 1955).

2. *Yuejue shu* (*SBCK ed.*), 1/3b, records that Wu Yuan (6th–5th century B.C.) stopped by a river where he saw a woman pounding rags (*jixu*) in the Lai River; *Zhuangzi* (*SBCK ed.*, 1/15b) says: "There was a man of the Song state who had a recipe for salve for chapped hands, and from generation to generation his family made their living by pounding and stirring rags in water (*pingpiguang*)"; *Shiji* (Tongwen shuju ed.), 92/lb, also says that Han Xin (d. 196 B.C.), Marquis of Huaiying, was fishing outside of the city, where he saw many women washing rags in the Huai River; one of them worked continuously for several tens of days.

3. There are two ways of removing fibers from water to make a sheet of paper. In one, the mold is dipped perpendicularly into water, and the macerated fibers lifted upon it horizontally. In the other the mold is held flat, and the water and fibres poured upon it. The latter method is apparently the more primitive, since more molds are required so that the fibres may remain on them to dry.

4. See Ding Fubao, *Shuowen jieji gulin* (Shanghai, 1930), 5901. The commentator Duan Yucai (1735–1815) says that the manufacture of paper originated from the process of pounding and stirring rags in water, after which the wadded pulp was placed on a mat.

5. The character *shan* has been written in various editions of the *Shuowen*. The Northern Song edition gives the form with the grass radical, but it was changed by others and again by Duan with the bamboo and water radicals in order to suit his interpretation of picking up the fibers from water with a bamboo mold. The use of a bamboo screen, however, developed later than in Han times.

6. *Erya*, compiled ca. 200 B.C., defines *zhan* as a white sheet for covering (*baigai*), and it was woven of rushes (*bian mao*), according to the commentator Xu Kai (920–974); see discussion in Tsien Tsuen-hsuin, *Zhongguo gudai shushi* (Hong Kong, 1975), 127, note 8.

7. A mold or woven cloth from Foshan, Guangdong, found by Dard Hunter during his field trip to the Far East in the 1930s, is kept in the Paper Museum in Appleton, Wisconsin, U. S. A.; see illustrations in his *Papermaking: the History and Technique of an Ancient Craft* (2nd ed., New York, 1974: reprint 1978), 84, 111–13. The stems of the day lily are said to have been used for making the screen in the Hebei area; see *Wenwu*, 1966, no. 3, 45, note 4.

8. Up to the time of this writing, at least seven discoveries of paper fragments from the Han period have been reported. Microscopic examinations of four Former Han specimens indicate that they were made of used hemp fibers; see Pan Jixing, *Zhongguo zaozhi jishu shigao* (Peking, 1979), 165; other tests by the Research Institute of Paper Industry and Technology, Ministry of Light Industry, Beijing, are reported in *Wenwu*, 1980, no. 1, 78–85.

9. There are three ways of making plant fibers into a sheet. It can be done by spinning and weaving into a textile, by soaking and beating into *tapa*, and by macerating and felting into paper. Because *tapa* has been used primarily for clothing rather than for writing, it has been called cloth. Because the process of making it is somewhere between weaving and felting, it should be considered a quasi-paper rather than cloth or true paper. For the manufacture of *tapa* in various places in the Pacific Islands and in Central and South America, see Hunter, op cit., 29–47; Fred Siegenthaler, "Tapa," in *Handmade papers of the world* (Tokyo, Takeo Co., 1978), 27–28.

10. *Shiji*, 129/15b. says that a town merchant managed in a year to sell "a thousand piculs of *tabu* and leather"; the term *dabu* is used in *Han shu*, 91/7b; and *dubu* in *Hou Han shu*, 24/2b.

11. See the biography of Cai Lun in the *Hou Han shu*, 108/5a-b; also Ling Chunsheng, *Bark-cloth, Impressed Pottery, and the Invention of Paper and Printing* (Taibei, 1963), 29–57.

12. Lu Ji (261–303) mentioned in his commentary on *Shi jing* that people south of the Yangtze River used the bark of *gu* (paper mulberry) to make cloth and also pounded it to make paper called *gubu zhi* (paper of paper-mulberry cloth); see *Maoshi caomu niaoshou chongyu shu* (*TSCC* ed.), 29–30.

13. In the search for fresh raw materials for papermaking, Dr. Jacob C. Schiffer (1718–1790) tells of testing over thirty kinds, including bark, straw, vines, seaweed, moss, walnut, potatoes, wood, and various other plants; he does not mention paper mulberry or bamboo, which have been the major raw materials used in papermaking

in China and other nations in East and South Asia; see Hunter, op. cit., 309ff.

14. In 1367, 31 quires of parchment, each containing 3 dozen sheets, cost 76 livres, 5 sous, 8 deniers in Tours; in 1359, 2 quires of paper cost 18 deniers; and in 1360, 4 quires of paper cost 2 shillings, 4 deniers; see Andre Blum, *On the Origin of Paper*, tr. by H. M. Lydenberg (New York. 1934), 62–63.

15. Paper was forbidden for official use by King Roger of Sicily in 1145, and again by Emperor Frederick II of Germany in 1221; cf. Ibid., 23, 30.

16. Cf. Ibid., 30.

17. Chemical microanalysis of the specimens of oracle-bone inscriptions indicates that the black is a carbon mixture of the nature of ink and the red pigment is cinnabar; see Roswell S. Britton, "Oracle Bone Color Pigments," *Harvard Journal of Asiatic Studies*, II (1937). 1–3.

18. *Xi'an Banpo* ed., the Institute of Archaeology, Academia Sinica (Beijing, 1963), 156.

19. Cf. James H. Breasted. "The Physical Processes of Writing in the Early Orient and Their Relation to the Origin of the Alphabet," *American Journal of Semitic Languages and Literatures* 32 (1916), 230–49; Frank B. Wiborg, *Printing Ink: A History* (New York, 1926). 7, 71–72.

20. The use of seals in China is considered one of the most important technical prerequisites for printing. For inscriptions of Chinese seals and sealing clay, see Tsuen-hsuin Tsien, *Written on Bamboo and Silk* (Chicago, 1962), 54ff.

21. Cf. E. Chiera, *They Wrote on Clay* (Chicago, 1956), 192.

22. For the development of cylindrical seals, see Gustavus A. Eisen, *Ancient Oriental Cylinder and Other Seals* (Chicago, 1940); Henry Frankfort, *Cylinder Seals* (London, 1939); and Donald J. Wiseman, *Cylinder Seals of Western Asia* (London, 1958).

23. For scarab seals and their religious meaning, see P. E. Newberry, *Scarabs: An Introduction to the Study of Egyptian Seals and Signet Rings* (Oxford, 1971); and J. Ward, *The Sacred Beetle: A Popular Treatise on Egyptian Scarabs in Art and History* (London, 1902).

24. Large charm seals used by Daoists in the fourth century contained 120 characters on a wood block 4 inches wide; see *Baopuzi* (SBCK ed.), *juan* 14, 104; tr. in Carter, op. cit., 13.

25. Cf. Constance R. Miller, "An Inquiry into the Technical and Cultural Prerequisites for the Invention of Printing in China and the West," Unpublished M.A. thesis, University of Chicago, 1975.

26. The earliest metal coins cast with inscriptions may have been made in the late Shang or early Zhou; see Wang Yuquan, *Early Chinese Coinage* (New York, 1950), 114. For the development of Chinese numismatic inscriptions, see Tsien, op. cit., 50–53.

27. Cf. Blum, op. cit., 21.

28. See Tsien, op. cit., 64ff.

29. Cf. David Diringer, *The Hand-produced Book* (New York, 1953), 44–45, 82, 358.

30. Confucian classics were engraved on stone seven times from 178–183 to 1791–1794;

the Han inscriptions contained over 200,000 characters. A total of 105 Buddhist sutras in over 4,200,000 words were engraved on some 7,000 stone tablets from the middle of the sixth through the end of the eleventh century. The engraving of Daoist canons on stone was made on a smaller scale, starting in the early eighth century.

31. In his review of Carter in *Journal of the Royal Asiatic Society* (1926), 141, A. C. Moule expressed doubts about the influence of rubbing on printing because the two processes are essentially different. However, the difference in one respect does not preclude influence on another, as can be seen in the fact that special reference to stone inscriptions was made when Confucian classics were first printed from woodblocks in the tenth century.

32. Inscriptions on stone are always cut into the surface in intaglio in the positive position, while writings engraved for printing are cut in relief in reverse. Rubbing obtains the duplications with white text on black background, while printing by applying ink on the block produces black text on white background.

33. Chinese characters have been composed of from one to more than thirty independent strokes, dots, straight or curved lines, and squares since their development into the clerical and regular styles from around the beginning of the Christian era.

34. For a comparative study of word-syllabic and alphabetic systems, see I. J. Gelb, *A Study of Writing* (2nd ed., Chicago, 1963).

35. Chinese book production was prominent before the end of the fifteenth century when printing was still not used in Europe on a large scale. In about 1450–1500, some 30,000 editions of incunabula were printed, a third of them in Germany alone, while Chinese book production has lagged far behind; see Tsien, op.cit., 4, note 4.

36. See Poon Ming-sun, "Books and Printing in Sung China, 960-1279." Unpublished doctoral dissertation, University of Chicago, 1979.

37. See Weng Tongwen, "Yinshuashu duiyu shuji chengben de yingxiang," *Tsing Hua Journal for Chinese Studies*, n.s., vol. 6, nos. 1/2 (1967), 35–43.

38. For instance, hand copying of *Yueshi jing*, 1 *juan*, cost 1,000 pieces of cash; *Fahua jing*, 7 *juan*, 10,000; *Daniepan jing*, 40 *juan*, 30,000.

39. Ye Dehui, *Shulin qinghua* (Taipei. 1961), 285–88, gives several stories concerning the *Tang yun*, hand copied by Wu cailuan (ft. 827-835), which was sold for 5,000 pieces of cash. According to its preface, this dictionary consisted of 42,383 words in 5 juan, an average of 8,500 words per juan.

40. The Japanese monk Ennin: (793–863) bought in China in 835 a Buddhist sutra in 4 *juan*, which cost 450 pieces or cash; see Edwin O. Reischauer (tr.), *Ennin's Diary* (New York, 1955), 48. Because of its cheapness in comparison with the copied manuscripts at that time, it is believed that this book must have been a printed edition; see Weng, op. cit., 38–39.

41. The printing of calendars by the Song government in 1042 cost 30,000 pieces of cash, while hand writing them in previous years cost ten times this amount. The Ming author Hu Yinglin (1551–1602) says a hand-copied manuscript cost ten times as

much as a printed edition; see Weng Tongwen, op. cit.

42. A *koti* is variously put at one hundred thousand, one million, and ten million.

43. See the translation of the *dharani* cited in Carter, op. cit., 50.

44. One million copies of four versions of the *dharani* printed ca. A.D. 764–770 were found in pagodas among ten Buddhist temples in Japan; see Carter, op. cit., 46–53. These samples of early printing were superseded as the earliest by another *dharani* in Chinese text, dating to 704–751, which was found in 1966 in Pulguk-sa in Korea; this is so far the world's earliest specimen of block printing; see L. Carrington Goodrich, "Printing: Preliminary Report on a New Discovery," *Technology and Culture* 8:3 (1967), 376–78.

45. See Henry N. Humphreys, *A History of the Art of Printing from Its Invention to Its Wide-spread Development in the Middle of the Sixteenth Century* (London, 1867), 20.

46. See W. A. Chatto and John Jackson, *A Treatise on Wood Engraving* (2nd ed., London, 1861; reprint 1969), 121–22. It says that of all the early typographers of Antwerp, only one may have been admitted to guild membership as a wood engraver, probably on account of the illustrations printed with his typography, between 1485 and 1590.

47. Cf. Douglas P. Bliss, *A History of Wood Engraving* (2nd ed., London, 1964), 10–11.

Published in Explorations in the History of Science and Technology in China, *compiled in honor of the Eightieth Birthday of Dr. Joseph Needham, FRS, FBA (Shanghai: Classics Publishing Co., 1986).*

11   WESTERN IMPACT ON CHINA THROUGH TRANSLATION

Translation is not only a science or an art, but a practical tool of international communication in the worldwide exchange of ideas. The importance of translation has grown with the increasing number of contacts among nations of widely divergent cultures. In the Western world, translation has been considered more frequently from the linguistic than the cultural point of view, for the West has a common pattern of culture underlying its linguistic variety. The communication problem between East and West is significantly more complex in that besides the language barriers there are divergent cultural patterns.

The translation of Western works into Chinese began near the end of the sixteenth century. Moved by religious enthusiasm, the Jesuits initiated the process and the Protestant missionaries soon followed. Since the middle of the nineteenth century, translation programs have been an aspect of Chinese governmental activity directed toward modernization. Both the subject matter translated and the languages from which they were translated are indicators of trends in modern Chinese thought as well as changing governmental policies. Moreover, the motivation of translation and the shifts in intellectual interests are reflected in the character and quantity of translations produced at different times.

The importance of translation is intensified by the fact that, as many modern political and intellectual leaders in China did not know a foreign language, Western knowledge was acquired largely through translated materials. Recognition of the importance of translation in China has been evidenced by the compilation of many general and special bibliographies of translations from various languages. The Chinese traditional concept of bibliography, which emphasized the importance of ideas as reflected in records of the past, is quite similar to the modern theory of statistical bibliography, which traces the growth of civilization through the analysis of bibliographical records.[1] This study is intended to investigate the Western impact on China as reflected in the history and analysis of translations.[2]

Jesuit Translations

The appearance of Western knowledge in Chinese intellectual circles at the end of the sixteenth century marked the beginning of the second great importation of foreign culture into Chinese history—the first being Buddhism. Over the next two centuries, at least eighty Jesuits of various nationalities participated in translating into Chinese more than four hundred works covering fields of knowledge new to the Chinese. More than half of these works relate to Christianity, about one-third are scientific literature, and the remainder concern Western institutions and humanities (Table I). It is obvious that the primary motivation of the Jesuit translators was religious. Among the earliest translations and writings by the Jesuits, a theological work on Christianity, *Shengjiao shilu* 聖教實錄, written by Michel Ruggieri in 1582 and printed in Canton in 1584, was the first book in Chinese produced by a westerner. In 1596, Matteo Ricci, in his *Tianxue shiyi* 天學實義, originated the technique of relating Christianity to Confucianism by quoting the Chinese classics in support of Christianity. But it was a point of Jesuit strategy to take advantage of the Chinese respect for astronomy and mathematics by focusing on translations in these fields to enhance the prestige of Western culture. When Euclid was first published in 1607, the work was considered as coming "very opportunely to lower the pride of the Chinese, for the best scholars had to admit that they had read a book printed in their language without being able to understand the meaning, even after applying themselves to it unremittingly."[3]

The translation program was supported by the importation of numerous Western books at the beginning of the seventeenth century. The miscellaneous materials brought by individual missionaries were augmented by a major acquisition of some seven thousand volumes in 1620. Recent discoveries concerning this collection indicate that they had been used for translation.[4] The collection, covering various subjects such as philosophy, theology, medicine, science, law, and music, was selected from Italy, France, Germany, and Belgium by Nicolas Trigault, who was primarily responsible for building up the collection and bringing it to China.[5]

Table I. Jesuit Translations and Compilations, 1584–ca. 1790

Subject	Number of Works Produced			Total	%
	16th c.	17th c.	18th c.		
CHRISTIANITY				251	57
Sacred Scriptures	--	3	3		
Theology	6	119	18		
Rituals	1	49	9		
History and Biography	--	23	6		
Miscellaneous		11	3		
HUMANITIES				55	13
Philosophy and Psychology	1	7	1	9	
Ethics	1	9	--	10	
Government	--	2	--	2	
Education	--	4	--	4	
Linguistics and Dictionaries	2	6	1	9	
Literature	--	1	--	1	
Music	--	1	1	2	
Geography and Maps	1	9	3	13	
Miscellaneous	--	5	--	5	
SCIENCES				131	30
Mathematics	--	16	4	20	
Astronomy	--	83	6	89	
Physics	--	6	--	6	
Geology	--	3	--	3	
Biology and Medicine	--	8	--	8	
Military Science	--	2	--	2	
Miscellaneous	1	2	--	3	
Total	13	369	55	437	100

Figures represent separate titles of printed books or manuscripts only. Reprinted editions are not included. Sources of data: Louis Pfister, *Notices biographiques et bibliographiques sur les Jésuites de l'ancienne mission de Chine, 1552–1773* (Shanghai: Imprimerie de la Mission Catholique, 1932–1934), 2 vols.; Henri Bernard, "Les adaptations chinoises d'ouvrages europeens, 1514–1688," *Monumenta Serica*, 10 (1945), 1–57, 309–388.

Chinese scholars with some knowledge of Western science aided the Jesuits with their translations. Without them, the introduction of Western ideas, many of which required the invention of new terms and the mastery of literary techniques, would have been much more difficult. At the same time, the Jesuits, who had been trained in special fields of science in Europe, took great pains to acquire a thorough knowledge of Chinese language and culture and built acquaintances and friendships with many noted Chinese individuals. Letters and poems of greeting from Chinese to the Jesuits are found in many literary collections. Hundreds of noted scholars were acquainted with them, and many assisted in adapting Jesuit writings in Chinese into an acceptable style. It was the common practice for the text to be orally translated by the foreigner, and for a native Chinese speaker then to dictate a corrected version. The first process was called *kou yi* 口譯 (oral translation) or *shou* 授 (to teach), and the second *bishou* 筆授 (received writing) or *yan* 演 (to elaborate). Among the translated works, some were partial or complete translations of individual originals, and others were based upon several different texts. Most of the translations were written in the classical language but were made as simple and readable as possible in order to have a wide appeal.[6]

Xu Guangqi 徐光啓 (1562–1633) was inspired by Ricci, and in 1605 he began to cooperate with him and others in translating scientific works. According to the bibliography compiled by his son, Xu produced no less than sixty works on various subjects including ten scientific translations.[7] Another Chinese scholar, Li Zhizao 李之藻 (1565–1630), impressed by Ricci's map of the world, devoted himself to the study of science, geography in particular. He is especially noted for his compilation of the *Tianxue chuhan* 天學初函 (1629), which was the first attempt to collect the works on Western studies in one edition. Wang Zheng 王徵 (1571–1644) was interested in applied sciences and attempted to improve agricultural implements by searching out information about mechanical contrivances used in Europe. He studied Latin under Trigault in 1625, but his mastery of the language was insufficient to translate without assistance.[8] He collaborated with Terrentius in translating a famous work on mechanics; some of the terminology established in this translation is still in use today.

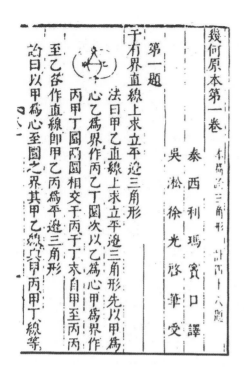

MATTEO RICCI'S HEADSTONE AND HIS TRANSLATION
OF CLAVIUS' *EUCLIDIS ELEMENTORUM*

Matteo Ricci wrote or translated more than twenty works into Chinese. His translation of Clavius' *Euclidis Elementorum* (1607) was regarded by Chinese scholars as "the crown of Western studies."[9] The first book in Chinese on psychology was his treatise on memory, *Xiguo jifa* 西國記法 (1595), in which he pointed out that the brain, not the heart, as indicated in Chinese traditional works, is the seat of memory.[10] Perhaps his most important contribution to China was the epoch-making map of the world (1584), based on, Ortelius' *Theatrum Orbis Terrarum*, by which Chinese knowledge of the world was broadened. Another Italian, Sabbathin de Ursis, is credited with the introduction of Western techniques of hydraulics, which appeared in *Taixi shuifa* 泰西水法 (1612) illustrated with machine designs. His *Yuelu shuo* 藥露說 (1617) is probably the pioneer work on Western pharmacology.

Another notable missionary was Trigault, who contributed to the phonetic study of the Chinese language. His lexicographical work *Xiru ermu zi* 西儒耳目資 (1626) was an early attempt to Latinize the Chinese language.[11] His inspired translation of Aesop's *Fables* (1625) was the first Western literary work to be introduced to China. Among his contemporaries were Nicholas Longobardi, whose *Dizhen jie* 地震解 (1626) gave a scientific interpretation of the earthquake of 1624, and Alphonse Vagnoni whose translation of Aristotle's *In libros Meteorum* (1633) was the pioneer work in Chinese on meteorology. The earliest account of European government is also credited to Vagnoni, whose *Xixue zhiping* 西學治平 (1630) was the first systematic work on Western political science written in Chinese. The pioneer work on Western education was that of Julius Aleni, who introduced the curricula of European universities in his *Xixue fan* 西學凡 (1623). He also wrote a companion volume to Ricci's world map, *Zhifang waiji* 職方外紀 (1623), which was the earliest treatise on world geography in the Chinese language. Western logic was introduced by Francois Furtado, who in 1631 translated *In libros Ethicorum Aristotelis ad Nicomacbum*. The translation in 1625 by Jean Terrentius of Kaspar Bauchin's *Theatrum Anatomicum* was the first introduction of Western scientific anatomy, which contrasted with the more speculative theories of Chinese medicine.[12] In 1627, Terrentius prepared a significant translation on mechanics, *Qiqi tushuo* 奇器圖說, which was based on four different originals.[13] By the time of Galileo's death in 1642, many of the new inventions in the physical sciences made by Galileo and others had been introduced to China. Among these were the telescope, proportional compass, thermometer, and barometer.

The downfall of the Ming dynasty and the coming of the Manchus made no great difference in the position of the Jesuits. Jean Adam Schall von Bell, for example, not only devoted himself to designing astronomical instruments and manufacturing weapons for both the Ming and the Manchus, but also produced the largest number of translations on a variety of subjects. Besides his contributions in astronomy, he imported to China the first telescope in or before 1626, when he translated Girolamo Sirturi's *Telescopio*. He rendered into Chinese and presented to the throne in 1640 Agricola's *De re Metallica*, which was the first work in Chinese to discuss the scientific exploitation of mineral resources. The famous work on fire-arms *Huogong qieyao* 火攻挈要, written in 1643 to aid the Ming defenses against the Manchus, was completed under the instruction of Schall. Of his contemporaries, Louis Buglio was the first to introduce Western zoo-logical works by translating from Ulisse Aldrovandi's *Historia Naturalis* the sections on the eagle and the lion when, about 1678, a live lion was brought to the capital by a Portuguese ambassador. The first to introduce spheri-cal trigonometry and logarithms was Jean-Nicholas Smogolenski, who initiated the European method of calculating eclipses in an astronomical work written about 1656.[14] Another influential Jesuit was Ferdinand Verbi-est, whose geographical treatise, *Kunyu tushuo* 坤輿圖說 (1672), furnished further information on world geography. His translation of *Anatomia Arti-fiziale dell'occhio Umano* (1682) is unknown today but is supposed to have been the first scientific work in Chinese on ophthalmology.

After Verbiest's death in 1688, though missionaries continued to ar-rive in China, their translations are relatively insignificant. The works pro-duced in the eighteenth century were mostly theological, and the energies of the Jesuits turned to translating Chinese works into European languag-es. One collective enterprise of the Jesuits in the early eighteenth century was the production of a general atlas of China.[15] From 1708 to 1718, more than ten missionaries participated in this work. It was the first attempt at a nation-wide survey of Chinese topography and became the primary source for later maps of China.

Protestant Missionaries and Translation

After an interval of a few decades at the end of the eighteenth and be-ginning of the nineteenth centuries, Protestant missionaries took up the work left off by the Jesuits. Though they generally followed the style and technique of the Jesuits, the nature and quality of their translations dif-fered. The Protestant missionaries established contact primarily with trad-ers and relatively less educated groups, while the Jesuits had cultivated the literati and government officials.[16] Consequently, Protestant transla-tions were mostly tracts of an elementary nature, and a majority of the non-religious works were used as textbooks for mission schools. Though more numerous, their general quality is not comparable with that of Jesuit translations. Perhaps this is because the Protestant missionaries, except for medical missionaries, were not trained in special fields of science as were the Jesuits, and their Chinese collaborators were not generally prominent scholars, as were those who cooperated with the Jesuits. Between 1810 and 1867, Protestant writings were devoted to Christianity except for 12% that touched on Western institutions and sciences (Table II). The abundance of religious material, supported by only a few scientific and educational subjects, indicates that the Protestant translators of this period paid scant attention to the interests of Chinese intellectuals and, therefore, made little impression on this group.[17] Although the missionaries called for the elimination of religious propaganda from scientific texts, "so that they may win their way into the interior, and be prized by native scholars . . . yet every suitable opportunity is to be taken to bring out the great facts of God, sin, and salvation, that the fragrance of our blessed religion may be diffused wherever they penetrate."[18]

The first Protestant publication in China was a translation of the *Acts*, which was revised from the old manuscript by Robert Morrison and first printed in 1810–1819. During the early years of Protestant activity in China, the missionary work was inseparably connected with translation of the Bible, since the Jesuits had not brought out a complete translation.[19] Marshman's, printed with movable type at Serampore, India, in 1822, and Morrison's at Malacca in 1823, were the first complete translations of the Bible into the Chinese language. Of the non-religious works, an interesting one is the *Comparative Chronology, Dongxi shiji hehe* 東西史記和合 (Batavia, 1829), compiled by Walter Henry Medhurst, which was one of the earliest known Chinese books printed by lithography. This book displays the Chinese and Western accounts of history in parallel columns, and attempts to show similarities between the Chinese records and the Scripture. It was said that "the work was drawn up to correct the vain boasting of the Chinese, and to show them that we possess records four thousand years earlier than the Christian era."[20] Another interesting work is the *Brief Geographical History of the United States of America, Yameilige heshengguo zhilue* 亞美利哥合省國志略 (1838), compiled by Elijah Coleman Bridgman, which was the first treatise to provide the Chinese

Table II. Protestant Translations and Compilations, 1810–1867

Subject	Number of Publications		Total	%
	Literary Style	Various Dialects		
CHRISTIANITY			687	86
Translation of Scriptures	28	37	6	
Commentaries on Scriptures	30	3		
Theology	344	74		
Sacred Biography	11	37		
Catechisms	37	16		
Prayers	17	14		
Hymns	18	21		
HUMANITIES			46	6
Government	2	--		
Economics	2	--		
Linguistics and Textbooks	11	8		
History	6	--		
Geography	14	3		
SCIENCES			47	6
Mathematics	8	1		
Astronomy	6	1		
Almanacs	12	--		
Physics	4	--		
Botany	2	--		
Medicine	13	--		
Miscellaneous	13	2	15	2
Total	578	217	795	100

Figures represent books and pamphlets only; translated articles in periodicals are not included. Source: Alexander Wylie, *Memorials of Protestant Missionaries to the Chinese* (Shanghai: American Presbyterian Mission Press, 1867), 314–331.

with a detailed knowledge of this country. Other works introducing Western nations are credited to Karl Frederick Gutzlaff, whose *History of England* (1834), *Universal History* (1838), and *Universal Geography* (ca. 1840), have been revised or reprinted one or more times. His *Outlines of Political Economy* (ca. 1840) and a *Treatise on Commerce* (1840), in addition to Morrison's *Summary of English Affairs* (Malacca, 1833), were the most important works on Western institutions introduced during the first half of the nineteenth century.

In the fields of mathematics, astronomy, medicine, and other sciences, important translations by Protestant missionaries appeared only after 1850. Alexander Wylie contributed many translations in mathematics, especially the completion of Books 7–15 of Euclid's *Elements of Algebra* (1857). In collaboration with Li Shanlan 李善蘭 (1810–1882), a noted mathematician, Wylie translated Augustus de Morgan's *Elements of Algebra* (1859), Elias Loomis's *Elements of Analytical Geometry and Differential and Integral Calculus* (1859), and John F. W. Herschel's *Outline of Astronomy* (1859). His translation of Newton's *Principia* was not finished. Li also cooperated with Joseph Edkins, who translated William Whewell's *An Elementary Treatise on Mechanics* (1858) and *Conic Sections* (1866), and with Alexander Williamson, who translated Lindley's *Botany* (1859). Many scientific terms established in these translations are still in use today.[21]

Protestant missionaries contributed much to the development of modern medicine in China. Dr. Benjamin Hobson's five major compilations: *Treatise on Physiology* (1851), *Natural Philosophy* (1855), *Fine Lines of the Practice of Surgery in the West* (1857), *Treatise on Midwifery and Diseases of Children* (1858), and *Practice of Medicine* and *Materia Medica* (1858), remained for many years standard works in China and subsequently were reproduced by the Japanese. In later years, Dr. John Glasgow Kerr engaged in the translation and compilation of fuller treatises on each branch of medicine, including surgery, *materia medica*, syphilis, ophthalmology, gynecology, and inflammatory diseases.[22]

The missionary translations and writings were all published by missionary presses that were first established outside of Chinese jurisdiction and moved to Chinese port-cities after the Anglo-Chinese War of 1842. At least fourteen establishments were reported in 1895.[23] The earliest to engage in translation work was the London Mission Press, which was originally established by Morrison and Milne at Malacca about 1818, in connection with the Anglo-Chinese College. The press was later transferred to Hong Kong and Shanghai, where it operated with the Chinese trade name Mohai Shuguan 墨海書館. Under the supervision of Alexander Wylie after 1847, it became the publishing center of missionary translations, until it was succeeded by the American Presbyterian Mission Press, which was established at Macao in 1844 and transferred in 1860 to Shanghai, where it operated under the name of Meihua Shuguan 美華書館. The press was supervised by William Gamble, who had been trained in a large publishing firm in Philadelphia. From 1891 to 1895, about 70% of the total output of this press were medical and scientific works, dictionaries, and educational materials.[24] Another noted missionary organization engaged in translation work was the Society for the Diffusion of Christian and General

像生先知樂林

YOUNG J. ALLEN

Knowledge, known in Chinese as Yizhi Shuhui 益智書會, later renamed the Christian Literary Society for China, or Guang Xue Hui 廣學會. It was founded in 1887 by Alexander Williamson (succeeded by Timothy Richard), for the purpose of preparing and translating a series of suitable textbooks and general reading materials for the missionary schools. This society was noted for its publication of many periodicals, including *The Chinese Globe Magazine*, a political and religious monthly edited by Young J. Allen; *A Miscellany of Useful Knowledge*, a scientific monthly; and the *Missionary Review*. *The Eastern Western Monthly Magazine*, founded in 1833, the first Chinese periodical published in China by the missionaries, was later carried on by this society.

Missionary publications were at first neglected by Chinese scholars because they considered them merely religious propaganda. But this attitude changed after 1895, when a reliable report on the Sino-Japanese War by Young J. Allen was published by the Christian Literary Society.[25] Later, the translation of Mackenzie's *History of the Nineteenth Century*, by Timothy Richard, was reported to have had a circulation of a million copies.[26] Because the missionaries needed large quantities of their publications, especially the Bible, they experimented with the application of Western techniques to Chinese printing by using movable type, casting from matrices, cutting steel punches, and using printing machines.[27] The facilities of the modern Chinese press, in regard to both typography and lithography, are largely to be credited to the religious enthusiasm of the missionaries, who introduced and adapted Western appliances to the Chinese printing industry.

Translation by Government and Private Agencies

The trends in translation shifted near the middle of the nineteenth century, when Chinese government agencies began to participate in the work. This new period was characterized by official sponsorship of translation and a general appreciation of the importance of Western scientific knowledge. Although it was recognized that Western ideas were potentially dangerous to the established order, Western techniques were greatly needed by the government for the defense of the country. With the increasing demand for modern technology, translation was generally motivated by the political and economic interests of the government rather than by the purely religious or intellectual enthusiasm of translators. During the latter half of the nineteenth century, as shown in Table III, there was a great increase of translations in natural and applied sciences, which comprised more than 70% of the total.[28] More than that, half of these were translated from English, but German, French, Russian, and Japanese were also included. The government established various institutions to train interpreters and translators, and students were sent abroad for further study. Many who had a competent knowledge of both Chinese and a foreign language became professional translators. Furthermore, the translated works had a more far-reaching effect than before as the press became an organized en-

Table III. Translations by Subject and Language

Subject	Language Translated from							Total	%
	Eng.	Am.	Fr.	Ger.	Rus.	Jap.	Other	Total	%
Philosophy	5	1	--	--	--	--	4	10	1.8
Religion	3	1	--	--	--	--	1	5	1.0
Literature	1	1	--	--	--	--	1	3	0.5
Fine Arts	1	--	--	--	--	--	1	2	0.3
History and Geography	25	10	1	1	2	16	2	57	10
Social Sciences	96	5	2	6	--	6	4	46	8.1
Natural Sciences	96	26	3	2	--	32	10	169	79.8
Applied Sciences	123	33	6	16	--	29	23	230	40.6
Miscellaneous	9	5	1	4	--	3	23	45	7.9
Total	286	82	13	29	2	86	69	567	100
Percent	50.5	14.5	2.3	5.1	0.3	15.1	12.2		100

Figures represent books only; compilations on Western subjects by Chinese authors and translated articles in periodicals are not included. Source of data: Xu Yisun 徐以孫(孫+心), *Dongxixue shulu* 東西學書錄 (Shanghai, 1899), 2 vols. The revised and enlarged edition of 1902, which adds some 300 titles, is not available for examination.

terprise and translations became easier to publish and so reached a wider audience through professional schools and government offices. Methods and techniques of translation were widely discussed: the selection of material, standardization of terminology, and subject specialization of various agencies.

Government participation in the translation of Western material was first begun in 1839, when Lin Zexu 林則徐 employed a corps of translators in Canton to gather information and intelligence by translating Western books and newspapers concerning the opinions and activities of the foreigners. Materials relating to China, tea, military affairs, and opium were especially collected and submitted to the throne. A digest of the foreign press on Chinese affairs, *Huashi yiyan luyao* 華事夷言錄要, was published and distributed among officials. Yuan Dehui 袁德輝, a senior interpreter, and three others were responsible for selecting and translating the material.[29] Several of these translations were included in the *Sizhou zi* 四洲 志(1841), which was based on Murray's *Cyclopaedia of Geography*. This work was later recompiled and enlarged with additional selections from translations of foreign periodicals by Wei Yuan 魏源, under the title *Haiguo tuzhi* 海國圖志 (1844). For about half a century it remained the most authoritative work on foreign countries and was widely read in China and Japan.

After successive wars with Western powers, the Chinese government decided in 1861 to establish a language school, known as the Tongwen guan 同文館, to train competent personnel and translators for government service.[30] This school was later expanded by including more foreign languages and new courses on science and institutions. According to the college calendar of 1888,[31] 125 students were enrolled with a teaching staff of nineteen, including eight of American, French, German, or English nationality. The library contained three hundred volumes in Chinese and seventeen hundred in foreign languages. Foreign newspapers and magazines in various languages were provided. A printing press was established in 1873 to publish translations of foreign books, which were sent to the governors of different provinces for distribution to local officials. Among the works translated, international law and legal codes were first introduced by William A. P. Martin, the president of the college after 1869. Other translations include works on Western institutions, history, and sciences. These works were all printed on the best paper, and some were presented to the throne. However, the contributions of the Tongwen guan in translation were comparatively insignificant in quantity. In a period of forty years, only about twenty-six works were translated, including some incomplete and unpublished works.[32]

In 1901, the Tongwen guan was ordered to be incorporated with the Peking Imperial University, in which a Translation School, the *Yixue guan* 譯學館, was set up in 1903 with an enrollment of 120 students. Five languages (English, French, German, Russian, and Japanese) were taught in addition to courses in the sciences, law, and diplomatic procedure. The period of training, however, was reduced to five years as compared with eight in the Tongwen guan. One of the special features of this school was the establishment of a Dictionary Bureau (*Wendian chu* 文典處) charged with the compilation of official dictionaries. They were to include English, French, German, Russian, and Japanese, with three dictionaries of each language: a Chinese-foreign, a foreign-Chinese, and a lexicon of scientific and technical terms with pronunciations and definitions.[33] Since the life of the school was very short, it appears to have achieved very little.

In Shanghai in 1869, the Jiangnan Arsenal, with its new Translation Bureau, merged with the Guang fangyan guan 廣方言館,[34] a foreign language school which had opened in Shanghai in 1863. These two institutions, one engaged in teaching and the other in translation, worked successfully and produced more works than any other government agency. The Translation Bureau, known as Fanyi guan 翻譯館, was, by 1871, publishing translations on science, engineering, military science, and other miscellaneous subjects. The initiation of this undertaking is credited to two Chinese scientists, Hua Hengfang 華衡方 and Xu Shou 徐壽, who were inspired by the Jesuit translations and Hobson's *Natural Philosophy* (*Bowu xinbian* 博物新編, 1855). A number of foreign and Chinese translators participated in the work, including John Fryer, Daniel Jerome McGowen, Young J. Allen, Xu Feng (a medical student returned from America), Zhao Xinghan (a Chinese medical doctor who wanted to study Western theories of medicine), Jin Buwei (a mathematician), and Xu Jianyin (Xu Shou's son who visited European factories between 1879 and 1884). Among these men, John Fryer, who became a professor at the University of California in 1896, contributed most, both in volumes produced and subjects covered. More than 130 works in various fields of science were translated by him in collaboration with Hua, Xu, Zhao, and many others.[35] According to the report made by Fryer in 1880, 156 works were translated by the Jiangnan Arsenal, of which 98 titles were published with a total distribution of 31,111 copies.[36] The translation service of the Arsenal was continued into the early years of the twentieth century, with a total of 178 works published from 1871 to 1905.[37]

The enthusiasm for translation at the end of the nineteenth century was reflected in the establishment of many privately supported societies devoted exclusively to translating Western works. One of the important organizations was the Scientific Book Depot (Gezhi shushi 格致書室), founded in 1884 by John Fryer, which translated and published many books on scientific and technical subjects. Among these, the *Xuzhi* 須知, or *The Essential Series*, and *Tu shuo* 圖說, or *The Illustrated Series*, were very popular.[38] Another privately supported institution was the Translating Society of Shanghai, known as the Yishu gonghui 譯書公會, which was established around 1897 by a number of Chinese scholars. The purpose of this society was to translate important works on Western history and institutions, because the government had devoted its interest to the natural and applied sciences. About thirty works were scheduled to be translated from French, English, and Japanese, and published in installments in a journal called the *Weekly Edition*, which had a circulation of 3,000 copies each issue.[39]

Many universities and Chinese publishers also participated in translation after 1895, through the encouragement of the Reform Movement. Translation departments were established in such universities as Nanyang College in Shanghai, Shanxi University in Taiyuan, and, as previously mentioned, the Imperial University in Beijing. At the end of the nineteenth and beginning of the twentieth century, at least forty official and private publishers were engaged in translation and publishing.[40] For example, the Xinxue huishe 新學會社 specialized in agriculture, the Guangzhi shuju 廣智書局 in history and institutions, and the Xiaoshuo lin 小說林 in fiction. Most of the publishers were set up in Shanghai, which became and remains a publishing center.

Twentieth-Century Translations

The twentieth century, the most revolutionary period in Chinese history, marked another stage in modern Chinese translation. Numerous changes in the institutions as well as in the intellectual life of China resulted from contact with the West. Changing interests were reflected in the translations, as the enthusiasm for natural and applied sciences of the past centuries shifted to the social sciences and humanities. This new emphasis exercised a great influence on the political and social developments of China in the following years. It also indicates a growing understanding by

Chinese intellectuals that the solution of China's fundamental problems did not depend purely upon military and technical knowledge, but rather upon a synthetic knowledge of Western political, economic, and social organization.

During the early years of the present century, the demand was for more translations in the social sciences, including government, law, economics, and education. From 1902 to 1904, almost half of the translated books were concerned with history and institutions (Table IV).

The interest in institutional reform and Japanese influence were dominant factors in translation during the early years of the twentieth century. After a period of agitation caused by the aggressive attitude of Japan toward China during the First World War, translation from English again led all others. After the May Fourth Movement of 1919, there was a notable growth of interest in the humanities. More than one fourth of all the books translated between 1912 and 1940 were Western literary works, of which about 90% was fiction, drama, and poetry, and the remainder literary theory and criticism. Western novels and plays translated into colloquial language have been influential both as entertainment and in education and propaganda. More than one third concerned the social sciences and history; especially significant were works on ideology. Marxism was first introduced to China at the beginning of this century, but the complete translation of works by Marx and Engels was not begun until about 1920.[41] During the later years, when the study of the "new social sciences" reached its highest peak, many Russian works on dialectics and materialism were translated. The introduction of this ideological literature laid the foundation for the development of the Communist movement in China.

With the increase of translation in various fields, great confusion arose in the choice of Chinese equivalents for Western terms, especially in scientific literature. This confusion was a serious handicap to the advancement of science in China. Earlier attempts at standardization of proper and technical terms were discussed by many scholars and institutions. Liang Qichao 梁啓超 suggested in 1896 that transliteration might be applied to personal and geographical names, translation of meaning to names of government offices, and new words created for technical terms.[42] At the beginning of the twentieth century, several government bureaus worked

Table IV. Translations by Subject and Language, 1902–1904

Subject	Language Translated from							Total	%
	Eng.	Am.	Fr.	Ger.	Rus.	Jap.	Other	Total	%
Philosophy	9	2	--	1	--	21	1	34	6.5
Religion	1	--	--	--	--	2	--	3	0.6
Literature	8	3	2	--	2	4	7	26	4.8
History and Geography	8	10	3	--	--	90	17	128	24.0
Social Sciences	13	3	3	7	2	83	25	136	25.5
Natural Sciences	10	9	5	--	--	73	15	112	21.0
Applied Sciences	3	3	3	14	--	24	9	56	10.5
Miscellaneous	5	2	1	2	--	24	4	38	7.1
Total	57	32	17	24	4	321	78	533	
Percent	10.7	6.1	3.2	4.5	0.7	60.2	14.6		100

Source of data: Gu Xiguang 顧錫廣, *Yishujingyanlu* 譯書經眼錄 (Hangzhou, 1935), 2 vols. This work is a continuation of the revised edition of Xu's bibliography (see Table III, footnote). Also, data collected from Pingxin 平心, *Shenghuo quanguo zongshumu* 生活全國總書目 (*A Classified Catalogue of Current Chinese Books with Index Translationum* (Shanghai: Life Publishing Co., 1935), which lists 4,159 translations out of about 20,000 new publications from 1912 to 1934, and from the *Quarterly Bulletin of Chinese Bibliography*, English edition, 1935–1940, which lists 1,140 works in the sections "Index Translationum." Figures represent books only. Periodical literature is not included.

on the problem of standardization. In 1918 a Committee on the Examination of Scientific Terms was organized through the co-operation of the Ministry of Education, the China Science Society, and many individual experts; it included special divisions on medicine, chemistry, physics, mathematics, botany, and zoology. Three lexicons on medical, biological, and chemical terms have been published since 1931.

An organized plan for the standardization of terms covering every field of science, however, did not begin until the founding of the National Institute of Compilation and Translation. Since its establishment in 1932, some thirty-seven different committees have been engaged in the work of the standardization of terms. Up to 1947, standardized Chinese scientific terms had been drafted and adopted by the Institute for a total of ninety-seven fields, thirty-five of which had been promulgated by the Ministry of Education and issued to the public.[43] Besides the activities on standardization, the principal function of the Institute was to translate and publish foreign works in Chinese and also Chinese works in Western languages. A Committee on Translation was set up to select books to be translated and to assign them to translators. Works on Western philosophy, history, and literature, including the great writings of Aristotle, Plato, Kant, Darwin, Shakespeare, Thackeray, Ibsen, and many others have been translated. Up to 1946, more than fifty classical works and popular treatises were published and more than one hundred titles were being either translated or printed.[44]

During the twentieth century, most translations have been made by Chinese without the participation of foreigners, and most Chinese translators have been trained in foreign languages and in the special subjects to be translated. Many writers have become professional translators and have made important contributions in the introduction of Western thought, literature, and technical knowledge. Among them, Yan Fu 嚴復 had an entirely different background from that of earlier translators; he had received the classical and the new education in China and further studied in England where he became familiar with Western philosophers. Stimulated by the defeat of China in the Sino-Japanese War of 1895, Yan began in 1896 to translate Huxley's *Evolution and Ethics*, through which Darwin's theory of the "struggle for existence" and "survival of the fittest" was first introduced to China. This was published in 1899 and has been widely read and used as a textbook. Yan then published his translations of Adam Smith's *Wealth of Nations* (1902), John Stuart Mills' *On Liberty* (1903) and *System of Logic* (1905), Herbert Spencer's *Study of Sociology* (1903), Edward Jenks' *A Short History of Politics* (1904), Montesquieu's *Spirit of Laws* (1906), and William Stanley Jevons' *Primer of Logic* (1908).[45] These eight Western classics have exercised great influence on modern Chinese thought. In translating, Yan set up three criteria—faithfulness, explicitness, and elegance—

and wrote in a classical style. He also introduced many illustrations and quotations from Chinese sources in order to please the reader and make the new ideas seem less alien. This method of translation, unfortunately, often distorts the author's original ideas. Wu Rulun 吳汝綸, then head of the faculty of Beijing Imperial University, commented in a letter to Yan: "If you write a book yourself, you may say what you like; but if you are translating Huxley, it is more appropriate to use the ancient quotations and illustrations from the West that are in the original work. It seems undesirable to exchange them for Chinese sayings, since those persons and things Chinese could not be familiar to Huxley."[46]

Among the early translators of fiction may be mentioned Lin Shu 林紓, who has had tremendous influence on Chinese readers of fiction. Before his time, there was no place for fiction in serious literature. Even in the early twentieth century, intellectuals would read a story only if it were both interesting and presented in a distinguished literary style. Lin used the classical language in translating Western literary works. Since he had no training in foreign languages, his translations were dependent upon collaborators for the selection of the text and the oral interpretation. His collaborators were not all well qualified, and his translations have, therefore, been criticized both for unwise selection and for inadequate technique. It was pointed out that his method was paraphrase rather than translation, and produced a restatement in Chinese based on the plot of a foreign story. These deficiencies, however, did not reduce his influence. Lin translated, during the late nineteenth and early twentieth centuries, no less than 171 works of Western fiction.[47] Though most of Lin's translations have been re-rendered by later translators, credit must be given to him for first introducing them to Chinese readers.

Many modern Chinese writers and translators are former students of science and technology who have turned to writing and translating in the humanities and literature. Zhou Shuren 周樹人, better known by his pen-name of Lu Xun 魯迅, who studied naval science and mining in China and medicine in Japan, started in 1903 by translating two short stories by Jules Verne. In 1909 he collaborated with his brother in publishing a collection of short stories by Andreyev, Chekhov, Sienkiewicz, Wilde, Poe, Maupassant, and others. They first used the so-called literal method in the classical style in their translation, but it was not acceptable to their readers. Only twenty-one copies of their first book were sold in the period of ten years following its publication.[48] Lu Xun's later translations in the colloquial style are mostly from Russian and Japanese authors and include short stories by Fadeev, Gogol, Gorky, and Panteleev, literary criticism by A. V. Lunacharsky, fairy tales by Eroshenko, and literary essays by Kuriyagawa Hakuson and Tsurumi Yūsuke. His brother, Zhou Zuoren 周作人, is especially noted for his translation of works by Eastern European authors.

Another medical student who turned to literature and writing is Guo Moruo 郭沫若, who translated Goethe's *Die Leiden des Jungen Werthers* in 1928 and *Faust* in 1932. Among his other translations were novels, dramas, and poems by Sinclair, Galsworthy, and Tolstoy and selections from English, German, and Russian poets.[49] Other noted translators are Tian Han 田漢, a pioneer of the modern Chinese drama, who has translated many plays by Shakespeare, Tolstoy, Wilde, and Maeterlinck; Fu Donghua 傅東華, an engineering student and translator of literary criticism; Liang Shiqiu 梁實秋, a Harvard graduate; Guan Qitong 關其桐, who has become famous as a translator of many Western philosophers, including Descartes, Francis Bacon, Berkeley, and Hume. In the field of science, most translators specialize in their own fields of study, but a few have covered a wide range of subjects.

Foreign Relations and Translation

The cultural interchange between two nations is tied up with their political and economic relationship. The closer their diplomatic relations, the more extensive are their cultural interchanges. The relationship between the Catholic Church and China from the sixteenth to the eighteenth centuries was, to a considerable extent, independent of the political and economic interests of European countries. This situation remained, however, only during the initial stage of European expansion. From the middle of the nineteenth century down to the present, we can see four distinct stages in Chinese foreign relations in which contacts with particular countries—Britain, Japan, America, and Russia—were close. These stages correspond with those in the history of translation. From the Anglo-Chinese War of

1842 to the Sino-Japanese War of 1895, almost half a century, British influence was dominant in China. Translations during this period reflected this fact. Among the 567 books translated from 1850 to 1899, 50% were from British sources (Table III). The earlier translations by Morrison, Milne, Medhurst, Gutzlaff, Muirhead, Wylie, and many others were mostly associated with British interests.

From the Sino-Japanese War of 1895, until the May Fourth Movement of 1919, the rise of a Westernized Japan served as China's chief stimulus. The reform program, stimulated by China's weakness in the face of the foreign powers, was largely aimed at imitating Japan. Students who wanted to secure new learning from Japan reached the greatest number in history. At the beginning of the twentieth century, more than ten thousand students flocked to Japan.[50] Many reformers stressed the importance of learning from an Eastern country and of translating Japanese works rather than those in European languages.[51] A rapid increase of translations from Japanese resulted, changing the proportion to 60% from Japanese. (Table IV).

Japanese aggression toward China, especially during World War I, which was the immediate cause of the May Fourth Movement of 1919, aroused hostility toward Japan. This event turned China back to Western countries. The American attitude toward China at that time won the friendship of the Chinese people, and the tendency was for students to come to the United States instead of Japan. Closer cultural relations stimulated the importation of American works of science and literature. Though there are no statistics that separate American from British authors, from the establishment of the Republic to 1940 these together constitute over 50% of the total number of translations.

China's relationship with Russia, both political and cultural, was insignificant during the nineteenth century, as were those with the other three countries. Few Russian works were translated until the 1920s, when the rising tide of Chinese translations of Russian literature and social sciences began to appear. From 1919 to 1949, about 650 titles were translated from Russian, representing 9.5% of 6,680 works translated during the period, in contrast to 67% from English.[52] With the establishment of the People's Republic of China in 1949 and closer political, economic, and cultural relations with Russia, the extensive translation of Russian works became part of the new government's policy. According to a report of 1950, about 2,147 translations on various subjects, mostly ideological and scientific litera- ture, were published during the year. Of these, 1,662 or 77.5% are from the Russian language, while translations from English dropped to 382 titles, representing 18% of the total.[53]

Other Western countries, including France and Germany, have been less important in terms of both their political and cultural relationships with China. Translations from German and French have always ranked after those from Britain, America, and Japan. A more complete record sets the German total at 540 works, of which 230 were in the humanities, 199 in the social sciences, and 111 in natural and applied sciences. [54] Translations from other countries represent authors of at least twenty-two nationali- ties,[55] including a considerable number from Italy.[56]

In the process of importing Western culture into China, Japan has played an important role as an indirect channel of acquisition. The history of Chinese translation from Japanese can be traced back to 1880, but the great period of translation began after the Sino-Japanese War of 1895. At first, when few competent Chinese translators were available, the transla- tion was done by qualified Japanese, and some works were even written in Chinese by Japanese authors. Since the early twentieth century, however, Chinese scholars have translated many works from the Japanese, espe- cially on economics, government and law, agriculture, and medicine. In the 1920s, Japanese literary works were introduced on a large scale by stu- dents returned from Japan. With the rising tide of left-wing literature in China around 1927, Japanese sources supplied a great deal of material for translation. Among the 2,204 works translated from Japanese from about 1880 to 1940,[57] the highest percentage was in the social sciences, followed by natural and applied sciences, literature, and other subjects.[58]

Because Japanese is easier for the Chinese to read and translate than European languages, many Western works were re-translated into Chi- nese from Japanese. For example, Lu Xun's translations of Russian works, more than seven different translations of Remarque's *Der Weg zurück*, and the six different translations of Karl Kautsky's Karl Marx' *oekonomische Lehren* were all re-translated from Japanese.[59] A modern writer has com- mented on the danger of retranslation: "Some changes, abbreviations, and mistakes in the Japanese version were in turn re-translated into Chinese with more changes, alterations, and mistakes. How could this work retain its original form? If a Russian work were translated into German or English with some mistakes, then, re-translated into Japanese with more mistakes, the Chinese translation from the Japanese would then be a collection of mistakes from mistakes."[60]

Conclusion

The total number of translations from the end of the sixteenth century to the present time has been estimated at more than ten thousand separate titles of books in addition to numerous articles. And of these the greatest number were produced during the last thirty or forty years. Although the data collected for tabulation in the present article are not complete, it is believed that the figures presented are representative enough to illustrate the subjects and languages prominent in various periods. The actual influence of these translations, academically and practically, cannot be accurately measured, but a quantitative analysis of the subjects and languages covered gives some indication of the type of influence exerted.

The subject matter of books translated reflects a picture of the needs and interests of the time. It is clear that humanities and social sciences have been predominant in translations of the past, since they account for 70% of the total, while the natural and applied sciences only amount to 27%. This may be explained partly by the fact that humanistic influence is perhaps more basic and fundamental than technical knowledge, and partly by the fact that the humanities and social sciences are a type of cumulative knowledge in which the old is not supplanted by the new as in the fields of science and technology.

Taking all subjects into account, literature ranks the highest. The vast amount of translation of literary works is probably motivated by the demand for political and social reforms rather than merely for entertainment. Literature as a popular medium of reading has been considered by many modern Chinese intellectuals as the best instrument for educating the great mass of people. As early as the end of the nineteenth century, translation of fiction had been suggested as a political weapon.[61] Early in the twentieth century, many students of science and technology turned their interest to literature as they believed that it was even more important to stir people out of spiritual apathy than to cure their physical ills.[62] It is no wonder that the great importation of Western literature has become an effective medium for advocating reform.

The sources of materials for translations have been selected from works representing more than twenty-five countries, with the English, Japanese, and Russian languages dominating. Many works have been re-translated from other versions rather than from the original text. Others which have been called original writings are actually based on a foreign work or works. In many cases there have been two or more versions of the same work, thus allowing some competition in the quality of the transla-tion. It is, however, a great waste to produce many duplications while leav-ing other important fields unexplored. Sometimes a translated work has been out of date for a long time, or is otherwise not the best selection on the subject. Nevertheless, translations during recent years show consider-able improvement in both selection and technique. Despite many short-comings and criticisms in one respect or another, the influence which translation has exerted in China cannot be denied.

Notes

1. Edward Wynham Hulme, *Statistical Bibliography in Relation to the Growth of Modern Civilization* (London: Grafton, 1923).
2. "Translation" is here defined as a rendering of foreign material into the Chinese language without altering its original idea. A compilation on Western subjects is not considered a translation, except for those earlier missionary writings as tabulated in Tables I and II, of which the originals cannot be completely identified. Material in the following tables represents the separate titles of books only; translated articles in peri-odicals are not included.
3. Henri Bernard, *Matteo Ricci's Scientific Contributions to China*, trans. by Chalmers Werner (Peiping: Henri Vetch, 1935), 68.
4. Hubert Verhaeren, "The Ancient Library of Pei-t'ang," *Quarterly Bulletin of Chi-nese Bibliography*, new series, 1 (1940), 124.
5. Edmund Lamelle: "La propaganda du P. Nicolas Trigault en faveur des missions de Chine (1616)," *Archivum Historicum Societatis Jesu*, 9 (1940), 71–75.
6. The Chinese characters for names of Ming and Qing scholars mentioned in this

article can be found in L. Carrington Goodrich and Fang Chao-ying, ed., *Dictionary of Ming Biography* (New York, 1976), 2 vols.; Arthur W. Hummel, ed., *Eminent Chinese of the Ch'ing Period* (Washington, 1944), 2 vols.

7. Fang Hao, *Hsu Kuang-ch'i* (*Biography of Xu Guangqi*), (Chungking: Victory Press, 1944), 90–91.

8. Chen Yuan, "Jingyang Wang Zheng zhuan" (*Biography of Wang Zheng of Jingyang*), *Bulletin of the National Library of Peiping*, 8:6 (1934), 12–15.

9. *Siku quanshu zongmu* (*Annotated Bibliography of the Complete Library of the Four Treasures*).

10. Fan Shi, *Mingji xiyang chuanru zhi yixue* (*Western Medicine Introduced to China at the End of the Ming Dynasty*) (Shanghai: Society of Chinese Medical History, 1943), 2/1a.

11. Luo Changpei, "Yesu huishi zai yinyunxue shang de gongxian" (*"Jesuit Contribution to Chinese Phonology"*), *Bulletin of the Institute of History and Philology, Academia Sinica* (1930) 1:3.

12. Fan Shi, *op cit.*, 3/1a–3a.

13. Hubert Verhaeren, "Wang Zheng suoyi Qiqi tushuo" (On the Translation of the *Illustrated Description of Mechanical Contrivances* by Wang Zheng), *Bulletin of the Institutum S. Thomae*, 2 (1947) 1, 26–36.

14. Alexander Wylie, *Notes on Chinese Literature* (Shanghai, 1922), 111.

15. Cf. Walter Fuchs, *Der Jesuiten-Atlas der Kanghsi Zeit* (Peking, 1943).

16. Kenneth Scott Latourette, *A History of Christian Missions in China* (New York: Macmillan, 1929), 226.

17. One scholar commented: "Religious (Christian) books are all superficial and unworthy to be studied; the style of translation is especially bad." Cf. Zhao Weixi, *Xixue shumu dawen* (*Answers about Bibliography of Western Studies*) (Guiyang, 1901), Preface, 1a.

18. A Report of the Committee appointed to take charge of the preparation of the series of school and text books by Alexander Williamson on July 15, 1878, published in the *Chinese Recorder*, 9 (1878), 307–309.

19. Wylie, *Memorials, op cit.*, 6: William Milne, *A Retrospect of the First Ten Years of the Protestant Mission to China* (Malacca, 1820), 83.

20. Wylie, *Memorials, op cit.*, 30.

21. James Thomas, "Biographical Sketch of Alexander Wylie," in *Chinese Researches*, (Shanghai, 1897), 7–8.

22. Liang Qichao, *Xixue shumu biao* (*Bibliography and Critical Notes on Western Studies*) (Shanghai, 1896), 1, 46–6a.

23. Gilbert McIntosh, *The Mission Press in China* (Shanghai: American Presbyterian Mission Press, 1895), 35–58.

24. Ibid., 38.

25. Yang Shouqing, *Zhongguo chuban jie jianshi* (*A Short History of the Chinese Press*) (Shanghai: Yong Xiang Press, 1946), 17.

26. Albert J. Garnier, *A Maker of Modern China* (London: Carey Press, 1945), 77.

27. K. T. Wu, "The Development of Typography in China during the Nineteenth Century," *Library Quarterly*, 22 (1952), 288–301.

28. The numbers of translations relating to religious subjects listed in Tables III and

IV are obviously too small. Many may have been omitted by compilers who shared the antagonistic attitude of Chinese toward Christianity.

29. Zhang Xitong, "The Earliest Phase of the Introduction of Western Political Science into China," *Yenching Journal of Social Studies*, 5 (1950), 1417–1444.

30. Knight Biggerstaff, "The T'ung Wen Kuan," *Chinese Social and Political Science Review*, 18 (1934), 307–340.

31. The school began in 1879 to publish a calendar, called *Tongwen guan timing lu* (*Calendar of Tongwen College*), which appeared every few years.

32. The fourth issue of the calendar, in 1888, contains a list in English, including translations of Wheaton's *Elements of International Law*, Woolsey's *International Law*, Bluntschli's *Droit international codifié*, Fawcett's *Political Economy*, the *Code Napoléon*, De Martens *Guide Diplomatique*, the *Penal Code of Singapore*, Tytler's *Universal History*, *A History of Russia*, Loomis's *Practical Astronomy*, Malaguti's *Chemistry*, and other compilations on natural history, chemical analysis, mathematical physics, and human anatomy.

33. *Yixueguan kaiban zhangcheng* (*Announcement of the Translation School*) (Peking, 1903), 18.

34. Feng Guifen, *Xianzhitang gao* (*Collected Works of Feng Guifen*) (1876), 10/18–20.

35. The translations made by Fryer have been kept in the East Asiatic Library of the University of California. The writer is indebted to Dr. Richard G. Irwin for the detailed information concerning the Fryer collection as described in his unpublished paper entitled, "John Fryer's Legacy of Chinese Writings."

36. John Fryer, "An Account of the Department for the Translation of Foreign Books at the Kiangnan Arsenal," *North-China Herald*, 24 (January 29, 1880); also published in Chinese in *Gezhi huibian* (*Chinese Scientific and Industrial Magazine*), third year, nos. 5–8 (1880).

37. These include 66 on natural science, 38 on military science, 35 on engineering and manufacture, 11 on medicine, 7 on agriculture, and 21 on history and institutions. A complete list was included in Wei Yungong, *Jiangnan zhizaoju zhi* (*An Account of the Jiangnan Arsenal*) (Shanghai, 1905), 2/15–22.

38. Zhou Changshou, "*Yikan kexue shuji kaolüe*" (A History of Translation of Scientific Works), in *Zhang jusheng xiansheng qishi shengri jinian lunwenji* (Essays Dedicated to Zhang Jusheng on His Seventieth Birthday) (Shanghai: Commercial Press, 1937), 425–28.

39. *Yishu gonghui bao* (Weekly Edition of Translation Society), no. 1 (1897), various pp.

40. Yang Shouqing, *op cit.*, 20–21.

41. Liang Qichao first mentioned Marx in *Xinmin congbao*, no. 18 (1902), 22. A more detailed discussion was included in the translations of several Japanese works, including Fukui Junzō's *Contemporary Socialism* (Shanghai: Guangzhi shuju, 1903), translated by Zhao Bizhen. A complete translation of the *Communist Manifesto* by Chen Wangdao appeared in 1920.

42. Liang Qichao, *Lun yishu* (*On Translation*), in *Yinbingshi heji* (*Collected Works of Liang Qichao*) (Shanghai: Zhonghua shuju, 1936), 1, 64–76.

43. Published terminologies include those of chemistry, pharmacy and pharmacol-

ogy, astronomy, physics, mineralogy, meteorology, geology, anatomy, bacteriology and immunology, pathology, electrical engineering, mechanical engineering, chemical engineering, general psychology, sociology, economics, education, statistics, etc. See *Zhonghua* (*Chinese Yearbook*), 1948 (Nanking, 1948), 2, 1773.

44. *Guoli bianyiguan gongzuo gaikuang* (*Report of the National Institute of Compilation and Translation*) (Nanking, 1946).

45. Wang Quchang, *Yan Jidao nianpu* (*An Annalistic Biography of Yan Fu*) (Shanghai: Commercial Press, 1936), 29–78.

46. Ibid., 35.

47. These include 99 by English authors, 20 by American, 33 by French, 7 by Russian, 2 by Swiss, one each by Belgian, Spanish, Norwegian, Greek, and Japanese, and five by authors of unknown nationalities. See A Ying, *Wan Qing xiaoshuo shi* (*History of Chinese Novels in the Late Qing Dynasty*) (Shanghai: Commercial Press, 1937), 277–80.

48. Ibid., 283–84.

49. Joseph Schynes, *1500 Modern Chinese Novels and Plays* (Peiping, 1948), 59–60. This work gives the Chinese characters for names of modern writers.

50. Shu Xincheng, *Jindai Zhongguo liuxue shi* (*History of Chinese Students Studying Abroad in Modern Times*) (Shanghai: Zhonghua shuju, 1933), 46.

51. Zhang Zhidong, *Zhang Wenxiang gong quanji* (*Collected Works of Zhang Zhidong*) (1928), 203/15a.

52. *Fanyi tongbao* (*Bulletin of Translation*), 3:5 (1951), 9.

53. Ibid., 10.

54. Wolfgang Franke and Dschang Schau-dien, *Titelverzeichnis Chinesischer Übersetzungen Deutscher Werke* (Peking: Deutschland-Institut, 1942).

55. Yang Jialuo, *Tushu nianjian* (Chinese Book Annual), 1933 issue, Chapter 6, 1–444.

56. Bi Shutang, *Catalogo di opere in Chinese tradotte dall' Italicano o riguardanti*.

57. Sanetō Keishū, *Nihon bunka no Shina e no eikyō* (*Cultural Influence of Japan on China*) (Tokyo, 1940), 8–9.

58. These works include 98 on philosophy and religion (4%), 697 on social science (32%), 257 on history and geography (11%), 267 on natural sciences (12%), 396 on applied sciences (18%), 288 on literature (13%), and 201 on miscellaneous subjects (10%).

59. Franke, op cit., 16.

60. Jiang Guangci, *Yixiang yu guguo* (*Strange Lands and Mother Country: Collected Essays*) (Shanghai: Xiandai Book Company, 1930), 131.

61. Liang Qichao, "Yiyin zhengzhi xiaoshuo xu" (1898) (*On Translation and Publication of Political Fiction*), in *Yinbingshi heji*, 2, 34–39; "Xiaoshuo yu qunzhi zhi guanxi" (*Fiction and Democracy*) (1902), ibid., 4.6–9.

62. Lu Xun, *Na han* (*Cheers on the Sidelines*) (Shanghai, 1926), iv.

Published in the Far Eastern Quarterly, *v. 14 (1954), 305–329.*

In 1956, a visiting scholar from India conducted a survey of undergraduate students in American colleges to determine how much American students knew about India. Among the questions asked was "What are the first two or three associations that come to mind when someone mentions the word 'India'?" A Princeton senior answered: "It is exotic; people are poor for the most part; it has a lot of tigers." Many of the students related their associations with such images as Marco Polo, rope tricks, jungles, and Yogis sitting on spikes, but only a few alluded to India's culture, her struggle for independence, or books by certain eminent authors. The implication of the survey's results was summed up by a Wellesley student: "It was rather embarrassing that the questionnaire showed me how little I really know about India." What is true of this survey about India might also be true about China, Japan, or other Asian countries if a similar survey were conducted among American students.

Asia in American Textbooks

The survey further indicates that more than one-half of the students questioned had heard about India for the first time in grade school through textbooks on geography and social studies. We may ask then, "How good has the treatment been of Asia in these textbooks, which provide the first seeds of knowledge about Asian countries?" This, however, is not a new concern of scholars and educators. As early as 1917, a Chinese scholar at Yale University, Timothy T. Lew, took the first critical look at the treatment of China in American textbooks. He felt strongly that American children were receiving an inadequate understanding of China and the Chinese people from their textbooks and that much of the material was producing racial prejudice and a patronizing attitude toward the Chinese. Some twenty-three years later, Alfred Madison Church of Harvard University made a similar study on the coverage of China and Japan in American schools. He discovered that the typical high school student probably spent less than one percent of the time on social studies relating to East Asia and that the students were definitely not well-informed about countries in that area of the world. A study on the Far East in nineteenth-century textbooks by Robert K. Dobberstein of the University of Chicago indicates that the poor treatment was the result of the author's failure to accept China and Japan as equal civilizations with values worthy of respect, and Western standards were constantly used to determine the value of East Asian cultures.

Since World War II, the quantity of information about Asia found in American textbooks has shown a notable increase, but the material is still considered to be slight, uncritical, and outdated. This conclusion was reached in a comprehensive study by the American Council on Education and the American Institute of Pacific Relations in 1946, which focused on the similar problem of inaccuracies, stereotypes, and lack of proper balance.

The findings in these surveys are perhaps still true even today. First of all, the quantity of the material about Asia and Asian relations with the world has always been scant. In 1917, it was found that only one out of twenty-three world history textbooks allotted as much as one percent of its content to China. In 1946, space allocated to the Asian nations was four to eleven percent in textbooks of geography; seven percent in world history; just over three percent in American history; and slightly more than one percent in civics books. Although the amount of material shows some improvement, it is neither adequately nor properly presented and a few items, such as the story of Marco Polo, are overused in a majority of the textbooks.

Secondly, there are incorrect statements, vague expressions, and omissions of facts which give wrong impressions to young readers. In reference to the variety of dialects in China, for example, one textbook author notes: "A few Chinese all over China have been educated in Peiping and can speak the Mandarin language." In some textbooks, certain stereotyped expressions such as "opening up," "backward," "China went to sleep," or "Yellow Kingdom" are frequently used. One history textbook, which includes a time chart of "Sixty Important Dates" of world history, lists only one event pertaining to Asia—the Meiji restoration of 1868 in Japan. This type of presentation and selection of material must certainly lead students to misunderstanding and even distortion of the facts.

Thirdly, there are uncritical and superficial judgments of Asian values.

The story of Asia is too often presented as that of a backward continent, and Westernization is equated with progress. Too many pictures present a tourist's point of view, stressing the exotic or unusual and atypical, and many of them are obviously outdated. One textbook author states: "We shall find it harder to understand the Chinese than to understand the Egyptians, the Babylonians, or the people of India." Another says: "Japan in a somewhat similar manner represents the Orient with its ways which are so unfamiliar to us." The stress and emphasis on the strangeness of other lands, peoples, and customs may discourage and hinder young people from understanding these countries about which they are prepared to learn. Furthermore, these statements should be severely questioned on their own merits for accuracy.

These shortcomings in the treatment of Asia in textbooks should be blamed not merely on the ignorance of the textbook authors or publishers, but also on the inaccuracies and obsolete sources upon which the writing of textbooks has generally been based. In the nineteenth and early twentieth centuries, we find that a large number of writings by missionaries and travelers included numerous superficial impressions, distortions, and sometimes patronizing attitudes towards the Asians. If such sources are used without critical evaluation and sound judgment, it is very easy to produce such over-simplified conclusions and incorrect generalizations as are reflected in the content of certain textbooks and thus accepted by the average American.

Beginnings of American Scholarship on Asia and India

During the nineteenth century, there were two major forces which promoted the study of Asia in America. One coincided with the extension of American missions to Asia and the other with the academic influence of European scholarship in American higher education, so that the academic tradition of European Sinology and Sanskrit studies was imitated in American colleges. At the end of the nineteenth and during the early part of the twentieth century, university chairs for Chinese and Indic studies, with the few exceptions of those occupied by former missionaries, were largely held by European scholars or by students who had been trained in

European universities. It is generally agreed that not until the late 1930s did American students of Asia begun to work along independent lines.

The beginnings of American scholarship in the Asian field centered on two major countries: India and China. As early as 1841, Sanskrit was first introduced into the curriculum of Yale University, but the inclusion of Chinese was not initiated until some thirty-five years later. In 1836, a young Yale graduate student, Edward Elbridge Salisbury, went to Europe to study Oriental languages. Five years later, Yale made him a professor of Arabic and Sanskrit, but it was not until 1843 that he returned to America and took up his post.

One of the few Sanskrit students that Salisbury had at Yale was William Dwight Whitney, who enrolled at Yale in 1849 and later went to Berlin to study. When he returned to America in 1854, he was made professor of Sanskrit and Sanskrit literature at Yale. For the next forty years Whitney remained there, publishing over 350 titles on Sanskrit and linguistic studies.

Another American student of Sanskrit was Fitzedward Hall, who graduated from Harvard in 1846 and later studied in India. In 1850, he was professor of Sanskrit at a government college in India, and he worked out a Sanskrit grammar that was the first of its kind to be produced by an American. In 1859, he went to Oxford, where he was given an honorary degree and a position on the faculty. Although he spent most of his productive years in England, his influence was widely felt in America.

Besides these academicians in Sanskrit studies, a number of missionaries also contributed to the understanding of India. Henry Richard Hoisington, who was a missionary to Ceylon (now Sri Lanka) and India, lectured on Hinduism at Williams College when he returned to America in the middle of the nineteenth century. He published two translations on Oriental astronomy and on Hindu philosophy. Other contributors include David O. Allen, whose large volume on India summed up the information he had gathered from a lifetime of work there; and William R. Alger, whose book on poetry includes translations from Sanskrit.

Throughout the nineteenth and early twentieth centuries, American universities had a significant tradition of Sanskrit studies and have maintained to this day some internationally known Sanskritists. Besides Salisbury and Whitney, there were Edward W. Hopkins at Yale, Maurice

Bloomfield at Johns Hopkins, Abraham V. W. Jackson at Columbia, Charles R. Lanman at Harvard, and Arthur W. Ryder at the University of California. These scholars attracted a number of students to the field of Indic studies; but there was no corresponding interest requiring specialists of this type until after World War II, when the interest in modern India and social science studies of its culture began.

American Pioneers in Chinese, Japanese, and Korean Studies

The interest of American scholarship in China started with the study of the language, followed by that of social customs, history, religion, and other subjects. As early as 1818, Thomas Jefferson wondered about the Chinese ideographic writing as a suitable medium of communication for scientific ideas. A similar curiosity about the Chinese language led Peter S. Du Ponceau, then President of the American Philosophical Society, to the publication in 1838 of *A Dissertation on the Nature and Character of the Chinese System of Writing*. The author apparently did not read Chinese but learned some of its principles from European writings and from certain reports that the peoples of China, Japan, Korea, Liuqiu, and Cochinchina understood each other by means of "common written characters," though they could not understand each other's languages. One of the first Americans to gain some real knowledge of spoken and written Chinese was William C. Hunter, who reached China in 1825 at the age of thirteen. After studying Chinese at the Anglo-Chinese College in Malacca, he wrote *The Fan Kwae at Canton* (1882) and *Bits of Old China* (1885), which became the source of many later works on early Chinese-American relations before the treaty days.

Among the few American missionary-scholars in the nineteenth century, three prominent names should be mentioned. Elijah C. Bridgman was the first American missionary to arrive in China; he had learned Chinese from William Hunter beginning in 1829. In 1832, Bridgman founded the first English-language periodical in China, the *Chinese Repository*, in which he contributed many writings, including his translation of Chinese elementary textbooks used in classical education. In 1841 he published *Chinese Chrestomathy in the Canton Dialect*, one of the early attempts to use romanization as a medium for the study of the Chinese language.

Another American pioneer in Chinese studies was Samuel Wells Williams, who went to China in 1833 as a printer for a missionary press and learned both Chinese and Japanese there. Later, he became an interpreter for Perry's expedition to Japan, secretary of the American Legation in China, and finally a lecturer, writer, and professor of Chinese at Yale University. He succeeded Bridgman as editor of the *Chinese Repository* between 1848 and 1851 and contributed many articles to it. His most influential writing is the *Middle Kingdom*, first published in 1847 and considered a standard work on China. His *Syllabic Dictionary of the Chinese Language*, published in 1874, was one of the early Chinese-English dictionaries used by students pursuing Chinese studies.

SAMUEL WELLS WILLIAMS

William A. P. Martin, a graduate of Indiana University, was another prominent missionary who was known as a scholar-politician. After several years of missionary work in the 1850s, he became an interpreter for the American Legation in Peking, and later professor of international law at Tongwen College. When Peking Imperial University was established, he was its first president. He wrote a number of books in both Chinese and English, including his memoirs, *A Cycle of Cathay* (1896), *The Siege of Peking* (1900), and *The Awakening of China* (1907). His activities in China, especially his associations with official Chinese circles, influenced the Chinese reform movement toward the end of the nineteenth century.

Other missionaries who contributed to Chinese studies include Calvin W. Mateer, whose *Mandarin Lessons* (1892) was a standard text for some time; Chauncey Goodrich, whose *Pocket Dictionary* (1891) has been a handy reference book for students of Chinese; and Frank H. Chalfant, whose study of oracle-bone inscriptions has been one of the few studies by a Westerner to clearly understand Chinese archaic writings.

American missionaries arrived in Japan slightly later than in China. Among the first who contributed to scholarship was James Curtis Hepburn, a medical missionary whose *Japanese-English and English-Japanese Dictionary*, first published in 1867, was not only the first of its kind, but its system of Romanization has been adopted as a standard system throughout the Western world.

The first and most influential work on Japanese history written by an American is *The Mikado's Empire* by William Elliot Griffis. Griffis was an English instructor at the Imperial University of Tokyo who wrote many books on Japan, Korea, and China. This work was very popular in the late nineteenth century, with its second edition appearing only four months after the initial publication in 1876.

There were a few books on Korea written by Americans during the nineteenth century. One of the earliest is *Corea: The Hermit Nation* (1882), also written by William S. Griffis. The individual who contributed most to early American studies of Korea was Homer B. Hulbert, a missionary who lived in Seoul for many years and had numerous associations with the king and the court. His works, including the "History of Korea" (1905) and many other articles, appeared in the *Korean Repository* (1892–1898) and the *Korean Review* (1901–1906), both of which he edited. These two periodicals included scholarly articles on Korean life and history, with excellent coverage of contemporary political events. This early interest in Korea, however, was interrupted by Japan's annexation in 1910. After that time, study of Korea was considered merely as an appendage to that of Japan until after World War II and the outbreak of the Korean War, when a long-neglected interest in Korean affairs was awakened.

Teaching and Promotion of Chinese and Japanese Studies

The teaching of Chinese has been included in American university curricula since 1876, when Yale established a chair for Chinese language and literature and made Samuel Wells Williams the first professor, although no student is known to have signed up for his courses. Three years later in 1879, Harvard secured the services of a Chinese scholar, Ge Kunhua 戈鲲化. His courses in Chinese instruction were supported by subscription largely payable in annual installments. The presence of this Chinese scholar and his family in Cambridge was a memorable event, which became, as described in the *Harvard Register*, "a mysterious link between the old nation from which he had come and the youthful one to which we belong." Unfortunately, Ge died three years later, and Chinese was not taught at Harvard again until the 1920s, when Zhao Yuanren 趙元任 and later Mei Guangdi 梅光迪 came to fill this post.

At the University of California, the Agassiz Professorship of Oriental Languages and Literature was established in 1890, because "the business between California and Asia is already very great," and "it is the duty of the University to supply this want." This position, however, was not filled until 1896, when a British educator, John Fryer, a noted translator of over one hundred Western works into Chinese, was appointed as chair. He served there until 1915, when a Chinese scholar, Jiang Kanghu 江亢虎, and later Edward Thomas Williams, succeeded him as chair.

At Columbia University, the Dean Lung Professorship of Chinese was established in 1901 by Horace Carpenter, a Columbia graduate, with a supplement from Dean Lung (Ding Liang 丁良) for the promotion of Chinese studies. In 1902, a German Sinologist, Frederick Hirth, was appointed chair, and a number of visiting scholars, including Herbert Allen Giles and Paul Pelliot, were brought from abroad to present lectures. This position was held briefly by Thomas F. Carter before L. Carrington Goodrich was appointed.

At the University of Chicago, Chinese studies was not formally inaugurated until 1936, when Herrlee G. Creel joined the faculty. Although one Chinese language course was taught as early as 1928 by Chen Shouyi 陳受頤, several courses on Asian history, religion, and international relations were offered by H. F. MacNair and others. In Chicago, there was the early leadership of Berthold Laufer, a German-born Sinologist who had an amazing knowledge of at least ten Asian languages and served at the Field Museum of Natural History beginning in 1898. Although he did not engage in actual teaching, his contribution was so great that, as Professor Latourette remarked, "his name has become a revered household word in Far Eastern scholarship, and in his chosen field no one in this country could then approach his stature. Nor have we since had his full equal."

The teaching of subjects on Japan in America was not begun until the turn of the twentieth century. About 1906, a Japanese scholar, Kan'ichi Asakawa, began to offer courses on Japanese history at Yale. About the same time, Stanford created a professorship in Far Eastern history, which was held by Payson J. Treat, author of several books on Japanese diplomatic history. In 1914, two Japanese professors of the Imperial University of Tokyo, Masaharu Anesaki and Unokichi Hattori, were invited to Harvard to lecture on Buddhism and Japanese culture. However, Japanese language was not taught until a later date.

The University of Hawai'i was probably the first university in America to offer courses on Japanese language and literature. As early as 1920, its program of Japanese and Chinese studies—including language, literature, and history—was initiated by Tasuku Harada from Japan and Wang Tianmu 王天目, a *jinshi* from China. Wang left in 1922 and was succeeded by Li Shaozhang 李紹章, who reorganized, in 1935, the Department of Oriental Studies into the Oriental Institute as an interdisciplinary organization for teaching and research. Other universities did not begin their Japanese-language programs until the 1930s, when courses were taught by Hideo Kishimoto at Harvard, Yoshi Saburo Kuno at the University of California, and Henry Saburo Tatsumi at the University of Washington. From that point, the Japanese language has been included in the curricula of a wide range of universities.

The interest of Asian studies in this country, specifically since the 1920s, was largely promoted by various organizations and institutions with the support of different foundations. Besides such established organizations as the American Oriental Society, which was founded in 1843, there were the Far Eastern Association (now the Association for Asian Studies, the American Institute of Pacific Relations), the Japan Society, the China Institute in America, and the Harvard-Yenching Institute, which were all founded in the first part of the twentieth century and have been engaged in the promotion of study and research in this area.

Besides these private agencies, the government has also been operating within various departments in the field of Asian studies and research. These agencies, concerned with political, economic, and strategic development in Asia, comprise principally the Department of Agriculture, the Department of State, the Department of Defense, the Census Bureau, the National Library of Medicine, and the Library of Congress as a central repository of publications for the government.

Asian Books and Art Objects in American Collections

With the increasing interest in Asian studies, literary and artistic materials from Asian countries have gradually been incorporated into American libraries and museums since the nineteenth century. The initiation of acquisitions can be traced back to 1869, when the Chinese government presented to the U.S. government some one thousand volumes of Chinese books on classical and scientific subjects in return for American gifts. These Chinese books, which were then shipped to America and shelved in the Library of Congress, constituted the first noteworthy acquisition of Asian materials by an American library.

In subsequent years, Chinese books were introduced to many university and public libraries, including Yale, Harvard, the University of California, Columbia, and the New York Public Library, through gifts and donations by both Chinese and American scholars. Japanese books, however, were not acquired until about 1906, when Yale and the Library of Congress began to build up their Japanese collections. At the same time, books in Manchu, Mongolian, and Tibetan languages were first acquired by Berthold Laufer for three institutions in Chicago during his travels in East Asia between 1907–1910.

The interest in East Asian studies was further encouraged by the establishment of several notable Chinese and Japanese collections in universities during the period between the two World Wars. These include the Wason Collection at Cornell University, the Gest Research Library at Princeton University, the Oriental Collection at the University of Hawai'i, and the Far Eastern Library at the University of Chicago, while those earlier collections were further strengthened by more systematic and large-scale acquisitions.

Since World War II, East Asian collections have grown rapidly and established collections have doubled or tripled their holdings along with the introduction in many universities of extensive teaching and research pro-grams on East Asia. Among the prominent collections built up during this period were those in the Hoover Institution at Stanford, the University of Washington, UCLA, and the University of Michigan. Minor collections are found in many other universities, including Colorado, Florida, Indi-ana, Kansas, Michigan State, Minnesota, Pittsburgh, USC, and Wisconsin.

According to a survey in 1984–85, there were about fifty major librar-ies in America, in addition to many small and private collections. Of these, about two-thirds are in Chinese, one-third in Japanese, Korean, and other East Asian languages. In South and Southeast Asian languages, collections were not begun in this country until the 1930s. These materials are repre-sented in the Library of Congress, Pennsylvania, Cornell, the University of Chicago, and the University of California. In addition, there are numerous volumes of books on Asia in Western languages held by many large and small institutions.

Museums were the first institutions to show an interest in Asia. As early as 1831, the Yale Art Gallery had already started to collect representa-tive items of Asian art, with emphasis on China and India. The Peabody Museum of Harvard, the Art Museum of Princeton, and the Pennsylvania University Museum all began their collections of Asian art at the end of the nineteenth century. Today, numerous museums include distinguished Asian collections, such as the Boston Museum of Fine Arts, the Metropol-itan Museum in New York, the Freer Gallery in Washington, the Detroit Institute of Arts, the Art Institute of Chicago, and the Nelson Gallery in Kansas City. These collections of Asian Art are among the most famous in the United States.

Asian Impact on America

What, if any, is the influence of Asia on America as a result of American efforts to study and understand Asia over a period of a century or so? It is generally known that many Asian traditions and inventions have been carried from China, India, and Japan to Europe and that Americans have received these contributions secondhand. However, a number of Asian ideas and institutions, as well as art and literature, have found their way directly to America and exercised a direct influence on American life and institutions. Not only has Asian experience in agriculture been fully exploited by both the American government and private enterprise, but the empirical knowledge of Asians in other fields has also been profitable to the American people.

The most interesting and significant case transmitted entirely through academic channels is the American adoption of the so-called "ever-normal granary," by which the government purchased grain from farmers in surplus years for storage and sold to the public at a fixed price in periods of crop failure. This Chinese economic theory, dating from the beginning of the Christian era, was first discussed in a doctoral dissertation by Chen Huanzhang 陳煥章 of Columbia University in 1911. This piece of research chanced to fall into the hands of Henry Wallace, who had held great admiration for this Chinese institution since 1918, when he was editor of a weekly paper. This alien idea was finally realized in America in 1933, when Mr. Wallace became Secretary of Agriculture. He applied this theory to control increasing surpluses of wheat and other commodities which had been piling up during the 1920s and which became one of the important causes of the depression of 1929. The first Agricultural Adjustment Act of 1933, which was an integral part of the New Deal Policy, embodied the general principle of this Chinese institution of the "ever-normal granary."

Asian art is another field that has enriched certain aspects of the American way of life. Not only is the Oriental motif very popular in decorative art and dress designs, but the basic concepts and techniques of Chinese and Japanese painting also have had significant influence on the form and content of modern American art. The intense interest in the so-called "calligraphic school" is but one illustration. Actually, American interest in Asian art can be traced back to the nineteenth century, although the influence was not as evident then. For example, George Innes, the American landscape painter, praised the "wonderful richness of rhythm in nature" in Chinese painting, and James McNeil Whistler became the ardent champion of "form" against "content," as he had learned to appreciate it in many expressions of Asian art. Asian influences may also be seen in American architecture. Oriental-type villas and gardens appeared in the midwest and south, where many planters' mansions were decorated with

Chinese wallpaper and trellises. In New England there are still many relics in homes and apartments from the days of the China trade.

In the field of literature, the transcendentalist movement in America was largely influenced by the Orient—writers such as Emerson, Thoreau, and Alcott were especially interested in Hindu and Chinese philosophy. The poets of the Imagist circle during the first generation of this century were moved by the discipline and imagery of Chinese poetry. Such notable poets as Ezra Pound and Amy Lowell were influenced by reading Western translations of Chinese classics and poetry. More recently, comparative studies of literature and philosophy, East and West, have interested students and teachers. Translations of and writings on Asian classics, philosophy, history, and literature have even invaded the mass-publication business of paperbacks.

Through the medium of both scholarly and popularized works, Asian ideas and Oriental ways of life have been relayed to the American public. Increasingly uneasy about Western deficiencies and imperfections in social and other problems, American people have begun to look to Asian formulae, especially in personal and family relationships, and emotional stability and moral standards, for help in adjusting to the inadequacies in everyday living. With increased opportunities of communication, perhaps more Americans will have the opportunity to study more deeply and observe Asian cultures first hand, so that they may become more critical of themselves and their own points of view. In this way, the impact of Asia will penetrate even more widely into American life.

A public lecture delivered at the Summer Institute on Asian Studies at the University of Hawai'i, 1959, published in Asian Studies and State Universities *(Bloomington: Indiana University, 1960), and further revised in 2010.*

No. 10 Two Inclosures   Mr. Haswell

Legation of the United States
Peking. April 18. 1868

Referring to your Circular
of June 13. 1867. relating to exchanges
of U. S. official documents, I have
the honor to inclose for your
information and the use of
Professor Henry. copy of a
correspondence which has passed
on this subject with the Chinese
officials. and my remarks on
what I have done and ascertained
in connection with carrying out
this liberal proposal of the United
States Government

I have the honor to be,
Sir
Your Obedient Servant
S. Wells Williams

Hon. William H. Seward
Washington

LETTER DRAFTED BY THE U.S. DELEGATION IN CHINA, 1868

13   FIRST CHINESE-AMERICAN PUBLICATION EXCHANGE

On the shelves of the Orientalia Division of the Library of Congress is a collection of almost a thousand Chinese volumes in 130 cases, each labeled: "Presented to the Government of the U.S.A. by His Majesty the Emperor of China, June 1869." These books, which crossed the Pacific over a century ago, formed the Library's earliest major acquisition in an Asian language and marked the beginning of Asian collections in America,[1] which have grown to millions of volumes today. Yet the history of this pioneer collection has been largely unknown;[2] even the nature of its accession was misconstrued as "a gift from the Emperor of China."[3] Information recently gathered,[4] however, reveals that these works were not exactly a gift from the Emperor, but an exchange from the Chinese Government in return for American gifts. This exchange of publications between the two governments was not only unprecedented in Chinese-American cultural relations, but also represents an early chapter in the history of America's expanding interest in Asia and Asian affairs.

This process, which took some two years of negotiation, resulted from the desire for Chinese publications of three different agencies of the United States Government. The Smithsonian Institution initiated the giving of American official documents in return for those of other countries, including China, in 1867. Since the Chinese reaction was lukewarm, the plan was shelved until late 1868, when the U.S. Department of Agriculture again expressed a desire to acquire Chinese books and plant seeds in this manner. The Chinese material was not sent until 1869, when another agency of the U.S. Government, the General Land Office, was in need of census and revenue data from the Chinese Empire. On this occasion the Chinese Government responded, though hesitantly. Although the quantity of the return was much greater than what the American Government had sent to China, the content of the publications apparently was not what the Americans had really wanted.

The story begins with an Act passed by Congress on March 2, 1867, which provided that fifty copies of all documents printed by the United States Government should be placed at the disposal of the Smithsonian Institution, to be used for exchange for the official publications of other nations. In accordance with this act, a circular from the Smithsonian Institution, concerning the implementation of the law for international exchange,[5] was transmitted by the Department of State to the American Legation in Beijing.

About a year after the receipt of the Smithsonian request, Samuel Wells Williams, then *chargé d'affaires* of the American Legation in China,[6] found a convenient opportunity to propose such an exchange to the Zongli Yamen 總理衙門 (Chinese Foreign Office) on March 27, 1868. He also personally explained the purpose, advantages, and expected results to one of its members, Dong Xun 董恂 (1807–1892), who was described by Williams as "the most learned and literary member of the foreign office" and whose name was well known to many Westerners for his Chinese version of Longfellow's "Psalm of Life."[7] Dong was said to be in favor of the plan, but he stated that its adoption depended upon another department, most likely the Court of Colonial Affairs, and it might not therefore immediately be accepted.

After the initial contact, Williams recommended a measured approach to the Chinese Government in terms of the exchange. In a letter to Professor Joseph Henry, then Secretary of the Smithsonian Institution, he wrote:

> The Chinese Government has from time to time published or aided works of value, but it issues nothing like our reports of departments, nor has it any official organ for making known its operations, decrees, or appointment. The three last Emperors have not equaled their predecessors in their patronage of letters, and if an exchange of a suitable selection of the books printed by order of Congress can, by and by, be made for some of the statistical and political works of former monarchs, the result would no doubt be mutually advantageous. At present, I do not think that there are a score of Chinese in the whole country who are able to fully understand them, but it is even more probable that there is not half that number of persons in the United States (not including Chinese) who could intelligently consult the works which this government might send to you in exchange. It is perhaps best then not to press the subject at present.[8]

About half a year after that recommendation, when John Ross Browne was appointed minister to China, the proposal was resumed. This action was apparently prompted by the U.S. Department of Agriculture, which was "especially desirous of obtaining information about Chinese agriculture, which had supported so large a population for so many centuries."[9] Col. Charles D. Poston was appointed as Commissioner to China to deal with agricultural matters. Since there had been an understanding that the matter of exchange would be accepted in principle but acted on at a future time, Col. Poston's sudden arrival seemed to be contradictory to the previous agreement. Browne explained "that reply had not been received at the date of Col. Poston's appointment, and he has now reached this city on his mission" in connection with the exchange of publications and seeds.[10]

Upon his arrival in Beijing, Poston brought with him, besides a collection of American seeds of grain, vegetables, and pulse, several books relating to agriculture, mechanics, and mining, and maps and reports connected with the survey of the Pacific Railroad, hoping to exchange these for similar materials from the Chinese Government. When Browne presented his credentials to the Chinese Government a few days after his arrival in Beijing on September 29, 1868, he spoke with several members of the Zongli Yamen, including Prince Gong 恭親王 (1833–1898), the Chief Secretary; Dong Xun; Bao Yun 寶鋆 (d. 1879); Tan Tingxiang 譚廷襄 (d. 1870); and Xu Jiyu 徐繼畬 (1795–1873). At the reception, the subject of the exchange of books and seeds was brought up. The American minister introduced Col. Poston, explained his duties in China, and expressed a desire to establish a system of exchange that might be mutually beneficial to the two countries. Browne told the Chinese officials that: "The object was to introduce a system of exchange by which the Government of the United States might render a special service to China and at the same time obtain better knowledge of the literary, educational, and financial systems of the Empire and a more direct acquaintance with its products and systems of agriculture."[11]

On October 19, 1868, Poston, accompanied by Williams, personally presented the books and seeds to Prince Gong, expressing the hope that similar objects would be sent in return to the United States.[12] Browne later remarked: "Although there are no members of the Imperial Government who can read books in English, many of the works presented contain maps, drawings and diagrams of machinery and mechanical instruments, which I have no doubt interested Prince Gong and his associates. The time may come when foreign works will be available as sources of knowledge to the Chinese. The grains and seeds of course require no great length of time to demonstrate their own utility."[13] The Zongli Yamen acknowledged to Browne on October 28, 1868, the receipt of the publications and seeds: "We beg to express our sincere thanks for the considerable kindness of the Government of the United States in sending the publications and seeds, which have been received, and which are regarded as objects for which similar things are to be exchanged. This act shows the great regard it has for the promotion of agriculture, and its desire to promote and strengthen the cordial relations existing between our countries."[14]

While the Zongli Yamen agreed in principle to the exchange of publications, its members were not sure whether it was in fact proper to present Chinese books to a foreign country or, if so, what type of materials should be sent. In order to justify this action, they searched for precedents so that they might avoid criticism for deviation in handling this unprecedented diplomatic affair. On November 17, Prince Gong and other members of the Zongli Yamen memorialized the Emperor:

> In the ninth month of this year [October 1868], the American Minister Laowenluosi 勞文羅斯 [John Ross Browne] sent your ministers a letter saying that his government has ordered Poshidun 薄士敦 [Col. Charles D. Poston] to present several books on agriculture, mechanics, and the geography of San Francisco, together with grain seeds, in the hope of negotiating an exchange for Chinese books and seeds. We found that in the twenty-fifth year of Daoguang [1845] when Russia made a presentation of books the case was memorialized by the Court of Colonial Affairs with an imperial rescript in file. We duly asked the Court of Colonial Affairs about this matter. In reply we received thereupon a copy of the original memorial in regard to the Russian presentation of books in the Daoguong period.
>
> From the Russian communication cited in the original memorial, we learn that the Senate of the said country presented us with Russian books because Chinese books had been bestowed on Russian residents in Beijing previously.[15] We accordingly inquired of the Imperial Household as to exactly what kind of books we had granted to

the Russian residents in Beijing during the Daoguang reign, but we have not yet received a reply from the Imperial Household. We have, however, established the fact that it was not until after we had given Russia a gift of books that they presented us theirs in return. In the present case, it is the Americans who presented books and seeds to us first. While this is similar to the Russian case, it differs in the order of procedure *per se*.

After examining the letter from the American Minister, we found his concern for agricultural crops and his hope to exchange for Chinese books to be sincere. Since its language is very cordial and respectful, it seems to be inappropriate to refuse his gift. We decided thereupon to keep these books and seeds temporarily at our office. As soon as we are notified by the Imperial Household, we shall submit a proposal as to how to send books and seeds to the Americans and will ask Your Majesty's further instruction.

Meanwhile, we shall deliver four volumes of books and fifty-two parcels of seeds to the Grand Council, while keeping the rest of the gift at our office. The original letter of the American Minister is hereby copied and respect fully submitted for Your Majesty's perusal.

The imperial endorsement remarked: "Noted. Seeds to be kept in Grand Council and books to be sent to said office for custody."[16]

While the Zongli Yamen was awaiting a reply from the Imperial Household, the U.S. State Department, at the request of the Commissioner of the General Land Office, further instructed the American Minister to China on March 25, 1869 to ask for Chinese publications. At this time the request specifically mentioned census data of the Chinese people, which were said to have been taken by the Chinese Government in 1851 or 1852. The Commissioner had tried to obtain these data from "the three envoys connected with the Chinese Embassy, when they were in Washington, but the multiplicity of their public duties had left them no leisure to attend to the matter."[17] Since the United States publications had been presented to the Chinese Government and no Chinese books had yet been seen in the United States, Browne requested that some of the official publications relating to the census and revenue of China might be furnished for the purpose of sending them to the government at Washington for its use.[18]

On the receipt of this letter, the Zongli Yamen decided to respond positively by sending some Chinese materials to the United States Government in return. In doing so, Prince Gong again made reference to the exchange with the Russians and requested imperial endorsement of his recommendations. His second memorial, dated July 4, 1869, stated:

> In the ninth month of last year [October 1868] when books and seeds were presented by the American Minister, Laowenluo 勞文羅 [John Ross Browne], we asked the Court of Colonial Affairs and the Imperial Household what kind of books were granted to the Russians in the Daoguang reign and requested replies for our consideration. The books and seeds were then sealed and sent to the Grand Council for inspection. According to the reply from the Court of Colonial Affairs, in the twenty-fourth year of Daoguang [1844], a Russian resident in Beijing, Dalama Dongzhengwu 達喇嘛佟正笏, asked for one set each of the Tibetan Kanjur and Tanjur. The matter was memorialized and the request granted.[19] In the second month of this year [March 1869], the American envoy sent a communication to your ministers' office, saying that they had only seen books from their own country, but not those from China. He also requested access to the census records for the Chinese population. We replied accordingly that the Chinese population data were reported annually from every province, but no record was printed by the Board of Revenue. We find that in the twenty-fourth year of Daoguang, subsequent to the grant of Buddhist sutras to the Russians, they presented books in return. Since we have accepted the American books and seeds at this time, it seems inappropriate not to give something in return. After several discussions, we reached the decision to buy, under the budget of this office, ten titles of Chinese books wrapped in one hundred thirty cases, sixteen kinds of Chinese grain and vegetable seeds packed in fifty-six boxes, and fifty kinds of flower seeds packed in fifty boxes. These gifts will be sent together to the American envoy as a return of thanks.

An Imperial endorsement was added. "Noted."[20]

Prince Gong further memorialized that the books and maps presented by the Russians were sent for custody in January 1858 to the Office of Military Archives. Since the Zongli Yamen was now managing all the negotiations with various countries, he proposed to transmit these Russian books and maps to his office for reference.[21]

With the endorsement of the Emperor, the Zongli Yamen then sent the books and seeds to the American Legation in Beijing on June 7, 1869, with a communication from Prince Gong saying: "I have, therefore, now to observe that as no return has yet been made for the publications so kindly sent to this Government, we have purchased and put up ten different works filling one hundred and thirty cases, as well as fifty-six sorts of grain and garden seeds and fifty of flower seeds, each kind in a separate box, which are all now sent to Your Excellency for the purpose of being forwarded to the Government of the United States as an expression of our appreciation of its kindness.[22]

While the American gifts of a few books and seeds were requited with more volumes and varieties of books and seeds, the request for census and revenue data was not granted. The Chinese communication explained: "In regard to the details of the population of China, it is the custom that the officers of each province prepare their reports annually and send them to the Board of Revenue, but these reports are not made up into books and printed."[23] The ten books mentioned in the Communication were woodblock prints of Chinese classical and scientific works of the fifteenth to nineteenth centuries. The subjects included Confucian classics, rituals, medicine, agriculture, language, acupuncture, mathematics, and metaphysics, running to 934 volumes wrapped in 130 cases. The contents of this collection were described in detail in the accompanying list,[24] which is reproduced verbatim as follows:

LIST OF TEN PUBLICATIONS

1. 皇清經解 *Huang Ts'ing King Kiai (Huang Qing jing jie)*. Imperial edition of the Thirteen Classics in 366 [actually 360] volumes, arranged in fifty cases. Published at Canton in 1829, under the supervision of Yuen Yuen (Ruan Yuan 阮元), the Governor general. The Thirteen Classics consist of the *Book of Changes, Book of Records, Book of Odes*, three works on the *Book of Rites*, three comments on the *Spring and Autumn Record, Filial Piety, Analects of Confucius*, the *Writings of Mencius*, and the *Wordbook* of the Han Dynasty 150 B.C. This edition comprises the commentary on each work deemed to be most instructive, with notes from other commentators.

2. 五禮通考 *Wu Li Tung K'ao (Wuli tongkao)*. Researches into the Five Rituals. 120 volumes arranged in 12 cases. Published in 1754 at Yanghu in

Jiangsu province. These five ancient works contain the ceremonies to be observed at marriages, funerals, military matters, visits, and joyful occasions.

3. 欽定三禮 *Kin ting San Li (Qinding sanli)*. Imperial edition of the Three Rituals, viz. *Rituals of Chou, Rules of Behavior,* and *Book of Rites;* some parts of this work are contained in the preceding. Printed in Peking in 1749 in 144 [136] volumes in 18 cases.

4. 醫宗金鑑 *I Tsung Kin Kien (Yizong jinjian)*. The Perfect Mirror of Medical Science or Authors. Printed at Peking in 1740 in 91 [90] volumes or 12 cases. Part of this work contains the medical writings of a physician who flourished A.D. 50; the remainder is a collection of rules in 58 volumes for all classes of complaints.

5. 本草綱目 *Pen Tsao Kang Muh (Bencao zongmu)*. General view of Plants, an herbal of Medical Plants. Printed in 1655 at Peking, in 48 volumes or 8 cases.

6. 農政全書 *Nung Ching Tsiuan Shu (Nongzheng quanshu)*. Encyclopaedia of Agriculture. Printed in 1857 in Kweichou (Guizhou) province, in 24 volumes or 4 cases.

7. 駢字類編 *P'ing Tsi Lui Pien (Pingzi leibian)*. Assorted Collection of Authorized Expressions. Printed by the Government in 1727 at Peking, in 120 volumes or 20 cases. This work contains myriads of phrases used in the Chinese language, with quotations from standard authors showing their use and meaning. They are arranged by subject.

8. 針灸大成 *Chin Kiu Ta Ching (Zhenjiu dacheng)*. Complete Treatise on the Acupuncture and use of Moxa. Printed in 1859 in Kiangsi (Jiangxi) in 10 volumes or 2 cases. A diagram of the human body shows the places for applying both needles and cautery.

9. 梅氏叢書 *Mei Shi Tsung Shu (Mei shi congshu)*. The Mathematical Course of Mei, a scholar in the reign of Kanghi (Kangxi). Printed in 10 volumes or 2 cases, in 1707 at Peking. It deals chiefly with the higher branches of mathematics, conic sections, and astronomical questions.

10. 性理大全 *Sing Li Ta Tsiuen (Xingli daquan)*. Collected Essays on Mental Philosophy. Printed in 1416 at Peking in 16 volumes or 2 cases, by order of the Yongle Emperor. It contains opinions and extracts from the works of 116 different authors, who lived in various periods of Chinese history, and wrote on politics, morals, and metaphysics.

Enclosure D
Resp. 50

List of the Ten Publications

1. 皇清經解 Hwang Ts'ing King Kiai. Imperial edition of the Thirteen Classics in 366 volumes, arranged in fifty cases. Published at Canton in 1829, under the supervision of Yuen Yuen, the Governor-general. The Thirteen Classics consist of the Book of Changes, Book of Records, Book of Odes, three works on the Rites of the ancients, three comments and the Spring and Autumn Record, Filial Duty, Analects of Confucius, the writings of Mencius, and the Wradows of the Han Dynasty B.C. 150. This edition comprises the commentary on each work deemed to be most instructive, with notes from other commentators.

2. 五禮通考 Wu Li Tung Kao. Researches into the Five Rituals. 120 volumes arranged in 12 cases. Published in 1755 at Yanghu in Kiangsu province. These five ancient works treat upon the ceremonies to be observed in marriages, funerals, military matters, visits, and joyful occasions.

3. 欽定三禮 Kin Ting San Li. Imperial edition of the Three Rituals, viz. Ritual of Chau, Rules of Behaviour and Book of Rites; some parts of this work are contained in the preceding. Printed at Peking in 1749 in 144 volumes put up in 18 cases.

4. 醫宗金鑑 I Tsung Kin Kien. The Perfect Mirror of Medical Science or Authors. Printed at Peking in 1740 in 91 volumes or 12 cases. Part of this work contains the medical writings of a physician who flourished A.D. 80; the remainder is a collection of rules in 58 volumes, for all classes of complaints.

LIST OF BOOKS PRESENTED BY THE CHINESE EMPEROR, 1869

It is interesting to note that the selection included only Confucian classics and works on a few scientific subjects, while the very numerous Chinese publications on the major philosophers, history, and literature were not represented. There is no clue to the intention of the Zongli Yamen; perhaps the books were picked to correspond with the scientific works presented by the American side, with the addition of Confucian classics and rituals.

The list of books was followed by four lists of the seeds of flowers, grain, pulse, and vegetables.[25] Upon receipt of these, Browne wrote to Prince Gong on June 10, 1869, saying:

> These articles have all been safely received, according to the list accompanying them; and I shall take a favorable opportunity to send them on to the Government for its library. It is not improbable, that, among the grains and garden seeds, some sorts, hitherto unknown in the United States, may be found; and they will be forwarded immediately to the Department of Agriculture, where they can be examined and properly used by those conversant with such subjects.
>
> The collection of books will, on its arrival, be carefully arranged and put up so that it can be easily examined by all who are acquainted with the Chinese language, and thus full advantage taken of the good feeling manifested in sending it. I beg, therefore, now to return Your Imperial Highness my best thanks for these articles. . . .[26]

After the receipt of these materials, no further evidence has been found to indicate when and how these books were shipped to the United States and finally deposited in the Library of Congress. However, Browne wrote in his last dispatch to the State Department, dated June 29, 1869: "It will require two months to classify and label the books. The seeds I hope to be able to transmit to Washington by the next California steamer."[27] The books are therefore believed to have been shipped to the United States and to have reached the Library of Congress sometime in the latter part of 1869.

Browne stayed in China for less than a year and returned to the United States in July, 1869, before the books were dispatched. When he went to say farewell to Prince Gong on July 1st, he expressed gratitude for the collection of books and seeds recently received from the Chinese Government, which indicated their friendly desire to reciprocate the advantages to be derived from an exchange of such articles. He told the Chinese officials: "If the books could not be read in America, the grains and flower and other seeds would no doubt speak for themselves, and would be highly appreciated there." He also said he "hoped that before long there would be many more persons in each country that could read the works of the other, for now there were not as many Americans in the United States who could read these books as there were states in the Union, though the number of Chinese who could understand English books was far greater; and a better knowledge of each other's literature would probably be productive of more mutual appreciation."[28]

This article is based on fifteen original documents from the American Legation in Beijing, dated 1867–1869, found in the National Archives in Washington D.C., and on the dates and personal names in the Chouban yiwu shimo 籌辦夷務始末, *juan 32, Tongzhi 7th year, 10th month, 4th day.*

EARLIEST CHINESE BOOKS AT THE U.S. LIBRARY OF CONGRESS

Notes

1. Dr. Arthur W. Hummel notes that "the first noteworthy collection of Oriental books to come to the Library of Congress was in the Chinese language, made in 1869," and that its Japanese collection started in 1906, South Asian in 1938, Near Eastern in 1945, and Korean in 1950; see "The Growth of the Orientalia Collections," *The Library of Congress Quarterly Journal of Current Acquisitions* 11.2 (February, 1954), 69–87. Besides the Library of Congress, Chinese collections started at Yale in 1878, Harvard in 1879, and the University of California in 1896, and the New York Public Library is known to have had some books in East Asian languages toward the end of the nineteenth century; see G. Raymond Nunn and T. H. Tsien, "Far Eastern Resources in American Libraries," *The Library Quarterly*, XXIX.1 (January, 1959), 28.

2. An exhaustive search at the Library of Congress has failed to reveal any information relating to the accession of these books. The Library's Exchange Book, 1862–1878 and 1878–1879, and the Letter Book of the Librarian of Congress, March 12, 1869 to January 10, 1871, contain nothing relating to these ten Chinese titles in 934 volumes. The Smithsonian Institution also has no record of them.

3. Hummel, cit., 70. The belief that this was a gift from the Emperor of China was apparently based on the statement on the labels of the book wrappers.

4. The information includes a dozen or so unpublished documents kept in the National Archives, Washington, D.C., primarily dispatches from the American Legation in Beijing to the Secretary of State and communications between the Chinese Foreign Office and the American Legation. In addition, two memorials to the Emperor from Prince Gong are to be found in the *Chouban yiwu shimo* 62.17a, 18ab; 66.1a–2b, but not in other collections of Qing documents.

5. The circular, dated May 16, 1867, is included in "History of the Smithsonian Exchanges," *Annual Report of the Smithsonian Institution, 1881* (Washington: Government Printing Office, 1883), 746–748.

6. Williams was appointed Secretary and Interpreter at the Legation in 1855 and, after the resignation of the Minister Anson Burlingame, was called upon in 1867 to take charge of the affairs of the Legation for the sixth time. When his successor, John Ross Browne, left China in 1869, Williams was urged by his friends to take the position of American Minister but did not receive the appointment. The Secretary of State is quoted as having said that the reason was that Williams was "altogether too good a man, too highly endowed, and in all respects too unexceptionable to receive the appointment"; see Frederick W. Williams, *The Life and Letters of Samuel Wells Williams* (New York: Putnam, 1889), 378.

7. Dong Xun, a native of Yangzhou, paraphrased an unrhymed translation of this poem by Thomas Wade into nine stanzas of four seven-word lines, each in classical style, entitled "Changyou shi" ["Tall Friend's Poem"]; see Fang Junshi, *Jiaoxuan suilu* (1872), v. 12, folio 37–40; also C. S. Ch'ien, "An Early Chinese Version of Longfellow's 'Psalm of Life,'" *Philobiblon* II.2 (March, 1948), 10–17.

8. A reply from the American Legation in China to the Smithsonian Institution, dated

April 17, 1868. The author is grateful to Mr. John DeGurse, Jr., Archivist of the Smithsonian Institution, for his search for this letter, which was enclosed in Williams' dispatch to William H. Seward, Secretary of State, dated April 18, 1868, but is missing from the archives and marked on the margin of the dispatch as "In closures to Prof. Henry, 24 July."

9.   Browne's interview with Prince Gong in a report to the Secretary of State, dated November 20, 1868.

10.   Browne to Prince Kong, dated October 19, 1868. It was translated into Chinese as an enclosure with Prince Kong's memorial to the Emperor, dated November 17, 1868; see *Chouban yiwu shimo*, 62.18ab.

11.   Browne's report to the Secretary of State, June 29, 1869.

12.   Browne's communication to Prince Kong, dated October 29, 1868.

13.   Browne's report to the Secretary of State, dated June 29, 1869.

14.   The Chinese Foreign Office's communication to Browne, dated October 28, 1868, translated as enclosure 4 of the U. S. Legation's dispatch to the Secretary of State, November 20, 1868.

15.   The Chinese-Russian exchange of books in 1845 is described in He Qiutao, *Shuofang beisheng* 39.125, with a list of 357 titles of Russian books translated into Chinese.

16.   *Chouban yiwu shimo* 62.17a18a. This and the following two documents in Chinese, which are translated here in full, are not found in *Da Qing shilu, Donghua lu, Donghua xulu*, or the diplomatic archives at the Academia Sinica.

17.   Browne to Prince Gong, dated March 25, 1869.

18.   Ibid.

19.   He Qiutao remarks that a copy of the *Tanjur* was requested by the Russians and that an edition in some 8,000 volumes, preserved in the Yonghegong, was granted. After a few months, when some Russian students came to study in Beijing, they brought with them and presented to China "all the Russian books they have in 357 titles, each work luxuriously bound and decorated in one volume, with text and illustrations; but all in the Russian language which no one could read," (*Shuofang beisheng*, 39.3ab).

20.   *Chouban yiwu shimo*, 66.1b2b.

21.   Ibid., 66.2b.

22.   Prince Gong to Browne, dated June 7, 1869.

23.   Ibid.

24.   The list of ten titles apparently was prepared and annotated by Williams. The total number of volumes according to this list is 949, while the actual count at the Library of Congress is 934. The dates given for different works also vary. Cf. Hummel, 70–71. The author wishes to thank Dr. Edwin G. Beal, Jr. and Dr. K. T. Wu of the Library of Congress for their help in verifying this collection.

25.   The "List of Fifty Sorts of Flower Seeds" with translation, perhaps also prepared by Williams, includes "marygold," larkspur, sunflower, daisy, lychnis, hollyhock, cocks comb, chrysanthemum, aster, balsam, touchmenot, begonia, four o' clock, magnolia *yulan*, betony, poppy, Prince's feather (polygonum), etc. Many items were not translat-

ed, and some were mistranslated. The "List of Seventeen Kinds of Grain" includes different species of wheat, millet, corn, cotton, sesamum, and "darnel" (probably a kind of millet). The "List of Fifteen Kinds of Pulse" includes different varieties of beans, peas, and "canary seed." The "List of Twenty-four Kinds of Vegetables" includes radish, turnip, celery, spinach, lettuce, cabbage, chives, mustard, caraway, squash, melon, cucumber, pepper, eggplant, and onion. The Chinese name *hsi hung shih* of a tomato is translated as "red persimmon."

26. Browne's reply to Prince Gong, dated June 10, 1869.

27. No further documents concerning these ten books have been found in the National Archives. Neither in the records of the Smithsonian Institution nor in the Library of Congress can anything further be located about the final transactions relating to this collection of books.

28. Notes of an interview with Prince Gong at the Chinese Foreign Office on July 1, 1869, as reported by Browne to the Secretary of State on July 3, 1869.

14   EAST ASIAN STUDIES IN AMERICAN LIBRARIES

Among the many non-Western language area collections in American libraries, the East Asian collection was the earliest to be established. Its growth since the 1950s has been especially rapid and spectacular. With the increasing interest in the study of world civilizations, these once exotic materials have become an integral part of many research collections in American libraries and are of national and international significance. This chapter attempts to summarize some of the highlights and point out certain special features that characterize the collection development of East Asian-language materials in North American libraries at different stages during the last one hundred years or so.

Briefly, the time from the first arrival of Chinese books in 1869 to the end of World War I in 1918 may be called the pioneer period, as a few collections began to grow accidentally in that era. The time between the two world wars from about 1920 to 1945 was a period of systematic development parallel to the growth of academic interest in the study of East Asia. From the end of World War II in 1945 to the present, it has been a period of rapid expansion with a tremendous increase in the number of collections as well as accelerated growth of the resources. Although from the year 1970 onward some signs of stagnation and retrenchment have appeared, the general trend of overall growth continues but has gradually been shifted from individual toward collective concerns among the East Asian library community.

Beginnings of East Asian Collections, 1869–1919

The first large acquisition of Asian books by an American library occurred in 1869, when some 1,000 Chinese volumes were "presented to the government of the U.S.A. by His Majesty the Emperor of China." This was not exactly a gift but an exchange, which took some two years of negotiations and involved at least three agencies of the U.S. government. The Smithsonian Institution initiated the exchange in 1867, when the Congress passed an act to provide fifty copies of U.S. government documents in exchange for official publications of other countries. A year later the U.S. Department of Agriculture requested information about Chinese agriculture, and on this occasion a special commissioner traveled to China, taking with him a collection of American plant seeds and some books on agriculture, mechanics, mining, and maps and surveys of the Pacific Railroad—all in the hope of exchanging them for similar materials from the Chinese side.

While the Chinese Foreign Office awaited instructions on what kind of materials to send, the U.S. General Land Office in 1869 further requested information on Chinese census and revenue data. The Chinese government responded by sending to the U.S. government some Chinese plant seeds and books, which included ten titles in 934 volumes on Confucian classics, philosophy, rituals, mathematics, agriculture, medicine, and acupuncture. These books are still on the shelves at the Library of Congress.[1] In subsequent years, several major gifts of materials in Chinese and other languages were added to the Library of Congress. These included the 2,500-volume collection of Caleb Cushing (1800–1879), added in 1879, and the 6,000-volume collection of William W. Rockhill (1854–1914) in 1901–1902; both men were American ministers to China. Also included were a gift from the Chinese government of 1,965 volumes from China's exhibit at the Louisiana Purchase Exposition held at St. Louis in 1904; a 5,040-volume set of the *Grand Encyclopedia* in 1908, in acknowledgment of the American return of the Boxer Indemnity Fund, and some 300 volumes of books and maps in 1909. During the next decade, Walter T. Swingle (1871–1952), a botanist at the Department of Agriculture, collaborated with the library in acquiring more than 23,000 volumes on Chinese agriculture, collectanea, encyclopedias, and especially local history—a collection that has since become the largest outside of China.

The books received earlier at the Library of Congress were mostly in Chinese, but there were also some in other East Asian languages. Included in the Cushing collection were thirty-five volumes of dictionaries, literature, and a translation of the Bible in Manchu; and in the Rockhill collection were 730 volumes of mostly Buddhist texts, some dictionaries, biographies, and medical and divinatory materials in Manchu, Mongolian, and Tibetan. The library did not acquire Japanese materials systematically until 1906, when Kanichi Asakawa 朝河貫一 (1873–1848) of Yale University selected a good working collection of 9,027 volumes on Japanese literature, history, and institutions, which was reported to be unequaled outside of Japan. Also, a year earlier Crosby S. Noyes presented a large collection of Japanese prints to the library's Fine Arts Division.[2]

After the arrival of Chinese books at the Library of Congress, other libraries also began to acquire materials in Chinese. In 1878, Yung Wing (Rong Hong 容閎, 1828–1912), the first Chinese graduate of Yale University and then a Chinese associate minister to Washington, presented to his alma mater a 5,040-volume set of the *Grand Encyclopedia*. A year later, Yale appointed Samuel Wells Williams (1812–1884)—who was *chargé d'affaires* in the Beijing Legation when the first exchange of publications was arranged—as its first professor of Chinese language and literature; but records indicate no students enrolled in his courses. After his death in 1884, Yale acquired his private collection. It was supplemented by further gifts from Francis E. Woodruff; Addison van Name, curator in 1890; and Kani'chi Asakawa, who acquired 1,350 volumes in Japanese and brought the initial Japanese collection at Yale to 3,578 volumes before he became its curator in 1907.

In 1879, the same year that Yale first offered Chinese language courses, Harvard College secured the service of a Chinese scholar, Ge Kunhua 戈鯤化 (d. 1882), for Chinese instruction. In 1914, two Japanese scholars, Hattori Unokichi 服部宇之吉 (1867–1939) and Anesaki Masahara 姉崎正治 (1873–1949), contributed some important Japanese works. These materials formed the initial Chinese-Japanese Collection at the Harvard College library.[3]

On the West Coast, increasing business contacts with Asia necessitated action by the University of California to supply needed training. In 1890, the university established the Agassiz professorship of Oriental languages and literatures but did not fill the position until 1896, when it appointed a British educator, John Fryer (1839–1928), who had served as an instructor at Tongwen College and as a translator at the Jiangnan Arsenal in China. Fryer brought with him his own library and the entire collection of Chinese translations of Western works then produced at the Jiangnan Arsenal. These constituted part of the early Chinese collection at Berkeley.

Fryer served at Berkeley until 1915, when a Chinese scholar, Jiang Kang-hu 江亢虎 (1883–1954), and later Edward Thomas Williams (1854–1944), succeeded him. Jiang donated his own collection of some 13,000 volumes to the library in 1916. All the pioneer teachers of Chinese, in addition to Michael Hagerty, who served as curator from 1916 to 1932, contributed to the original collections at Berkeley, making a total of 22,541 volumes in East Asian languages at the end of the early period.[4]

Columbia University established the Dean Lung professorship of Chinese in 1901 in memory of Dean Lung (Ding Liang 丁良) with a donation of $200,000 by Horace W. Carpenter (1824–1918) to his alma mater, supplemented by a gift of $12,000 from Dean Lung himself, for the promotion of Chinese studies. In conjunction with the teaching program, the university established a Chinese library in the following year. Also, the university received from the Chinese government a 5,040-volume set of the *Grand Encyclopedia*, valued at $7,000 in 1902. This acquisition was initiated by university president Seth Low (1850–1916), who expressed his belief that China and the United States were destined to be thrown into closer contact with each other in the near future.

In the Midwest, there was the leadership of Berthold Laufer (1874–1934), who served at the Field Museum of Natural History beginning in 1908 and acquired a large collection of materials in all East Asian languages for three libraries in Chicago during his travels in 1907–1910. He returned with 12,819 volumes of works on social and natural sciences for the John Crerar Library, which were transferred to the Library of Congress in 1928; 21,403 volumes of Chinese classics, philosophy, history, belles lettres, and art for the Newberry Library,[5] which were acquired by the University of Chicago in 1945; and some 5,000 volumes on archaeology and anthropology for the Field Museum, where the original collection is still kept intact. These three collections made Chicago one of the major centers for East Asian studies at the beginning of this century.

Similar interest in East Asia was also reflected in the teaching programs and library development at Cornell University during this early period. Cornell pioneered Chinese-language instruction in the 1870s and added other course offerings in such fields as history and international relations toward the end of the century. Library development began with gifts of some 350 books in Chinese by Chinese students in 1912, and 1,500 volumes in Japanese by the Reverend William E. Griffis (1843–1928) in 1916. The most important event at Cornell was the donation in 1918 by Charles William Wason (1854–1918) of his 9,000-volume private collection on China and the Chinese in Western languages, together with an endowment of $50,000 for supplementary acquisitions. His collection became distinguished not only in Western-language materials on China but also by its inclusion of such rarities as the fifteenth-century Chinese encyclopedia *Yongle dadian* 永樂大典, in three manuscript volumes, and the original papers relating to Lord Macartney's embassy to China in 1792. Also included were well-kept and well-bound sets of English-language periodicals and newspapers, pamphlets, off-prints, and other ephemeral materials, which are unrivaled in American libraries.[6]

By the turn of the century, materials in Chinese, Japanese, and other Asian languages are known to have been held also by the New York Public Library and a few others in the United States. Toward the end of this pioneer period, there were some ten major collections in American libraries with a total of at least 150,000 to 200,000 volumes in a variety of East Asian languages, in addition to many on the area in Western languages.

Generally speaking, these collections were in most cases built up accidentally without definite plans, primarily through gifts and exchanges, or collected by individuals as hobbies or for special interests. They were not much used, or used by very few; they were not systematically processed and sometimes were only briefly described by volunteer scholars.

Period of Systematic Development, 1920–1945

The growth of East Asian collections during the period 1920–1945 marked the second stage of development. In comparison with the earlier period, collections were built in a more purposeful and systematic way to support academic programs in teaching and research, mostly in universities and colleges with a few in art museums. These new collections, in addition to those established before, made more extensive acquisitions primarily through purchases, incorporated a number of distinguished private collections, and began to devise new systems for bibliographic control.

This development paralleled the increasing interest in popular and academic fields of Asian studies in the United States. This awareness of needs was promoted primarily through the efforts of various professional organizations and institutions with the support of private foundations, especially Rockefeller and Carnegie, and of individual donors. There have existed such organizations and institutions as the American Oriental Society; the American Council of Learned Societies; the Far Eastern Association, now the Association for Asian Studies; the American Institute of Pacific Relations; the Japan Society; the China Institute in America; the Harvard-Yenching Institute; and a number of concerned agencies in the federal government. As a result, formal instruction in the languages and special subject disciplines, especially in the humanities and history, was incorporated into or expanded in the university curricula. More extensive library collections were required to support these teaching and research programs.

The establishment of the Harvard-Yenching Institute in 1928 was a significant event in the development of Chinese and Japanese studies and of the East Asian collections in the United States. Not only did it create a center for East Asian studies at Harvard, but the establishment of the Harvard-Yenching Library with A. Kaiming Chiu 裘開明 (1898–1977) as its librarian also set an example by devising new systems for processing traditional Chinese and Japanese materials. Its classification system and catalog cards printed with characters and romanized entries were influential at the time and were adopted by most of the libraries during this period.

Some of the distinguished collections then and now began with the incorporation of private collections, which were built up around personal interests with special concentrations and strong financial backing. The Wason collection was one and the Gest collection another. The Gest Oriental Library was founded by Guion Moore Gest (1864–1948), a Canadian engineer with a curiosity about Chinese medicine. Over the years, the Gest collection acquired some 500 works in 2,000 volumes on this subject and now constitutes the largest such collection in the West. Gest entrusted the acquisitions to a retired U.S. Navy officer in Beijing, I. V. Gillis (d. 1948), who enlarged the scope of the original collection into a general research library.

In 1937, the entire Gest collection was acquired by the Institute for Ad-

HARVARD-YENCHING LIBRARY READING ROOM

vanced Studies at Princeton with the support of the Rockefeller Foundation. At the time of transfer, the collection consisted of some 102,000 volumes, forty percent of which were old manuscripts, early printings, and other rare editions. Especially important was the collection of some 24,000 volumes of Ming printing, which has become one of the largest in the West.[7]

Three years later, another Chinese collection was acquired by a Canadian institution. This was the private collection of Mu Xuexun 慕學勳 (1880–1929), a staff member of the German Legation in Beijing, whose collection of some 40,000 volumes was sold for $10,500 to the Royal Ontario Museum in Toronto after his death in 1929, through the arrangement of Bishop William C. White of the Anglican Church in Henan. This collection, which consisted of 371 titles in 4,182 volumes of Song, Yuan, and Ming editions, as well as some rather rare manuscripts, remained in Beiping for cataloging until 1935, when White added some 10,000 more volumes.[8] Together with its rich collection of oracle bone inscriptions and other archaeological objects, the Toronto collection has become an im-

GEST COLLECTION IN CANADA (NOW HOUSED AT PRINCETON)

portant center for Chinese studies in North America.

In the Midwest, the University of Chicago introduced a program of Chinese studies in 1936, with the appointment of Herrlee G. Creel to the Department of Oriental Languages and Literatures. Along with courses on the Chinese language and history and a project of compiling a series of Chinese-language textbooks, the university established a Far Eastern library. With support also from the Rockefeller Foundation, the collection grew rapidly. With the acquisition of the Laufer Collection from the Newberry Library in 1945, the total holdings of the Chicago collection numbered about 70,000 volumes at the end of the war, with special strength in Confucian classics, archaeology, and works for the study of ancient China.[9]

Several circumstances made possible the rapid growth of a research collection of this size within less than a decade. The supply of materials on the book market was plentiful, and the cost low during a time of war in China. Many rare materials, such as clan records, not available in peacetime, began to be sold by private families. With the cooperation of the National Beiping Library, the Peking Union Bookstore acted as an agent for several libraries in the United States, including Chicago, Columbia, Cornell, and the Library of Congress. It selected and specialized in all materials for them—local histories for the Library of Congress, Ming-Qing documents and clan records for Columbia, and classics and ancient history for Chicago—thus making each a specialized concentration, in addition to a basic collection for general research.

Besides these collections, a few other notable libraries were built up during the 1920s and 1930s. The University of Hawai'i initiated its Oriental library in 1925, and it has grown steadily into one of the major collections in the Pacific. On the West Coast, the Claremont Colleges established their Chinese collection in 1933, in conjunction with a bequest of $50,000 by James W. Porter for interpretation of Chinese culture to Americans and in promoting practical Sino-American friendliness, understanding, and mutual appreciation. In the same year, another collection was established at Northwestern University in Evanston, Illinois by William Montgomery McGovern to support his teaching and research on Japanese government, with Chinese materials added later.

In 1938, Henry Moore of Norfolk, Connecticut presented his Chinese library of some five thousand volumes on Chinese history, art, and culture to Trinity College. This collection was transferred to Central Connecticut State College in New Britain in 1970. At the same time in 1938, a Chinese collection was developed at the University of Pennsylvania to support its programs in Chinese studies. Under the initial direction of Professor Derk Bodde, it has grown into a well-balanced and serviceable collection.

During this period from 1920 to 1945, collections doubled to approximately twenty. These included a few in such museums as the Cleveland, Field, Fogg, Freer, Metropolitan, Nelson, and the Royal Ontario. They possessed a total of more than a million volumes in East Asian languages, with an average annual addition of about thirteen thousand volumes mostly acquired during the 1930s before the outbreak of the Pacific War.

Era of Rapid Expansion, 1945–1975

The years from 1945, following World War II, brought a new era of library development, characterized by rapid expansion not only in the number of new collections but also in the size and type of new acquisitions. These resulted from the demand for more language-area specialists in both academic and professional fields and from the shift from a traditional to a new approach for the study of East Asia. Unlike the purely academic interest in the 1930s, the postwar development created a growing awareness of practical problems focusing on the social sciences within the modern and contemporary scene of this area. This new discipline of foreign-area studies is one of the most important American contributions to postwar higher education.

The years 1958–1959 saw the beginning of massive support of Asian and other area studies in the United States from the government, foundations, universities, and other institutions. This resulted in a tremendous increase in non-Western-language materials in American libraries. In 1930 there were about 400,000 volumes in a dozen collections. The total holdings had increased to more than one million in some twenty collections by 1945, to two million in thirty collections by 1960, and to nearly seven million in more than sixty sizable collections (more than 10,000 volumes) by 1975, and to probably more than 10 million at the end of the twentieth century. The average annual additions were 45,000 volumes in 1930–1945; they doubled in the 1950s and sextupled in the 1960s through the 1970s with an average annual addition of 300,000 volumes.

As pointed out in earlier surveys, the year 1960 may be used as a benchmark for the development of East Asian collections in American libraries. The acquisitions made during the decade 1960–1970 equaled the total number of volumes accumulated over the 100 years preceding 1960, and as many new collections have been established since then as those founded before that date.[10] The growth of East Asian collections indicates a trend toward doubling in size every ten years between 1930 and 1955, and fifteen years between 1955 and 1975.

During the fifteen years between 1945 and 1960, ten new collections were organized, including those in the Hoover Institution at Stanford, the University of Washington at Seattle, the University of California at Los Angeles, and the University of Michigan, all of which were founded in the 1940s, and Virginia, Georgetown, Seton Hall, and British Columbia in the 1950s.

The East Asian Collection at the Hoover Institution was established in 1945, with emphasis on twentieth-century materials on China and Japan. Included are the notable collections of Harold Isaacs on Chinese Communism, of Nym Wales on the Chinese revolution, and of Webster on Chinese guerrillas in Malaya, as well as Japanese materials on student and left-wing movements.[11] The total holdings at Hoover were about 100,000 volumes in 1960 and more than 235,000 volumes in 1975.

The East Asian collection at UCLA was organized in 1948, when the Department of Oriental Languages was inaugurated. Its original collection, acquired by Professor Richard C. Rudolph, is strong in art, archaeology, literature, history, folklore, and Buddhism. With the deposit of some 80,000 volumes from the *Monumenta Serica* collections in the 1960s, the total holdings numbered more than 150,000 volumes in 1975.

The Far Eastern Library of the University of Washington at Seattle was established in 1947. With the support of the Rockefeller Foundation, it acquired two private collections from George Kerr and J. F. Rock. This library emphasizes nineteenth-century China and its border regions and is especially rich in Chinese local history of the southwestern provinces. This collection consisted of 86,000 volumes in 1960, and more than 200,000 volumes in 1975.

The Asia Library at the University of Michigan was formally organized in 1948, after the Center for Japanese Studies was established. It started mainly as a Japanese collection, with the acquisition of about 10,000 volumes from the Washington Documentation Center in 1949 and the Kamada Library in 1950. Its holdings in 1954 numbered 40,000 volumes in Japanese and 800 in Chinese.[12] With additional support during the 1960s, the growth of its Chinese collection was so rapid that by 1970 its holdings of 200,000 volumes contained more in Chinese than in Japanese. By 1975 its total holdings numbered more than 300,000 volumes. It was probably the most rapidly growing collection of all those established during the postwar period.

Along with the rapid expansion in the United States, there was similar growth in Canadian libraries. One of the most important developments was the establishment of the Asian Studies Division in the University of British Columbia at Vancouver, which acquired in 1959, with support of the Friends of the Library, the noted Puban 蒲板 Chinese Library of Yao Junshi 姚鈞石 from Macao. Yao, a physician in training, built his private library in Canton and moved to Macao in 1939. At the time of transfer, the library contained about 45,000 volumes, including some 300 rare items of Song, Yuan, and Ming printing and manuscripts and 86 gazetteers on Guangdong.[13] It was one of the most important private collections acquired after the war, when all sources of supply from China were closed. Its total holdings grew from 70,000 volumes in 1960 to more than 185,000 volumes in 1975.

The East Asian Library at the University of Toronto has been expanded since 1953 into a general research collection, with the addition of many works in modern editions. The original Mu collection at the Royal Ontario Museum, except for materials on art and archaeology and some 5,000 items of rubbings, was integrated into the new collection of some 60,000 volumes bought with a Carnegie grant. Its total holdings consisted of 50,000 volumes in 1960 and passed the 100,000-volume mark in 1975. The nature of the library has gradually changed in recent years from that of a traditional depository to a working research collection.

With the initiation of many private and state universities and the federal support of language-area centers under National Defense Education Act (NDEA) matching grants, more than thirty new collections have been established since 1960. These included those in such private institutions as Brown, Dartmouth, Denver, Oberlin, Pittsburgh, St John's, and Washington (St. Louis), and such state universities as Arizona, California at Davis and Santa Barbara, Colorado, Florida, Illinois, Indiana, Iowa, Kansas, Maryland, Michigan State, Minnesota, Nebraska, North Carolina, Ohio State, Oregon, Rochester, Rutgers, and Wisconsin.[14]

A few noted collections were acquired by some of these libraries. For example, the Prange collection of Japanese publications under U.S. occupation between 1945 and 1949, including about 13,000 periodicals, 11,000 newspapers, and 50,000 monographs, which were submitted to the Civil

Censorship Detachment of the headquarters for pre- and post-publication censorship, was deposited in the East Asian Library of the University of Maryland. The private Chinese collection of Ma Kiam (Ma Jian 馬鑑) was acquired by the Oriental collection of the University of Virginia Library in 1964.

During this period, the expansion of some of the old collections was even more extensive than that of the newer ones, since they already had a well-established base in addition to generous support from various sources. The most significant development in the history of the Library of Congress was probably the rapid expansion of its collection of Japanese materials. As a consequence of the Allied occupation of Japan, several collections that had been gathered by Japanese military agencies were transferred to the Washington Documentation Center, from which some 300,000 volumes, mostly in the fields of economics, science, and technology, were added to the Library of Congress Japanese collection, which had some 50,000 volumes before the transfer. With the creation of a Korean unit in 1950 and further acquisitions in Chinese and Japanese over the postwar years, the Orientalia Division increased its holdings in these languages from about 250,000 volumes in 1945 to more than a million in 1975, a fourfold increase in thirty years.

At Harvard, an intensive program of modern and contemporary studies of China, Japan, and Korea was added through the establishment of the East Asiatic Regional Studies program in 1948. For this program the university library has been buying books in Chinese and Japanese on the contemporary scene and the recent past. The Harvard-Yenching Library was also enriched during the postwar period by the acquisition of several private collections such as those of Henry H. Hart on Chinese literature and of Qi Rushan 齊如山 on Chinese drama and novels. In addition, there were those acquired earlier, such as the Petzold Buddhist collection in some 6,500 volumes and the manuscript collection of the Qi family in Nanking, which included many unpublished manuscripts and autographs, documents, examination papers, theatrical handbooks, and records of old-style business shops.[15] The growth of the Japanese collection was also impressive, from 15,000 volumes in 1945 to 140,000 in 1975, a tenfold increase in thirty years.

The expansion of the East Asiatic Library at Berkeley during the postwar period was very significant. At least three major acquisitions were made between 1948–50. These included the Mitsui Bunko with diversified materials, the Murakami Library on Meiji literature in some 11,000 volumes, and the Asami collection of classical Korean materials in 4,150 volumes. The total holdings at Berkeley increased from about 75,000 volumes in 1945 to 370,000 volumes in 1975, a fivefold increase in thirty years.

The expansion of the East Asian collection at Yale University since 1961 has been equally impressive. With substantial financial support from its Council on East Asian Studies under its chairman Arthur Wright, an Asian Reading Room was opened in 1963, incorporating hitherto scattered collections into one location. The total holdings increased from 35,000 volumes in 1945 to more than 264,000 volumes in 1975, a more than sevenfold increase in thirty years.

In Chicago the growth of the Far Eastern Library at the University of Chicago was rapid before and during the war but slowed down after the war until 1958, when the establishment of a Japanese collection and the expansion into the study of modern and contemporary China began. With substantial support from the government and the Rockefeller Foundation, as well as the university's own resources, the collection has grown rapidly. Over the last twenty years it has built up a distinguished collection in Japanese that is especially strong in literature, history, and religion; a periodical collection of more than 5,000 titles; a collection on Chinese local history in some 3,000 titles and on local administration in 2,500 volumes; a special collection of specimens of old inscriptions, manuscripts, and early printing; and an additional rare book collection of more than 2,300 volumes of Ming prints from the private library of the late Professor Li Zongtong 李宗侗, acquired in the 1960s. The total holdings increased from 70,000 volumes to nearly 350,000 volumes in 1975, a fivefold increase in twenty-eight years.

Summary and Prospects

Generally speaking, the prewar period before 1945 created a solid foundation for the development of East Asian collections in American libraries.

Except for very few, almost all of these collections have grown continuously and expanded into major centers, playing dominant roles in supporting the language-area studies programs in American higher education. Collections since World War II have experienced unprecedented growth both in terms of their numbers and in the size and diversity of new acquisitions. The shift in emphasis from humanities to social sciences and from classical to modern and contemporary interests has brought about the establishment of separate collections within each collection.

The larger growth of materials in Japanese than in Chinese immediately following the war and, during more recent years, the establishment of Korean and other East Asian-language collections, along with the inclusion of such materials in public libraries, indicate new trends in collection building during the postwar period.

Most of the resources are concentrated in fifteen major collections, which contain 4.7 million volumes, or 70 percent of the total holdings of all libraries in 1975. They each have acquired from a few thousand to as many as 30,000 volumes a year, with an average annual addition of 150,000 volumes, or 60% of the total acquisitions. With more new collections established, such concentration has gradually been dispersed from over 90% before 1960 to just over two-thirds in 1975.

Many rarities and specialty items in East Asian languages have been built up in a number of distinguished collections. At least thirty rare book collections and eighty large subject concentrations in individual collections currently are found in American libraries. Included in this number are more than 100,000 volumes in Chinese printed in the tenth to seventeenth centuries, 13,000 manuscripts and 2,000 volumes of early and fine printing in Japanese, some 10,000 volumes of movable-type printing in Korean, and nearly 5,000 items of rubbings from stone inscriptions in Chinese and other languages. Xylography and manuscripts in Tibetan, Mongol, Manchu, and Moso are also represented.

The large subject collections include almost every possible kind of material in different languages and areas on such broad or specific subjects as Confucian classics, Buddhism, genealogy, maps, local history, and science and technology, as well as sources on modern and contemporary affairs. All of these are believed to be either unique or not likely duplicated elsewhere in American libraries.

The field in general has received more support since the 1960s than at any time before from individual institutions as well as outside sources. The total expenditures for 1975/76 came to eight million dollars, one-third of which were for materials and supplies and two-thirds for personnel. This ratio has not changed much since the 1960s. This total includes four percent from the federal government and seven percent from foundations, especially Ford, Mellon and, more recently, Japanese sources. Although outside funding has always been around ten percent of the total investment, encouragement in the form of matching and developmental funds has stimulated institutional initiatives.

The sources of support for future developments are rather uncertain. While federal and foundation money may be available for the initial cost of some of the national programs, as the American Council of Learned Societies steering committee report indicates,[16] the basic resources for long-term support of individual collections will have to come from the institutions themselves. How to use this limited support to meet the increasing needs of the academic community is a common problem that must be solved. The prospects of the East Asian collections as a field depend upon the future needs of the academic community, the potential sources of additional support, and the cost-effectiveness for the operation of the collections. Cooperation and coordination in the field will be key for any future development. In other words, individual collections must be strengthened in order to meet local needs. At the same time, new systems and national programs should be worked out through regional, national, and international cooperation for the benefit of all.

Published as "Current Status of East Asian Collections in American Libraries,"
in Journal of Asian Studies, *v. 36, no. 3 (May, 1977).*

Notes

1. Tsuen-hsuin Tsien, "First Chinese-American Exchange of Publications," *Harvard Journal of Asiatic Studies* 25:19–30 (1964–1965).

2. Arthur W. Hummel, "The Growth of the Orientalia Collections," *Library of Congress Quarterly Journal of Current Acquisitions* 11:80 (February 1954).

3. Serge Elisséeff, "The Chinese-Japanese Library of the Harvard-Yenching Institute." *Harvard Library Bulletin* 10:73 (1956).

4. Elizabeth Huff, "Far Eastern Collections in the East Asiatic Library of the University of California," *Far Eastern Quarterly* 14:443 (1955).

5. Berthold Laufer, *Descriptive Account of the Collection of Chinese, Tibetan, Mongol, and Japanese Books in the Newberry Library* (Chicago: Newberry Library, 1913).

6. Richard C. Howard, "The Wason Collection on China and the Chinese," *Cornell University Library Bulletin* 193:36–43 (January 1975).

7. Hu Shih, "The Gest Oriental Library at Princeton University," *Princeton University Library Chronicle* 15:113–141 (Spring 1954).

8. Raymond W. H. Chu and S. Uyenaka, "East Asian Library Collection in the University of Toronto," *Pacific Affairs* 46:548–556, (1973–1974).

9. T. H. Tsien, "The Far Eastern Library of the University of Chicago, 1936–1956," *Far Eastern Quarterly* 15:656–658 (May 1956).

10. Tsuen-hsuin Tsien, "East Asian Library Resources in America: A New Survey," *Association for Asian Studies Newsletter* 16:1–11 (February 1971); also occasional surveys in *Library Quarterly* 29:7–12 (1959); 35:260–282 (1965); and *Committee on East Asian Libraries Newsletter* 16 (October 1966); 22 (December 1967); 29 (May 1969); 33 (December 1970); and 50 (July 1976).

11. "Far Eastern Collections in the Hoover Library, Stanford University," *Far Eastern Quarterly* 14:446–447 (February 1956).

12. G. Raymond Nunn, "Far Eastern Collections in the General Library of the University of Michigan," *Far Eastern Quarterly* 12:381–382 (May 1954).

13. Yi-t'ung Wang, "The P'u-pan Chinese Library at the University of British Columbia," *Pacific Affairs* 34:101–111 (1961–1962).

14. See Tsuen-hsuin Tsien, "Current Status of East Asian Collections in American Libraries, 1974/75" (*Washington, D.C. Center for Chinese Research Materials*, Association of Research Libraries, 1976), Table 1.

15. A. Kaiming Ch'iu, "The Harvard-Yenching Institute Library," *Far Eastern Quarterly* 14:147–152 (1954).

16. *East Asian Libraries: Problems and Prospects: A Report and Recommendations*, prepared by the Steering Committee for a Study of the Problems of East Asian Libraries (New York: American Council of Learned Societies, 1977).

HOW CHINESE RARE BOOKS CROSSED THE PACIFIC

In 1941, just before the outbreak of World War II, some 30,000 volumes of Chinese rare books were shipped from China to the United States for safekeeping and microfilming. This was an important event in the history of Chinese-American cultural relations and also for the international sharing of Chinese rare resources, yet very few people know the story of how these rarities were able to cross the Pacific Ocean during a time of world crisis. Twenty-six years later, I recalled this incident in an article revealing how I risked my life in order to accomplish this difficult mission.[1] In that account, I mentioned how an accident made this shipment possible and that it remains a mystery how the last shipment reached the States, since the vessel supposedly carrying the rare books was captured by the Japanese navy.

After the war in 1947, I was commissioned by the Chinese government to go to the United States to bring back these books, but the outbreak of civil war in China prevented their return. Instead of going to Washington, D.C., I ended up in Chicago. Before my arrival in Chicago, I worked at the Nanjing and Shanghai offices of the National Beiping Library (now the National Library of China) for ten years. The two branches were established in 1934, when many rare books were moved to the south for safekeeping after the Japanese occupation of Manchuria. Among them were some 60,000 volumes of old printings, manuscripts, and Dunhuang documents, as well as artifacts, maps, and rubbings, in addition to many complete sets of foreign periodicals, which were then stored secretly in several locations in the International Settlement and French Concession in Shanghai. In 1937, when the Japanese occupation of northern China was imminent, the headquarters of the National Library was moved from Beiping to the remote cities of Changsha and then Kunming, and I was assigned to work in Nanjing and later in the Shanghai office undercover.

Besides the custody of rare books, my job in Shanghai consisted of publishing the *Quarterly Bulletin of Chinese Bibliography*, contacting libraries and cultural institutions in the West for supplies of research materials, and acquiring publications under the Japanese occupation. The most difficult and exciting task assigned to me during this period was the shipment of rare books then stored in Shanghai to the Library of Congress in Washington, D.C., under an agreement between the Chinese and American governments.[2]

In those days, the shipment of antiquities to the U.S. was all but impossible since the Shanghai harbor and customs were already under Japanese control. There was no way of getting rare materials out of the city without approval from the Japanese authorities.

Many attempts had been made by the State Department in Washington, D.C., through the American Consulate General in Shanghai and by myself to negotiate with the Director-General of the Shanghai Customs, but they all ended in failure. Nevertheless, an accidental and unexpected turn of events enabled the books to be shipped out of Shanghai without any approval from the higher authorities, but at great risk.

It happened one day that one of my wife's former schoolmates was visiting us and, from our conversation, we learned that she had a brother working as an inspector in the Shanghai customs bureau. She arranged for me to meet him and he expressed his patriotic sympathy about the shipment and agreed to help on the condition that we kept it top secret. The books were already packed in 102 wooden crates and sealed inside with galvanized iron sheets except for two that had already been shipped by the American Consulate in Shanghai. This inspector suggested that the rare materials should be sent in installments at intervals and disguised as if they contained new books that were being acquired by U.S. libraries. I acted as the book dealer and made out an invoice for large sets of new publications. Each time I accompanied the crates, which were loaded on a hand-pulled cart, to the customs office when this particular inspector was on duty. The crates of rare books were then examined by him and immediately cleared as ordinary cargo. About ten crates were sent each time, so it took almost two months to complete the shipment of books. The final batch was understood to have been shipped by the SS President Harrison and delivered on December 5, 1941, just two days before Japan's surprise attack on Pearl Harbor and the beginning of World War II, followed by the immediate occupation of Shanghai, Hong Kong, Singapore, the Philippines, and other parts of Southeast Asia by the Japanese army.

A few days later, it was reported in the newspaper that the SS President Harrison, which was supposed to have been carrying the last shipment from Shanghai, had been captured by the Japanese navy outside Shanghai. We were all extremely anxious, believing that the last shipment must have been either seized or destroyed by the Japanese. Six months later, to my great surprise, a dispatch from Lisbon by a German news agency reported that the U.S. Library of Congress had announced that all 102 crates of Chinese rare books had arrived safely in Washington, D.C., and that microfilming had already begun.[3]

In order to help solve this puzzle, Dr. Edwin G. Beal, Jr., the former Head of the Chinese and Korean Section of the Library of Congress, made an inquiry in 1983 to find out when precisely the SS President Harrison had left Shanghai and whether it had been seized by the Japanese or had reached San Francisco.[4] After combing its archives, the American President Lines, Inc., released some exciting information concerning the fate of the ship during the war, together with the names of the Master and one of the crew of the vessel and their reflections at the time of the capture. According to this information, on December 8, 1941, just after the outbreak of war, the SS President Harrison was on its way from Manila to Qinhuangdao in northern China in order to evacuate American marines stationed in Beiping. As the vessel approached Shanghai, it was trapped by a Japanese cruiser and the Japanese liner Nagasaki Maru about forty miles off the coast of Shanghai. The Master of the vessel ran the ship aground on Shewieshan Island at full speed, hoping to prevent the Japanese from using it. Afterwards, however, a Japanese salvage firm succeeded in refloating the ship, which was renamed the Kakko Maru and later, Kachidoki Maru. It was used by the Japanese until September 12, 1944, when it was torpedoed and sunk by an American submarine in the South China Sea. At the time, it was transporting some 900 U.S. prisoners of war from Singapore to Japan, among whom only about 500 were rescued.

It seems quite clear, however, that the last shipment of Chinese rare books was not on board the President Harrison, which was scheduled to run between Shanghai and San Francisco but had apparently been recruited by the U.S. government for the evacuation of Americans in China before the outbreak of the war. The last shipment of ten cases of rare books must have been placed on another ship sailing from Shanghai, though this transfer was not reported, nor could the name of the ship be traced.

Dr. Beal reported that he had also examined the documents at the Library of Congress, hoping to find bills of lading or other indications of how the final shipment had arrived and by which vessel. Though his search did not answer all the questions, it is now understood that all the crates reached San Francisco and were in temporary custody at the University of California at Berkeley before they reached their final destination in Washington, D.C. However, the puzzle remains unsolved as we do not know how the final shipment arrived, though it seems clear it could not have done so on the President Harrison, since the latter never reached Shanghai or ever again came near San Francisco.

After a quarter of a century in the U.S., these books re-crossed the Pacific in 1965 and were transferred to the National Central Library in Taiwan for temporary custody at the request of its former director, Dr. Chiang Fu-tsung.[5] They were shipped on board the U.S. naval vessel, General H. Guffey, together with other rare materials from Taiwan exhibited at the World's Fair in New York. After being verified against the original packing list drawn up in Shanghai, a separate rare book catalog of the National Beiping Library in the custody of the National Central Library was published in 1969.[6]

After Dr. Chiang became Director of the National Palace Museum in Taiwan, these books, packed in the 102 original crates, were moved to the new building of the Museum in Taibei. I visited the Museum in 1987 and was very impressed by the physical facilities of its rare book stacks. The books have been well cared for with excellent security and the proper temperature and humidity control in the Museum's rare books building. I was also surprised to see that all of the original labels, which had been used to seal the crates in Shanghai fifty years ago, were still there. It is hoped that these rare materials, China's national treasures from thousands of years and numerous dynasties, will eventually be returned to their original home.

Notes

1. T. H. Tsien (Qian Cunxun), "Beiping tushuguan shanben shuji yunMei jingguo," *Zhuanji wenxue*, 10, no. 2 (February, 1967), 55–57.

2. For details of the negotiation, see Margaret C. Fung, "Safekeeping of the National Peiping Library's Rare Chinese Books at the Library of Congress, 1941-1965," *Journal of Library History*, 19, no. 3 (1984), 359–372.

3. A total of 2,070 titles were transferred to 1,070 reels of microfilm on master film at the U.S. Library of Congress.

4. I am grateful to Dr. Beal for sending me his correspondence with Ms. Collette Carey of the American President Lines' Archives, together with all of the related documents.

5. For the return of this collection to Taiwan, see "Youguan Beitu cun Mei shanben yun Tai dang'an," *Guoli zhongyang tushuguan guankan*, v. 16, no. 1:1964; Chiang Futsung (Jiang Fucong), "Yunguei Guoli Beiping tushuguan cun Mei shanben gaishu," *Zhong Mei yuekan* 11, no. 3 (1966), 5–7; Chang Bide, "Guanyu Beiping tushuguan jicun Meiguo de shanbenshu", *Shumu jikan*, v. 4, no. 2 (1969.12), 3–11;

6. *Guoli Zhongyang tushuguan 'diancang' Guoli Beiping tushuguan shanben shumu*, 1969.

Published in the Bulletin of East Asian Libraries, *no. 101 (February 1993).*

16

Before the 1930s, only a few American universities offered courses on China based on the tradition of European scholarship, instead providing a rather superficial coverage of Chinese language and culture. Most instructors were either from Europe or missionaries familiar with the Chinese language. It was in the 1930s that American scholars began to study in China with the encouragement of academic organizations and foundation support. After returning, they taught at American universities, cultivating later generations of young sinologists, which contributed to the cultural exchange between the United States and China. Herrlee G. Creel (1905–1994) was one of these sinologists, dedicating his entire life to teaching and research and leaving behind numerous works of significance.

Education and Academic Background

Dr. Creel was born in Chicago on January 19, 1905. After graduating from high school, he focused on writing and became a journalist, for which he had particular talent. He studied at two midwestern universities before transferring to the University of Chicago, specializing in philosophy and the history of religion, receiving his B.A. in 1926, M.A. in 1927, and Ph.D. in 1929. He became interested in the teachings of Confucius, studied Chinese with a Chinese student, and wrote his doctoral dissertation on Chinese intellectual thought. After graduation, he taught English and psychology in various colleges. An accidental encounter with the German sinologist Dr. Berthold Laufer (1874–1934) led him to a scholarship from the American Council of Learned Societies and enrollment in Harvard University in 1930–1932 to study classical Chinese under Mei Guangdi 梅光迪 (1890–1945).

From 1932 to 1935, he went to China with support from the Harvard-Yenching Institute to study inscriptions with Liu Jie 劉節 (1901–1977), then head of the Department of Bronze and Stone Inscriptions at the National Beiping Library. He made several archaeological trips to the Shang ruins in Anyang, Henan Province and became acquainted with Chinese scholars of Chinese archeology. It was at this point that Dr. Creel started his collection of ancient Chinese materials, research on Chinese history, and publication of books and articles in academic journals, including some written in Chinese under his Chinese name Gu Liya 顧立雅.

Dr. Creel returned to the U.S. in 1936 and was appointed as an instructor to the Department of Oriental Languages and Literatures and the Department of History at the University of Chicago, teaching courses in Chinese language, philosophy, and history. He was promoted to assistant professor in 1937, associate professor in 1940, and full professor in 1949. During this time, he established the Far Eastern Library, visited China again in 1939–1940 to acquire Chinese books, and returned to the U.S. via Korea and Japan. During World War II, he was drafted and became an army major in the intelligence division. He returned to campus in 1945.

After 1958, the Department of Oriental Languages and Literatures was divided into three departments: Near East, Southeast, and Far East. Since He was for many years chairman of the Department of Far Eastern Languages and Civilizations and the Committee on Far Eastern Studies. In 1964, he became the Martin Ryerson Chaired Professor, a title he held until his retirement in 1973. He worked at the University of Chicago for a total of thirty-seven years, making a tremendous contribution to the studies of China and East Asia.

Writing and Research

Dr. Creel was a prolific writer and had published eight monographs, three textbooks, and dozens of essays, which were translated into Chinese, Japanese, French, Italian, and Spanish. His interest in China started with his doctoral dissertation—*Sinism: A Study of the Evolution of the Chinese World View* (Chicago: Open Court, 1929). During his study in China, he published several articles on Chinese language, history, and philosophy.

He was most well known for *The Birth of China: A Survey of the Formative Period of Chinese Civilization* (London: Jonathan Cape, 1936; New York: John Day, 1937), a comprehensive introduction to the society, politics, economy, culture, and art of the Shang Dynasty. He did extensive research on authenticating texts with archaeological materials, which were incorporated into his *Studies in Early Chinese Civilization*, First Series (American Council of Learned Societies, 1937), which has become an important work for many topics in Chinese history.

Dr. Creel possessed unique insights into histories from the Shang and Zhou dynasties to the pre-Qin schools of thought. His other monographs included: *Confucius: the Man and the Myth* (New York: 1949; London: 1951; Tokyo: 1961); *Chinese Thought: From Confucius to Mao Tse-tung* (New York: 1953); *What Is Taoism? And Other Studies of Chinese Cultural History* (Chicago, 1970); *The Origins of Statecraft of China: Western Chou Empire* (Chicago, 1970), and *Shen Pu-hai* (申不害): *A Chinese Political Philosopher of the Fourth Century* B.C. (Chicago & London: 1974), which was a by-product of his many years studying Chinese intellectual history. He not only gave a very positive appraisal of the political achievements of the father of the Legalist School, but also extensively collected his writings with detailed translations, which marked the last of his scholarly publications.

Teaching and Other Academic Activities

Besides his research publications, Dr. Creel also composed a series of textbooks: *Literary Chinese by the Inductive Method* (Chicago, University of Chicago Press, 1938–1952), including three traditional Chinese beginner's texts: v. 1, *Hsiao Ching* (孝经, *Book of Filial Piety)*; v. 2, *Lun Yu* (论语, *The Analects of Confucius*); and v. 3, *Mencius* (孟子). These three volumes each give an introduction of the book with full or selected text, detailed notes on each new character in the text with examples to illustrate its uses, grammar, order of writing, romanization, and English translation of single and compound words and exercises. This invaluable set of textbooks applied a scientific method to the study of early Chinese language, thought, and history. They were extensively adopted by many universities in the West.

These three volumes provided the student with around 3,000 commonly used Chinese characters in texts. Students would read the *Zuo zhuan* (左传, *Spring and Autumn Annals according to the Zuo commentary*), and *Shiji* (史记 *Records of the Grand Historian*), as well as other texts before they could do specialized research and write dissertations.

Besides teaching, research, and administrative duties, Dr. Creel also participated in other academic activities, including the presidency of the American Oriental Society (1954–1956). In 1980, he attended an International Conference of Sinology in Taiwan and read a paper on the metamorphosis of Daoism, discussing the content of the writings of Laozi, Zhuangzi, and other schools of thought, as well as their influence.

Since 1958, enormous changes have taken place in the study of China in the American scholarly community. For instance, language teaching has expanded from the literary to the vernacular, the period of study from ancient to modern times, the research of subjects in the humanities to include social sciences, and the curricula from graduate school to college level. To meet the new trends, Dr. Creel invited administrators of various universities for a symposium on whether universities should add courses on Chinese culture for undergraduates, which resulted in the volume *Chinese Civilization in Liberal Education* (Chicago, 1958).

The early stages of Chinese language instruction at the University of Chicago included three periods: ancient, medieval, and modern. Dr. Creel taught first year Chinese, ancient Chinese history, and philosophy; Edward A. Kracke Jr. (1908–1976) taught second year Chinese, medieval history, and political institutions; and Ssu-yu Teng 鄧嗣禹 (1906–1988) taught on modern and contemporary Chinese, as well as other subjects. I came to the University of Chicago in 1947 and taught courses on Chinese bibliography and historiography beginning in 1949.

Besides my work in the Far Eastern Library and research in the Graduate Library School, I also took seminars with Dr. Creel, under whom I wrote my Ph.D. dissertation, titled "The Pre-printing Records of China: A Study of the Development of Early Chinese Inscriptions and Books" (later renamed *Written on Bamboo and Silk,* published by the University of Chicago Press in 1962, revised ed. 2004). He paid close attention to the choice of words and terms, style of expression, translation, and authenticating sources, making very detailed comments and corrections. His style of scholarship greatly influenced my later writings and scholarship.

In Celebration

In 1975, to celebrate Dr. Creel's 70th birthday, David Roy, then chairman of the Department of East Asian Studies, and I invited sixteen scholars from around the world to write papers on the philosophy, literature, history, and archaeology of the pre-Qin and Han Dynasties for a volume titled *Ancient China: Studies in Early Civilization* (Hong Kong, 1978). It was presented to him at a party in honor of his lifelong devotion to teaching and research in Chinese culture and for his mentorship of scholars.

In 1986, at the annual conference of the Association for Asian Studies in Chicago, a discussion group was held to celebrate the 50th anniversary of the publication of Creel's *The Birth of China* and to discuss the impact of this book on international sinology. He gave the speech, "The Birth of *The Birth of China*," reminiscing about how he had met Dr. Laufer, who wrote a letter of recommendation for him to receive financial assistance to study Chinese at Harvard University, and how he finished the book in six months in China. In the same year, to celebrate the 50th anniversary of the founding of the East Asian studies program and the Far Eastern Library, the University of Chicago held a celebratory dinner party, which included a speech by then-president Hanna Gray, who praised Dr. Creel for championing East Asian studies at Chicago. At the same function, I also was honored as one of the early participants in the program.

Dr. Creel donated to the David and Alfred Smart Gallery his collections—including bone, bronze, clam, and jade utensils, pottery and tortoise shell pieces, all from the Shang and Zhou Dynasties. These items that he had brought back from China to facilitate his teaching had never been viewed by the public. The Smart Gallery opened a special collection for the preservation of these items, including a catalogue and the publication *Ritual and Reverence* (1989). Professor Edward Shaughnessy later deciphered the inscriptions on the forty-three pieces of tortoise shells that Dr. Creel had collected, and published an essay in the *Tushu wenshi lunji* 圖書文史論集 (*Literary and Historical Essays on Chinese Books*. Taipei, 1991; Beijing, 1992). Through this Dr. Creel's collections were made known to the public.

THE AUTHOR WITH DR. CREEL (1947)

Dr. Creel continued writing after his retirement, though he soon grew physically weak and eventually went blind. He died on June 1, 1994, at the age of 89. Mrs. Creel passed away December 12, 1995. After Dr. Creel's death, major newspapers carried obituaries that praised him as a towering figure in the field of international sinology. The University of Chicago held a memorial service for him on November 3, 1994, in which over 200 scholars from around the world participated. At the service I gave a speech reminiscing about my arrival in Chicago in the fall of 1947, when he was still young and energetic, well dressed, decisive, and universally respected by colleagues. Apart from all of these accomplishments, it was his arrangement of my permanent stay in Chicago, and his assistance in bringing my family to the U.S., that perhaps had the greatest impact on my career and family.

Published in Chinese in Lishi yanjiu, *January, 1997, and translated by Professor Diana Chen Lin of Indiana State University, with revisions by Ma Tai-loi.*

17　WORKING WITH JOSEPH NEEDHAM

Joseph Needham (1900–1995) and I first became acquainted in 1964, when he wrote a review of my book, *Written on Bamboo and Silk: The Beginnings of Chinese Books and Inscriptions* (Chicago: University of Chicago Press, 1962) in the *Journal of Asian Studies* v. 23, no. 4, 1964. He praised my book as a companion volume to Thomas F. Carter's classic *The Invention of Printing in China and Its Spread Westward*, saying "we may say at once that it need not fear any comparison with that wonderful book," and "the text is a model of clarity and brevity in good Cartesian style." Because one chapter of my book covered paper and paper scrolls, Needham wrote me for the first time in October 17, 1967, inviting me to write parts of the fifth volume of his *Science and Civilisation in China* on the subjects of paper, inkmaking, and printing. He wrote: "Your special knowledge of paper and its predecessors, as well as of seals, writing and printing in general, makes you one of the most obvious people in the world to be approached in this way, and I do hope that you will consider the matter very seriously."

Although I was flattered, some colleagues and friends advised me not to accept the offer. They were concerned that Needham was not a sinologist by training and he had been attacked by other British scholars, also he was being watched closely by the CIA. If I were to collaborate with him, I might be inviting trouble. Even though I had limited knowledge of him, I was impressed by his goodwill towards China, his sense of justice during the Korean War, and his anti-war stance on the Vietnam War. After some thought, I accepted his invitation to visit Cambridge and discuss the matter before making a decision. With the support of the American Association of Learned Societies, I was also able to visit continental Europe in September 1968.

When I arrived at Cambridge, Needham, then Master of Gonville and Caius College, and Lu Gwei-djen 魯桂珍 (Lu Guizhen, 1904–1991), his assistant, came to meet me at the bus station; he carried my luggage, walking rapidly in front of me. I was put up in an old building in the college, and every morning, a specially prepared breakfast was sent to my room.

Lunches were usually with Needham, his wife Dorothy, and Lu Gwei-djen, and we would have afternoon tea at 4 PM. For dinner, I was occasionally invited to sit with the robed fellows and professors on the upper level of the dining room, while students ate at the tables below.

Needham was a very candid and sincere person, easily approachable, simple, honest, and warm. He admired everything about China and was a true "China fan." Tall and casually dressed, he often wore a long blue Chinese robe and cotton shoes at home. Scrolls of his own Chinese calligraphy hung on the walls. His spoken Chinese was limited, so when we talked he would usually write down those Chinese characters that he was unsure of. All of the research materials he collected, whether quotations or notes, were written on single sheets or cards, placed in topical folders, and filed by category in his cabinets for easy access. He lived a simple life and worked with unbelievable efficiency. Such an enormous research project was assisted by only one secretary and a part-time librarian. He undertook almost all of the clerical work, including the typing, correspondence, and other miscellaneous work. This gave me a glimpse into the admirably simple style of European scholars.

Modesty and Courtesy

After exhaustively explaining his research plan to me, Needham brought out materials that he had already collected and told me that besides paper and printing, this part of volume five would also include topics on textiles, pottery, and gunpowder. He had tentatively titled the volume "War and Peace." He thought that what I had assembled for *Written on Bamboo and Silk* on paper, plus an additional narrative on printing, should be sufficient for the chapter, which he imagined would be about one hundred pages. Instead, my research led me deeper into an extensive array of sources, and my chapter grew well beyond initial expectations. I eventually spent fifteen years on the book, and the manuscript expanded from the original plan of one hundred pages to a monograph of 300,000 words.

In the process of writing, I would usually draw up an outline for each chapter, including subtopics and descriptions of details, for his approval. He never commented on the outlines and always encouraged me to continue. When I finished drafts for the three chapters on papermaking in 1972, it was already over 200 pages. When I asked him whether he would like me to reduce the content after I sent him the draft, he replied that he believed in Daoism, which abided by nature and does not put limits on things. Therefore, I proceeded with the following chapters as I did with the three on papermaking.

There were few original sources for the section on printing, and many problems with this subject arose along the way, in part because of the enormous amount of material on the worldwide transmission and influence of printing. The complexity of research, in addition to my heavy workload at the University of Chicago, gave me little time to write. I was fortunate to obtain funding from the National Science Foundation and the National Endowment for the Humanities, which partly relieved me from my administrative duties at the university and enabled me to hire graduate research assistants. I also offered a seminar on the History of Chinese Printing three times in the Graduate Library School, using the opportunity to conduct discussions on the research and also to train a number of young scholars to conduct research on this specialized field.

Although I did not meet with Needham that many times, I corresponded with him often and accumulated many letters from him. He would forward to me all of the inquiries and collected subject materials. His letters were often written in a beautiful running script, and I was moved by his warmth. I was not used to addressing him as "Joseph," generally calling him "Dr. Needham." And he always used his unique Chinese spelling of my name—Chhien Tshun-hsun.

Many times I raised this issue, arguing that my English publications always used Tsuen-hsuin Tsien, and if I published under Chhien Tshun-hsun it would be hard for readers to identify my other works. He finally agreed to a compromise: in the Chinese-language part of the bibliography, he used his spelling of my name, and in the English-language part of the bibliography and on the title page, he used my spelling. On other occasions, he still preferred to place his spelling in brackets after Tsuen-hsuin Tsien. In this way, he maintained his style of romanization and respected my name in English, the way it had been spelled since my college days.

Authorship of the Volume

When the manuscript *Paper and Printing* was completed in mid-1982, I traveled to Cambridge again in order to discuss its publication. Following the precedents of the already published volumes of *Science and Civilization in China*, I put Joseph Needham and Tsuen-hsuin Tsien as joint authors on the cover page. Although he did not refuse then, in the published volume 5, part I of the series, my name was printed as the sole author, and his name was placed below as the series editor, which became the template for later volumes in the series. This made me admire him all the more for his modesty. He always thanked all of his collaborators, including the individuals who did the indexing, typing, proofreading, or writing of Chinese characters. As for Chinese scholars, he would always insert the Chinese characters after the romanization. His respect for others and his sincere modesty contrasted with the style of earlier Western sinologists such as James Legge in the nineteenth century, who never mentioned a word about the numerous Chinese scholars who had collaborated with him.

Although my volume on paper and printing was not co-authored with Needham but included in his series, it was positively reviewed. One book review from the *London Times* commented that my work gave a thorough account of the topic and it would no doubt be well-received. As part of the *Science and Civilization in China* series, it was to become a classic. According to a report from Cambridge University Press, the book was sold out before its publication in 1985, a second printing came out in 1986, a third revised edition in 1989, with more reprints since then, and it remains the best-selling book in the series. Because readers on this topic are wide-ranging, the book will serve as an eternal memorial to him.

First Honorary Degree from the U.S.

One of the most unforgettable events was his visit to the United States, which he considered to be the happiest and most symbolic among the many trips he took late in life. This visit transpired some thirty years after he had left the U.S. to study and teach. By then he already had received over ten honorary degrees from many countries throughout the world, but not a single honorary degree from an American university.

The story began in 1976, when the University of Chicago proposed to invite Needham for a lecture and to confer an honorary doctoral degree on him in recognition of his outstanding contributions to international scholarship. There were several problems, however. First, the nominees were usually young scholars, as a way to encourage their continued excellence in their fields, and Needham was already over seventy-five years old. His nomination was further complicated by politics, due to his charge that the United States had used germ warfare during the Korean War. This statement, in addition to his opposition to the Vietnam War, had placed his name on the blacklist of the U.S. government.

After the University of Chicago decided to confer the degree on him, I was asked to write to see if he would be interested in coming to the United States. He replied immediately that he would be happy to come but that there might be complications in obtaining a U.S. visa. He enclosed a letter signed by the American senator William Fulbright inviting him to come to the U.S. as a major speaker at the thirtieth anniversary celebration of the Fulbright-Hayes Act organized by the U.S. congress, a trip for which he was denied a visa. He wrote, "If my American friends invite me to the U.S., I hope they would first clear the way with the American State Department." After negotiations between the University of Chicago Board of Trustees and the State Department, he was finally able to come with Lu Gwei-djen to the United States.

In mid-June of 1976, the University of Chicago conferred on Joseph Needham an honorary degree of Doctor of Humane Letters at its graduation ceremony. In my speech to introduce him on behalf of the Department of East Asian Languages and Cultures at the ceremony conferring the honorary degree, I said:

Dr. Joseph Needham has made outstanding double contributions to international scholarship. He is a biochemist, and his chemical embryology paved the ground for this field of study. He is also the founder of the historical study of Chinese science and technology. His thirty-plus volume work of Science and Civilisation in China *makes an immortal contribution to twentieth century scholarship. His analysis of the convergence of heaven and man in Chinese philosophy helped to explain hitherto little known Chinese science*

THE AUTHOR WITH LU GWEI-DJEN AND NEEDHAM

and technology, much of which was borrowed in the West. His research has impacted the world, and he is the greatest scholar who has introduced Chinese culture to the world, a rapidly growing field internationally.

His trip to the U.S. was undoubtedly successful and important. He was welcomed not only by the American scholarly community, but also by other cultural organizations and business groups. Because of the mass media coverage, his activities in the U.S. were followed widely. These events could be considered a correction to the attacks and prejudices he had suffered in the past. After that point, the door of the United States was reopened to him, and he was invited many more times to visit, give speeches, and to mobilize financial support so that his research projects and new research institute buildings could receive funding from American foundations, financial groups, and businesses.

Translated by Diana Chen Lin of Indiana State University and published in the Journal of East Asian Libraries, *no. 146, October, 2008.*

18

Professor Tung Tso-pin (Dong Zuobin 董作賓, 1895–1963) came to the University of Chicago in 1946–1948 to assume the Visiting Professorship of Chinese Archaeology in the Department of Oriental Languages and Civilizations. For two years he was honored and acclaimed in the American academic world before he returned to China in the fall of 1948. The experiences he gained in the United States during this period were considered among the highlights of his academic career and life.

I came to the University of Chicago from China in the fall of 1947. With the help of Professor Tung, I obtained accommodations in the same house at 6137 S. Kenwood Avenue, where he resided during his stay. This house belonged to a graduate student of the University and was later sold to Mrs. Graham, who lived with her daughter Fern. Working with him in the same building at the university and sharing our leisure time together, I had the privilege of his friendship over that year.

Daily Life at the University

On my first day in the Oriental Institute building, as I began to enter my office in room 226, I saw approaching me an elderly Chinese gentleman of medium height with wind-blown hair, dressed in a brown suit with a bronze-colored necktie. He was holding a teapot in his hand, looking serene and amiable. Seeing that I was about to knock at the door, he greeted me by saying: "Are you Mr. Tsien? I heard that you would be coming in today." Then he introduced himself "I am Tung Tso-pin. My office is just next door, room 230. Please come over and have some tea with me a little later."

Even though I had heard his name when I was in China, we had never met. My first impression of him was that he was gentle, cordial, and sincere. At noon that day I stepped into his office. He was busy cooking Chinese noodles over a hot plate. There was an aroma of spice and garlic. He told me that he had to cook his own food because he was not accustomed to the cafeteria food in the States. He insisted that I should have a bowl of noodles, too. Though I could not refuse his hospitality, I doubted that he was supposed to be cooking in the office. The office was very spacious with a large desk in the center of the room. Scattered over the desk were books, manuscripts, and various kinds of drawing paper, on some of which were unfinished calligraphy with shell-and-bone inscriptions. On the back of the desk was a long table with books on one end and an electric plate on the other. I was amazed by the fact that there was a canvas bed in front of the desk. I had never before considered whether it was customary to sleep in one's office in America.

Yes, the freedom of a professor is respected and protected in America, especially the freedom of a visiting professor from another country to live how they so choose. In this case, his office served as a combination study and living room. He arrived at the office around ten in the morning. There he worked, interviewed, dined, and rested until he went home late at night. He spent over twelve hours a day in this overseas *pinglu* 平盧, or "ordinary cottage," as he modestly referred to his office.

T. H. TSIEN AND TUNG TSO-PIN

Course Work

Professor Tung offered four courses at the University of Chicago: "Research in Ancient Chinese History" in the spring quarter; "Research in Chinese Archaeology" in the summer, 1947; and in the winter quarters of that year and the next, he collaborated with Professor H. G. Creel in offering "Bronzes of the Zhou Dynasty" and "Chinese Paleography." Mr. Tung prepared his own lecture notes, dictographed from his own handwriting, and lectured in Chinese with assistance from Dr. Creel and Miss June Work, an assistant to Dr. Creel.

There were three or four graduate students who did research work under him, including John H. Dyer, Charles O. Hucker, and William J. McCoy. Mr. Hucker continued his work in Taiwan and Japan after receiving his doctorate in Chinese from the University of Chicago. He was the chairman of the Department of Far Eastern Languages and Literatures at the University of Michigan and later at the University of Arizona, and one of the most active sinologists in America. Mr. McCoy wrote a master's thesis, "Some principles of evolution in form as found in the bronze inscriptions of the Zhou dynasty," which was completed in 1948. Mrs. H. G. Creel (Lorraine), also a Chicago Ph.D. in Chinese, often came to consult Mr. Tung for her research on bone and bronze inscriptions. She reconstructed over one hundred pieces of fragmented bones, although her work remains unpublished.

At that time there were other students, including Arthur W. Hummel, Jr. and John A. Lacy, who were doing Chinese studies, specializing in Ming, Qing, and modern history; all of them had some association with Mr. Tung. Mr. Hummel, Jr., the son of Arthur W. Hummel, Head of the Orientalia Division at the Library of Congress, worked at the State Department after graduation and became the second Ambassador to China in the 1980s. Mr. Lacy was Consulate-General in Hong Kong and Singapore after graduation from the University.

Research and Studies

Professor Tung's research work during his stay in America consisted of two phases. Primarily, he continued his research on bone inscriptions and a Chinese chronology. In addition to that, he conducted research on the history of Chinese painting. A student at the University of Chicago had bought a Chinese scroll in Beijing right after the Second World War and brought it back to America. One day he showed the scroll to Mr. Tung, requesting him to give an evaluation, as an art museum had offered to buy it if it was genuine. When Mr. Tung saw the painting, he could hardly let go of it, for it was not only the world-famous scroll "Spring Festival at the River" 清明上河圖 (Qingming shanghe tu) supposed to have been painted in the Song dynasty, but it was also a panorama of the city Kaifeng, where he had spent his childhood years.

He asked me to find for him in the Chinese library all the references relating to that scroll. When he went to New York City later, he made a special trip to the Metropolitan Museum of Art and found several hand copies of this painting. Later on he found two more copies in U. S. private collections. He compared and studied them carefully. Then he took the original painting for his examination to be photographed in sections. He counted some 1,162 people in the scroll and made an analytical study of their costumes, poses, and distribution in the painting. He also made notes of the houses, decorations, boats and carriages, utensils and implements, recreation activities and performances, store signs in the market place, and other details. With these notes, he proceeded to do an enormous amount of painstaking research backed by historical references. The result was the book *Spring Festival at the River*, first published in Taiwan in 1953. The original scroll went with the owner when he left Chicago, and its whereabouts are since unknown.

Traveling

While in the United States, Professor Tung took several trips in which he visited sinologists in different colleges and universities, examined Chinese collections in major libraries and museums, and toured scenic spots and factories. In the summer of 1947, he visited Dr. Homer H. Dubs, an authority on Shang chronology, at Hartford Seminary. In September, he took a trip to the Library of Congress in Washington, D.C. During the Christmas vacation of that year, he invited me to accompany him to Washington, D.C., New York City, and New England to visit Columbia, Harvard, and Yale Universities. Mr. Tung so enjoyed seeing his old friends that he lingered long with each visit. He took his third trip in the summer of 1948 to New York, where he toured the Ford Automobile factory and saw Niagara Falls, from which he wrote a long letter to me with great excitement.

Collections

Professor Tung was interested in collecting practically everything and working on calligraphy. His collections included Christmas and New Year greeting cards; different kinds of bottles, cans, boxes; or even pieces of paper with artistic appeal. As for calligraphy, his specialty was writing in the shell-and-bone style. He used pieces of colored paper for his calligraphy, then he framed, and gave them as gifts. Dr. Hu Shi 胡適 once remarked that very rarely did he not see the bone inscription calligraphy of Mr. Tung in the homes of Chinese and American friends when he traveled from coast to coast in America.

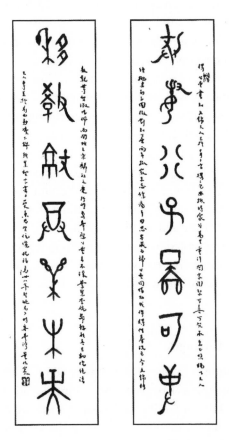

ORACLE BONE INSCRIPTION SCROLL BY TUNG TSO-PIN

After he returned to China, he favored me with letters, books, poems, and calligraphy for occasional and seasonal greetings. What I treasured most was a pair of scrolls that he sent me on that first Christmas after he arrived in Taiwan, after learning that my wife and children had joined me in Chicago. The scrolls read: "Desertion of the family is excusable; Family reunion will certainly be happy forever," with the following postscript: "I was happy to learn from your letter that Wen-ching (Mrs. Tsien) and your three children have gone to Chicago to join you. My hearty congratulations to you on this joyous reunion. Your quoting of Wen-ching's comment 'Photo of Deserted Wife and Children' on the recent family reunion picture shows that the sadness and loneliness which you suffered in the absence of your family still lingers in your memory. I am most grateful that sympathetically you helped me join my family in China. I admire the wisdom and devotion of Wen-ching in making it to Chicago. She is a match for the wives of many of our friends. Now you can rejoice with them for many days of wedded bliss in the future. The scrolls serve as my congratulations to you, sent from Taiwan, on the night before Christmas in the year 1949. Signed, Tung Tso-pin."

Prior to my leaving Shanghai to come to the United States, I accompanied my family to Guiyang, where they were to stay with my mother and my brother's family. Later, my wife sent me the family picture taken at my departure with the comment "Picture of Family Desertion" 抛妻別子圖. I showed it to Mr. Tung and we both lamented over this for a long time, since he was also separated from his family. In 1949, my family joined me in Chicago, and his family went with him to Taiwan. I sent our new family picture with the old comment to amuse Mr. Tung, hence the scrolls and the postscript.

Friends in Chicago

The names mentioned in the postscript were some of his friends in Chicago. At that time there were about sixty Chinese scholars at the University of Chicago. His wit and humor brought a sparkle to any gathering. He gave several lectures on the discoveries at the Yin ruins and on Shang writings to this group of Chinese scholars in Chicago.

In December 1948, he flew back to Shanghai with the hope of returning to the States with his family at a later date, but for some reason this
plan never materialized. He continued to send me letters, books, magazines, and inscriptions written in his own handwriting. His friendship and
devotion reflected what he wrote in my album before he left Chicago, "A
friend in need is a friend indeed." This may be about his only handwriting
in English, written with a Chinese brush, and left to be treasured by the
admirers of a scholar of our times.

BRUSH WRITING BY TUNG TSO-PIN

Published in the Newsletter of the Midwestern Student
and Alumni Association, *n.s., v. 10, no. 1, January, 1967.*

19

YUAN TUNG-LI AND INTERNATIONAL EXCHANGE

In the course of modern Chinese library development, Yuan Tung-li (Yuan Tongli 袁同禮, *t.* Shouhe 守和, 1895–1965) was the indisputable leader of his time. He not only excelled at both Chinese and Western modes of learning, but he was also endowed with foresight and vision in the realms of management and public service. These qualities enabled him to combine a traditional Chinese background with the best qualities of Western library management as he guided the direction of the modern Chinese library movement and laid the foundation for the National Library of China. His outstanding contributions included the planning and overseeing of construction of the National Beiping Library built in the 1930s, featuring both Chinese and Western elements of design. He also widely collected Chinese and Western books for the collection, hired top professionals from different disciplines, and emphasized research and publication as an integral aspect of the National Library. These qualities enhanced the Chinese library's importance in both international scholarly development and cultural exchange.

Hosting Foreign Scholars and A Research Center

Mr. Yuan possessed a unique scholarly breadth and talent for establishing both institutional and personal relationships with foreign scholars. Many of the Western scholars who returned to their home countries left with a deep empathy for China that would be reflected in their writings or other contacts with China. In particular, the older generation of Western scholars who studied in China enjoyed a feeling of being "home away from home," because of Mr. Yuan's cordial and hospitable nature.

The first generation of American scholars who established sinological studies arose only during the 1930s. At precisely this time, Mr. Yuan was presiding over the freshly established National Beiping Library. Under his direction, the library operations became ever more efficient. As the National Beiping Library had a rich collection of books as well as wonderful facilities, it was an indispensable resource for sinologists and graduate students who came to study in China.

The many American and European scholars hosted by Mr. Yuan included John K. Fairbank of Harvard University, Herrlee G. Creel at the University of Chicago, Derk Bodde of the University of Pennsylvania, Homer Dubs, the translator of the *History of the Han Dynasty*, Arthur W. Hummel of the Library of Congress, and the writer Pearl Buck. Furthermore, Wolfgang and Herbert Franke from Germany, Walter Simon from Britain, André Dubosque from France, and Lionello Lanciotti from Italy all developed a deep affection for and friendship with Mr. Yuan through their scholarly contacts. The National Beiping Library at this time was the focal point of international sinological studies, but its role could not be separated from Mr. Yuan's generosity and expertise.

Acquisitions and Publication Information in Foreign Libraries

Around the 1930s, there were about twenty Chinese libraries in the U.S., including those at the Library of Congress, Columbia University, Cornell, and the University of Chicago, which received assistance from the National Beiping Library with their book purchases. At the time, a most effective deputy in external relations was Mr. T. K. Koo, who used the name of Datong Bookstore to help several American libraries acquire books and periodicals. With awareness of particular fields of emphasis, he would purchase for each library on the basis of its research needs. He would add a 10% service charge to the actual price and used the bookstore's surplus to buy books and other materials for his own library, the National Beiping Library.

The Far Eastern Library at the University of Chicago was a good example of how its core collection was built with the help of the National Beiping Library. Because the University chose pre-modern Chinese history as its focus for teaching and research, most of the early acquisitions were traditionally designed books, many of which were excellent editions of top quality from private collections. Starting from 1936 until 1947, there were almost 70,000 volumes in the library, including 20,000 volumes in Chinese, Japanese, Manchu, Mongolian, and Tibetan purchased from the Berthold Laufer collection of the Newberry Library in Chicago. Among these materials, the section on the Classics was the strongest and should rank as the premier collection in the West. There were few duplications, and the collection was well represented in all categories.

In order to provide news of Chinese publications and scholarly activities for both domestic and foreign scholars, Mr. Yuan started in 1934 the *Quarterly Bulletin of Chinese Bibliography* in both Chinese and English editions. The contents included articles, book reviews, introductions to new books and journals, special columns on academic news, and Chinese translations of Western books. Both editions placed particular attention on Chinese scholarly research results and the introduction of newly published books. Although Mr. Yuan initiated the journal, his name did not appear in the journal until it was resumed in Kunming from 1939, as the Managing Editor with me as its Manager, since it was actually published in Shanghai. Both the Chinese and English editions ended in 1947, when Mr. Yuan went abroad.

Chinese and Foreign Scholarly Exchange

Mr. Yuan cultivated his junior staff by sending them abroad for advanced professional training. Because of his international reputation and the friendships he had established with foreign librarians and scholars, he was able to recommend more than ten staff members to go abroad for advanced training on exchanges or fellowships. These staff members eventually were to have an enormous impact on the future development of both Chinese and foreign library enterprises.

The earliest agreement Mr. Yuan signed with an American institution was with Columbia University, which involved having a member of the National Beiping Library staff work at the university library and simultaneously take advanced courses at its Library School. Each staff person was to stay for two years. He also set up similar arrangements with the Library of Congress and several other universities, including for Yan Wenyu 嚴文郁, Wang Zhongmin 王重民, Yue Liangmu 岳良木, Li Fangfu 李芳馥, Zeng Xianwen 曾憲文, and others. I was perhaps the last staff member who came to the U.S. under this arrangement.

Among those dispatched to Europe on such exchanges were Wang

Zhongmin to France, and Xiang Da 向達 and Yu Daoquan 于道泉 to Britain, as well as the aforementioned Yan Wenyu to Germany as well as the States. Among the Europeans who came to the National Beiping Library to study were Dr. Walter Simon from Germany and Mlle. Marie-Roberte Dolléans from France. Both Mr. Wang and Mr. Xiang brought back from Europe considerable materials related to the treasures of Dunhuang, and their writings opened the entirely new fields of Dunhuang studies and the history of Sino-Western cultural exchange. Their work indeed was of long-lasting importance. But it was Mr. Yuan who early on saw the importance of Chinese documents and records that had been scattered abroad, and it was his foresight and vision to dispatch scholars to go to these countries to study them. Thus in the promotion of Chinese scholarship, his contribution was enormous.

Foreign Language Materials and Microfilming Rare Books

The National Beiping Library inherited from the former Imperial Library much of its book collection, most of which consisted of rare editions. As a national library, it was tasked with collecting publications from countries around the world. Early in the establishment of the library, Mr. Yuan set up an office for international library exchange to collect foreign library publications to bolster his library's holdings; at the same time he sought to purchase foreign government publications, reports from academic organizations, conference records, and even entire sets of scientific and technical journals, as well as academic journals and special monographs relating to sinology and Oriental Studies written in Western and Japanese languages. It was extremely difficult to collect complete sets of sequential publications; nevertheless, the National Beiping Library possessed no fewer than several hundred such academic publications, many of which dated from the early nineteenth century. Hence, when the rare books were moved south in 1934, entire sets of these academic journals also accompanied them southward for the sake of safety.

During the war, with the Library's headquarters moving to Kunming, Mr. Yuan kept in touch with the British and American embassies and received books as well as instruments from these two countries' aid program for China. Moreover, using his title as the Chairman of the Board of Directors of the Chinese Library Association, he wrote for aid to various library associations, universities, and academic and cultural organizations of various countries. The library associations of the United States and Britain immediately responded by initiating a book acquisition campaign and before long gave several tens of thousands of books and periodicals to China. The British for their part also contributed cash for the purchase of books and instruments. All of these accomplishments can be traced back to the institutional and personal friendships Mr. Yuan established with foreign libraries and sinologists, which helped engender this outpouring of enthusiasm.

Moreover, Mr. Yuan reached an agreement with the Library of Congress to receive the National Beiping Library's rare books, which had been previously stored in Shanghai for temporary safekeeping and to make microfilm copies for permanent preservation and usage accessibility. Begun in 1942 and finished in 1946, this microfilming work amounted to 2,500,000 pages, resulting in 1,070 reels of microfilm that measures 101,920 feet. The master copies were deposited at the Library of Congress with three sets of positive films presented to China. There are no fewer than 200 important libraries in various countries around the world that have such sets. The fact that such rare treasures have been preserved through the ages and can be consulted with ease for research throughout the world is truly a gift brought about by Mr. Yuan's foresight.

Bibliographies and Academic Exchange

Mr. Yuan's publications consisted primarily of textual studies, research on lost works, and compilations of bibliographies. Among the Chinese publications are included his investigation of the extant volumes of the *Yongle Encyclopedia*, research on private library holdings during various dynasties, and editing of the *Collectanea of Materials on Xinjiang*. After his arrival in the U.S., he compiled several bibliographies in Western languages on China and the doctoral dissertations of Chinese students in the U.S. and Europe. He also tracked down the Chinese names of Chinese authors who used only Western names, a feature not often found in other bibliographies. The most important of his publications in Western languages can be grouped under the following three categories:

1. General bibliographies:

a)   *China in Western Literature 1921–1958*. New Haven, 1958; This was a supplement and continuation of the *Bibliotheca Sinica* by Henri Cordier, listing some 18,000 monographic works in English, French, and German.

b)   "Sinological Literature in German, 1939–1944," Quarterly Bulletin of Chinese Bibliography, n.s. 7 (1947): 21–64; *Russian Works on China, 1918–1960*. New Haven, 1961.

2. Specialized bibliographies:

a)   *Economic and Social Development of Modern China: A Bibliographical Guide, 1918–1960*. Lists monographs, pamphlets, journals, and reference books in English, French, and German that relate to statistics, economics, finance, regional studies, and social development.

b)   *T. L. Yuan's Bibliography of Chinese Mathematics, 1918–1960*. Provides materials for research into the history of Chinese science.

c)   *The T. L. Yuan Bibliography of Western Writings on Chinese Art and Archaeology* (London, Mansell, 1975). Contains 1,500 monographs and articles in Western European and Russian languages on calligraphy and painting, architecture, sculpture, ceramics, bronze objects, engraving, and crafts. The materials originally collected had a cutoff date of 1955, before the author died. Subsequently, Professor Harrie Vanderstappen of the Art Department at the University of Chicago updated it to 1965. I added an introduction to its contents and to Mr. Yuan's contributions to Chinese studies through his compilation of many bibliographies.

3. Bibliographies of doctoral dissertations by Chinese students abroad:

a)   *A Guide to Doctoral Dissertations by Chinese Students in America, 1905–1960*. Contains 2,779 titles, 1,914 of which were in the fields of science, engineering, and medicine; those in the humanities and social sciences numbered 875 titles.

b)   *Doctoral Dissertations by Chinese Students in Great Britain and Northern Ireland, 1916–1961*. Contains 346 titles.

c)   *A Guide to Doctoral Dissertations by Chinese Students in Continental Europe, 1907–1962.* Contains 1,574 titles.

From these last three bibliographies, we know that during the fifty to sixty years of the first half of the twentieth century, no fewer than four to five thousand Chinese students received their highest academic degrees in Europe and America, which contributed significantly to China's modernization. Mr. Yuan's investigation and listings are the most detailed and important records of this kind.

Translated by Tsing Yuan from Biographical Literature, *68:2 (February, 1996), with modifications by Ma Tai-loi.*

Wu Kuang-tsing (Wu Guangqing 吳光清, h. Ziming 子明, known as K. T. Wu), was the first Chinese scholar to use English in all of his writings on Chinese librarianship and one of the earliest Chinese to receive the highest degree in library science. He was also a pioneer who assumed major positions in national libraries in both China and the United States. His fluency in English enabled him to propagate to the Western world the history of Chinese scholarship, printing, publishing, and the development of libraries. He was kind, modest, dependable, and tolerant—a prototypical Chinese gentleman.

K. T. Wu was born December 5, 1905, in Jiujiang, Jiangxi Province. After graduating from primary school there, he was admitted into the Middle School of the University of Nanking (Nanjing University), where he was formally enrolled in 1923, majoring in education and English, with elective courses in library science. He was an excellent student and graduated in the fall of 1927. After teaching at a middle school for the next two years, he obtained a fellowship from the Carnegie Foundation in 1930 to study library science at Columbia University, where he received his B.A. in 1931. He went on to the University of Michigan for graduate study and received an M.A. degree in library science in 1932.

After returning to China, he was appointed the Librarian of the Ginling Women's College from 1932 to 1935, before assuming the position of Head of the Cataloguing Department at the National Beiping Library, and editorship of its library journal. In 1938, with the financial support of the Rockefeller Foundation, he came to the Oriental Department at the Library of Congress as an intern. Later, he was admitted to the Graduate Library School at the University of Chicago for the doctoral program, specializing in the history of printing under William Butler, an authority on this subject. He received his Ph.D. degree in 1944, becoming only the third Chinese Ph.D. in library science.

He continued to work at the Library of Congress in charge of Chinese reference books and cataloguing. His *Chinese Books Classification,* compiled in 1945, was adopted by the Library of Congress for cataloguing Chinese books until 1957, when the *Classification System of the Library of Congress* was adopted for cataloguing books in all languages. In 1966, Dr. Wu became the Head of the China/Japan/Korea section in the Oriental Department, a position he held until his retirement in 1975. He worked at the Library of Congress for thirty-seven years, and after retirement, he was appointed an honorary consultant of Chinese bibliography for another three years.

Dr. Wu's writings can be divided into two periods: work published in China and abroad. His first paper in English was published in 1929 in an English quarterly in Shanghai. In 1935, at the invitation of the Chinese Association of Library Science, he wrote and published a comprehensive history of Chinese libraries in English to commemorate the association's tenth anniversary. He then became a chief contributor to the English monthly *Tien Hsia,* edited by Lin Yu-tang in Shanghai. Most of his publications in America appeared in the *Harvard Journal of Asiatic Studies* and publications through the Library of Congress. Later, his publications were mostly work-related, including annual reports of the Library of Congress collections.

Dr. Wu's doctoral dissertation, entitled "Scholarship, Book Production and Libraries in China, 678–1944" included ten chapters in about 100,000 words. Besides the introduction and conclusion, other chapters covered the period from the Tang to the Ming Dynasty, public and private book collections, publishing, and textual criticism, which made it the first Chinese intellectual history in English and a significant work for the study of Chinese cultural history.

I began studying at the University of Nanking in the summer of 1927, as well as working in the Ginling Women's College Library. At that time Mr. Wu was nearing graduation. He was a classmate and good friend of my older brother T. D. (Qian Cundian 錢存典, 1905–1992) from high school through college, and my academic mentor. Wu helped me not only with my scholarly work, but also with my job, as he introduced me to T. L. Yuan (Yuan Tongli 袁同禮, 1895–1965), Director of the National Beiping Library, who offered me the directorship of its Nanjing branch in 1937 and later transferred me to its Shanghai office for ten years. After I came to work and study in the U.S. in 1947, he also gave me much assistance and encouragement. He read my Ph.D. dissertation and other manuscripts before publication, and I dedicated my book *Paper and Printing* in the *Science and Civilisation in China* series to my three advisers, including K. T. Wu.

Upon my retirement, he sent a telegram in which he wrote: "By happy coincidence, our schooling at Nanking and Chicago, our professional service in bibliographical history, are almost identical." Actually, we have had five things in common: we both graduated from the University of Nanking, both worked for Ginling Women's College Library, both were on the staff of the National Beiping Library, both received a Ph.D. degree from the Graduate Library School of the University of Chicago, and both shared an interest in the history of Chinese books and publishing. Indeed, not only were our academic and work careers similar, but our work and research interests were very close, too.

Besides our common professional interests, we were also very close friends. His wife, Amy Chen, was introduced to him by my wife Wenching and myself. In 1949, Amy came to the U.S. from Japan to study at the College of Education in Chicago. Her former colleague in Tokyo and our good friend, Mr. Liu Linsheng 劉麟生, asked us to look after her, and it so happened that at the same time K. T. Wu was looking for a girlfriend. They eventually became lifelong partners. Mrs. Wu is a multi-talented woman and used to work for the federal government in the field of education.

Dr. Wu led a very healthy lifestyle, but later in life he began fainting often, which his doctors could not explain. He died in October 1998 at the age of 93. A special memorial service was held for him by the Library of Congress in 2000 during the annual meeting of the Association for Asian Studies in Washington, D.C.

LIST OF PUBLICATIONS by K. T. Wu

Compiled by Ming-sun Poon

1929

Wu, K.T., "A Brief Study of Chinese Lexicography," *China Journal of Science and Arts* 11 (1929), 169–172.

1936

Wu, Kuang-tsing, "The Chinese Book: Its Evolution and Development," *T'ien-hsia Monthly* 3 (1936), 25–33, 137–160.

Wu, Kuang-tsing, "The Development of Printing in China," *T'ien-hsia Monthly* 3 (1936), 137–160.

1937

Wu, Kuang-tsing, "Libraries and Book-collecting in China Before the Invention of Printing," *T'ien-hsia Monthly* 5 (1937), 237–260.

1940

Wu, Kuang-ts'ing, "Cheng Ch'iao, A Pioneer in Library Methods," *T'ien-hsia Monthly* 10 (1940), 129–141.

Wu, Kuang-tsing, "Color Printing in the Ming Dynasty," *T'ien-hsia Monthly* 11 (1940), 30–44

1943

Wu, Kuang-ch'ing, "Ming Printing and Printers," *Harvard Journal of Asiatic Studies* 7 (1943), 203–260.

1944

Wu, Kwang Tsing, "Scholarship, Book Production, and Libraries in China (*618–1644*)", Thesis (Ph.D.)—University of Chicago, Graduate Library School. 291.

Wu, K. T., "Books on East Asiatic Music in the Library of Congress: Works in Chinese," Compiled and annotated by K. T. Wu; in Hazel Bartlett, *Catalogue of Early Books on Music (before 1800)—Supplement (Books Acquired* by the Library 1913–1942) with a List of Books on Music in Chinese and Japanese (Washington, D.C., U.S. Government Printing Office, 1944), 121–131.

1945
Wu, Kuang-ch'ing, *Books on East Asiatic Music in the Library of Congress Printed Before 1800,* Washington, D.C., U.S. Government Printing Office, 1945. 121–133.

1950
Wu, Kwang-tsing, "Chinese Printing Under Four Alien Dynasties (916–1368 AD)," *Harvard Journal of Asiatic Studies* 13 (1950), 447–523.

1952
Wu, Kuang-tsing, "The Development of Typography in China During the Nineteenth Century," *Library Quarterly* 22 (1952), 288–301.

1955
Wu, K. T., "China (Annual Report: Library of Congress)," *Library of Congress Quarterly Journal* 12 (1955), 59–64.

1961–1969
Wu, K. T., "Report on Orientalia: China," *Quarterly Journal of the Library of Congress* (February 1961–April 1969).

1969
Wu, K. T. and S. Sakanishi, "A List of Books on Music in Chinese [by K. T. Wu] and Japanese [by S. Sakanishi]"; in Julia Gregory and Hazel Bartlett, *Catalogue of Early Books on Music (Before 1800),* New York, Da Capo Press, 1969. *Notes: Prepared under the direction of O. G. Sonneck. This Da Capo Press edition is an unabridged republication, in one volume, of the 1913 Catalogue and of the 1944 Supplement.*

MEMOIR OF A CENTENARIAN

FRIENDS AT A DINNER IN CELEBRATION OF THE AUTHOR'S CENTENARY BIRTHDAY
(*from the right: Ching-Mei Tsia, Ted Foss, author, Hui-Xin Lei and Mrs. Wang; standing: Ming-Sun Poon, David Tsai, James Cheng, Chester Wang, Tai-loi Ma, Preston Tobert, Yuan Zhou, Hui-Chun Lei, and Xiaowen Qian*)

21

EARLY YEARS IN CHINA

I lived my youth in China during an era of social transformation, political corruption, and revolution. This was the time of the overthrow of the last imperial dynasty and the establishment of a republic. Shortly afterwards, the country was carved up by warlords, and civil wars spread throughout the nation; while the foreign powers looked on, China faced extinction. Social values were undergoing reassessment and the traditional family system was crumbling apart. My youth was spent under one of the darkest ages in Chinese history.

I was born during the reign of the last Emperor of the imperial dynasty. According to the lunar calendar, my birth fell on the first day of the twelfth month of the first year of the last Manchu emperor, which, according to the Gregorian calendar, was January 11, 1910. Since the Chinese custom at that time favored the lunar calendar, I reported December 1, 1909 as the birth date in my passport, and it has become my official birth date.

Family Background

Many people in China would recognize my family as being descendants of a royal family, or a family of distinguished scholars. According to the Qian family genealogical records, the founder of the family was Qian Liu 錢鏐 (852–934), King of the Wuyue Kingdom, one of the ten kingdoms established in the tenth century after the fall of the Tang dynasty. Qian Liu was well versed in both the arts and military affairs. He brought the most prosperous region in China under his control, including present-day Jiangsu and Zhejiang provinces, and part of Anhui province on the eastern coast. It was not until the reign of the fifth ruler that the kingdom united with the central government of the Song dynasty. The Qian family controlled this region for nearly a hundred years. It became a model for the peaceful unification of the country, and is praised as such to this day. It also explains the large number of memorial halls dedicated to King Qian in the famous West Lake area in what was then the capital city of

PORTRAIT OF QIAN LU   SEAL OF WUYUE   QIAN FAMILY TEMPLE
                   KINGDOM

Hangzhou, as well as in many other parts of China. These were the stories I learned as a boy; they taught me patriotism and family pride.

As for the well-known family of scholars, my great-grandfather, Qian Guisen 錢桂森 (1827–1899), successfully passed the highest imperial examinations as a *jinshi* scholar in 1850. Among the posts he held were those of Junior Editor of the Imperial Hanlin Academy, Vice Minister of the Department of Rites, Education Commissioner of Anhui province, and Examiner in six other provinces. Many important personages, including an early President of the Republic and several provincial governors, were his students.

STONE RUBBING OF A POEM WITH CALLIGRAPHY BY QIAN GUISEN (1831)

Qian Guisen was the author of several works, including the *Yisong-xuan shigao* 一松軒詩稿, his collected poems, and *Duan zhu Shuowen kao* 段注說文考, a critical study on the *Annotations of the First Dictionary*. He was the owner of the famous private library of the Jiaojing Tang 教經堂 (Hall of Teaching Classics), which was noted for its collection of rare

FAMILY RESIDENCE IN TAIZHOU, NOW DESIGNATED AS A CULTURAL RELIC

editions. The ancestors of this branch of the Qian family originally lived in Henan Province but later moved to Hailing 海陵 (present day Taizhou 泰州 in Jiangsu Province). The biography of Qian Guisen can be found in several sections of the municipal records of the *Taizhou Gazette*. An honest and upright official in the national government, he also participated in local affairs and was praised by the local people. For that reason, the street on which our ancestral home stood was known as "Excellency Qian's Boulevard." This building, my family's former residence and my birthplace, was designated by the municipal government of Taizhou for preservation as a cultural relic in 1988 and re-dedicated by municipal dignitaries in 2008.

Taizhou is now no longer a small town but a major industrial city on the north bank of the Yangtze River. My family's old residence is located on the northeast corner of North Hailing and Dongjin Roads near the city center. The house will be restored to its original form together with other nearby residences as a historic area for tourists. When the project is completed, my family's books, documents, and artworks of historic significance will be restored and exhibited in the house.

My grandfather, Qian Xiheng 錢錫恒 (z. Zijiu 子久) died at a young age. His brother Qian Xitong 錢錫彤 (z. Qisi 屺思) was an excellent calligrapher and painter. My father, Qian Weizhen 錢慰貞 (z. Ganting 幹庭, 1883–1931), was an only child who was recognized as the son and heir of both the two brothers' families. Later in life, he studied Buddhism under the Buddhist Elder Taixu 太虛, a most respected Buddhist scholar, and edited the Buddhist journal *Haichao yin* 海潮音 (*Voice from the Sea Tide*), which he founded. My mother, Xu Zhuanshi 許篆詩 (1884–1970), a beautiful lady from a famous Hangzhou family, was a dutiful wife and mother who raised her children and educated them in preparation for their careers in this time of transition.

Mine is the 35th generation of the direct descendants of King Qian Liu. There were eight siblings in my line: five boys and three girls, and all shared the middle character *tsuen* (chun or cun 存, "to preserve") in our given names. We had formerly lived together in one household in Taizhou, but eventually no one was left in the ancestral home. Thus, my generation witnessed the break-up of China's tradition of the large multi-generational family living under one roof.

My eldest brother T. D. Tsien (Qian Cundian 錢存典, 1903–1992), graduated from the University of Nanking (now Nanjing University) in 1927 and won top place in the first National Civil Service Examination offered by the Nationalist government in 1928. As the first-place winner of this prestigious competition, he was appointed in 1929 to the position of Personnel Director in the Foreign Ministry. In 1936, he was assigned to the Chinese Embassy in Great Britain, where he was promoted to First Secretary and then Cultural Attaché. In 1947, he was appointed to the Chinese Embassy in India as *chargé d'affaires* and then Ambassador *ad interim*.

My second brother Chien Chun-mo (Qian Cunmo 錢存謨, 1906–

2002), was Assistant Manager of the Bank of China's Tianjin Headquarters. I was the third son of the family. My fourth brother, Chien Chun-kao (Qian Cungao 錢存誥, 1913–2008), was also a banker, serving as manager of the Bank of China of Guiyang city. My fifth and youngest brother, Qian Cunxue 錢存學 (1923–), was an activist in the student movement in Shanghai against the corrupt Nationalist government in power in the late 1940s. Later, he spent a number of years in Europe, first as the Vice President of the International Students' Union and later as a Deputy Director and member of the Chinese delegation to UNESCO under the new government.

FAMILY GATHERING IN NANJING, 1931 (*author at the far right*)

My eldest sister, Chien Chun-shu (Qian Cunshu 錢存淑, 1902–1956), married a landowner from the Taizhou countryside. During the anti-Japanese War of the 1930s, the whole family, numbering over a dozen people, fled from the cities to take refuge in her home, narrowly avoiding being victims in the Nanjing Massacre. My second sister, Chien Chun-shen (Qian Cunshen 錢存慎, 1916–1947), married a diplomat and lived for many years in the Philippines, Australia, and India. She died young after an unsuccessful operation. My youngest sister, T. R. Tsien (Qian Cunrou 錢存柔, 1918–), is a retired Professor of Microbiology at Peking University (Beijing University). Her husband, the late Professor Xing Qiyi 邢其

毅 (1911–2002), a noted chemist, was a member of the Chinese Academy of Sciences and twice served as a member of the Chinese People's Political Consultation Conference.

Beginning with my generation, my siblings and I gradually left our ancestral home and moved elsewhere to study or work. Eventually, my parents also moved away from Taizhou and lived in various parts of the country, including Nanjing, Shanghai, Guiyang, Tianjin, and Beijing, following their children. From this time on, the Hailing or Taizhou branch of the Qian family scattered all over the country or abroad.

Early Education in China

I first studied under a private family tutor and then attended the Taizhou County Primary School. In 1922, I entered the Huaidong Middle School, now known as Taizhou Middle School. (The Chinese President Hu Jintao 胡錦濤 is an alumnus of the class of 1959). The years during my studies were full of national tragedies. In this fiery atmosphere, I joined a group called the Youth Society and served as editor-in-chief of the *Youth Fortnightly*, a periodical advocating national revolution. As a result, I was arrested together with the headmaster of the school by troops of the warlord in Taizhou. The headmaster was executed. I was spared because my family bribed a corrupt officer, who set me free on condition that I leave Taizhou.

As I could no longer live in my hometown, I decided to join the Nationalist Revolutionary Army. On the Northern Expedition from Nanjing to Beijing, we overpowered the warlord, and our garrison was stationed in the palatial domicile of a former prince near the Imperial Palace. We then moved to a town outside of Tianjin and engaged in propaganda work.

Eventually my eldest brother called me back in 1927 to study at the University of Nanking (now Nanjing University), where he was appointed the new registrar after his graduation, so he was able to pay my tuition. He also arranged a part-time job for me at the library of the nearby Ginling Women's College, where I earned 25 cents an hour for my living expenses. The curator of the library went abroad to study, and the president of the college appointed me the Acting Head of the library, which was a very positive step for my future career.

DRAWING BY THE AUTHOR OF GINLING WOMEN'S COLLEGE FIGURES (1930)
(*from right*): MINNIE VAUTRIN, DEAN; TSENG HSU-PEI, PROFESSOR;
WU YI-FANG, PRESIDENT; MS. SPALDING, PHYSICAL EDUCATION DIRECTOR;
MS. KU, DORMITORY WARDEN

While I was working at Ginling Women's College, I was permitted to take courses there for credit at my university. I decided to take one course in translation, taught by Tseng Hsu-pei (Zeng Xubai 曾虛白, 1895–1994), a noted journalist. For class I translated Bertrand Russell's "Differences of Happiness between the East and West" and Dorothy J. Orchard's "China's Use of the Boycott as a Political Weapon," both of which were later published in popular periodicals and stimulated my further interest in translation.

The University of Nanking was one of several missionary universities in China founded by the United Board of Christian Higher Education in New York City. My major was history, and I minored in library science. Besides the required courses in Chinese, English, mathematics, and sciences, I took a number of courses offered by Dr. M. S. Bates (Cambridge), including European history, history of Russia, history of India, and history of Japan. I also took such elective courses as Chinese philology, philosophy, political science, sociology, and history of books, as well as other courses in library science. The combination of my studies in history and library science furthered my interest in research for my graduate studies and greatly influenced my career.

The University of Nanking was the first university to offer courses in library science in China. Such courses were first taught in 1913 by Harry Clemens, the university librarian, former Reference Librarian of Princeton University and Director of the University of Rochester Libraries. He trained a number of China's early specialists in the field. In 1927, the Department of Library Science was formally established at the University, and I was one of the first students enrolled in the department.

My overall college grades were average, but outstanding in library sci-

FIRST LIBRARY SCIENCE CLASS OF THE UNIVERSITY OF NANKING (1927)
(*Author second from left in the front row*)

ence. One class paper on "Libraries and Scholarly Research" was published in 1931 in the *Journal of the University of Nanking, Division of the Humanities* and it became my first published paper. It was later selected for a collection of works by former staff members in celebration of the 75th anniversary of the National Library that was published in 1987. The editor made special mention of this article in his preface, saying: "Tsuen-hsuin Tsien's essay was a class paper, but his description of the functions of scholarly research and the library has stood the test of time and still has practical value today. It goes to show that the author, though still a youth at the time, already held mature views of scholarship in library science."

Five Years at National Jiaotong University

After I graduated from the University of Nanking in the spring of 1932, I was recommended to Mr. Du Dingyou 杜定友, Director of National Jiaotong University Library, who put me in charge of books in Western languages. During my years at National Jiaotong University, I compiled its cataloguing rules for Western-language books and published its *Catalogue of Books in Western Languages* in five volumes. In 1932, Mr. Du established the China Library Service, which specialized in selling college textbooks and books on library science, as well as library supplies and furniture. He asked me to be the manager of this business. Every day after my library work, I had to go from the western suburbs to the office, located in the city center of Shanghai, where I gained much of my business experience. Three years later, I left the position, which was taken over by a man who later established his own press, the Longmen Bookstore, which has become a major publisher in China.

AUTHOR (*left*), LIU GUOJUN AND DU DINGYOU ON A TRAIN (1932)

Mr. Du had a quick mind and was a fluent and prolific writer. In 1936, he published a monograph, *Du's Collected Writings*, of which I was editor and contributor of an article on his writings. At that time, he had already published ten monographs and over two hundred articles. His productivity no doubt influenced my later interest in writing.

My Family Life

While I worked in Shanghai, I was able to visit my mother every weekend in the nearby city of Suzhou, where she lived after my father died in 1931. There I met Hsu Wen-ching (Xu Wenjin 許文錦 1906–2008), who later became my life-long companion for over seventy years. I made the two-hour train trip from Shanghai to Suzhou every weekend. She loved new literature, especially by the noted woman writer Bingxin 冰心, who later became my relative, the aunt of my youngest sister-in-law. So I often brought books by many modern authors for her to read. For my return trip to Shanghai, she would send along all kinds of famed Suzhou delicacies.

Wen-ching had a very good memory and recalled many interesting stories from her earliest years. For example, she remembered when she was two years old, playing with a balloon while in her mother's arms. Suddenly, the balloon burst and she began to cry. Her mother comforted her

AUTHOR AND HSU WEN-CHING IN SUZHOU (1933)

and promised to buy her more balloons. She said such is a mother's love. She lost her mother at the age of nine. After that, she became "hostess" for her father, a high government official who often entertained guests.

She was such a gifted child that her father was her personal tutor. Not only was her calligraphy excellent, but she could also compose poems with couplets in a traditional style that had very strict rules. It was said that when she was ten years old, sitting at the dinner table as her father was entertaining guests, he suddenly pointed to a bowl of dried lilies, known as *jin zhen cai* 金針菜, "Golden needle vegetable," and asked her to match it in a couplet. She instantly replied *yu zan hua* 玉簪花, "Jade hairpin flower," pairing precious material to precious material, needle to needle, and vegetation to vegetation. All the guests were amazed at her quick response and talent.

Not only was Wen-ching the top student in all of her classes at school, but she also excelled in oration, dancing, and acting. Unfortunately, she lost her father at the age of eighteen, and then she took on the additional responsibility of raising her brothers and sisters, so she did not enjoy the normal life of other teenagers.

As I continued to visit Suzhou over five years, Wen-ching and I grew very close. On August 31, 1936, we were married in the chapel of Ginling Women's College. We began our married life back in Shanghai in the attic of a house where we lived for one year before I left for another job in Nanjing. Over the next few years, we had three daughters: Ginger (Xiaoqin 孝芩), born in 1937 in Nanjing; Gloria (Xiao-E 孝峨), in 1941, and Mary (Xiaoyue 孝岳), in 1944, both born after we returned to Shanghai.

Work at the National Library

In 1937, I received an offer from the National Beiping Library for a position as the Head of the Nanjing Engineering Reference Library, which was set up by the National Library in 1934, when the Japanese invasion of North China was imminent. The office was located in the newly built Institute of the Academia Sinica. The holdings of the Nanjing library consisted of entire sets of periodicals on science and technology and several thousand volumes of reference materials on engineering, as well as over seven thousand old maps formerly belonging to the imperial cabinet. Only a week after I had begun work at the Nanjing Library, Japanese troops crossed the Marco Polo Bridge into North China, and fighting soon erupted in Shanghai and Nanjing.

The headquarters of the National Library in Beiping was moved south to Kunming in Yunnan province, while the Nanjing Branch Library was ordered to close. I was then transferred to the Shanghai Office, which had also been established as one of the branches of the National Library in the south. I arrived in Shanghai in the spring of 1938, when Shanghai had already been occupied by Japanese troops, except in the foreign concessions due to the interests of the Western powers. Refugees were crowded into there, prices of commodities skyrocketed, and housing was especially hard to come by. Japanese influence was everywhere, but communication with free China via British Hong Kong and the hinterland were still intact.

The Shanghai Office was located in the French Concession, where some ten thousand volumes of complete sets of periodicals in foreign languages were housed. In addition, over 60,000 volumes in 5,000 titles of Chinese rare books, 9,000 rolls of manuscripts from Dunhuang, and numerous pieces of bronze inscriptions and stone rubbings were stored in a warehouse in the International Settlement. In addition to preserving rare books, the Shanghai Office was also responsible for the acquisition of rare and unique editions of old books on the market, publishing the *Quarterly Bulletin of Chinese Bibliography* in both Chinese and English editions, and collecting the publications by the Japanese occupation forces that were to be transferred to the Library headquarters in free China. In order to avoid

AURORA UNIVERSITY

CHINESE SCIENCE SOCIETY, SHANGHAI
OFFICE OF THE NATIONAL LIBRARY
(1934–1945)

the attention of the Japanese and its sponsored government, everything was done surreptitiously.

The mood in Shanghai's foreign concessions became increasingly tense. The rare books moved to the south were no longer safe. Library

Director T. L. Yuan in free China contacted the U.S. Library of Congress through the Chinese Embassy for permission to ship the rare books in Shanghai to the U.S. for safekeeping.

In early 1941, the Library of Congress agreed to send a staff member to select a total of 2,720 titles in some 30,000 volumes; these consisted of 200 volumes printed in the Song and Yuan Dynasties, about 2,000 volumes from the Ming Dynasty, and 500 manuscripts, most of which were from the former Imperial Library. They were packed into 102 wooden crates lined with metal sheets to protect the volumes from moisture.

My Fortune Foretold

I lived under harsh circumstances in Shanghai under Japanese occupation for five years. Prices soared from morning to evening. All daily necessities were rationed with coupons. My salary at the National Library was insufficient to support my own family, let alone the expense of caring for nearly a dozen other relatives under my care. So I had to work several other jobs concurrently to earn enough money to support my large family.

Every day I felt depressed and that the future was hopeless. In early 1941, a friend of mine told me that his father, Pan Yuqie 潘予且, a well-known author in Shanghai, was also a gifted fortune-teller. He offered to predict my future. So I gave him the year, month, day, and time of my birth according to the Chinese calendar. Soon, a sheet was returned with his calculations, as follows: ". . . This year (1941), summer is not as good as the coming winter (夏不如冬). Wait patiently for change. Age 42 surely gains satisfaction (當然得意). Age 46 sees a brighter career (事業更見輝煌). Age 52 will step up to a much higher level (層樓更上) . . ."

At that time I thought fortune-telling was merely superstition and useless for solving problems, so I ignored the predictions and set it aside.

One day after I came to the States, by chance I found an envelope in an old folder with handwriting on it that said: Stay Relaxed and Anticipate a Better Life (居易以俟) by Hall of Flower Dyke Surrounded with Water (水繞花堤館) with the predictions on a sheet of decorated letter-paper inside. The fortune-teller's predictions seemed to match the events in my life almost exactly. For example, he wrote: "For this year (1941), summer is not as good as the coming winter." It happened that in the summer of 1941, shipping the rare books to the U.S. for safekeeping, which became the major accomplishment of my career in China, appeared hopeless; but the task was accomplished—albeit inadvertently—that very winter. As for the ages of 42 and 46, they were the years that I would receive my two advanced degrees and progress in my career. At age 52, I was promoted to

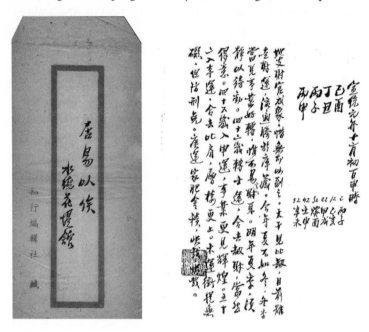

ENVELOPE AND FORTUNE-TELLING SHEET (1941)

full professor at the University of Chicago.

In accordance with the predictions, my fortune improved every ten years of my life: I received my university education in 1927; started to work in the National Library in 1937; came to the U.S. in 1947; received my Ph.D. in 1957; was invited by Professor Joseph Needham to join his research project in 1967; received two grants from the National Science Foundation and the National Endowment for the Humanities in 1977; was invited by the National Library of China to participate in the celebration of its 75th anniversary and entertained as a guest of high honor in 1987; was named a distinguished alumnus by the University of Chicago in 1997; and was honored with the opening of the T. H. Tsien Library at Nanjing University in 2007. It seemed every major promotion or honor matched the fortune-teller's calculation in 1941.

Later, I read an article by Dr. Ho Peng-Yoke (He Bingyu 何丙郁, 1926–), a noted scientist and successor of Dr. Joseph Needham as Director of the Needham Research Institute, in which he asked: 'Is fortune-telling a school of science?' He answers: "Fortune-calculation is based on the principle of Chinese traditional Man-Nature theory . . . an operation to predict future happenings . . . such as weather forecasts, prediction of the financial market, or national elections, etc. . . . It is the same as religion for advising people to be good. . . ." (*Science and Culture in Ancient China: Selected Works of Ho Peng-Yoke*, Liaoning, 2001, 522–538). Therefore, I wish to add this story of fortune-telling to my memoir as a prediction of my life before and after coming to the United States.

PHOTO OF "DESERTED WIFE AND CHILDREN" (1947)

22

ARRIVAL IN CHICAGO

In 1947, after the war against Japan had ended, I was assigned by the Ministry of Education to bring the rare books back to China that had been shipped from Shanghai in 1941 for deposit at the Library of Congress in Washington, D.C. Just when all of the preparations were being completed, civil war broke out and the return of the books was cancelled. As a result of the travel interruption, I accepted an invitation from the University of Chicago and settled down in the Windy City, where I have lived ever since.

Exchange Scholar from China

In 1947, the University of Chicago asked the National Beiping Library to recommend one of their experienced staff members to come to Chicago to catalog the University's Chinese books, collected from China beginning in 1936. With the recommendation of the Library Director, T. L. Yuan (Yuan Tongli 袁同禮, 1895–1965), I received an invitation from the University to work in its Far Eastern Library as an exchange scholar for two years with permission to take courses in the Graduate Library School for advanced studies. This arrangement was to begin immediately.

Professor Herrlee G. Creel of the Department of Oriental Languages and Literatures of the University of Chicago, who invited me to the U.S., was the earliest sinologist in America to specialize in ancient China. He had spent three years in China studying Chinese history and philology. When he returned to the U.S in 1936, he initiated the teaching program in Chinese and founded the Far Eastern Library at the University of Chicago.

After accepting the offer from the University, my first task was to make arrangements for my family in Shanghai. Because my appointment was temporary, and because very few Chinese scholars took their families overseas at that time, I made plans to send my wife and our three daughters to Guiyang to be taken care of by my younger brother, who was the local manager of the Bank of China. He had a spacious residence on the scenic bank of the Yangming River, where my mother had relocated.

However, Wen-ching had collapsed from exhaustion during WWII and was bedridden for two years after victory. She had taken care of dozens of people of all ages in our large family during the war, and due to the stress, as well as lack of adequate nutrition, she fell seriously ill. Nevertheless, when I was ready to leave for the U.S., though physically weak, she agreed to be separated for two years. I escorted her and our three girls from Shanghai to Chongqing by plane and then by car to Guiyang. After two weeks in Guiyang, I went back to Shanghai alone and prepared for the journey to the U.S. Before my departure, we took a family picture together and Wen-ching wrote on its back: "Photo of Deserted Wife and Children." These few bitter words left me feeling selfish and full of regret for the rest of my life.

In mid-September 1947, I boarded the transport U.S. Marine Swallow in Shanghai, bound for the U.S. with hundreds of other Chinese scholars and students on board. After experiencing stormy weather at sea for fifteen days, I arrived in San Francisco on October 1st. Then, after another three days and two nights on the transcontinental train of the Western Pacific Railroad, I finally arrived in the largest city in the Midwest.

Upon arrival at the University of Chicago campus, I was put up at the Brent House, a church dormitory in the neighborhood. Then I moved to

CHINESE STUDENTS AND SCHOLARS ON THE MARINE SWALLOW (1947)

a rental house at 6133 South Kenwood Avenue. The bedrooms were upstairs, with a living room downstairs that was shared by all residents. The landlady served breakfast in the morning, and I had lunch and dinner at the campus cafeteria. At that time, a sandwich cost twenty-five cents and two quarters could buy a good meal. Every day I made the long walk to my office at the Oriental Institute on East 58th Street.

On the first day at the Oriental Institute, I met Mr. Tung Tso-pin (Dong Zuobin 董作賓, 1895–1963), who came from the Academia Sinica of China in 1946 as a visiting professor in the Department of Oriental Languages and Literatures. His office was two doors from mine in Room 226. He usually arrived at work at 10AM and went home at 10PM. I used to chat with him during breaks, and since he was the one who referred me to the house on Kenwood where he resided, we would walk back there together in the evening. He visited the East Coast twice to meet old friends in Washington, D.C., New Haven, Boston, and New York City. I was always his companion and translator, and we became very close friends.

A year later, in 1948, Mr. Tung went back to China and I moved to the International House on campus, where many Chinese students and visiting scholars stayed. It was a period of political crisis in China. Many residents at the International House met daily to discuss the domestic situation. Some were preparing to return to China. Others who could not were facing great hardship since domestic support was cut off. Later, the American government helped: for those who planned to go back, the U.S. State Department provided travel expenses; for those who chose to stay, it provided tuition and living expenses so they could continue their studies. I considered going back, but the University convinced me to stay.

Permanent Residence in the U.S.

I worked full-time in the Far Eastern Library while taking courses in the Graduate Library School. I had planned to return to China after two years. But after the first year, Professor Creel asked me to extend my stay and teach part-time in the Department of Oriental Languages and Literatures. Although the offer was attractive, I had little interest in accepting and was planning to go back as soon as possible. But Mr. Creel had already received approval for the extension of my stay from the National Library. However, I felt very hesitant to stay for many reasons.

First, my original status was on official business, having been sent to the U.S. by the Chinese government. Although the mission had been cancelled, I still held an official passport with a temporary visa in the U.S. Mr. Creel had telegraphed me that he would apply for a work visa for me, but I replied that all plans for coming to Chicago were already under way. At that time, friends back in China had told me that an official passport was the most convenient, with which I could either work or study in the U.S. But it was a benefit offered only during wartime to U.S. allies and cancelled when the war was over. Therefore, with the status of a foreigner on an official passport, one could not work in the U.S., nor could one receive a salary. As a result, Mr. Creel paid my living expenses for the first year at the University out of his own pocket. This made me feel very embarrassed. Second, my family was temporarily staying with my brother in Guiyang after I came to the U.S. The photo of "Deserted Wife and Children" came to mind time and time again. I had promised to go back in two years and I was determined to keep my word.

Third, even though I was able to bring my family to the U.S., I had no money for their travel expenses. Furthermore, renting an apartment was difficult not only because of racial discrimination, but also because families with children were not welcome. After listening to my concerns, Mr. Creel promised to take care of all the issues.

He arranged with an attorney at the University of Chicago, through Illinois Senator Paul Douglas, to introduce a special bill in Congress that would grant me permanent residence status in the U.S. American immigration law was very strict then, and only two kinds of foreigners could work in the U.S.—pastors or professors. After the permanent residence bill for me was passed, to qualify for this, the University of Chicago offered me the title of Professorial Lecturer in the Department of Oriental Languages and Literatures and Curator of the Far Eastern Library. In addition to an annual salary of $4,000, the entry-level pay for an Assistant Professor, the University also paid for my family's travel expenses from China. Looking back, this offer was the best that could be expected at that time, but I wasn't completely happy and accepted reluctantly.

American immigration law then stipulated that the status of a person could not be changed after arriving in the U.S. Therefore, one had to leave the country and get a new visa before returning. To meet this requirement, Mr. Creel arranged with the University of Toronto to invite me to give a lecture. Afterwards, I could visit the Royal Ontario Museum in Toronto to see its rare book collection as well as its shell and stone inscriptions that had been collected by the late Rev. Frank H. Chalfant. After two weeks, I could pick up the new visa from the U.S. consulate in Toronto to return to the U.S.

I obtained permanent residence status in June 1949, and immediately telegraphed my brother in Guiyang to send my family to the U.S. Unfortunately, it was the peak of the civil war, and all traffic in China was interrupted. It was not only difficult for anyone to leave the country but almost impossible to get out of Guiyang. My brother was busy evacuating his staff at the Bank of China, but when he received my message, he immediately turned his attention to making every possible arrangement for my family's departure. Quite unexpectedly, he discovered that there was a chartered plane scheduled to pick up the family of a high official of Guizhou province leaving Guiyang. With the approval of this high official, Wen-ching and our three daughters were permitted to board his chartered plane and get out of the city. The charter was a non-pressurized cargo plane with no passenger seats and they sat on wooden benches. My youngest daughter, Mary, cried the entire way from the pain in her ears. But my family and I felt extremely fortunate and grateful that they were able to leave.

The family first arrived in Canton in June, then transferred to Hong Kong where they stayed with relatives to await visas and a ship bound for the U.S. There were so many people trying to leave China that my family had to wait three months to secure passage on the ocean liner President Wilson, finally departing Hong Kong in mid-September 1949. After enduring storms at sea for two weeks, just as I had, they finally arrived in San Francisco. From there they boarded a transcontinental train and arrived in Chicago at the beginning of October. It was precisely the anniversary of my own arrival in the U.S. two years prior. We were overjoyed, having experienced inconceivable coincidences, ingenuity, and kindness on the part of friends and relatives that allowed us to meet again.

Life in Woodlawn and Hyde Park

Our daughters grew up in Shanghai and spoke the Shanghai dialect. After two years in Guiyang, they had picked up the Guizhou dialect. I did not expect that they would also learn Cantonese after staying in Hong Kong for only three months. When we saw each other again, we felt like strangers, speaking different dialects; our two years' separation had made a world of difference. The family reunion was the most joyful occasion in our lifetime. It was beyond all my expectations that the University not only paid for my family's travel expenses, but was able to settle us on the third floor of a newly-renovated university apartment near the campus at 6020 South Ingleside Avenue in the Woodlawn area. Our apartment was very spacious, with three bedrooms, a living room, a dining room, a study, and a large kitchen in a quiet neighborhood that rented for only $60 per month. For all this I felt very lucky and thankful.

FAMILY REUNION IN CHICAGO (1949)

In those years, the University neighborhood was quite safe. No one locked their doors at night. I usually took a walk with the family after dinner; we could see well-furnished rooms through the windows of brightly-

6020 INGLESIDE AVENUE, MY FIRST HOME IN HYDE PARK, CHICAGO (1949)

lit homes. The shopping center was nearby on 63rd Street, with a variety of shops, stores, restaurants, and movie theaters. My three daughters attended Fiske Elementary School one block away. Mrs. Ruth Mills, a former missionary to China, tutored the girls in English. During the eight years of the war against Japanese aggression, we had fled from one place to another and lived a homeless life with a dozen of my family and relatives. Now we finally had a place of our own to settle down. These were the most peaceful and happy days of my life.

Though I was extremely busy with my work and studies, I was able to take the family shopping or go to the movies during the weekend. Every Friday, we would see the classic movies from the '40s and '50s. We also attended parties with friends and went on picnics or took part in other activities, such as picking soybeans on a nearby farm. At that time, very few families owned a car, and we had to depend on those families with transportation for our many outings.

After two years, we were able to buy a second-hand Pontiac. During the summer, we went touring around. The place we most frequently visited was Canada, since it was quite convenient to cross the border without a visa or passport. And from time to time, there were Chinese expositions there, such as the World's Fair Expo in Quebec and the Chinese Science and Technology History Exhibit in Toronto. On our way, we visited scenic spots and museums on the East Coast and in the Midwest. We especially enjoyed Niagara Falls, where we lingered over its magnificence and beauty.

Looking back, I cannot help but be extremely grateful to Professor Creel for his arrangements. His fervent commitment to help us not only changed my life and career but also created opportunities for my family to work and study. Beginning in 1953, Wen-ching worked in the Far Eastern Library for three years. In 1957, she was recruited to teach modern Chinese in the Department of Oriental Languages and Literatures for five years. Wen-ching was beloved by her students for her thorough knowledge of Chinese culture and language; her humor and patience with American students who had difficulty picking up this exotic language is remembered by her former students even today.

My three daughters all graduated from the Hyde Park High School. When they attended college, the University waived half their tuition since I was a faculty member. Ginger, my eldest daughter, received her degree in Biopsychology at the University, and worked as a research assistant in Otolaryngology in the University Hospital under world-renowned Drs. César Fernández and Jay M. Goldberg. Gloria, my second daughter, studied fine art and fashion design at the School of the Art Institute of Chicago, in a joint academic program with the University of Chicago. She exhibited her dynamic and colorful abstract paintings both in the U. S. and China. Mary, the youngest, received her BA and then her MAT in Russian on a Ford Fellowship at the University. She taught Russian at the University Laboratory School for nine years and was selected to be a participant on several teaching exchanges to the Soviet Union. On the U.S. government-sponsored International Research and Exchange program at Moscow State University, she met and later married Alexander Dunkel, a professor of Russian at the University of Arizona. After Mary moved to Arizona, she worked as the Marketing Director of Tucson Pepsi-Cola. So my daughters covered the fields of science, art, linguistics, and business through the education they received in Chicago.

HYDE PARK HOME

In 1961, we purchased our first home in Hyde Park, a cooperative townhouse designed by I. M. Pei when he was with the firm of Harry Weese as part of the Hyde Park Redevelopment Project. I still live in this house; the neighborhood now well known because President Barack Obama and his family own a home there.

After-Hours Activities

During the war when I lived in Shanghai, I seldom attended any group activities. After coming to the U.S., I started to follow the progress of the Chinese political situation in discussion groups and other organizations. Early in 1949, I joined the American Association of Overseas Chinese Scientists to assist Chinese scholars and students in the U.S. to return to China. Many of them who could not leave found it difficult to work and study in this country because they had no way to deal with illness, accidents, or other misfortunes. In 1959, I joined the reorganization of the Midwest

Newsletter of the Midwest Chinese Student & Alumni Services

New Series, Vol. IX, No. 2   January, 1966

WISHING

YOU

A

HAPPY

AND

GALLOPING

YEAR

A poem in her own handwriting by Chang Ch'ung-ho 張充和 (Mrs. Hans Frankel), a most talented scholar, poet, calligrapher, painter, and opera singer. She performed a K'un-ch'ü play at the International Art Fair in Chicago a few years ago. Her paintings have been exhibited at several art museums in this country. She now lives in California, where Dr. Frankel is a professor of Chinese literature at Stanford University. Above is her picture (right) taken at the Berkeley campus with her old schoolmate, Mrs. Tsien, to whom this poem is written.

MIDWEST CHINESE STUDENTS AND ALUMNI SERVICES NEWSLETTER

Chinese Students and Alumni Services (CSAS), originally a missionary group, to assist in solving such problems. This organization also published a newsletter, organized musical concerts, and sponsored a summer family camp to promote the welfare of the Chinese community. I was the Director for two years (1966–1968) and the editor of the CSAS Newsletter for ten years. This was the only social welfare organization for Chinese in America, until CSAS closed down in the 2000s.

Although I did not know much about the arts, I became involved after I came to the States. In 1948, when I resided at the International House, I sponsored an exhibit of brush paintings with a demonstration by Wang Jiyuan 王濟遠 (1893–1975), then president of the Shanghai Institute of Fine

Arts. In 1950, I sponsored another exhibit by David Kwo (Guo Dawei 郭大維 1919–2003), a student of the internationally renowned painter Qi Baishi (齊白石, 1864–1957). His paintings were exhibited at the Art Institute of Chicago, and I wrote the preface to his first album of paintings. Later I arranged a joint exhibit for him and my daughter Gloria in Montgomery Hall at the University of Illinois. The exhibit was very well received by visitors and art critics alike. I also sponsored shows for several other noted artists, including Huang Junbi (黃君璧 1898–1991) from Taiwan, Chiang Er-shih (Jiang Eshi, 蔣諤士 1913–1972) of Paris, and Zhao Shao'ang (趙少昂 1905–1998) from Hong Kong, a member of the Lingnan School of Painting, which introduced modern ideas into traditional Chinese art.

After Wen-ching arrived in Chicago in 1949, she was invited to join a Christian fellowship on the University campus. This group later formed a congregation with Sunday services in a nearby church. In 1955, the Home

CHRISTIAN REFORMED CONGREGATION

Mission of the Christian Reformed Church sent Rev. Isaac Jen to establish a church and be the full-time minister. I was baptized in this church in 1959. After Rev. Jen left for an assignment in Taiwan, Rev. Paul Han from California became the pastor. He bought an old building on 52nd Street and Cornell Avenue, which was later demolished. A new building was completed in 1973, and that is where it stands today. When Rev. Han retired in 1985, he was succeeded by other Chinese ministers. Following Wen-ching's lead, my family and I were among the first to become members of this church.

STUDENTS AT THE HYDE PARK CHINESE LANGUAGE SCHOOL (1960)

In the mid-1950s, Wen-ching organized a Chinese Language School in the church building to teach children of the Chinese community spoken Chinese, reading, writing and calligraphy, with songs, speeches, and other performances in Chinese on Saturday mornings. There were about 50 students in the school, divided into six classes. She was the headmaster for ten years with other members in the community serving as teachers or music directors. A parent-teacher meeting was held every quarter; students would exhibit their calligraphy, give speeches, perform songs, and demonstrate the Chinese language skills and knowledge acquired in these Saturday classes. The Chinese community in the Chicago area and elsewhere in the U.S. embraced this pioneer school that taught the heritage and culture of the homeland in America.

Founded in 1928, the University of Chicago's Graduate Library School (GLS) from its inception had been accredited and considered a leading institution of librarianship. The emphasis of the School was on research rather than merely training students in library techniques. Programs were organized along the lines of academic disciplines in the humanities, social sciences, and science and technology. It was also the first library school to confer doctoral degrees in library science, beginning in 1928. The GLS required full-time students to take 18 courses with a thesis to complete a master's program and another nine courses in residence with a dissertation for the Ph.D. degree. In my case, due to the demands of full-time working and teaching, I could only take one course each quarter with a total of four courses each year, including the summer. As a result, it took me five years to receive my M.A. in 1952, and five more to obtain my Ph.D. in 1957.

JOSEPH REGENSTEIN LIBRARY, WHERE THE GLS AND
FAR EASTERN COLLECTIONS WERE LOCATED

Inspired by my undergraduate course on the history of Chinese books at the University of Nanking, I decided to focus my graduate studies in Chicago on the history of books and printing. My very first mentor was Professor Pierce Butler, whose work *The Origin of Printing in Europe* was the classic in its field. However, he retired the year after my enrollment in 1947. At that time the library science program was experiencing a

AUTHOR AFTER RECEIVING HIS PH.D. (1957)

transition from the humanities to social sciences, so the courses shifted emphasis to such fields as textual readability, content analysis, statistical application, and mass communication. In the 1950s, the emphasis shifted again to computer technology. Because the University established the Department of Computer Science, and for various other reasons, the GLS was closed in 1994.

Among many notable GLS faculty members under whom I studied was Herman H. Fussler, the Library Director and a pioneer of the preservation of library materials in microform. I took his course "University and Academic Libraries" in order to better understand the functions and operations of the University Library where I was working. With Leon Carnovsky, I took "Library Survey," which I later applied to my surveys of East Asian library resources in America and Europe since 1959.

Lester Asheim was another instructor whose courses on content analysis and mass communication taught me new research methodologies. I used the quantitative method in writing my master's thesis, "Western Impact on China through Translation: a Bibliographical Study," in which I collected some 8,000 titles of Chinese translation of foreign books from the 16th through the 20th centuries for analysis of their original languages, subject matter, quantity and dates of translation, to interpret the motivations, influences, and intellectual trends prevailing at different periods of time in China. The abstract of this thesis was published in the *Far Eastern Quarterly* in 1954 with commendation by its editor as a new approach to the study of modern Chinese history.

Professor Howard W. Winger, who was my closest teacher, mentor, and friend, joined the GLS faculty in 1953 and offered courses on library history, the history of books, and history of printing. Upon his recommendation in 1962, GLS offered me a joint professorship and concurrently a position on the Editorial Board of the *Library Quarterly*, assisting him in reviewing submitted articles. He also helped me in supervising the Joint Program on Far Eastern Librarianship, of which I was Director in 1962; organizing the GLS annual conference on Area Studies and the Library in 1964; and assisting me as Director of the Summer Institute for Far Eastern Librarianship, supported by the U.S. Department of Education in 1969. At my retirement reception, he presented me with a woolen scarf that he had knit himself and recited a poem he had composed. His untimely death in 1985 was a shock to everyone.

Because my doctoral program was interdisciplinary, involving the GLS and East Asian studies, I also took a seminar with Professor Creel and wrote a paper on the classic *Zhanguo ce* 戰國策 (*Strategy of the Warring States*, 468–221 B.C.). Due to his influence, I shifted my interest to the study of ancient China and wrote my doctoral dissertation under his supervision.

Work in the Far Eastern Library

I spent the first ten years working in the Far Eastern Library almost single-handedly completing the cataloging of the entire collection of about 70,000 volumes. In 1958, financial support became available for expansion of the library resources, but the major supplier from China was cut off because the diplomatic relations between the U.S. and China had been terminated, and the anti-China atmosphere in the U.S. had grown worse. However, I did my best to acquire books from other sources to build up the library in Chicago, and it grew from a minor collection to a major center of East Asian studies in the U.S. It has since become a miracle in librarianship and been praised by the scholarly community around the world.

READING ROOM OF THE FAR EASTERN LIBRARY
IN THE REGENSTEIN BUILDING (1970)

The University's Far Eastern Library, now renamed the East Asian Collection, began in 1936 to meet the needs of teaching Chinese language and history. At the beginning, the focus of the acquisitions was on basic materials of the early period as well as general reference tools.

Instrumental in establishing the library was Professor Herrlee G. Creel, who emphasized the study of ancient China. As a result, the Chinese collection was especially strong in Confucian classics, and history, archaeology, local gazetteers, genealogy, and reference books on various subjects were all well-represented. With a Rockefeller Foundation grant, the Library was able to acquire some 1,000 titles in about 5,000 volumes annually, most of them in traditional thread-bound format. In 1945, the library acquired from the Newberry Library in Chicago approximately 20,000 volumes of books in Chinese, Japanese, Manchu, Mongolian, and Tibetan languages. With this acquisition the scope of the library collection expanded to include works in all Northeastern Asian languages.

Dr. Berthold Laufer, the renowned German sinologist, originally acquired the books purchased from the Newberry Library during his trips to China and Japan in the early 20th century on behalf of three Chicago libraries. After his return, books on science and technology went to the John Crerar Library and were later taken over by the Library of Congress. About 5,000 volumes of books on archaeology and 2,000 rubbings of Chinese bronze and stone inscriptions were offered to the Field Museum of Natural History in Chicago. The works in the humanities were placed in the Newberry Library. This was one of the earliest large-scale acquisitions of East Asian language publications in America. In those early days, however, very few people made use of these books, and there were no special personnel to take care of these collections. Thus, with the exception of the books and rubbings remaining in the Field Museum, other institutions eventually acquired the books in the Newberry Library and the John Crerar Library.

The primary part of the Chinese-language collection of the Far Eastern Library was acquired during the late 1930s prior to WWII with the help of the National Library in Beiping. Thus all titles of early acquisitions for the Chicago collection are basic and standard works for research, including a number of titles from notable private collectors. All books had thread-stitched bindings with fine quality paper and ink contained in blue cloth cases with handwritten titles. Book prices at that time were very low. On the average, a volume of Qing printing cost less than ten cents, until the late 1950s. Even during the 1960s, Ming editions cost only two to four dollars in Taiwan, Hong Kong, or Japan, when such books were prohibited for export from mainland China.

From 1958 until 1978, when I retired, the annual acquisition of new publications stood at about ten thousand volumes. According to the 1974–1975 survey, the Far Eastern Library collection of the University of Chicago contained some 300,000 volumes, with two-thirds of them in Chinese. The collection had more than quadrupled from the 70,000 volumes in the Library when I arrived in 1947. As compared with other major East Asian collections in American universities, the Chicago collection, which was founded much later than those at Harvard, Yale, Columbia, and Berkeley, ranked among the five largest East Asian collections in all U.S. universities, with many unique materials not found in other collections.

Rare Book Collections

The Far Eastern Library at the University of Chicago was especially strong in Chinese classics. This collection not only surpassed other libraries in the number of titles, but also contained a number of rare items, some of which are the sole surviving copies today. These rare titles were examined during the 1960s–1970s by experts in the field, including Peter Chang of the Palace Museum in Taiwan, and Shen Jin of the Shanghai Library (now at Harvard), who published abstracts of some of these rare titles in 1998. According to Shen's estimate at that time, the Chicago collection of Chinese Classics consisted of 91 titles on the *Book of Changes*, 80 on the *Book of History*, 109 on the *Book of Poetry*, 113 on the *Book of Rites*, 102 on the *Spring and Autumn Annals*, 16 on the *Book on Filial Piety*, and 297 in the *Four Books* section. Out of the thirty-two rare titles specially selected by him, eleven are not listed in the national bibliography of the Qing dynasty, and a number of titles are not in any current library collections in mainland China or Taiwan.

Among other materials in the Chicago collection were original editions of local gazetteers, the number of which ranked third behind the Library of Congress and Harvard at that time. The collection of local gazetteers of several particular provinces was especially rich, with 161 titles on Hebei, 153 on Zhejiang, 149 on Henan, and 106 on Shaanxi. The collection of genealogical publications also ranked third, behind Columbia University and the Library of Congress. Overall, the rare book collection in Chicago may not be the largest in terms of number of titles, but it includes some extremely rare material.

In total, the Far Eastern Library's rare book collection consists of more than 500 titles of Yuan and Ming editions in some 15,000 volumes (both in printed and manuscript form), and about 500 editions dating from the early Qing until 1795, in more than 7,000 volumes. All of these rare books have been examined and authenticated.

Laufer had purchased several rare works, including a Ming edition of the Buddhist Tripitaka and the *Collected Poems of Hang Huai* 杭淮, printed in the early 16th century with a seal of the Imperial Library in Manchu and Chinese characters and a handwritten postscript by the noted scholar Zhu Yizun 朱彝尊 (1629–1709), dated 1701. The Tripitaka set in 6,361 chapters is known as the *Northern Edition of Buddhist Sutras*, and has 7,929 volumes in 792 yellow silk brocade cases, dating from the 15th century. It was issued by the Imperial Court, with supplements dating from the 16th century. This collection in its entirety is very rare even in China.

One of the major acquisitions was from the private collection of the late professor Li Zongtong 李宗侗 (z. Xuanbo 玄伯, 1895–1974) of Taiwan University. This collection numbered more than two hundred volumes of Ming editions, manuscripts, and drafts. In addition, the collection has 528 letters of personal correspondence between Pan Zuyin 潘祖蔭 (1834–1890), the Minister of Works, and Li Hongzao 李鴻藻 (1829–1897), the Minister of Personnel; 201 telegram drafts by Liang Dingfen 梁鼎芬 (1859–1919), Surveillance Commissioner of Hubei Province; manuscripts by Zhao Liewen 趙烈文 (1832–1893), prefect of Yizhou; and a poetry manuscript by Weng Tonghe 翁同龢 (1830–1904), tutor to the Guangxu Emperor. Among other important materials in the Far Eastern Library are the *hishi* copies of rare Chinese books from collections in Japan.

Last but not least, the Library owns some samples relating to the early history of Chinese books and printing. For example, ten official sealing clays from the Han dynasty, dated around the beginning of the Christian era, were purchased from a private collector in Paris during my European tour in 1968. The Buddhist sutra printed in 956 by the Qian family and recovered from an old pagoda in Hangzhou is one of the earliest examples of printing; formerly owned by Kang Youwei 康有爲 (1858–1927), it was acquired in Hong Kong. The three rolls of the Buddhist sutra *Lianhua jing* 蓮華經, written in the 9th century and discovered in Dunhuang, was acquired in Taiwan. The Far Eastern Library also owns some loose-leafs of a Song dynasty printing; paper money printed in 1368; paper vouchers of the 19th century; and woodblocks used in printing the famous novel *Dream of the Red Chamber*. In addition, the library has 39 issues of the *Beijing Women's Daily*, a newspaper published by women for women during the 19th century. These rare materials came from various sources, with different provenances at the time of their acquisition.

Along with these are some three hundred souvenirs I collected during WWII in the 1940s in Shanghai. Included are items circulated by the Japanese army, such as ordinances, announcements, leaflets, slogans, posters, maps, military flags, paper money, ration coupons, and archives relating to the surveillance of foreigners by the Japanese military police in Shanghai, as well as documents from the Nanjing and Shanghai governments sponsored by the Japanese, and underground newspapers and propaganda materials. In addition, there are documents, paper money, stamps, and commemorative medals with Mao Zedong portraits from the Border Regions in the northwest under the control of the Communist party in the 1930s. Also included are propaganda posters and leaflets from student demonstrations and protests in Beijing and Tianjin during the years 1947–1948. These are all very rare materials vital to the study of the rise of the Communist Party in China.

Acquisitions During the Embargo

The main collection of the Far Eastern Library in the early days was books focused on the ancient period. However, after WWII, especially since the founding of the People's Republic of China in 1949, the scope of Chinese studies in American universities has greatly expanded from the areas of language, history, and philosophy to the social sciences, including contemporary politics, economics, social studies, law, and other subjects. The teaching and research trends in other disciplines required

LOTUS SUTRA, 9TH CENTURY MANUSCRIPT

these additional materials to meet the demands of different faculties and students.

Expansion in the scope of the collection was particularly necessary, as from 1958 the library began to receive substantial funding from the U.S. government, the Ford Foundation, and the University's special subsidies. While filling the gaps in the collection of classics, special efforts were made to acquire entire runs of periodicals, government bulletins, local documents, and works of social science and contemporary art and literature published since the 1920s. As for the publications from mainland China since 1949, acquisitions were made by way of book dealers and private collections in Hong Kong, Taiwan, Japan, and Europe.

From the 1950s through 1978, during my term as Curator of the Far Eastern Library, U.S.-China diplomatic ties were broken and acquisitions were severely challenged by the anti-China movement as a result of the Korean War. Any communication with mainland China was considered collaboration with the enemy. Library readers of books, periodicals, and newspapers published in mainland China were often under surveillance.

Communication between the United States and mainland China was completely severed.

Compounding the U.S. embargo against China and the blockade of communications between the two countries, the Library also faced difficulty in sending money to acquire publications. Any remittance sent to mainland China had to have the approval of the Department of Treasury and had to be a limited amount. Despite the complicated procedures, the Library was able to overcome various difficulties for acquiring important publications from mainland China.

Beginning in the late 1960s, the United States resumed contact with mainland China, but many important materials were prohibited from export by the Chinese side. It was impossible to acquire books published before the Republican period, even reprints or microform copies. As a former staff member of the National Library in Beijing, I was able to make arrangements with its International Exchange Bureau to establish an exchange program with publications of the University of Chicago Press. Even during the time of the Cultural Revolution in China, when all scholarly publications had completely ceased, the exchange on our part continued. In the 1980s, when directors of the National Library of China visited the University, they expressed special thanks to the University for our part of the contributions during that period. Consequently, the University of Chicago Library received on exchange more journal titles than any other institutions in the U.S.

Far Eastern Library Staff

Prior to my coming to Chicago, Prof. Creel had warned me that all the main tasks of the library would have to be done by one person, unlike in China where there were assistants. Thus, after I came to the Far Eastern Library, I was the sole staff member dealing with every aspect of the library's operation from cataloging and classification to writing and duplicating catalog cards, labeling, shelving, and answering reference questions. It was only after five years that my wife Wen-ching was added to the library staff to handwrite the catalog cards. Her calligraphy was admired and praised by colleagues in other libraries. She had worked in the library for three years (1953 to 1957) when she was appointed Lecturer of Chinese language in the Department of Oriental Languages and Literatures.

The year 1958 was crucial in the development of the Far Eastern Library; processing of the original collection was completed, and financial support became available. Thus, both the collection and staff of the Far Eastern Library were greatly expanded. By this time, the Far Eastern Library consisted of two major sections: Chinese and Japanese, plus the circulation desk. The number of professional staff had gradually increased to more than ten, including heads of each section and catalogers of different languages, with supporting staff in each unit and the circulation desk. At the time of my retirement in 1978, a total of over one hundred people had worked at one time or other in the Far Eastern Library. Among them were students in the Joint Program of Far Eastern Librarianship under my direction, whose work-study program was hands-on training in the Far Eastern Library.

During my tenure both in the Library and GLS, about 30 students received master's or doctoral degrees under this program and have taken various teaching or administrative posts all over the world. Among them are Lucie Cheng (1940–2010), former professor at UCLA and Director

WEN-CHING HSU WORKING IN THE FAR EASTERN LIBRARY
AT THE ORIENTAL INSTITUTE (1953)

of the Information School of the New World University and Proprietor of the Biographical Literature Co. in Taiwan; Shiow-jyu Lu, professor in the Department of Library and Information Science, National Taiwan University; James Cheng and Tai-loi Ma, now respectively heads of Harvard-Yenching Library and Princeton University's East Asian Library; Ming-sun Poon, together with David Tsai, Lily Kecskes, and Paul and Anna Ho, are senior staff members at the Library of Congress in Washington, D.C.

Students from other departments also worked at the Far Eastern Library for financial assistance while pursuing their advanced studies. Among them was Leo Ou-fan Lee, who became a professor of Chinese literature at Harvard University. In his book *My Years at Harvard* (Taipei, 2005), he wrote, "It was Professor Tsien, Curator of the Far Eastern Library at the University of Chicago, who had reserved a position even before my arrival, thus solving my urgent day-to-day financial needs . . . Prof. Tsien was not only my benefactor and inspiring teacher of Sinology, he was also instrumental in my successful application to Harvard; his letter of recommendation played an important role. With his 'authoritative' recommendation, I was equipped with the necessary qualifications to be a Ph.D. student in Chinese culture."

Services and Facilities

One of the most important tasks of the Far Eastern library was to respond to requests and inquiries of university faculty and students from various academic institutions. Even individuals and institutions in the Chicago area received assistance, including help with the translation of writings and reading seal inscriptions on paintings and calligraphic works.

The Far Eastern Library also published reference lists and book catalogs, including the Book List of New Publications, Chinese-Japanese Language Book Catalog (18 volumes with supplements), Catalog of Ikeda Bunko in Japanese, Catalog of Chinese local gazetteers, List of Far Eastern periodicals, Catalog of Exhibitions of Far Eastern Books in the University Library, and List of Doctoral Dissertations on East and South Asia. The Library has also compiled and published catalogs of materials in Manchu, Mongolian, and Tibetan.

The offices of the Far Eastern Library were originally located in the Oriental Institute, with space borrowed from the library reading room. The book collection was in the basement, exposed to dust and vermin, in a very limited space. In 1958, the Library was moved to the second floor of Harper Library with the addition of a Japanese collection, and later, a Korean collection. In 1970, when the new building of the Joseph Regenstein Library was completed, the Far Eastern Library moved again, this time to the fifth floor of the building, with spacious offices, temperature-controlled book stacks, a reading room, and seminar rooms.

Thinking back, these were acute reminders of the difficulties inherent in the development of the collection. Not only were library source materials scarce, but there were many restrictions in terms of their processing. It was particularly difficult to do everything manually, in contrast to the modern-day computerized processes.

The principle of collection development at Chicago has been based mainly on research needs. The selection of materials has had no political agenda or geographical bias. Over the years, many Russian scholars came to Chicago from faraway points in the former Soviet Union because they were unable to acquire books and journals published in Taiwan; or else scholars from Taiwan visited because they were unable to access recent publications from mainland China. Numerous scholars from around the globe benefited greatly from these overseas collections. In the future, researchers from both coasts will most likely continue to rely on materials in the overseas collections to gain a complete picture of Chinese publications.

AUTHOR AT WORK IN HIS REGENSTEIN OFFICE (1972)

24 TEACHING, RESEARCH, AND PUBLICATIONS

In 1949, I began teaching in the Department of Oriental Languages and Literatures at the University of Chicago. In 1958, the Department was divided into three entities: Far East, Near East, and South Asia, each with a newly established center for area studies. Far East then was changed to East Asia and later assumed the names "Department of East Asian Languages and Civilizations" and "Center for East Asian Studies." The Center includes faculty members in different departments who teach languages and literatures, history, political science, sociology, economics, art, and other subjects relating to China, Japan, and Korea.

I was promoted to Associate Professor in 1958 and to full professor of the Department of Far Eastern Languages and Civilizations and the Graduate Library School (GLS) in 1962. Also in that year, the Department and the GLS jointly formed the Center for Far Eastern Librarianship, and I was appointed its Director. I devoted half of my time to teaching and research and the other half to managing the library. In 1978, I retired from the Library, and the following year from the Department. Since then, my title has been Professor Emeritus of the Department of East Asian Languages and Civilizations and Curator Emeritus of the East Asian Library.

Beginning of Chinese Studies

The Department of Oriental Languages and Literatures of the University originally focused its program on the Near East. In 1936, the department expanded to include the Far East, when Herrlee G. Creel was appointed an instructor in Chinese with other faculty members added later.

The Chinese language class began with literary Chinese, using the textbook *Literary Chinese by the Inductive Method*, compiled by Creel and others in the Department. It consisted of three Chinese traditional primers, *Xiao jing* 孝經 (*Book of Filial Piety*), *Lun yu* 論語 (*Confucian Analects*), and *Mengzi* 孟子 (*Book of Mencius*). The beginning Chinese language class with *Xiao jing* and *Lun yu* and courses on ancient Chinese history and philosophy, were taught by Creel. The intermediate language class with *Mengzi* and selected reading of other classical works, as well as history of the middle period, were taught by Edward A. Kracke, Jr. The

EARLY FACULTY MEMBERS OF CHINESE STUDIES
AT THE UNIVERSITY OF CHICAGO (1947)
(*from right*) TENG SSU-YU, DR, AND MRS. EDWARD KRACKE, JR.,
DR. AND MRS. H. G. CREEL, WANG CHI-YUAN (VISITOR),
T. H. TSIEN, LUCY DRISCOLE (ART) AND VISITOR

advanced class on the modern period and courses on research methods were taught by Teng Ssu-yu (Deng Siyu 鄧嗣禹). Shortly after my arrival, Prof. Teng left the University, and I was asked to take over the two courses he had taught on Chinese bibliography and Chinese historiography.

The objective of the above-mentioned courses was to teach graduate students in Chinese studies how to collect source materials and write their theses, but Teng did not leave notes on the courses, so I had to create my own lectures. The University of Chicago has a quarterly system, with eleven weeks in each quarter. Accordingly, I prepared ten lectures with topics for each course and used the remaining week for review and examinations.

The Chinese bibliography course consisted of three parts: part one included the definition, scope, and functions of bibliography, history of the book, glossary, and terminology. Part two discussed methodology,

CLASSROOM DISCUSSIONS WITH GRADUATE STUDENTS
(*Author second from left against the blackboard*)

which included data gathering, the organization of sources, and writing style. The third part dealt with reference tools, including bibliographies, indexes, dictionaries, and collections to enhance the students' ability to utilize these reference materials. In addition to classroom discussions, each part also included assignments for practice.

The other course on Chinese historiography provided a systematic introduction to content in different types of historical documents, such as official histories, annals, chronicles, lists of officials, biographies, records on economics and finance, geography, and reference books. The two courses together offered the basic knowledge that would help students to select their thesis topics, collect sources, write outlines, compile bibliographies, and prepare to begin writing.

The courses began with choosing a topic, researching various bibliographies and indexes, verifying what others had already written to avoid duplication, or finding related topics for reference. Based on the number of primary sources gathered, the student could further expand or limit the scope and write the outline with sub-titles. He would then state the definition, scope, and importance of this topic, list the relevant reference materials, and compile a bibliography for the thesis in a standard style. These preparatory assignments, following the steps that had been discussed in the classroom, helped to formulate the thesis plan and eventually led to writing the thesis, after the Department's approval and oral examinations.

Most graduate students in the Department and the Graduate Library School, after taking these courses, were well-trained for writing their master's theses and doctoral dissertations. Students who had not been trained systematically were often in a hopeless tangle. This practical training saved them a lot of time. Thus from 1958 on, these courses were required for all doctoral candidates in the Department and the Graduate Library School, which incorporated the courses into their curricula.

Besides teaching the above courses, I also offered at least once other courses such as "Chinese Literature in Translation," "Selected Readings of Chinese Classics," "Introduction to Chinese Reference Tools," and several graduate seminars. At the Graduate Library School, I offered the "History of Chinese Printing" four times to train young scholars doing in-depth research on related topics of their own choice.

Visiting the University of Hawai'i

In the summer of 1959, I accepted an invitation to be a visiting professor in the Summer Institute of Asian Studies at the University of Hawai'i. There, I made the acquaintance of several internationally renowned scholars, including Hu Shi 胡適 (1891–1962) and Suzuki Daisetsu 鈴木大拙 (1870–1966), who were attending the East-West Philosophers' Conference in Oahu. This was the first time since coming to the U.S. that I had left Chicago to teach at another school. It was one of the most delightful summers for my wife and I, including a very busy social schedule.

The initial objective of the University of Hawai'i was to offer me a permanent position to teach and to take charge of the long-established Asia Library. Since I was not familiar with the university, I hesitated to

AUTHOR AND MRS. TSIEN IN HONOLULU (1958)

accept. The Dean, therefore, invited me to be a visiting professor for the Summer Institute, so that I could get to know the University.

The main subject of the summer session was Asian studies. Attending the Institute were some 150 students, most of them undergraduates, high school teachers, and U.S. military officers, including a general and a number of field officers. I taught two courses: "History of Modern Chinese Culture" and "East Asian Bibliography," each for five hours a week for six weeks, equivalent to a regular semester's work. I also delivered a public lecture, entitled "Asian Studies in America," highlighting the reasons for the American general public's lack of knowledge and its misunderstanding of Asian culture, and emphasizing the importance of Asian studies.

Hawai'i is a scenic spot for tourism and relaxation, but it lacked the intense academic atmosphere that I was used to. So, after careful consideration, I declined the University's offer but agreed to be a supporter of the proposed East and West Center to be established on the University campus. I returned to Chicago at the end of the Summer Institute, and the University of Chicago promoted me to Associate Professor with tenure.

Research and Writing

There were several reasons for my research and writing: 1) preparation for my dissertations and their related studies; 2) papers delivered at academic conferences; 3) institutional assignments for research reports; 4) requests for contributions to biographical dictionaries, encyclopedias, or collected essays; and 5) personal interests. The main subjects of my research centered around my master's thesis on translation as a medium for international cultural exchange and my doctoral dissertation on the history of the Chinese book, which resulted in several monographs and dozens of articles.

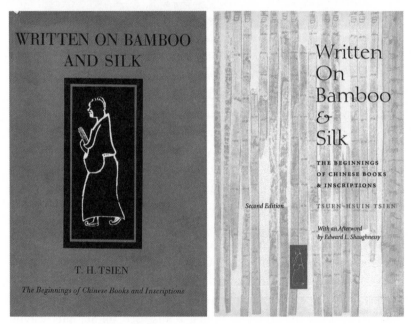

WRITTEN ON BAMBOO AND SILK, 1ST (1962) AND REV. ED. (2004)

Written on Bamboo and Silk: the Beginnings of Chinese Books and Inscriptions was my first published monograph. It was originally my doctoral dissertation, titled the "The Pre-printing Records of China: a Study of the Development of Early Chinese Inscriptions and Books," which was recommended by the Dean of the GLS for publication by the University of Chicago Press, but it was first rejected as the market appeared to be very limited. It was then revised with a new title, and the GLS made an offer to subsidize the printing cost for inclusion in its Studies in Library Science series.

Quite contrary to everyone's expectations, the first printing of this book sold out just three months after publication, with additional reprints in 1963 and 1969. A new, revised edition was published in 2004, with an afterword by Professor Edward Shaughnessy.

The book consists of nine chapters, with the first chapter outlining the significance and social background of the written records in ancient

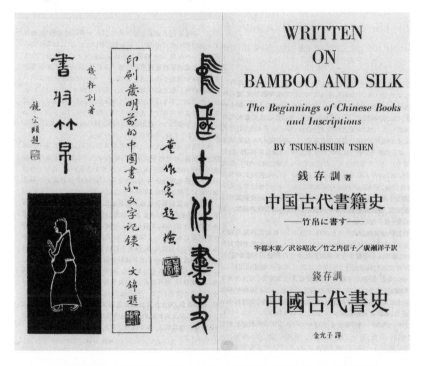

WRITTEN ON BAMBOO AND SILK IN VARIOUS LANGUAGE EDITIONS

China, and the other chapters each describing the various media of the documents, including bones and shells, bronze and pottery, jade and stone, bamboo and wood, silk, paper, and writing tools. The concluding chapter points to continuity, popularity, and productivity as the major functions of Chinese writing. It is a manifestation not only of the richness and permanence of the Chinese culture, but also of its unique character and vast influence on world civilizations.

The Chinese edition of this book was first published by the Chinese University of Hong Kong Press in 1978, with a reprint in 1981; a revised edition was published with simplified characters in Beijing in 1988; the third revised edition was published in Taiwan in 1996, using the original version for the title from *Mozi* of the fifth century B.C. In 2002, the Shanghai Bookstore published its fourth revised and enlarged edition; two years later, the Shanghai Century Publishing Group reprinted this book in its Century Series as one of its world classics. The Japanese edition of the book was published in 1980, and the Korean edition in 1990, with the addition of fifteen color illustrations, and again reprinted in 1999.

After the publication of the English edition, there were some 30 very favorable reviews in academic journals around the world. Dr. Joseph Needham of Cambridge University wrote, "This should be considered the companion piece to Thomas Carter's classic *The Invention of Printing in China and Its Spread Westward*. We may say at once that it need not fear any comparison with that wonderful book . . . The entirety of the book is written clearly and nimbly. The text as a whole is a model of clarity and brevity." His high regard for this book led to his invitation for me to collaborate with him on his multi-volume series *Science and Civilisation in China*.

Paper and Printing

In October 1967, I received an invitation from Dr. Needham to contribute sections on paper and printing for the fifth volume of his series. In his letter, he writes, "Your special knowledge of books and printing is just what we are seeking in the world. We hope that you will consider our request very seriously." After careful consideration, I accepted his offer. In August 1968, I visited Cambridge and discussed the plan with him. With a grant from the Council of American Learned Societies, I was also able to visit libraries and museums in England and on the European mainland to collect sources for my writing. Subsequently, the materials I gathered became ever more extensive and the content further expanded. It took me fifteen years to complete the book, which developed from the 100 pages as originally planned to a monograph of over 300,000 words.

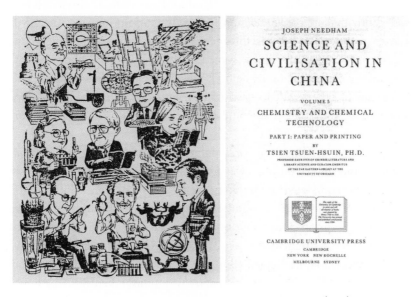

THE NEEDHAM TEAM AND PAPER AND PRINTING (1985)
(*from top left*) KENNETH ROBINSON, T. H. TSIEN,
DOROTHY NEEDHAM, JOSEPH NEEDHAM, LU GWEI-DJEN,
HO PENG-YOKE, NATHAN SIVIN, AND WANG LING.

The volume consists of ten chapters: the first chapter is an orientation, outlining, and evaluation of relevant sources, and discusses factors contributing to the early invention of paper and printing in China; three chapters each deal with paper and printing (including inkmaking and bookbinding), and two chapters deal with the worldwide spread and influence of paper and printing. The concluding chapter discusses the contributions of these two Chinese inventions, paper and printing, and their impact on world civilizations.

In particular, I emphasized that the impact of printing on China and the West led to two similar but differing results. In the West, printing had a profound effect upon European thought and society, intellectual trends, the development of national languages and literatures, and the establishment of independent nations, while printing in China played an opposite role. Not only did printing facilitate the continuity and universality of the Chinese language, but it also became an important vehicle for sustaining Chinese cultural traditions. There is also a definite and mutually-supportive relationship between printing and the civil service examination system, thus acting as one of the vital elements in the relative stability of Chinese society. Printing became a solid basis for the unity of Chinese national culture. The view in my conclusion differed from that of others, but it was highly regarded by Dr. Needham, who viewed it as something that would provide him with further thought for the conclusion of his series.

I worked on the book only intermittently alongside my official teaching and library duties; I was finally able to concentrate entirely on writing and completed the book only after my retirement. With grants from the National Science Foundation and National Endowment for the Humanities from 1977 to 1980, I was able to hire research assistants. Two years after my retirement, the ten draft chapters were finally completed. Next I collected and arranged almost two hundred plates and figures for illustrations and a bibliography of nearly two thousand entries. The book was completed at the end of 1982 and published in 1985 by Cambridge University Press, as Chapter 5, Part 1 of the series *Science and Civilisation in China*. The price of the book was set at £66, or about $100, which was quite expensive. Unexpectedly, all 1500 copies of the first edition were ordered prior to publication. It sold out again after three subsequent printings, and this volume has become one of the bestsellers in the series.

In the preface, Dr. Needham writes, "We were able to persuade our dear friend Professor T. H. Tsien (Chhien Tshun-Hsün), of the University of Chicago, one of the world's most eminent authorities on the subject, to accomplish this task in our series. We greatly admire what he has done . . . I suppose that no theme could be more important for the history of all human civilization than the development of paper and printing . . . In the present volume readers will be able to follow all the vicissitudes of paper and printing during those Chinese centuries when Europe knew nothing of such arts."

Dr. Needham was very satisfied with the achievement of the collaboration. Thus, in 1985, with the approval of the Board of Trustees, he extended a special invitation for me to join his Research Institute of the History of East Asian Science and Technology (the name has now been changed to the Joseph Needham Research Institute) as a 'Research Fellow *en permanence*'. This was indeed an exceptional honor for me and I gratefully accepted. At the same time, this volume was receiving unanimously good reviews in international academic circles, which referred to it as "authoritative" and "encyclopedic."

The Chinese Academy of Sciences in Beijing first selected this volume to be translated into Chinese for presentation as a gift to Dr. Needham on his 90th birthday in 1990. It was later translated into Chinese again in Taiwan and published in 1995. Another revised Chinese version, *Zhongguo zhi he yinshua wenhuashi* 中國紙和印刷文化史, or *Chinese Paper and Printing: a Cultural History*, based on my notes in Chinese and translations by others, was published in 2004. It received very good reviews and was noted as one of the ten best publications in the social sciences in China, with due attention in the field. That year, the Chinese Society of Printing Technology and the Society of the History of Chinese Printing held a symposium in Beijing, discussing the nature and international impact of this book. It was translated into Japanese in 2007 and Korean in 2008.

Other Compilations and Publications

In addition to these two monographs, I have also published a number of other works in English. Among these is *China: an Annotated Bibliography of Bibliographies*, including more than 2,600 selected titles on Chinese studies in Chinese, Japanese, and European languages, with annotations by James Cheng and published by G. K. Hall in Boston in 1978.

Area Studies and the Library (Chicago: University of Chicago Press, 1966) was a collection of papers delivered at the 1965 symposium sponsored by the Graduate Library School of the University of Chicago with myself and Howard Winger as chairmen. The conference was inspired by the growing interest in area studies in higher education in the U.S., which influenced the nature of contents of library collections. The conference included ongoing studies on seven language areas of East Asia, South Asia, Southeast Asia, Africa, the Middle East, Soviet Union, and

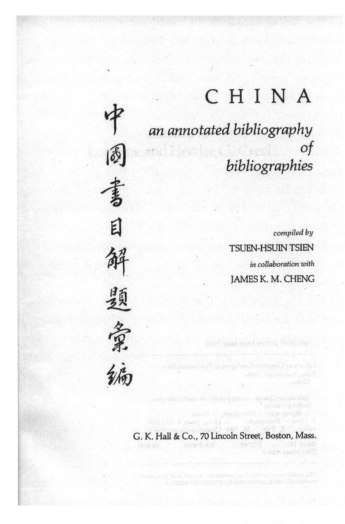

CHINA

中國書目解題彙編

an annotated bibliography
of
bibliographies

compiled by
TSUEN-HSUIN TSIEN
in collaboration with
JAMES K. M. CHENG

G. K. Hall & Co., 70 Lincoln Street, Boston, Mass.

CHINA: AN ANNOTATED BIBLIOGRAPHY OF BIBLIOGRAPHIES (1978)

Latin America, and their impact on American libraries, which had earlier only been oriented towards Western languages. Included was my paper, "East Asian Collections in America," which was published in different languages for various other occasions as well. In 1979, when I visited China as a member of the American Library Delegation, I delivered this paper with an updated revision in Chinese both in Beijing and in Shanghai.

Ancient China: Studies in Early Civilization (Hong Kong: Chinese University of Hong Kong, 1978) is a collection of papers which David T. Roy and I compiled for presentation to Professor Creel on the occasion of his seventieth birthday. It includes sixteen research papers by international scholars on the language, literature, philosophy, history, and institutions of the pre-Qin, Qin, and Han periods.

In addition, there were a number of articles that I had been requested to write for dictionaries, encyclopedias, and a collection of biographies of famous personalities. For example, I contributed a chapter on China to *A Guide to Historical Literature*, published by the American Historical Society in 1961. I was the author of an article on the "Chinese Library Association" in the *Encyclopedia of Library and Information Science*, published in 1970. For the *Dictionary of Ming Biography, 1368–1644*, edited by L. Carrington Goodrich and Chaoying Fang, (2v. New York: Columbia University Press, 1976), I contributed two articles on Hua Sui 華璲 and An Guo 安國, who were the first to use metal movable type for printing in China. I wrote biographies of Qi Baishi 齊白石, Gao Jianfu 高劍父, Gao Qifeng, 高奇峰 and Feng Chengjun 馮承鈞 for the *Biographical Dictionary of Republican China* (5v. New York: Columbia University Press, 1967–1979). I also contributed an essay on "The Evolution of the Nine Classics and Three Commentaries" in the *Sung Bibliography*, edited by Yves Hervouet (Hong Kong, 1978). My paper on the *Zhanguo ce* 戰國策 (*The Stratagem of Warring States*) is included in *Early Chinese Texts: a Bibliographical Study*, edited by Michael Loewe of Cambridge University and published in Berkeley, 1995.

Papers I delivered at international conferences formed another category of my writings. Among the conferences and symposia I attended were the International Conference of Oriental Studies, the International Conference on the History of Science in China, annual meetings of the Association for Asian Studies, the American Oriental Society, and the American Library Association. Early in 1958, I was responsible for the section on China in the survey of "Far Eastern Resources in American Libraries," published in the *Far Eastern Quarterly*, January, 1959. Twice I was requested to survey the East Asian collections in America. *Present Status and Personnel Needs of Far Eastern Collections in American Libraries* prompted the U.S. Department of Education to sponsor the University of Chicago Summer Institute for Far Eastern Librarianship in 1969. The other report, *Current Status of East Asian Collections in American Libraries, 1974-1975*, published by the Association of American Research Libraries in Washington, D.C., provided the basis for subsequent surveys by the Council on East Asian Libraries.

I also wrote numerous prefaces, postscripts, book reviews, commemorative essays, and biographies, including an essay on "Beauty Contests in Imperial China," based on a Ming record describing the selection of imperial wives, which was published in the Midwest CSAS Newsletter, 1965; and a paper on "China: the Birthplace of Paper,

AUTHOR (*at center*) AND MEMBERS OF THE SUMMER INSTITUTE
FOR EAST ASIAN LIBRARIANSHIP (1969)

Printing and Movable Type," published in fifteen different languages at the request of the *UNESCO Courier* for the 1972 International Book Year.

While I was reading the immense series "Chinese Diplomatic Relations *Chouban yiwu shimo* 籌辦夷務始末," I came upon a memorial by a brother of the Emperor Tongzhi, in which he requested an exchange of books with the United States. His petition was first denied, but later the Emperor Tongzhi agreed to decree a gift of one thousand volumes to America. Based on the names in Chinese and the dates in the memorial, I was able to find in the National Archives in Washington D.C. an exchange of fifteen official documents between the U.S. State Department and the American Embassy in China from 1865–1867. Based on these primary sources, I wrote an article, "The First Exchange of Sino-American Publications," published in the *Harvard Journal of Asiatic Studies*, (vol. 25, 1964/1965). In this article I traced the beginning of the Sino-American cultural exchange and also confirmed the year of 1869 as the beginning of a large-scale Chinese language collection at the Library of Congress. Based on this article, the Library of Congress held a special exhibition with these gifts displayed in 1969, in commemoration of its centennial. The National Central Library in Taiwan followed suit and held a commemorative event where my article, printed in a Chinese booklet, was distributed, catching the attention of both Chinese and American audiences.

Collected Writings in Chinese

Besides my publications in English, I also have published over 100 articles in Chinese, or translated into Chinese, some of which were collected and published in several collections. *Zhongguo shuji, zhi mo ji yinshua shi lunwen ji* 中國書籍紙墨及印刷史論文集 (*Collected Studies on the History of the Chinese Book, Paper, Ink, and Printing*), was published in Hong Kong in 1992; a revised and enlarged edition in simplified characters, *Zhongguo gudai shuji, zhi mo ji yinshuashu* 中國古代書籍紙墨及印刷術 (*Ancient Chinese Books, Paper, Ink, and Printing*), containing 40 essays in two parts, was published by the National Library Press in Beijing in 2002. These collections were, in fact, a by-product of my monographs in English on the history of the Chinese book, paper, and printing. Due to stylistic reasons, some of the issues could not be discussed in detail in the monograph, but it was necessary to do thorough research before I could come to any conclusions. For example, I had to do original research on the origin and usage of sealing clays, bookknives and paper, as well as the techniques for woodblock printing, prior to writing the monograph.

Regarding the origin of paper, it has been proven that paper was already in use in the second century B.C., but the character *zhi* 紙 (paper) was found on a bamboo strip of the third century B.C., so I had to do

COLLECTIONS IN CHINESE WITH COVER BY NOTED CALLIGRAPHERS
(*left*) STUDIES ON CHINESE BOOKS, PAPER, INK AND PRINTING
BY PROFESSOR TSENG YU-HUO; (*right*) SINO-AMERICAN CULTURAL
RELATIONS BY PROFESSOR CHOW TSE-TSUNG

further investigation on the origin of paper. As for the various uses of paper, there had not been any systematic studies. I checked documents and archaeological discoveries to trace the origin of paper used in the everyday life of the Chinese family and society, giving evidence that prior to the influx of paper into Europe in the twelfth century, China had already used paper for writing depositions, decorations, trade, rites, sacrificial offerings to the deceased, household use, and entertainment.

On the technique of woodblock printing, first invented in China, there had been no record in published books. For my monograph *Paper and Printing*, I checked all of the relevant Chinese and Western documents, visited print shops, interviewed old wood-carving masters, took photographs with drawings, all to describe in detail the materials, step-by-step processes, and methods of printing blocks, the number of impressions that could be made from each block, and the number of copies of each book that could be printed from the woodblocks. It was the first work with such details on the technique of woodblock printing.

The other collection in Chinese, published in Taiwan in 1998, is the *Zhong Mei shu yuan* 中美書緣 (*Sino-American Cultural Relations*), which contains sixteen articles on cultural exchanges between China and the United States. The primary information in these articles is in the summary of my master's thesis, "The Impact of Translations on the Modernization of China," my lecture on Asian studies in Hawai'i, my research on the Chinese books given to the United States from the Chinese Emperor Tongzhi, the history of Chinese rare books in America, my survey report on Chinese and Asian resources in American libraries, and cherished memories of my Chinese and Western teachers and friends. The revised and expanded edition, with a new title *Dongxi wenhua jiaoliu luncong* 東西文化交流論叢 (*East-West Cultural Exchange*) in simplified characters, was published by the Commercial Press in Beijing in 2009.

Summary and Reviews

Dr. Ming-sun Poon has compiled two bibliographies of my publications, one in chronological order, beginning with my first essay published in 1931 until 2008, with 16 monographs and some 150 articles. The other is by subject: 1) History of the book, paper, ink and printing, 2) Sino-Western cultural exchanges, 3) Bibliography, 4) East Asian library resources, and 5) History, biography, and miscellaneous. Since I came to the United States, I have written mostly in English with my first paper published in 1952. Since then I have written in English for international conferences or replying to invitations to submit papers. These papers have been translated into Chinese, Japanese, Korean, and numerous other languages. If I had only worked in a library, without doing scholarly research, or if I had only taught without having worked in a library, it would have been more difficult to have had so many relevant sources at hand. Looking back, my early decision to combine library science with history greatly benefited my career and academic life.

As mentioned earlier, my two major monographs were well received. Ms. Bie Liqian of Peking University wrote her master's thesis on "Prof. T. H. Tsien's Contribution to the Study of the History of the Chinese Book" (June 1998), and she later published an article on the "International Review

EXHIBITION OF AUTHOR'S PUBLICATIONS
AT THE UNIVERSITY OF CHICAGO LIBRARY (2006)

of the Works of Prof. T. H. Tsien" (2006), in which she wrote:

"Up until now, the author has gathered almost 100 published reviews on Tsien's works, a phenomenon rarely seen for scholarly books by others. The widespread influence of Tsien's work is obvious from the fact that these reviews are written in different languages and published in China, the U.S., England, France, Germany, and Italy. In particular, Prof. Tsien's well-organized methodology and his application of comparative studies to introduce the Eastern cultures to Western scholars have furthermore given abundant confirmation of his achievements. The overall success of Tsien's works are unanimously acclaimed. Words of admiration, such as 'authoritative,' 'classic,' 'encyclopedic,' and 'model for posterity,' appear frequently in these reviews."

25

TRAVEL AND WRITING
AFTER RETIREMENT

In the 1970s, the mandatory retirement age in the U.S. was sixty-five. How-ever, two years before I reached that age, the University President sent me a letter to extend my contract for three more years. So I retired in Decem-ber 1978, after thirty-one years of service at the University of Chicago. A farewell lunch party was held in my honor with over a hundred people in attendance, including colleagues from the University Library, Department of East Asian Languages and Civilizations, Graduate Library School, and my family and friends from across the States.

AUTHOR AT HIS RETIREMENT PARTY (1978);
(*Mrs. Tsien on his left and Mrs. Regenstein on the right*)

Mrs. Helen Regenstein, donor of the Regenstein Library building, showed up in person and presented me with a silver pen. Jeanette Elliot, a student of my wife's, endowed a special fund to the East Asian Library for the acquisition of books relating to my specialty. James Cheng, then a col-league of mine, wrote a biography of my life and career. Professor Howard W. Winger, Dean of the Graduate Library School, presented me with a scarf that he had knitted himself and read a poem that he had composed. Library colleagues gave me an electric IBM typewriter so that I could continue my writing.

Other friends called or sent congratulatory telegrams, which warmed my heart. The professorship was a tenured position and I was asked to continue teaching for another year. I then became Professor Emeritus of the Department of East Asian Languages and Civilizations and the Graduate Library School of the University of Chicago. The Library also gave me the honorary title of Curator Emeritus of the East Asian Library, with an office in the Regenstein Library. Since then I have not only enjoyed the university facilities and privileges, but also have been supported by the Library administration to attend conferences overseas. I am extremely grateful for all of these privileges.

After retirement, I visited Japan, Europe again, mainland China on several occasions, Taiwan for the first time, and several other sites around the world. Thanks to grants from the National Science Foundation, the National Endowment for the Humanities, the Needham Research Institute in Cambridge, and the Center for East Asian Studies at the University of Chicago, I was able to go overseas to visit scholars, gather information, and hire assistants to continue my research and writing. As a result, I have published and revised several monographs and scores of articles. Other than reading books and newspapers, I have continued working at least six to eight hours every day until midnight. Friends often ask me about life after retirement. I enjoy retired life, but I am actually much busier than before, since I no longer have an assistant to handle my correspondence and other routine work.

Visiting Japan

In order to write the volume *Paper and Printing* in the Needham series of *Science and Civilization in China*, I had visited major libraries and museums in Europe and America, but not countries in Asia, where more documents are concentrated. Therefore, I stopped in Japan for a week before joining the American Library Delegation in China in 1979.

I visited Tokyo, Kyoto, and Nara, all of which was arranged by Dr.

Kuroda Yoshinobu, Director of the Japanese Office of the U.S. Library of Congress. In Tokyo, I visited the National Diet Library, Seikadō Bunko 靜嘉堂文庫, Tōyō Bunko 東洋文庫, and the Paper Museum. The Japan Diet Library pioneered the automated and computerized library system. I examined their facilities, listened to reports, and attended a banquet hosted by the Library. The Seikadō Library has the largest collection of Chinese rare books in Japan; there I examined several Song prints and other rare editions. The Tōyō Bunko, or Oriental Institute, showed me its collection of all the Qian family records and different editions of Taizhou gazetteers in order to verify my great-grandfather Qian Guisen's biographies.

AUTHOR (*second from right*) AT THE JAPAN DIET LIBRARY (1979)

The next day, Professors Akira Utsugi 宇都木章 and Harutsugu Sawaya 沢谷昭次 along with two women from the Oriental Institute, who had translated my book *Written on Bamboo and Silk* into Japanese, met me for breakfast at the Shinbashi Daiichi Hotel. The Japanese translation added references in Japanese, indexes by subject and author, and prefaces by Professor Takeo Hiraoka 平岡武夫 of Kyoto University and myself. I gave them a copy of the Chinese edition of the book, which had just been published in Hong Kong. The Japanese translation was published in 1980.

The Paper Museum (Kami no Hakubutsukan 紙の博物館) in Tokyo carried a variety of paper and paper products, including paper specimens as well as charts and books on paper. They had various kinds of paper products, including paper clothes, hats, blankets, nets, paper models, and paper toys. The paper products of the twelve Chinese zodiac symbols are especially interesting. I took a picture of a paper tiger for an illustration in my book. Although paper was invented in China, it did not have a similar museum at that time. To my knowledge, only a few countries in the world have paper museums, most of which are attached to paper manufacturing companies. In 1974, I visited the Dard Hunter Paper Museum in Appleton, Wisconsin, where the displays were collected by Mr. Hunter when he was traveling in China and other parts of Asia. This collection had limited displays of paper specimens and paper products, far fewer than the Paper Museum in Japan.

AUTHOR AND PROFESSOR TAKEO HIRAOKA
OF KYOTO UNIVERSITY (1979)

After two days in Tokyo, I went to Kyoto by bullet train and was met by Professor Takeo Hiraoka. I was warmly welcomed by him with a lunch and dinner, and I was then taken to the Tōdaiji 東大寺 Temple, the University of Kyoto Library, and the Institute of Oriental Studies of Kyoto University.

I stayed in Kyoto for one day before my trip to the former capital city of Nara 奈良, where I visited a sacred Jinja shrine 右宮神社, Kōfukuji 興福寺 National Treasure Hall, and the famous Shōsōin 正倉院 Imperial Household Agency. I saw many Chinese relics of the Sui and Tang dynasties, including an enlarged facsimile of the Jiexianjin 劫賢經, a sixth-century manuscript from China. The watermarks of the paper still could be seen clearly, and I asked for permission to use the picture as an illustration in my book.

Back to Mainland China

I returned to Tokyo from Nagabe on September 12 to join other members of the American Library Delegation to fly to Beijing. I felt both excited and nervous, as it was the first time I would be stepping onto my native soil after an absence of 32 years. Over those two weeks I visited Beijing, Xi'an, Nanjing, Shanghai, and Guangzhou, returning to the U.S. via Hong Kong. The delegation was well-hosted, accompanied by the head of the Foreign Affairs Office of the National Library throughout the trip. I stayed in Hong Kong for a week before returning to Chicago.

AMERICAN LIBRARY DELEGATION RECEIVED BY THE CHINESE VICE-MINISTER IN BEIJING, 1979; (*author second from right in front row*)

During the week in Beijing, the delegation stayed at the famous Peking Hotel, and was received by Vice-Premier Fang Yi 方毅 at the Great Hall of the People. We visited the National Library, Peking University, Tsinghua University, the Chinese Academy of Sciences, the Chinese Academy of Social Sciences, the Imperial Palace Museum, the Great Wall, the Imperial Tombs of the Ming Emperors, and the Sixth National Sports Meeting in the capital. I presented a report at the Capital Library with over 1,000 people in attendance. During the visit to the National Library, I presented them with my personal copy of a rare manuscript, *Jiangcun shuhua mu* 江村書畫目, which had been given to me by a relative as a souvenir when I left for the States. It is a catalog of paintings and calligraphy in the collection of Gao Shiqi 高士奇 (1645–1703), an influential art critic and consultant to Emperor Kangxi. The catalog recorded over 500 items of art works from the Jin and Tang to the early Qing dynasties, including their ratings and prices at that time. The most interesting part of this catalog is that the art works marked "Bequest to the Emperor" were fakes, with prices of only one or two taels of silver, while those most treasured had a price as high as 500 taels, which were kept for his personal collection. This catalog, together with some of my manuscripts, are now kept in the Rare Books Department of the National Library as a token of my ten years' of service in its Nanjing and Shanghai Offices from 1937–1947.

After Beijing, the group visited the city of Xi'an for two days, Shanghai for three days, Nanjing and Guangzhou for one day each, with a warm reception wherever we stopped. While in Shanghai, I met my old friend Mr. Gu Tinglong 顧廷龍, who was then Director of the Shanghai Library. On behalf of the University of Chicago, I presented its duplicate collection of over 600 volumes of books in English on hi-tech subjects to the Shanghai Library, and Mr. Gu gave me a poem written with his archaic calligraphy on a scroll. I also presented the Shanghai Library with a photocopy of the earliest existing piece of printing that dates to the early eighth century, which was discovered in Korea in 1966; included were news reports and commentaries by international and Korean scholars. This discovery of the earliest example of printing was, at the time, a shock to the rest of the world, but it was not reported in China during the Cultural Revolution. These materials were later translated into Chinese by the

Library and resulted in heated debates over this specimen's origin by scholars in China.

During my stay in China, I visited Rongbao zhai 榮寶齋 in Beijing and Duoyun xuan 朵雲軒 in Shanghai to learn the techniques of making woodcuts and watercolor printing from surviving technicians at these stores. I also collected examples of carving and printing tools for my study and writing. In addition, I saw many relatives in Beijing, Tianjin, Xi'an, Shanghai, and Nanjing, whom I had not seen for more than thirty years. I saw so many relatives and their offspring that it made me feel as if I were in the famous Tang poem:

> Left home when young and back when old,
> With accent the same but hairs turned white.
> Children I meet don't recognize who I am,
> And ask: where does this guest come from?

In 1984, I went to Beijing again to attend the 3rd International Conference of the History of Chinese Science and Technology, sponsored by the Chinese Academy of Sciences. I was appointed chairman of the Section on Technology and read my paper "The Chinese Background of European Printing." Both Needham and Lu Gwei-djen were present at the conference, and I accompanied them to Shanghai for a celebration of Lu's 80th birthday after the meeting.

My third visit to China was with my nephew Victor in 1987 for the celebration of the 75th anniversary of the National Beijing Library and the opening ceremony of its new building. I was invited as a dignitary, put up in the Diaoyutai National Guest House, and was very much impressed by the immense dimensions of the new building with its full array of facilities. I also met many other dignitaries from all over the world. This was my last trip back to China, and I have not traveled overseas since.

In the summer of 1988, I was invited by the University of Washington in Seattle to lecture at the Summer Institute for Far East Librarianship. I later went to the University of California, Los Angeles where I was received by my former students, James Cheng and Professor Lucie Cheng. Afterwards, I traveled to San Diego to attend the 5th International Conference of the History of Chinese Science and Technology, where I chaired the section on "Printing in Chinese Culture" with ten panelists from the U.S, China, Taiwan, Hong Kong, and Korea. This was the first international conference to include a panel on printing.

AUTHOR OUTSIDE THE NEW NATIONAL LIBRARY (1987)

Visiting Taiwan

In November 1984, I was invited to Taiwan to speak at a seminar on the preservation of rare books held at the Palace Museum in Taipei. The seminar lasted for three weeks with more than thirty participants from around the world. I delivered two lectures, on the "East Asian Collections in Europe and America" and "History of Movable-type Printing in China." During my stay, I also gave a talk at the invitation of the Department of Library and Information Science of Taiwan University and visited the Academia Sinica in Taipei, where the second century A.D. wooden tablets discovered at Juyan, Gansu were displayed. Afterwards, I was accompanied by the Assistant Director of the Museum to visit other spots around Taiwan, including Hualian on the coast. There I was received by Professor Huang Shixiong 黃世雄 of Tamkang University, an alumnus of the University of Chicago.

UNIVERSITY OF CHICAGO ALUMNI RECEPTION IN TAIWAN (1984); SHAW YU-
MING (*second from right*), LIEN CHAN (*at center*), JAMES SOONG (*next to Chen*), LU
SHIOW-JYU (*seated*), AND AUTHOR (*second from left*)

I met the Director of the Palace Museum, library leaders, and many
relatives in Taiwan. I was also invited to a dinner by University of Chicago
alumni Lien Chan, James Soong, Shaw Yu-ming, Lu Shiow-jyu, and several other individuals.

During this visit I had the opportunity to inspect the rare books of the
National Library of Beiping, which I myself had shipped from Shanghai to
the Library of Congress for safekeeping some forty years before. In 1966,
these books had been sent to Taiwan into the custody of the National Central Library and were later transferred to the Palace Museum in Taipei. I
was overwhelmed to see these books in their original crates with the sealing tape of the National Library still on them.

Europe Revisited

My first visit to Europe was at the invitation of Dr. Needham of Cambridge
University in September 1968 to discuss writing the section on *Paper and*

AUTHOR IN TAIWAN WITH RARE BOOKS FROM THE NATIONAL
LIBRARY OF BEIPING RESCUED IN WWII (1984)

Printing in his series. I had agreed to submit the manuscripts to him in person when I finished writing. In October 1982, when the work was finally completed, I went to Cambridge again to discuss its publication and stayed for two weeks. I visited the British Museum and Oxford University and went to Eastbourne, Sussex, near London to meet my eldest brother, T. D. Tsien. He had retired from a diplomatic career and was managing the Summer Palace Restaurant at this beach resort, one of England's tourist centers.

From there I went to Amsterdam to visit Leiden University, where I was received by John Ma, curator of the Asian collection, who showed me around the city. Then I visited the International Book Exhibition in Frankfurt, Germany; there I met Dr. S. S. Taubert, who had written a long review of my book *Written on Bamboo and Silk*. I stopped over in Paris to see my younger brother, Qian Cunxue, the Assistant Head of the Chinese Delegation to UNESCO, where I learned much about their varied activities. I also paid a visit to the Bibliothèque nationale de France and Guimet Museum in Paris, which has a large collection of Chinese documents and cultural relics.

China Publications Service

AUTHOR AND QIAN CUNXUE AT UNESCO IN PARIS (1982)

During my visit to China in 1979, I gave a report at the Capital Library in Beijing on East Asian libraries in the U.S., with a list of about one hundred such libraries. The Chinese Ministry of Culture was establishing the China Publications Trading Company to promote the export of books and periodicals published in China. The company sent one of its senior staff to attend the lecture. Afterwards, the company wrote me for assistance.

Back then, East Asian libraries in America had an annual budget of about ten million dollars, a large part of which was for Chinese publications. Since diplomatic relations between the U.S. and China had been broken off for quite awhile, the acquisition of publications was done primarily through agents in Hong Kong, Japan, and elsewhere. It was not only indirect but incomplete. Therefore, I recommended that the company participate in book exhibits in the U.S., so that American scholars and library staff could understand the progress of publishing in mainland China. The company agreed, but it could not participate due to political difficulties. They suggested that I organize a book company in the U.S. to join the exhibits, and the company in China would supply about 2,000 books and periodicals.

In 1982, I registered the China Publications Services in Illinois to participate in the book exhibit at the annual meetings of the Association for Asian Studies in America. A book catalog was published each year for distribution at the exhibit. A few years later, the company in Beijing was able to join the exhibit as a co-sponsor. These joint exhibits have continued for many years since publications from mainland China have become available to American scholars and libraries. This is how I unexpectedly became involved in a business venture after my retirement. Although other book companies came to join the exhibits later, China Publications Services was the first agency to introduce publications from mainland China to American libraries and academic circles.

Publications

The majority of my books and essays were started, expanded, and published after my retirement in 1978. Although I began writing *Paper and Printing* in 1970, it was only after my retirement that I was able to concentrate fully on it. I spent four more years on the first draft of the volume, completed in 10 chapters with 300,000 words. Then I added about 200 illustrations and 2,000 titles to the reference lists. In 1982, I was able to send the complete draft to Needham for review; the work was published by the Cambridge University Press in 1985.

Although the Chinese and English versions of the book *Written on Bamboo and Silk* were published before my retirement, the revision and translation into other languages were all accomplished afterwards. The English version was revised in 1998 and published by the University of Chicago Press in 2004. Since library materials were no longer close at hand after my retirement, it was difficult to access new sources. Therefore, I spent most of the time revising my early writings with the support of friends and relatives.

Honors

Of my honorary titles and awards, a few deserve special mention. I received the first Outstanding Service Award in China from the Ministry of Education in 1941, for risking my life under Japanese occupation to smuggle rare books from the National Library out of Shanghai to the Library of Congress for safekeeping. Later, I received more distinguished service awards from both China and the U.S, including one from the National Library, with a special delegation sent to Chicago to present the award in 1999.

Another honor was being elected to the Chicago Senior Citizens Hall of Fame in 1978. Mayor Daley himself presented the award. This was the first time that an Asian-American had been elected to this organization, so the Chinese Chamber of Commerce held a big party to celebrate the occasion; this news was reported by the media both in the U.S. and abroad. In 2006, a special Lifetime Achievement Award was bestowed upon me by the U.S.-China Friendship Foundation in Washington, D.C.

In addition, I was honored with the publication of three festschrifts on my birthdays. For my 80th birthday, *Zhongguo tushu wenshi lunji* 中國圖書文史論集 (*Collection of Essays on Books, Literature, and History*), edited by Dr. Tai-loi Ma, was published in Taipei in 1990 and in Beijing in 1991 with 30 essays contributed by my friends and students. On my 95th birthday, another collection titled *Nanshan lunxueji* 南山論學集 (*Collection of Essays for Advanced Age*), edited by Dr. Ming-sun Poon, was published in Beijing in 2006, with 28 articles on art, literature, history, books, and bibliography. There was also a special issue published in honor of "Professor Tsien Tsuen-hsuen's 95th Birthday" in the *Bulletin of the Library Association of China (Taiwan)*, no. 74 June 2006, in which nine articles were contributed by friends in Taiwan, mainland China, and America. I felt particularly honored by these works and extend my thanks to the editors and contributors.

I am very much honored also by the two memorial library collections named for me. At the time of my retirement, an American student donated a special fund to the University of Chicago Library to set up a T. H. Tsien Book Fund to buy books related to my areas of interest. In November 2007, the T. H. Tsien Library was formally opened at my alma mater, Nanjing University, at its newly established Advanced Research Institute of Liberal Arts and Social Sciences.

The last honor was from U.S. presidents who sent congratulations on different occasions. When Wen-ching and I celebrated our 60th anniversary in 1996, President Bill Clinton and First Lady Hillary Clinton sent us a letter of congratulations. Ten years later when we celebrated our 70th anniversary in 2006, we received another congratulatory letter from President George W. Bush and First Lady Barbara Bush. And on the occasion of my 100th birthday in 2009, I received congratulations from President Barack Obama and First Lady Michelle Obama. Over the years, we received greetings from three American presidents, two Democrats and one Republican. Thus, I wish to use these honors as the conclusion of my memoir of more than sixty years of life in the United States of America.

THE WHITE HOUSE

WASHINGTON

October 20, 2009

Professor Emeritus Tsuen-Hsuin Tsien
1408 East Rochdale Place
Chicago, Illinois 60615

Dear Professor Tsien:

Happy 100th Birthday! We wish you the very best on this
momentous occasion.

You have witnessed great milestones in our Nation's history,
and your life represents an important piece of the American story.
As you reflect upon 100 years of memories, we hope that you are
filled with tremendous pride and joy.

Congratulations on your birthday, and may you enjoy many
more happy years as a centenarian.

Sincerely,

Barack Obama *Michelle Obama*

CONGRATULATORY LETTER FROM PRESIDENT AND MRS. OBAMA (2009)

26

T. H. TSIEN LIBRARY AT NANJING UNIVERSITY

T. H. TSIEN LIBRARY READING ROOM IN NANJING

On November 1, 2007, the opening of the T. H. Tsien Library was formally held in Nanjing University, Nanjing, China. To celebrate this event, Nanjing University and the University of Chicago Library co-organized a two-day international symposium on November 1–2 in Nanjing University. A total of forty-seven scholars, librarians, and university administrators from mainland China, Taiwan, and the United States attended the celebration and symposium. A good number of graduate and undergraduate students from Nanjing University also participated in this festive event.

Professor Tsuen-Hsuin Tsien, Curator Emeritus of the East Asian Library and Professor Emeritus of the Department of East Asian Languages and Civilizations at the University of Chicago, is one of the most accomplished and respected scholar-librarians in the field of East Asian librarianship. He came to the University of Chicago in 1947, and has worked on campus ever since, for more than 60 years. From 1949 to 1978, Dr. Tsien served as the first Curator of Chicago's East Asian Library and taught as a faculty member both in the Department of East Asian Languages and Civilizations and the Graduate Library School in the University. During his tenure at the University of Chicago, Tsien not only built successfully one of the finest East Asian collections in North America but also trained a generation of East Asian librarians and scholars. Many of his students are library leaders and faculty members in institutions of higher education in the U.S., Taiwan and elsewhere.

Dr. Tsien also made great achievements in research and scholarship. He is the author of more than 150 scholarly publications including two very influential monographs on the history of Chinese books, paper, and printing, *Written on Bamboo and Silk: The Beginning of Chinese Books and Inscription* (University of Chicago Press, 1962; 2nd revised edition, 2004) and *Paper and Printing* (Cambridge University Press, 1985) in Joseph Needham's *Science and Civilisation in China* series. Tsien is also well-known for his initiation of statistical surveys in the 1950–1970s on East Asian library resources in North America, the predecessor of today's CEAL statistics.

Nanjing University (formerly University of Nanking) is Tsien's alma mater—he graduated from the University in 1932 with a major in history and minor in library science. In 2006, Professor Tsien decided to donate his private collection to Nanjing University. The Institute for Advanced Studies in Humanities and Social Sciences (IAS), a newly established research institute in Nanjing University, was chosen to house Tsien's donation, which contains more than 6,000 volumes of publications in Chinese, Japanese, and English. The donated books were shipped to China from New York through the "Books-for-China Project," organized by John Ma, formerly librarian of Cornell, the Hoover Institute, and

OPENING OF THE T. H. TSIEN LIBRARY IN NANJING

Leiden. To honor Dr. Tsien's distinguished career, renowned scholarship, and generous donation, the IAS of Nanjing University decided to name its new facility the "T. H. Tsien Library."

To celebrate the grand opening of the Tsien Library, the University of Chicago Library and Nanjing University worked together to organize an international symposium held in Nanjing with a grant from the Chiang Ching-Kuo Foundation for International Scholarly Exchange. This meeting, entitled the *International Symposium on Sino-American Cultural Exchange and Library Development*, was co-hosted by the University Library, the Institute for Advanced Studies in Humanities and Social Sciences (IAS), the Institute for Publishing Research, and the Department of Information Management of Nanjing University.

The two-day conference began with a keynote speech by Professor Choyun Hsu, Professor Emeritus of the University of Pittsburgh and Visiting Professor of the Nanjing University's IAS. His introduction was followed by welcome remarks and opening speeches by Professor Zhang Yibin, Vice President of Nanjing University, Professor Hong Xiuping, Director of Nanjing University Library, Mr. James Cheng, Librarian of Harvard-Yenching Library, Harvard University, and Ms. Xiaoshan Qian,

Professor Emeritus of Nanjing Normal University and the representative of the Tsien family. Vice President Zhang and Professor Qian unveiled the name plaque of the T. H. Tsien Library and announced its opening.

Twenty-four papers were presented over the two-day conference. Among them, nine were given by the participants from the United States including Dr. Hwa-wei Lee, Chief of Asian Division, Library of Congress, Mr. James Cheng, Librarian of Harvard-Yenching Library, and Dr. Tai-loi Ma, Director of East Asian Library, Princeton University. Four presentations were made by the attendees from Taiwan, and the rest (eleven) were given by scholars and librarians from Beijing, Shanghai, Guangzhou, and Nanjing. The papers were well received by the audience and generated interesting discussions in the sessions as well as during the tea breaks, lunches, and dinners. The conference was concluded by Dr. Tsien's video presentation.

Published in Journal of East Asian Libraries,
no. 144, February, 2008

27

From China to Chicago he made his scholar's way,
With cakes of ink and classics and charm of old Cathay.
From Upper Song to Lower Song and majesties of Ming,
Of their calligraphy and thought he was acknowledged King;
For there were scholars in his line and culture in his blood.

This poetic excerpt was composed by Professor Howard W. Winger, former Dean of the Graduate Library School, University of Chicago, on the occasion of Dr. Tsuen-Hsuin Tsien's retirement from the University in 1978.

Reading and working with books, as well as teaching and writing about books, have been the life-long interests and career of Dr. Tsien, a scholar-librarian loved and respected by the many colleagues, friends, and students who have known him well. For over a quarter of a century, he has provided distinguished service and admirable leadership to the University of Chicago, the field of East Asian studies, the profession of East Asian librarianship, and to East Asian collections across America.

He has offered the library profession fifty years of devoted service in both China and the United States, and to the world of scholarship a better understanding of China's contribution to the history of the book and printing. He merges the qualities and abilities of scholar, teacher, librarian, and administrator—a combination that is rarely achieved.

Family and Early Life in China

Born January 11, 1910 (December 1, 1909, according to the Chinese calendar) in Taizhou, Jiangsu province, China, Tsuen-Hsuin Tsien 錢存訓 (Qian Cunxun) came from a family of scholars. His great-grandfather, Qian Guisen 錢桂森 (1827–1899), was a scholar-official who served in the Hanlin Academy and as Commissioner of Education and Chief Civil Service Examiner in Anhui and other provinces. He was also the author of a volume of collected poems and a book on etymology published by the private library Jiaojing tang 教經堂. His father, Qian Weizhen 錢慰貞 (1885–1935), was a Buddhist scholar and an editor of the Buddhist journal *Haichao yin* 海潮音, which he worked on under his Buddhist name, Chengshan 誠善.

Tsien began his formal education in 1916 with a private tutor at home. He entered the Taizhou Number 2 Secondary School in 1918 and studied at Huaidong High School (now Taizhou High School) between 1922 and 1926, during which he was active in the student movement and edited a youth periodical, *Qingnian Xunkan* 青年旬刊 (*Youth Fortnightly*). Afterward, he joined the Northern Expedition Army, then enrolled at the University of Nanking (now Nanjing University) in 1926 and worked part-time in the Ginling Women's College Library, first as a cataloger and later as Acting Librarian. He graduated from the University in 1932 with a B.A. in history and a minor in library science. His course with Professor Liu Guojun on the history of the book sparked an interest that he has carried with him to the present. While working at the Ginling Women's College Library, he took a course on translation, for which two of his class papers were later published in influential magazines in China, an experience which greatly encouraged his interest in writing and publishing.

After graduation, Tsien worked as Assistant Librarian at the National Jiaotong University Library in Shanghai (1932–37) under its director, Du Dingyou 杜定友, one of China's early leaders in the modern Chinese library movement. Tsien was also manager for three years of the China Library Service, an agency specializing in publishing books and periodicals on library science and in providing library supplies and equipment. In 1936 he married Hsu Wen-ching in Nanjing and his three daughters—Ginger, Gloria, and Mary—were all born in China.

In 1937 Tsien joined the National Library of Beiping under the direction of T. L.Yuan, Head of its Nanjing Branch, where complete sets of scientific and technical journals in foreign languages were transferred from the headquarters in Beijing before the outbreak of the Sino-Japanese War. Shortly after, he was transferred to the Library's Shanghai Office where he became custodian of the Chinese rare books moved from Beijing. For ten years, he also worked as manager of the *Quarterly Bulletin of Chinese*

Bibliography, taking charge of liaison work with foreign libraries and collecting materials published in the Japanese-occupied area of China.

In 1941, just before the attack on Pearl Harbor and under extremely dangerous conditions, Tsien supervised the covert shipping of 30,000 volumes of Chinese rare books to the U.S. Library of Congress for safekeeping and microfilming. For this complex task, he was awarded the Distinguished Service Award from the Chinese Ministry of Education in 1943 and again in 1999 from the National Library in Beijing. In 1947 he was commissioned by the Chinese government to travel to Washington, D.C., to oversee the shipment of the return of these rare books, but by that time communications in China had broken down due to the outbreak of civil war, and the return shipment was cancelled.

Work and Study at the University of Chicago

Tsien joined the staff of the University of Chicago in the fall of 1947 as an exchange librarian from the National Library of Beiping. He began processing the Chinese collection started by Professor Herrlee G. Creel in 1936, which had grown over the intervening ten years to nearly 70,000 volumes. Tsien almost single-handedly brought the entire collection under bibliographic control, thus laying the foundation for its rapid and systematic expansion over the following decades.

In 1949 Tsien was promoted to Curator of the Far Eastern Library and concurrently served as Professorial Lecturer in Chinese Literature in the then Department of Oriental Languages and Literatures. During this time, he worked full-time in the library while teaching part-time in the department and also studying part-time in the Graduate Library School, from which he received his M.A. in 1952 and Ph.D. in 1957. He was promoted to Associate Professor in 1958 and full Professor in 1964 jointly with the Graduate Library School. At the time of his retirement in 1978, he was named Professor Emeritus in the Department of East Asian Languages and Civilizations and the Graduate Library School, as well as Curator Emeritus of the East Asian Library.

Over the thirty-one years of Tsien's tenure, he built an outstanding Far Eastern collection at the University of Chicago. During the first ten years of his service, from roughly 1947 through 1958, he concentrated his efforts on bringing the initial collection of classical literature, including more than 20,000 volumes acquired from the Berthold Laufer Collection of the Newberry Library, under proper bibliographic control. Over the following two decades, he oversaw the acquisition of research materials on modern China, especially periodicals, official gazettes, materials relating to local administrations, and original documents published during the 1920–1930s, during an extremely complicated time when U.S.-China relations were being terminated. It was also during this period that a Japanese collection was established with initial acquisitions of literature and history, plus complete sets of collected works and learned journals. At the same time, the acquisition of rare materials continued, including over 200 Ming editions, rare manuscripts, *hishi* copies of rare Chinese books in Japanese collections, local histories, official administrative codes, and samples for the study of the history of the Chinese book, such as sealing clays of the Han dynasty, Dunhuang manuscripts, bamboo tablets in facsimile, movable type, paper money, and various samples of early printing.

Tsien also planned and executed the move of the Far Eastern Library from the basement of the Oriental Institute building to the Harper Library in 1958, and finally to the present spacious quarters in the Joseph Regenstein Library in 1970. With holdings of nearly half a million volumes, the Far Eastern Collection has many unique items and covers areas that are not likely to be duplicated elsewhere. The Chinese collection started in 1936 is especially strong in classics, philosophy, history, local gazetteers, archeology, art, and literature; the Japanese collection, built up since 1958, has distinguished holdings in literature, history, fine arts, history of religion, sinology, and journals. The acquisition of the Berthold Laufer Collection from the Newberry Library in 1943 added many rarities to the collections in different Far Eastern languages, including Manchu, Mongolian, and Tibetan.

Professor Chauncy D. Harris, former Vice-President for Academic Resources at the University of Chicago, made the following remarks on the occasion of Tsien's retirement:

> I wish to express both my great pleasure at having worked with you over
> the years and official gratitude for the outstanding leadership which you

have provided for building up the Far Eastern Library of the University of Chicago. You have played the key role in the transformation of a small collection on China into a major national library on the Far East. You have also provided national leadership in the coordination of efforts by Far Eastern librarians. You have happily combined the roles of scholar and librarian. The Far Eastern field, the Library, and the University have all been greatly enriched by your many contributions. Your thirty years of devoted service leave behind a priceless heritage. I count it as a high privilege to have been associated with you over these years.

Teaching and Promotion of East Asian Librarianship

As a teacher, Tsien has guided many students through their programs in East Asian studies and East Asian librarianship since he joined the faculty of the University of Chicago in 1949. His courses on Chinese bibliography and historiography were very popular among graduate students, whose dissertation topics were often developed in his classes through systematic searches of source materials. These courses proved to be so useful that they have been required for all Ph.D. students at Chicago since 1958. From 1964 until his retirement, Tsien directed the Program on Far Eastern Librarianship, a joint degree graduate program between the Graduate Library School and the Department of Far Eastern Languages and Civilizations. Over the years, more than thirty students have graduated with master's or doctoral degrees from this program and are serving in various positions in East Asian collections or teaching in America and elsewhere. A number of their theses or papers have been published by the Chinese Materials Center in the series, *Studies in East Asian Librarianship*, with an introduction to each volume by Tsien. And in 1969 Tsien directed a Summer Institute for Far Eastern Librarianship, sponsored by the U.S. Office of Education, in which thirty-one in-service librarians and students in East Asian studies participated.

Over the past thirty years Tsien has also lectured at Columbia University, the University of Illinois, Indiana University, the University of Minnesota, Ohio State University, the University of Pittsburgh, and the University of Wisconsin. He was Visiting Professor in Asian Studies at the University of Hawai'i in the summer of 1959. In 1982 he was appointed a Fellow of the Joseph Needham Research Institute in Cambridge, England. In 1984 he attended the third International Conference on the History of Chinese Science in Beijing, chaired its section on the History of Chinese Technology, and presented a paper "The Chinese Background of the Beginnings of European Printing." And in November–December 1984, he was invited to attend the "Workshop on the Authentication and Preservation of Rare Materials" held in Taipei, Taiwan, at which he presented the lectures "Chinese Rare Books in European and American Collections" and "Chinese Movable-Type."

As a librarian, Tsien has not only built a first-rate Far Eastern library at the University of Chicago but has also made outstanding contributions to East Asian librarianship as a whole, especially in the development of the Committee on East Asian Libraries (CEAL), which acquired its name and by-laws under his chairmanship from 1966–68. He also served as its Executive Member (1971–74), Chairman of its Subcommittee for Liaison with Chinese Libraries (1968–73), and Subcommittee on Resources and Development (1974–80). Another invaluable tradition he developed for CEAL is the periodic survey of East Asian collections in American libraries undertaken during the past thirty years. These surveys have carefully documented the history and development of all East Asian collections between 1869 and 1975; they have been extensively used by library administrations and funding agencies in the planning and support of East Asian libraries in North America.

In recognition of his contributions, Tsien was presented with a Distinguished Service Award by CEAL at the Association for Asian Studies Annual Meeting in 1978. He also received a Distinguished Service Award from the Chinese-American Librarians Association at the American Library Association Summer Conference in 1985. Beyond these awards, Tsien has served as a member of the China and Inner Asia Council when it was first organized by the Association for Asian Studies (1970–72); executive member of the Asian and African Section, Association of College and Research Libraries (1972–73); member of the Advisory Board, International Association of Oriental Librarians (1968–72); advisor to the National Central Library in Taiwan since 1970; advisor to the Government-Academic Interface Committee on International Education, Task Force on Library and

Information Resources, American Council of Education (1974); member of the ACLS-SSRC Task Force on (Chinese) Libraries and Research Materials (1974–75); consultant to the National Library of Iran (1975); and as a representative to CEAL for the Association of College and Research Libraries, American Library Association.

He was part of one of the first American Library Delegations to travel to China, visiting Beijing, Xi'an, Nanjing, Shanghai, and Guangzhou for two weeks in 1979, and he was invited to be an honorary member during the celebration of the 75th Anniversary of the founding of the National Library of China at the opening ceremony of its new building in 1987. Tsien initiated and later served as advisor to the International Union Catalog of Chinese Rare Books Project under the Research Library Group beginning in 1988. He was elected to the Chicago Senior Citizens Hall of Fame in 1989; received a Distinguished Alumni Award from the University of Chicago Alumni Association in 1996; served as advisor to the East Asian Group of the International Association of Libraries in 1996; and advisor to the China Printing Museum in 1998. He also received a Distinguished Service Award from the National Library of China in 1999; served as advisor to the Editorial Committee of Compiling Supplements to *Siku Quanshu* (1994–1998); was appointed advisor for the National Library of China in 2002, and received a Distinguished Service Award from the U.S.-China Policy Foundation, Washington D.C. in 2002. His book collection, donated to the Advanced Institute of Humanities and Social Sciences of Nanjing University, opened in 2007 as the T. H. Tsien Library.

Research and Publications

Like every serious scholar, Tsien is a prolific writer who has made tremendous contributions to the world of scholarship. He has published more than 160 books, articles, and book reviews in Chinese and English, many of which have been translated into Japanese, Korean, and other languages. His works on the history of the book, paper, and printing in China have shed much light on our understanding of these great Chinese contributions to world civilization. His book, *Written on Bamboo and Silk: The Beginning of Chinese Books and Inscriptions*, published by the University of Chicago Press in 1962, has since gone through several printings with a new edition in 2004. It is the first comprehensive study on the history of Chinese books, documents, and inscriptions before the invention of printing, covering a period from about 1400 B.C., when the earliest known Chinese writing is found to have been recorded, to about A.D. 700, when printing was about to begin in China. "Written in a simple and direct style, for the layman as well as for the scholar, it will find a hospitable place on many shelves," wrote Arthur W. Hummel in his review of the book in the *American Historical Review*. "Tsien's study is a triumph of modern sinology. . . . It is as definitive as extant research data will permit," declared the review in *Library Journal*.

Among other reviews, Joseph Needham wrote in the *Journal of Asian Studies*: "From its character and its size, it was evidently conceived as a companion volume to T. F. Carter's classic *The Invention of Printing in China and Its Spread Westward*, and we may say at once that it need not fear any comparison with that wonderful book." So it was no wonder that a revised Chinese edition, entitled *Zhongguo gudai shushi* 中國古代書史, was published by the Chinese University Press of Hong Kong in 1975; and yet other revised Chinese versions were published in Beijing, Taipei, and Shanghai, incorporating new archeological data unearthed in recent years. A Japanese edition, translated by Professor Akira Utsugi and Harutsugu Sawaya, with two others from the Tōyō Bunko, was published by the Hosei University Press in Tokyo in 1980, and a Korean edition in Seoul, Korea in 1990, reprinted in 1999. Moreover, Tsien has published more than fifty monographs and articles on the origin and development of paper making and printing in China, including one in a special issue for the International Book Year of the *UNESCO Courier*, published in 1972 in fifteen different languages.

His most significant contribution to the field is the study of paper, ink, and printing in Chinese civilization. In 1967 Dr. Joseph Needham of Cambridge University invited Dr. Tsien to join the East Asian History of Science Project to contribute a section on this subject. With a grant from the American Council of Learned Societies (1968–69), Tsien visited Cambridge and numerous libraries and museums in Europe and America to assemble research material. During the next few years, basic sources were collected and screened, lecture-discussion sessions were held at several universities, and a seminar on the history of Chinese printing was developed at the University of Chicago for a systematic examination of the source materials and discussion of the various issues.

Since his retirement in 1978, Tsien has been able to concentrate most of his time and energy on this study, again supported by several research grants, including from the National Science Foundation and the National Endowment for the Humanities, the Center for East Asian Studies of the University of Chicago, and the East Asian History of Science Trust at Cambridge, all of which made it possible for him to complete the work after another visit to Cambridge in 1982. This book, in some 300,000 words with 2,000 bibliographic entries and 200 illustrations, took him almost fifteen years to prepare for publication.

The volume *Paper and Printing* was published as Part I of Volume V in the *Science and Civilisation in China* series by the Cambridge University Press in 1985. This was the first volume written by a single author rather than in collaboration with others, as Needham points out in his Foreword. The book has been extremely well received, with the first printing selling out prior to publication. So far, it is the most comprehensive and up-to-date treatise on these subjects and a standard reference work for students in the field. As one reviewer commented in the *Printing Historical Society Bulletin*: "No short review can do justice to so notable a book about so remarkable a chapter of history, providing so great a display of historic detail from more than a thousand years of Oriental printing, and explaining the nature, method, materials, circumstances, and effects of mankind's most enduring form of communication." Or from another review in *Fine Prints*: "He brings his thorough knowledge of the subject to the Western reader with a clear and precise style. It is a rare talent, and one that makes this important book also genuinely enjoyable to read."

Another area of Tsien's interest is the topic of East-West cultural relations. His master's thesis was entitled "Western Impact on China through Translation," a version of which was published in the *Far Eastern Quarterly* in 1954. His research on the first Chinese-American exchange of publications in 1869, published in the *Harvard Journal of Asiatic Studies* in 1964/65, not only traced the origin of the Orientalia Collection at the

Library of Congress, but also highlighted a centenary celebration by the two countries in 1969. A collection of papers on this subject in Chinese, *Zhong Mei shuyuan* 中美書緣, was published in Taipei in 1998 and a revised edition in Beijing in 2008.

Tsien is also credited with a pioneering role in the introduction of area studies into American librarianship. In 1965 he was co-director, with Howard Winger, of the 30th Annual Conference of the Graduate Library School, University of Chicago, "Area Studies and the Library," the proceedings of which were published by the University of Chicago Press in 1966. This marked the first time that the area studies of East, South and Southeast Asia, Africa, the Middle East, Latin America, Eastern Europe and the Soviet Union and their impact on traditional Western librarianship were formally discussed by scholars and librarians. The conference drew the attention of library administrators and educators. Tsien has also published a large body of articles on East Asian librarianship, bibliography, and historiography. His reference work *China: An Annotated Bibliography of Bibliographies*, in collaboration with James K. M. Cheng, was published by G. K. Hall of Boston in 1978. Another scholarly work, *Ancient China: Studies in Early Civilization*, co-edited with Professor David T. Roy of the University of Chicago, was published by the Chinese University Press of Hong Kong in 1978.

It is heartening to note that Professor Tsien has retired only from his administrative and teaching duties at the University of Chicago. His wise counsel will be available for a long time to come as he remains active in the profession and in his own research. He continues to lecture by invitation and to revise and edit his monographs and articles for publication. His memoir in Chinese of his life in the United States, titled *Liu Mei zayi* 留美雜憶 (*A Memoir of Sixty Years in America*), tells the story of his life, family, study, and work in China and Chicago, with editions published in both Taiwan and mainland China. An English version, *Memoir of a Centenarian,* is under preparation.

This article was first published in English in the CEAL Bulletin, no. 81, 1987; revised in Chinese in a Festschrift in honor of Professor Tsien's 80th Birthday, (Taipei, 1991; Beijing, 1992), and again in another Festschrift in honor of his 95th Birthday (Beijing, 2006; Taipei, 2006) and finally revised in English in 2009.

28 AN INTERVIEW WITH T. H. TSIEN

Chang Pao-San

In the summer of 2002, I was invited by the Center for East Asian Studies at the University of Chicago to conduct research as a visiting scholar. It was during this time that I had the opportunity to meet Professor Tsien. The interviews took place at his home in the Hyde Park neighborhood of Chicago between November 7, 2002 and January 9, 2003.

Q: Professor Tsien, before coming to the United States, you had completed your college education and had also worked in China. Would you please talk about your education and work experience in China?

A: I started my education at home with a private tutor. Later I entered the Second Elementary School of Taizhou and in 1926 graduated from Huaidong Middle School (now Taizhou Middle School, where Chinese president Hu Jingtao also graduated from in 1959). In 1927, I entered the University of Nanking (now Nanjing University) while working part-time in the library of Ginling Women's College. This marked the beginning of my involvement with the library profession.

At that time, President Wu Yi-fang of Ginling College allowed me to take classes at her college for credit at my university. I took a Chinese history course taught by Professor Miao Fenglin and a translation course by Professor Zeng Xubai. As assignments for Zeng's class, I translated Bertrand Russell's "The Different Concepts of Happiness between the East and West" and Dorothy J. Orchard's "China's Use of Boycott of Foreign Goods as a Weapon." These translations were published in popular journals. These publications marked the beginning of my translation work.

At the University of Nanking, my major was in history and minor in library science. I took courses on the histories of Europe, Russia, India, and Japan given by Dr. M. S. Bates, and on the history of Sino-Japanese cultural relations and the history of modern China taught by Chinese professors. In addition to the required courses in Chinese, English, mathematics, physics, chemistry, and so on, I also elected to take Chinese philology, political science, sociology, population study, history of books, and other library science courses. The combination of library and history courses has had a significant influence on my career and research interests. Later, I spent most of my life with books and wrote my master's and doctoral dissertations on these subjects at the University of Chicago; all can be attributed to the courses I took during my undergraduate years.

After graduation from college in 1932, I joined the library of National Jiaotong University in Shanghai, where I gained much experience in library management and techniques under the guidance of Du Dingyou, director of the library. Five years later, I was appointed head of the Engineering Reference Library in Nanjing and later of the Shanghai office of the National Library, which were established for moving rare materials southward before the Sino-Japanese War. The Shanghai branch of the National Library kept some 60,000 volumes of Chinese rare books, 9,000 rolls of Dunhuang manuscripts, and several hundred items of stone and bronze rubbings, in addition to some 10,000 volumes of the complete sets of science and Oriental studies journals in Western languages. At that time, my work in Shanghai, besides the custody of these rare materials, included publishing work for the *Quarterly Bulletin of Chinese Bibliography*, collecting materials in the Japanese-occupied areas, and serving as liaison with libraries abroad.

Before long, security inside the foreign settlements in Shanghai increasingly became a problem. Therefore, the Chinese and U.S. governments agreed that part of these cultural treasures were to be moved to the U.S. Library of Congress for temporary custody and microfilming for preservation and circulation. Although the agreement was in place, the books could not be moved out of Shanghai because the customs service was under the control of the Japanese army. Fortuitously, I was able to contact a field inspector of the Shanghai Customs, who helped me ship these rare materials in one hundred cargo containers. After that two more containers were sent by the U.S. Consulate-General in Shanghai, which was all that could be managed. This very difficult task was completed just two days before the Japanese attack on Pearl Harbor in December 1941.

Upon the conclusion of the war, I was assigned by the Chinese government to go to Washington, D.C. to bring the books back to China, but the outbreak of civil war prevented this. I was, however, invited to Chicago, where I have now lived for over half a century.

Q: Why did you come to the University of Chicago?

A: I came to the University of Chicago as an exchange scholar from the National Library of Beiping in the autumn of 1947 to catalog the Chinese books acquired by the Far Eastern Library since its founding in 1936, as well as to engage in advanced studies at the Graduate Library School. After a year, Professor Herrlee G. Creel, who had invited me to the University, asked me to extend my stay and to teach courses in the Department of Oriental Languages and Literatures and offered to bring my family to Chicago. Upon the approval of the National Library of Beiping, the University of Chicago offered me a Professorial Lectureship at the Department with a concurrent appointment as Curator of the Far Eastern Library. Soon after, my family joined me in Chicago; this was a very peaceful time that allowed me to settle down with my family and engage in my work and studies after eight years of hardship in Shanghai during the war.

Q: How were your studies structured at the University of Chicago?

A: My plan was to spend most of my time working in the Far Eastern Library and to take classes part-time in the Graduate Library School. The University of Chicago was under the quarter system, which required three courses each quarter for full-time students. Because I was working full-time and studying part-time, I could take only one course each quarter with four courses per year, including the summer quarter. Therefore, it took me five years to earn my master's degree in 1952 and another five years for the doctorate in 1957.

Q: Would you please talk about the professors who influenced you the most during your graduate work at the University of Chicago?

A: I became interested in library science mainly because I worked in a library during my college years. I was also greatly inspired by a course "History of Books" with Professor Liu Guojun. After coming to the University of Chicago, I decided to focus my study on the history of books and printing. The first teacher who taught me the history of printing was Professor Pierce Butler, whose book *The Origins of Printing in Europe* was a classic in the field. Unfortunately, he retired a year after I arrived, and most of the classes I took were taught by other professors.

Among these classes were Jesse H. Sherra's "Theory and Practice of Classification," Leon Carnovsky's "Library Survey," Herman H. Fussler's "College and Research Libraries," and Lester E. Asheim's "Readability of Books, Popular Media, and Content Analysis." The focus of librarianship at that time was switching from the humanities to the social sciences. These new trends and methodologies had significant impact on my master's thesis, which was entitled "Western Impact on China through Translation: a Bibliographical Study."

When I started my doctoral program, Professor Howard W. Winger, whose specialization was in the history of Western libraries, books and printing, was appointed to the Graduate Library School in 1953 and became my advisor. His scholarly background and his manner with his students influenced me greatly in my studies, research, and personal conduct. In addition, my doctoral program consisted of a double major in library science and East Asian Studies and I therefore had seminar courses with Professor Creel and wrote a paper "Zhanguo Ce: Strategies of the Warring States," (later published in *Early Chinese Texts: A Bibliographical Study*, edited by Michael Loewe. Berkeley, CA, 1993). Subsequently, I completed my doctoral dissertation, "The Pre-printing Records of China: A Study of the Development of Early Chinese Inscriptions and Books," also under the advisorship of these two professors.

Q: You were the Curator of the Far Eastern Library for many years. Could you please talk about your work experience?

A: The Far Eastern Library (now the East Asian Library) of the University of Chicago was established in 1936 to collect basic reference works and materials to support the needs of Chinese teaching and research. Because the founder of the program, Professor Creel, emphasized ancient Chinese history and culture, the collection was especially rich in Confucian classics and documents, as well as such materials as collectanea, classified encyclopedias, local gazetteers, and complete sets of academic journals. In 1945, it also acquired the original collection of the Newberry Library of over 20,000 volumes of Chinese, Japanese, Manchu, Mongolian, and Tibetan books collected by Dr. Berthold Laufer, a German sinologist, during his trip to the Far East in the early 20th century.

When I arrived in late 1947, the total collection had grown to over 70,000 volumes. I spent about ten years completing the cataloging of the entire original collection. I accomplished this work largely by myself, from verification of the contents, cataloging, and classification, to making catalog cards, writing and attaching labels to bookcases and shelving. Five years later, my wife, Wen-ching, came to the library to assist me, but soon she was appointed lecturer to teach spoken Chinese in the Department of Far Eastern Languages, established in 1958. Up until then, Chinese language at the University of Chicago had focused on classical Chinese; this was the beginning of teaching modern Chinese as a result of changes in academic disciplines in U.S. higher education.

The Far Eastern Library was originally located in the basement of the Oriental Institute, but moved to the second floor of the Harper Library in 1958 and to the newly completed Joseph Regenstein Library in 1970. Now the East Asian Library has a collection of over 600,000 volumes, including over 15,000 volumes of editions and manuscripts from the Yuan and Ming Dynasties as well as about five hundred titles or seven thousand volumes of early Qing editions printed in or before the 18th century.

Since World War II and especially after 1949, Chinese studies in the United States have expanded from the traditional disciplines of language and history to modern politics, society, economy, law, and other areas of the social sciences. After 1958, the Far Eastern Library received substantial funding from the U.S. federal government and the Ford Foundation, as well as special support from the university administration. In addition to classical materials, it also acquired journals, government documents, social science publications, and new literary works published since the

1920s. Due to the Korean War and anti-China attitude in the U.S., acquisition of Chinese books ran into many difficulties in the 1950s, as the main supply source to the library was cut off. Despite this, we worked hard to overcome the challenges and to acquire important titles from Hong Kong, Taiwan, Japan, Europe, and other sources.

Because the present collection of modern publications in the East Asian Library at Chicago has no particular political affiliation and is without regional bias, numerous important research materials have been collected, many of which are perhaps not in mainland China or Taiwan. This is the collection development principle of the East Asian Library of the University of Chicago, which also mirrors the general acquisition policy of other collections in Western libraries.

Q: Would you please talk about your teaching experience?

A: In 1949 I began teaching courses on Chinese bibliography and Chinese historiography in the Department of Oriental Languages and Literatures. The purpose of these courses was to train graduate students to collect source materials for dissertations.

The course on Chinese bibliography included three parts: Part one covered the definition, scope, history of books and printing, and the terminology of bibliography. Part two focused on research methods, including acquisition, classification, cataloging, indexing systems for Chinese characters, styles of writing, and organization of materials. Part three then discussed reference tools, including bibliographies, indexes, dictionaries, encyclopedias, and collectanea, all of which were intended to develop students' understanding and ability to collect materials for their research. In addition to class discussions, there were practical assignments for each section.

The second quarter focused on methods of Chinese historical research. Because the graduate students of Chinese studies at that time usually wrote their dissertations on literature or history, this course was focused on the review of major historical works and reference tools. Actually, these two classes were the introduction of sinological methods, which assisted students in selecting a research topic, collecting sources, making detailed outlines, understanding writing styles, and compiling bibliographies for a proposed topic in a standard format. Since 1958, the Department of Far Eastern Languages and Literatures has made these courses required for doctoral students. So the initial stages of their dissertation research usually started with exercises in these two courses.

I also offered seminars on the history of Chinese printing at the Graduate Library School in the 1970s, through which I shared with the graduate students research materials that I was collecting for writing *Paper and Printing* for the Needham series, and at the same time trained a group of young scholars engaged in advanced studies of the subject. This is the only course on this subject ever offered in any American university.

In 1958, the Department of Oriental Languages and Literatures was divided into Far East (later changed to East Asian), Near East, and South Asian departments. The interdisciplinary center for Far East (later East Asian) Studies was established. I was promoted to associate professor in 1959 and to full professor in the Department of East Asian Languages and Civilizations and the Graduate Library School in 1962. I spent half of my time on teaching and research and the other half on library administration until my retirement in 1978. The university has continued to provide an office for me in the library, so that I can continue my research.

Q: Other than library work and teaching, you have also put emphasis on research and publishing and thus have enjoyed a distinguished reputation in the field. Would you please talk about your experience in writing and publishing the book *Written on Bamboo and Silk*?

A: *Written on Bamboo and Silk: The Beginning of Chinese Books and Inscriptions* was first published in English by the University of Chicago Press in 1962. This book was based on my doctoral dissertation, "The Pre-printing Records of China: A Study of the Early Development of Chinese Inscriptions and Books," which was intended to provide information about the dissemination and continuation of Chinese culture for understanding Chinese contributions to the world history of books. After completion, it was recommended for publication by the Graduate Library School to the University of Chicago Press.

At that time, however, the study of China in the West was receiving little attention. The press was reluctant to accept it, concerned that the book was too specialized and wouldn't have many readers. The press finally accepted it for publication after the GLS offered to pay one-third of its printing cost. To the surprise of many, the first edition sold out within three months of its publication, and was reprinted twice in 1963 and 1969. It was highly regarded in the international academic world and recognized as a companion piece to Thomas Carter's classic work, *The Invention of Printing in China and Its Spread Westward*. Moreover, interest in it has been shown by scholars in such disciplines as Chinese archaeology, paleography, and cultural history, as well as the history of books. The English edition was recently revised with a long Afterword by Professor Edward Shaughnessy as a classic of Chinese paleography and published by the University of Chicago Press in 2004.

Over the past forty years, it has circulated widely and has been translated into other languages, including Chinese, Japanese, and Korean. As Professor Hiraoka Takeo comments in the preface of the Japanese translation, the book "can be regarded as the entire history of Chinese writing during the significant period between the Yin Dynasty ruins and Dunhuang. . . . It aims at revisiting the culture of Chinese characters. . . . This is a fortunate book that continues to grow. In other words, it is a book filled with life."

Q: You have also written other books, such as *Paper and Printing; Studies on the History of the Chinese Book, Paper, Ink, and Printing;* and *Chinese-American Cultural Relations.* Would you please talk about these books?

A: *Written on Bamboo and Silk* covers the period from about 1300 B.C. to A.D. 700 in the early Tang Dynasty. After its publication, I considered writing a sequel to this volume to cover the entire history of the Chinese book. Coincidentally, in 1967 I received an invitation from Dr. Joseph Needham of Cambridge University to contribute sections on paper and printing for the series *Science and Civilisation in China.* At that time, he was approaching retirement age and hoped someone could collaborate with him in the remaining years of his life to complete his monumental work. I accepted his invitation to visit Cambridge in the autumn of 1968 to discuss the work and also to visit libraries and museums in Britain and other European countries where I began to collect material for the book. Later I visited many other places in the world to collect material, which grew immensely, along with the scope of the project. Consequently, it took me fifteen years from drafting the outline to completing the book, and the work expanded from the original plan of one hundred pages in a single chapter to a full-length monograph of 300,000 words. This far exceeded our original expectations.

The volume has ten chapters, with three chapters each on paper and printing (including inkmaking and bookbinding). One chapter includes an introduction to source materials and my reasoning for why the two major inventions of paper and printing took place in China instead of in other civilizations. The final chapter concludes by discussing the functions and impact of both inventions. I point out in particular that the functions of printing in China and the West are similar, but that their impact is quite different. Although my conclusion disagrees with that of others, Dr. Needham praised my scholarship, believing that it would provide him with strong ideas for his overall conclusions in the series.

I began writing the volume in my spare time, which is why it took so many years to complete. It was only after my retirement that I was able to concentrate fully. Thanks to grants from the National Science Foundation and the National Endowment for the Humanities, I was able to hire research assistants to help with the work. Two years after my retirement, I finally completed the first draft of ten chapters. It also has two hundred illustrations and a bibliography of about two thousand entries.

In September 1982, upon completion of the book, I visited Cambridge again to discuss its publication with Dr. Needham. The book was finally published by Cambridge University Press in 1985. It was priced at 66 pounds, equivalent to $100 at that time, which was very expensive, but the first edition of fifteen hundred copies sold out before the book was even published, and there have been three more printings since then. This volume is the best seller in the entire series. Dr. Needham was delighted with our collaboration and, with the approval of the board of trustees, he appointed me Research Fellow *en permanence* of his Institute. This was a special honor for me, which I happily accepted. Meanwhile, the book received very positive reviews internationally and was regarded as the authoritative work in the field as well as an encyclopedia on the subject of paper and printing.

The Chinese Academy of Sciences in Beijing had the volume translated into Chinese, published jointly by Shanghai Guji Press and Beijing Science Press in 1990, for presentation as a gift to Dr. Needham on his 90th birthday. About the same time, another translation was published in Taiwan. A third Chinese version, based on my Chinese draft, was published in 2004. Japanese and Korean translations were also published recently.

Studies on the History of the Chinese Book, Paper, Ink, and Printing, published in Chinese by the Chinese University Press in 1992, includes articles that were mostly byproducts of the research for my two monographs, which are limited in scope and style and so did not include individual details of various studies. Yet, certain issues must be explored before a conclusion can be made in the monograph. For example, the discussion on book knives only fills two pages in *Written on Bamboo and Silk*; but in the anthology, the article "A Study on Book Knives in Han China" comes to more than twelve pages. This book was revised and enlarged into two sections with twenty articles each and was published by Beijing Library Press in 2004.

Chinese-American Cultural Relations, published in Taiwan in 1998, includes articles, reports, and essays relating to the cultural exchange between China and the United States, or East and West. On the whole, this book is about another theme of my research and writing. They not only record and report historical facts but also include my personal experience and opinions on this subject. I have also co-edited two other books: *Ancient China: Studies in Early Civilization*, which includes sixteen articles on pre-Qin, Qin, and Han thought and institutions, and *Area Studies and the Library*, which includes proceedings of the conference on the impact of area studies—such as East, South and Southeast Asia, Near East, Latin America, the Soviet Union and Eastern Europe—upon the traditional management of Western collections.

Q: What has been the impact of the University of Chicago on your scholarship?

A: When I was in China, I published a few articles and translations, but they were mostly class assignments from my early college years and could not be considered serious research. Since arriving at the University of Chicago, I have made significant progress, including selecting research topics, collecting research materials and research methods, and especially improving my own writing in English. In addition, I have gained years of teaching experience, which has helped with my scholarship and research. For example, in selecting a research topic, I have learned to take new in-depth approaches and identify topics that had yet to be explored, so that I could fill in the gaps or expand on less studied and seemingly less significant topics.

For example, my M.A. thesis, "Western Impact on China Through Translation," used quantitative methods to analyze about 8,000 books listed in the bibliographies of translations from the 16th to the 20th centuries. This thesis analyzed the subjects, where the originals came from, the quantity of translations, their publication dates, and so on in order to understand the impact of Western culture on modern Chinese society. This study was actually inspired by E. W. Hulme's *Statistical Bibliography* (London, 1924), which used statistical methods to analyze the contents of over 20,000 incunabula to determine the impact of printing on Western civilization. The Chinese concept of bibliography emphasizes the recorded contents of the books, which is actually the method of content analysis, i.e., to use the analysis of the contents of the bibliography to further track the origins of cultural growth. The use of quantitative methods for the study of modern Chinese history was new in the field and it was highly regarded by the editor of *Far East Quarterly* who published the abstract of my thesis.

Another article, "A History of Bibliographical Classification in China," discussing the similarities and differences of classification concepts between China and the West, also used such comparative methods. In this article, I point out that the classification of knowledge of the British philosopher Francis Bacon (1560–1626), dividing human knowledge into the three categories of Memory, Imagination, and Reason, formed the triadic foundation of Western classification systems. This is almost identical to the Chinese fourfold classification of Classics, History, Philosophy, and Belles-lettres. Bacon further divided philosophy into Divinity, Nature, and Humanity, which is in accord with the Chinese divisions of Heaven, Earth, and Humanity. Bacon frequently cited Chinese inventions and other developments in his works. Consequently, I believe that Bacon's triadic system was influenced by the idea of Chinese classification.

Another article that discusses printing also employs comparative methods. The question posed in this article is why printing was invented in China instead of in the West. It has been generally accepted that the foundation of printing technology is based on the use of stamps. But the use of stamps in the West occurred earlier than in China and might have already been popular in Mesopotamia and Egypt before the invention of writing. Why, then, did Western stamps not lead to the invention of printing? Detailed comparative studies show that the Chinese stamps not only used the same materials but that they were also used for similar purposes. Western seals were mainly cylindrical in shape and had to be rolled on the surface of clay or wax to produce impressions, whereas the Egyptian seals were flat and contained mostly graphics without any writing. Chinese seals were mostly square or rectangular in shape, were flat on the bottom with reversed characters carved into them, and applied to silk or paper. Sometimes a stamp could have more than 100 characters carved onto it. Because this process is very similar to printing, that it paved the way for printing technology is not difficult to understand.

Q: What principles and research methods learned from your experience and scholarship do you believe to have been the most important?

A: My scholarship and research methods have been chiefly learned from my experience in writing my dissertations in graduate school. Before writing, I had to read extensively the related materials, and my writing was more or less illuminated by the viewpoints and methods of these references. My writing style perhaps was inspired and influenced by my daily reading of newspapers. Journalistic style is usually a succinct, fluent, and clear narrative. The opening generally presents the theme and a concise summary, followed by detailed factual elaborations, which leads to a conclusion. Such a three-part style is also common for scholarly writing. Reading newspapers has perhaps influenced me in organizing my writing systematically and coherently.

Some reviewers have commented that my writing is well-structured and rich in sources; my chapters are organically connected, and classic material is presented in the author's own words. I think these types of comments are important. As for sources, I first collect all materials related to the theme and then make selections for a reference bibliography. As for the structure, I usually plan the overall layout of the book from chapters down to individual paragraphs. After the first draft is completed, I go back to revise, polish, and adjust each chapter so that each part is an appropriate length. The beginning and ending of each chapter also correlate to each other, so that the narrative of the text continues seamlessly. As for the content of each chapter, it is mostly arranged according to the amount of material available and the nature of the discussion.

For example, I was aware when I wrote *Written on Bamboo and Silk* that bronze and stone inscriptions are traditionally treated as one group, but the amount of material on these two was substantially too much to balance with the other chapters. Therefore, I combined bronze with pottery inscriptions and stone with jade inscriptions to make two chapters of about equal size. Although pottery and bronze are very different materials and it seemed improper to group them together, I explained in the opening of the chapter the relationship and origins of the two so that it does not sound farfetched. As for citing Chinese classics, when writing in English, one must fully understand the original texts to be able to translate each word and sentence and then represent it in one's own words. This is different from writing in Chinese, where when citing classics, even if you do not fully understand, you still can cite. Therefore the degree of difficulty of writing in a non-Chinese language is much higher.

In general, I believe the principle of scholarship is to open new areas of research to avoid repetition. Therefore, the use of bibliography becomes the first step in any research. From selecting a topic, to drawing an outline, searching for material, writing and even compiling references, all must start with the bibliography to determine if others have done similar work. Thus we can avoid duplication and also finalize our themes and adjust the scope. When drawing an outline, a bibliography can lead to similar work and studies that enrich the content of one's own research. As for collecting material, we must rely on the various types of bibliographies; otherwise, it is impossible to have a complete idea of the sources. When using bibliographies, the first step is to check the bibliography of bibliographies. Bibliography is the foundation of scholarship and a vital research guide, so that when using any bibliography, first consult the instructions of the bibliographies. In that way, the point is not overlooked.

When I compiled teaching materials for the course "Chinese Bibliography," I collected over 2,500 titles of bibliographies of bibliographies about China in various languages. Later, this part was developed into a monograph, entitled *China: An Annotated Bibliography of Bibliographies*, which was annotated by James Cheng and has become an important reference tool for any study about China. The sources I use in my writings are considered by others to be relatively complete; an important reason for that is my extensive use of bibliographies.

Q: In your research areas, what are the questions that still require exploration? What directions should future research take?

A: My research mainly focuses on two major areas—the history of writing in China and the cultural exchange between China and other countries. The combination of the two, if looked at from a certain perspective, may lead to conclusions regarding the characteristics of Chinese culture and its position among world civilizations. In the conclusion of *Written on Bamboo and Silk*, I point out that the continuity, productivity, and universality of Chinese writing are the cornerstones of Chinese culture. This is unique in the history of world cultures. This is the conclusion that I have drawn through my study, observation, and analysis. But limited by the overall form of the monograph, I was only able to briefly address these points instead of fully elaborating on them. I believe there is much room for further investigation on this issue, and more detailed analysis, examples, and comparison may discover more on these points. This is a great project, which I hope aspiring future researchers will continue to explore.

Previous Chinese scholarship on the history of books and printing can be generalized into two major trends. One is the traditional approach of bibliography or bibliology, which emphasizes the recording, discerning, circulation, and textual criticism of books. The other main trend, under Western influence, is contemporary scholarship on the origin, development, technology, and dissemination of printing. I think future research should focus more on the issues of the cultural aspects of printing history, especially the relationship between printing and social developments. I have raised this question in my *Paper and Printing* and compared the functions and impact of printing in traditional Chinese and Western societies. My conclusion is that they had similar social functions but to varying degrees.

The impact of printing in Chinese and Western societies is not only quite different but in complete opposition to each other. In the West, the invention and spread of printing promoted the development of national languages and literatures, which encouraged nationalism and the establishment of new nation-states. Yet in traditional Chinese society, printing united with the civil-service examination system, which not only assisted in the continuity and dissemination of Chinese writing but also became an important factor in the relative stability of traditional Chinese society; it is also an important device in maintaining Chinese culture. Although my viewpoint differs from those of many others, this question must be further analyzed from social, economic, and political perspectives in order to arrive at any final conclusion. I think this is a new direction that warrants emphasis in the study of the history of books and printing.

The last question worth mentioning here is whether the methods for recording human thought are related to forms of media. In my conclusion to *Written on Bamboo and Silk*, I state that the invention of paper and printing did not change the depth and significance of the contents of the books. The traditional thoughts that influenced Chinese society for thousands of years—including Confucianism, Daoism, and the Legalist school—are all immortal works written on bamboo and silk. Another example is Sima Qian's *Shiji* (*Records of the Grand Historian*), an important work written on perhaps some 50,000 bamboo strips, which generations of historians have looked to as an historical standard. No works produced since the invention of paper and printing have surpassed these thoughts and doctrines, which have been circulating broadly through the eras. Even today in the computer age, we have yet to see a single historical record that surpasses the *Shiji* in terms of style, scope, and creativity. Sima Qian's record covers every aspect of history—surface, line, and point. What exactly is the relationship between the ability of human thought and the media of writing? This is also an important topic that warrants continued deliberation.

This interview was published in Chinese in the Newsletter of Chinese Studies *(Taipei), v. 22, no. 1, February, 2003; translated into English by Zhijia Shen, University of Colorado, in 2004; edited and updated by Alexander and Mary Tsien Dunkel of the University of Arizona in 2008; and published in the* Journal of East Asian Libraries, *no. 146, October 2008.*

29 PUBLICATIONS

Ming-Sun Poon

Professor Tsuen-Hsuin Tsien published his first article in Chinese in 1931. From that time until December 2008, he authored 169 separate works, including eighteen monographs, seven pamphlets, six instructional compilations, fourteen book reviews, thirteen prefaces and postscripts, and 111 articles and miscellaneous writings. Based on the tables of contents, these 169 works can be grouped into five subject categories: (1) History of books, paper, and printing, 59; (2) China-foreign cultural relations, 16; (3) Library science and bibliography, 18; (4) East Asian library resources, 30; and (5) History, biography, and miscellaneous topics, 46.

Tsien's publication career began in college when his paper, "Tushuguan yu xueshu yanjiu" 圖書館與學術研究 ("Libraries and Scholarly Research"), was published in his university journal in 1931. This work was selected, half a century later, for the *Anthology of Writings by Colleagues of the National Library of Beijing* (Beijing, 1987), in which the editor points out in the preface that this article "has stood the test of history, bearing relevance for the present day. It is testimony to the fact that the author demonstrated mature academic ability even during his early college years." A few years after this first publication, two other pieces, translations of a selection from Bertrand Russell's *The Conquest of Happiness* and Dorothy J. Orchard's "China's Use of Boycott of Foreign Goods as a Weapon," appeared in periodicals with wide circulations, sparking Professor Tsien's work on translation.

In the 1950s, Professor Tsien began to publish in English after moving to the United States. His first English article, "A History of Bibliographic Classification in China," which appeared in *Library Quarterly*, October 1952, was written when he was a student in the Graduate Library School of the University of Chicago. Two years later, an abstract of his master's thesis, "Western Impact on China through Translation: a Bibliographical

Study," was published in the academic journal *Far Eastern Quarterly*, May 1954. His subsequent study of the cultural relations between East and West was a continuation of this research topic.

In the 1960s and 1970s, Professor Tsien was invited by the Council on East Asian Libraries of the Association for Asian Studies to conduct surveys on East Asian library resources, personnel needs, and financial concerns across North America. Based on these surveys he published a series of reports that American higher education administrations and foundations continue to use as a basis for funding East Asian studies and library development. An annual conference held at the University of Chicago, on the theme of "Area Studies and the Library," was co-organized by Professor Tsien in 1965. Papers presented at this conference, which were subsequently collected in the conference proceedings, became important directives for librarianship on non-Western language resources. The conference was a landmark event as it initiated a dialogue between librarians and academicians in non-Western area studies to address issues of mutual concern. Later on, monographs such as *Ancient China: Studies in Early Civilization* (Hong Kong: Chinese University Press, 1978) and *China: an Annotated Bibliography of Bibliographies* (co-authored by James K. M. Cheng, Boston: G. K. Hall, 1978), along with a wide range of instructional materials that were the fruition of Professor Tsien's academic endeavors, all appeared in English.

Professor Tsien's doctoral dissertation, "The Pre-printing Records of China: A Study of the Development of Early Chinese Inscriptions and Books," eventually appeared in book form as *Written on Bamboo and Silk: The Beginnings of Chinese Books and Inscriptions* (Chicago: University of Chicago Press, 1962). It was reprinted numerous times until an enlarged and revised edition was published in 2004, forty-two years after the first edition. The book continues to enjoy international esteem as a classic text on the history of the Chinese book, civilization, archaeology, and paleography.

Joseph Needham's 1967 invitiation for Professor Tsien to participate in Needham's *Science and Civilisation in China* series marked another advancement in his research activities. From the moment that he began to write *Paper and Printing*, through its publication in 1985, and until very recently, Professor Tsien's publications have focused almost exclusively on the history of Chinese books, paper, inkmaking, and printing.

From the 1950s to the 1980s, Professor Tsien's publications were written primarily in English, targeting a Western and international readership. Many of these English publications have been translated into Chinese, Japanese, and Korean and published in Hong Kong, Beijing, Taipei, Shanghai, Tokyo, and Seoul. Particularly notable is an introductory article on the Chinese invention of printing that appeared in *UNESCO Courier*. This article was published simultaneously in fifteen different languages, in addition to the Chinese translation.

Since Professor Tsien's retirement in the 1980s, a majority of his publications have been written in Chinese, including *Zhongguo gudai shushi* 中國古代書史 and *Shu yu zhubo* 書於竹帛, published in Hong Kong, Beijing, Taipei, and Shanghai. Translations into Japanese and Korean were published in Tokyo and Seoul respectively. Chinese versions of his collected writings were also gathered into collections published as *Zhongguo shuji zhi mo ji yinshuashu* 中國書籍紙墨及印刷術 (Hong Kong, 1992; rev. ed., Beijing, 2002), and *Zhong Mei shuyuan* 中美書緣 (Taipei, 1998; rev. ed., *Dongxi wenhua jiaoliu luncong* 東西文化交流論叢, Beijing, 2009). Three Chinese versions of his *Paper and Printing* have been published since 1990, including the most recent edition *Zhongguo zhi he yinshua wenhuashi* 中國紙和印刷文化史 (Guilin, 2004), which was cited as one of the ten best books in the social sciences published in 2004, and was translated into Japanese and Korean in 2007–2008. This book proved to be so influential that a symposium was called in Beijing in 2004 to discuss its worldwide importance.

Yet another recent book by Professor Tsien is his memoir of life in America, *Liu Mei zayi* 留美雜憶 (Taipei, 2007; Beijing, 2008), in which he retells the story of his life, family, education, and career. Besides the current volume, *Collected Writings on Chinese Culture*, another Chinese monograph, *Huigu ji* 回顧集 (*Looking Back*), edited by friends and students, was published in celebration of his 100th birthday in 2010 and 2011.

Chronological Bibliography

The following list of Professor Tsien's publications is arranged in chronological order with monographs in bold to show the development of his scholarship.

1931　〈圖書館與學術研究〉，《金陵大學文學院季刊》，第1卷第2
　　　期 (1931)，頁280–92；收入《北京圖書館同人文選》
　　　(北京，1987)，頁165–72。

1931　〈中國以抵制外貨為對外武器〉，《時事月報》，第5卷第2
　　　(1931.8)，頁96–102。譯自Dorothy J. Orchard, *Industrialization of
　　　the Far East* (New York, 1930) 之一章。

1932　〈東北事件之言論索引〉，《中華圖書館協會會報》，第7卷第
　　　5期 （1932），頁11–24。

1933　《中文圖書館編目規則》，上海交通大學圖書館，1933。

1934　〈東西快樂觀念之歧異〉，《世界雜誌》，第2卷第4期
　　　(1934.10) 頁617–23。譯自Bertrand Russell, *The Conquest of
　　　Happiness* (New York, 1930) 之一章。

1935　《普通圖書館圖書選目》，與喻守真合編，上海中華書局，
　　　1935。446頁。

1936　《杜氏叢箸書目》，錢存訓主編，上海中國圖書館服務社，1936。
　　　100+40 頁。

1942　〈隋唐時代中日文化關係之檢討〉，署名「宜叔」，《學術界》，第
　　　1卷 (1942) 第4期，頁39–46；第5期，頁51–60；第6期，頁
　　　55–65。

1952　"Western Impact on China through Translation: A Bibliographical
　　　Study." M.A. Thesis, The University of Chicago, March, 1952, 245 pp.

1952　"A History of Bibliographic Classification in China," *Library Quarterly*,
　　　22:4 (Oct., 1952), 307–24.

1954　"Western Impact on China through Translation," *Far Eastern Quarterly*,
　　　14:3 (May, 1954), 305–29.

1954　[Review] *Code of Descriptive Cataloging*," by Charles E. Hamilton,
　　　Library Quarterly, 24:4 (Oct., 1954), 414–15.

1955　"An Introduction to David Kwo and His Paintings," in *Modern Chinese
　　　Painting* by David Kwo. Chicago: Art Institute of Chicago, 1955.

1956   "The Far Eastern Library of the University of Chicago, 1936–1956,"
       Far Eastern Quarterly, 15:3 (May, 1956), 656–58.

**1957   "The Pre-printing Records of China: A Study of the Development
       of Early Chinese Inscriptions and Books." Doctoral Dissertation,
       University of Chicago, 1957, 302 pp.**

1957   [Review] "Chinese Bronze Age Weapons," by Max Loether, *Library
       Quarterly*, 27:2 (April, 1957), 109–10.

1958   [Review] "Annals of Academia Sinica, no. 3, Presented in Memory of
       the 20th Anniversary of Late Secretary-General V. K. Ting's Death,"
       ed. by Li Chi, *Journal of Asian Studies* 17:4 (August, 1958), 623–25.

**1959   *Library Resources on East Asia* [editor]. Zug, Switzerland: Inter
       Documentation Co., 1959.**

1959   "Far Eastern Resources in American Libraries," co-authored with G.
       Raymond Nunn. *Far Eastern Quarterly*, XXIX: 1 (January, 1959), 27–42.

1959   〈美國圖書館中的極東資料〉，木寺清一譯，《圖書館界》，第
       11卷，第3期（1959.9），頁124–34。

1959   "Asian Studies in America: A Historical Survey," in *Asian Studies and
       State University* (Bloomington: Indiana University, 1959), 108–21.

1960   "Chinese Studies in America," *Newsletter of the Midwest Chinese
       Student & Alumni Services*, n.s., IV:3 (Dec., 1960), 3–4.

1960   [Preface] *Chinese Local History in the Far Eastern Library, University
       of Chicago*. Chicago: University of Chicago Library, 1960.

1961   〈美國早期的亞洲研究〉，洗麗環譯，《大陸雜誌》，第22卷第
       5期（1961.3），頁147–52。

1961   〈漢代書刀考〉，《中央研究院歷史語言研究所集刊》，外編第
       4號，下冊 (1961)，頁997–1088；收入劉家璧編《中國圖書
       史資料集》(香港，1974)，頁159。

1961   "China," in *American Historical Association: A Guide to Historical
       Literature*. New York: Macmillan, 1961.

1961   "The Lingnan Painters," *Newsletter of the Midwest Chinese Student and
       Alumni Services*, n.s., IV:4 (March, 1961).

**1962   *Written on Bamboo and Silk: The Beginnings of Chinese Books and
       Inscriptions*. Chicago: University of Chicago Press, 1962; 3rd
       printing, 1969, xiii, 233 pp. 28 plates; 2nd revised edition with
       Afterword by Edward L. Shaughnessy. Chicago: University of**

Chicago Press, 2004. xxiv, 323 pp. 30 plates, tables.

1962 "Silk as Writing Material," *Midway*, 11 (1962), 92–105.

1962 "*The University of Chicago Doctoral Dissertations and Master's Theses on Asia, 1894–1962*," compiler with preface. Chicago: Committee on Far Eastern Civilizations and Committee on South Asian Studies, University of Chicago, 1962.

1962 [Review] "*A Guide to Doctoral Dissertations by Chinese Students in America. 1905–1960*, by T. L. Yuan," *Library Quarterly*, 32 (July, 1962), 241–42.

1963 [Review] "Chinese Calligraphy and Painting in the Collection of John M. Crawford. Jr.," ed. by Laurence Sickman, in *Paper of the Bibliographical Society of America* (Summer, 1963), 249–51.

1964 "First Chinese-American Exchange of Publications," *Harvard Journal of Asiatic Studies*, vol. 25 (1964–1965), 19–30.

1964 *Present Status and Personnel Needs of Far Eastern Collections in America: A Report for the Committee on American Library Resources on the Far East of the Association for Asian Studies.* Washington, D.C., 1964.

1964 "Chinese Libraries in Chicago," *Newsletter of the Midwest Chinese Student & Alumni Services*, n.s., 7:45 (May, 1964), 3.

1965 "East Asian Collections in America," *Library Quarterly*, 35:4 (Oct., 1965), 260–82.

1965 "Beauty Contests in Imperial China," *Newsletter of the Midwest Chinese Student & Alumni Services*, n.s., IX:1 (Oct., 1965), 2.

1965 [Review] "Intrigues: Studies of the Chan-Kuo-Ts'e," by J. I. Crump, *Journal of Asian Studies*, 24 (1965), 34–39.

1966 *Area Studies and the Library*, co-ed. Howard W. Winger. Chicago: University of Chicago Press, 1966. 184 pp.

1966 〈美國的東亞書藏〉，居蜜譯，《出版月刊》，第11卷第1期 (1966)，頁69–77。

1966 〈董作賓先生訪美記略〉，《董作賓先生逝世三週年紀念集》 (臺北，1966)，頁328–39，《傳記文學》，第9卷第5期 （1966.11） 頁 49–52。

1967 "Tung Tso-pin in America," *Newsletter of the Midwest Chinese Student & Alumni Services*, n.s., X:1 (Jan., 1967), 2–3.

1967 [Review] *"Specimen Pages of Korean Movable Types," by M. P. McGovern. Library Quarterly,* 37 (1967), 40–41.

1967 〈國立北平圖書館善本書籍運美經過〉,《傳記文學》, 第10 卷第2期 (1967.2), 頁55–57;《思憶錄—袁守和先生紀念冊》(臺北, 1967), 頁114–18。

1967 "[Biographies of] Ch'i Pai-shih 齊白石, Kao Chien-fu 高劍父 and Kao Ch'i-feng 高奇峰, Feng Ch'eng-chun 馮承鈞" in Howard L. Boorman, ed., *Biographical Dictionary of Republican China* (5v. New York: Columbia University Press, 1967–1979).

1968 [Review] "Contemporary China: A Research Guide," by Peter Berton & Eugene Wu, *Library Quarterly* 38:3 (July, 1968), 276–77.

1969 〈中美書緣—紀念中美文化交換百週年〉,《傳記文學》, 第14 卷第6期 (1969.6), 頁6–9;又中央圖書館複印單行本。

1969 〈美國遠東圖書館概況〉, 成露西節譯,《東海大學圖書館學報》, 第9期 (1969), 頁197–200。

1969 〈論明代銅活字版問題〉(Movable-type Printing in Ming China),《慶祝蔣慰堂先生七秩榮慶論文集》(臺北, 1969), 頁127–44;收入劉家璧編《中國圖書史資料集》(香港, 1974), 511–26;《圖書印刷發展史論文集》初編 (臺北, 1957), 頁 356–66;《學術集林》, 卷7 (1996.4), 頁107–29。

1969 *Chinese Library Resources: A Syllabus,* prepared with K. T. Wu. Chicago: Institute for Far Eastern Librarianship, University of Chicago, 1969. 40 pp.

1969 *A Guide to Reference and Source Materials for Chinese Studies,* prepared with Weiying Wan. Chicago: Institute for Far Eastern Librarianship, University of Chicago, 1969. 114 pp.

1970 "Chinese Library Association," in *Encyclopedia of Library and Information Science,* vol. 4 (New York: Dekker, 1970), 656–57.

1971 〈中國古代文字記錄的遺產〉, 周寧森譯,《香港中文大學中國文化研究所學報》, 第4卷第1期 (1971.4), 頁273–86.

1971 "A Study of the Book Knife in Han China," translated by John H. Winkelman. *Chinese Culture,* 21:1 (March, 1971), 87–101.

1971 "East Asian Library Resources in America: A New Survey," *Association for Asian Studies Newsletter,* 16:3 (Feb., 1971), 1–11.

1972 "Education for Far Eastern Librarianship," *International Cooperation in Oriental Librarianship* (Canberra: National Library of Australia, 1972), 108–16.

1972　"China: The Birthplace of Paper, Printing and Movable Type," *UNESCO Courier*, vol. 25 (December, 1972), 4–11. 此文為聯合國教科文組織《信使月刊》慶祝「國際書年」特約撰述，同時以15種語文發行。Reprinted in *Pulp and Paper International* (Brussels, Feb., 1974), 50–56.

1972　〈中國對造紙術和印刷術的貢獻〉，馬泰來譯，《明報月刊》，第7卷第2期 (總84 期，1972. 2)，頁2–7。

1972　*Terminology of the Chinese Book, Bibliography and Librarianship.* Chicago: Graduate Library School, 1972. 22pp.

1972　[Review] "Directory of Selected Scientific Institutions in Mainland China," *Library Quarterly* 42:4 (Oct., 1972).

1973　[Preface] Far East: *An Exhibition of Resources in the University of Chicago Library.* Chicago: Committee on Far Eastern Studies and Committee on South Asian Studies, University of Chicago, 1973,

1973　[Introduction] *Author-title Catalog of the Far Eastern Library, University of Chicago.* Boston: G. K. Hall, 1973. 18v.

1973　"Raw Materials for Old Papermaking in China," *Journal of the American Oriental Society, 93:4 (Oct.–Dec.,* 1973), 510–19.

1973　〈英國劍橋大學藏本《橘錄》題記〉，《清華學報》，新第10卷第1 (1973.6)，頁106–14；附英文提要。

1973　〈中國古代的簡牘制度〉，周寧森譯，《香港中文大學中國文化研究所學報》，第6卷第1期 (1973.12)，頁45–60；收入《圖書印刷發展史論文集・續編》（臺北，1977），頁17–32。

1974　〈中國古代的造紙原料〉，馬泰來譯，《香港中文大學中國文化研究所學報》，第7卷第1期 (1974.12)，頁27–39；收入《中華文化復興論叢》，第9集 （臺北，1977），頁664–79；《圖書印刷發展史論文集・續編》（臺北，1977），頁33–42。

1974　〈譯書對中國現代化的影響〉，戴文伯譯，《明報月刊》，第9卷第8期 （總104期，1974.8），頁2–13；《文獻》1986年第2期（總第28期），頁176–204。

1975　《中國古代書史》，附勞榦後序，香港中文大學，1975，187頁，圖版28幅；1981再版。

1975　[Review] *"Chinese Colour Prints from the Ten Bamboo Studio"* by Jan Tschichold, translated by Katherine Watson. *Journal of Asian Studies,* 34:2 (Feb. 1975), 513–15.

1975 [Preface] *T.L. Yuan Bibliography of Western Writings on Chinese Art and Archaeology*, compiled by Harrie Vanderstappen. London: Marshall, 1975.

1976 "[Biographies of] An Kuo 安國 and Hua Sui 華燧" in *Dictionary of Ming Biography*, 1368–1644, ed. by L. Carrington Goodrich & Chao-ying Fang. 2v. New York: Columbia University Press, 1976, 9–12; 647–50.

1976 *Current Status of East Asian Collections in American Libraries, 1974/75*. Washington, D.C.; Center for Chinese Research Materials, Association of Research Libraries, 1976, 67pp.

1976 "Current Status of East Asian Collections in American Libraries: A Note on the Final version," *Committee on East Asian Libraries Newsletter*, no. 50 (July, 1976), 45–47.

1977 "Current Status of East Asian Collections in American Libraries," *Journal of Asian Studies*, 36:3 (May, 1977), 499–514.

1977 [Preface] *Far Eastern Serials in the University of Chicago Libraries*. Chicago: Far Eastern Library, University of Chicago, 1977.

1977 [Preface] *Daisaku Ikeda Collection of Japanese Religion and Culture. Chicago*: Far Eastern Library, University of Chicago, 1977.

1977 *Introduction to Chinese Bibliography: Outline and Bibliography*. Chicago: Graduate Library School, University of Chicago, 1977.

1977 *Chinese Bibliography and Historiography: Outline and Bibliography*. Chicago: Graduate Library School, University of Chicago, 1977.

1977 *History of Chinese Printing and Publishing: Outline and Bibliography*. Chicago: Graduate Library School, University of Chicago, 1977.

1978 *Manual of Technical Processing*. Chicago: Far Eastern Library, University of Chicago, 1978.

1978 *China: An Annotated Bibliography of Bibliographies* 《中國書目解題彙編》. In collaboration with James K. M. Cheng 鄭炯文. Boston: G. K. Hall, 1978. xxviii, 603pp.

1978 "*Chiu Ching San Chuan Yen Ko Li* 九經三傳沿革例," in *Sung Bibliography* 《宋代書錄》 ed. by Yves Hervouet. Hong Kong: The Chinese University Press, 1978.

1978 〈書籍、文房及裝飾用紙考略〉，馬泰來、陳雄英譯，《香港中文大學中國文化研究所學報》，第9卷上冊（1978），頁87–98。

1978 *Ancient China: Studies in Early Civilization* 《古代中國論文集》 co-ed. with David T. Roy. Hong Kong: The Chinese University Press, 1978, 370 pp.

1979　[Review] "Chinese History: Index to Learned Articles, 1905–1964," by P. K.Yu, *Harvard Journal of Asiatic Studies* 33 (1979), 291–94.

1979　"Trends in Collection Building for East Asian Studies in American Libraries," in Wason Collection 60th Anniversary Conference: *Cooperation Among East Asian Libraries* (Ithaca: Cornell University Libraries, 1979), 7–34; *College and Research Libraries* 40:5 (Sept., 1979), 79, 405–15.

1979　〈美國圖書館中東亞資源現況調查〉，李連揮譯，《圖書館學資訊科學》，第5 卷第2期（1979.10），頁38–40。

1980 《中国古代書籍史：竹帛に書す》，宇都木章、澤谷昭次、竹之内信子、 廣瀬洋子合譯，平岡武夫序。東京法政大學出版局，1980。xvii，258，xxii頁，圖28幅。

1982　"Why Paper and Printing were Invented First in China and Used Later in Europe," *Explorations in the History of Science and Technology in China* (Shanghai, 1982), 459–70.

1983　〈竹簡和木牘〉，《中國圖書文獻學論集》（臺北，1983），頁647–78。

1982　[Review] "Cambridge Texts in the History of Chinese Science on Microfiche," *Chinese Science*, no. 5 (June 1982), 67–70.

1983　〈遠東圖書館員的專業教育〉，潘銘燊譯，《中國圖書館學會會報》，第35期（1983.12），頁93–98。

1983　[Preface] "An Introduction to Studies in East Asian Librarianship," in the *Asian Library Series*, published by the Chinese Materials Center, San Francisco & Taipei, 1983.

1984　"Technical Aspects of Chinese Printing," in *Chinese Rare Books in American Collections*, ed. Soren Edgren. (New York: China Institute in America, 1984), 6–25.

1985 *Paper and Printing*, in Joseph Needham, *Science and Civilisation in China*, vol. V, part I, Cambridge & New York: Cambridge University Press, 1985, revised 3rd printing, 1987, xv, 485 pp, Illustrated.

1985　〈歐美地區古籍存藏現況〉，《古籍鑑定與維護研習會專集》（臺北，1985），頁25–46。

1985　〈中國歷代活字本〉，《古籍鑑定與維護研習會專集》（臺北，
　　　　1985），頁211-23。

1985　〈歐洲印刷術起源的中國背景〉，《東方雜誌》，復刊第19卷第5
　　　　期（1985.11），頁18-23；《中國印刷》，第18期 (1987.11)，頁
　　　　86-91；《第三屆國際中國科學史會議論文集》(北京，1990)
　　　　頁251-56。

1986　〈歐美各國所藏中國古籍簡介〉，《明報月刊》，第21卷第1期
　　　　(總241期，1986.1)，頁105-116；《圖書館學通訊》1987年
　　　　第4期，頁57-67。

1986　〈中國發明造紙和印刷術早於歐洲的諸因素〉，金永華譯，《明
　　　　報月刊》，第20卷第6期 (總234期，1985.6)，頁69-72；《中國
　　　　科技史探索》〔中文版〕(上海，1986)，頁 443-52。

1986　〈家庭及日常用紙探原〉，《中國造紙》，第5卷第4、6期
　　　　(1986.8,10)，頁58-61，頁63-66；《紙史研究》，第2期
　　　　(1986.10)，頁30-39；《明報月刊》，第21卷第9-10期 （總
　　　　249-250期，1986.9-10），頁74-77，頁96-100；《漢學研
　　　　究》，第5卷第1期 （總第9號，1987.6），頁75-93。

1986　〈"なせ"中国ほ—ロッバすも早く紙と印刷術を発明こた
　　　　が〉，澤谷昭次譯，《山口大學教養部紀要》，第20卷人文科學
　　　　篇（1986），頁1-12。

1987　〈中國雕版印刷技術雜談〉，《蔣慰堂先生九秩榮慶論文集》（臺
　　　　北，1987)，頁23-37；《明報月刊》，第23卷第5期（1988.5），頁
　　　　103-108；《中國印刷》，第20期 （1988.5），頁85-90；《雕版印刷
　　　　源流》（北京，1990），頁319-29。

1987　[Review] "Chinese Handmade Paper," by Floyd Alonzo McClure, *Fine
　　　　Print* (San Francisco), vol. 13, no. 3 (July, 1987), 156, 172.

1987　〈張秀民著中國印刷史序〉，《文獻》，1987年第2期 （總32期），
　　　　頁209-12；《中國印刷》，第16期 （1987.5），頁91-92；《中國古
　　　　代書籍、紙墨及印刷術》（北京，2002），頁284-87。

**1987　《印刷發明前的中國書和文字記錄》，鄭如斯增訂，北京印刷工
　　　　業出版社，1987。ix，180頁，圖版27幅。附錄：勞榦後序，李
　　　　棪、李約瑟、及平岡武夫評介。**

1988　〈芝加哥大學遠東圖書館所藏封泥題記〉，《董作賓先生誕辰紀
　　　　念集》（臺北，1988），頁91-94。

1988　"Sealing Clays in the University of Chicago Library," *Committee on*

East Asian Libraries Bulletin. No. 83 (February, 1988), 15–16, Illustrated.

1988 〈中國的傳統印刷術〉，高熹異譯，《故宮文物》，第5卷第11
期（總52，1988.2），頁110–7。

1988 〈中國墨的製作和鑑賞〉，高熹異譯，《故宮學術季刊》第5卷
第4期（1988.9），頁67–84。

1988 〈墨的藝術〉，《明報月刊》，第23卷第12期（1988.12），頁77。

1989 〈中國墨的起源和發展〉，高熹異譯，《文獻》，1989年第2
期，頁233–49。

1989 〈造紙與印刷：自敘〉，附李約瑟博士序言，《中國印刷》，第
23期（1989.2），頁80–83。

1989 〈對中國圖書館出版工作的幾點建議〉，《出版參考》，18
（1989.9.15），頁2–3。

1989 〈《中國手工造紙》評介〉，《漢學研究》，第7卷第2期（總第
14號，1989.12），頁423–32。

1989 〈現存最早的印刷品和雕板實物略評〉，《國立中央圖書館館
刊》，新第22卷第2期（1989.12），頁1–10；《中國印刷》，第
28期（1990.5），頁103–8。

**1990 《中國科學技術史：紙和印刷》，劉祖慰譯，北京科學出版社、
上海古籍出版社，1990。xix，472頁，插圖182幅。**

**1990 《中國古代書史》（韓文），金允子譯，漢城，東文選，1990；
1999再版，225頁，圖版28，彩色插圖15幅。**

1990 〈中國印刷史簡目〉，《國立中央圖書館館刊》，新第23卷第1期
（1990.6），頁179–99；《中國印刷》，第35–36期（1992）；《中國印刷
史料選輯》，第4冊（北京，1993），頁456–82。

1990 〈印刷術在中國傳統文化中的能〉，《漢學研究》，第8卷第2期
（總第6號，1990.12），頁239–50；文獻》，1991年第2期，頁148–59。

1991 "Recent Discovery of Earliest Movable-type Printing in China: An
Evaluation," *Committee on East Asian Libraries Bulletin*, no. 92
(February, 1991), 6–7, Illustrated.

1991 〈封泥小識〉，《明報月刊》1991.6；《上海高校圖書情報學刊》
第20期（1995.4），頁51–52。

1991 〈潘銘燊著《非花軒雜文》序〉，溫哥華，楓橋出版社，1991。

**1992 《中國書籍、紙墨及印刷史論文集》，香港中文大學出版社，
1992。x，330頁，插圖50幅。**

1993 "Chan Kuo Ts'e," in *Early Chinese Texts: A Bibliographical Survey*, ed.

Michael Loewe, (Berkeley, CA., 1993), 1–11.

1993 "How Chinese Rare Books Crossed the Pacific at the Outbreak of World War II: Some Reminiscences," *Bulletin of East Asian Libraries*, no. 101 (February, 1993), 109–112.

1994 〈中國印刷史研究的範圍、問題和發展〉,《中國印刷》,第12卷第2期（1994.2）,頁9–12;《中國印刷史學術研討會論文集》（北京,1996）,頁7–14。

1995 《中國之科學與文明：造紙及印刷》,劉拓、汪劉次昕譯,臺北商務印書館,1995。vi,610頁。

1995 〈珍貴的書緣、難忘的友誼：悼念李約瑟博士〉,《明報月刊》,1995年6月號,頁64–67。

1995 〈悼念中國科技史大師李約瑟博士〉,《歷史月刊》,第90期(1995年7月號),頁116–121;《文獻》,1996年第3期,頁53–59。

1995 〈日軍侵華史料舉證〉,《明報月刊》,第30卷第8期（1995.8）,頁58–60。

1995 〈抗日戰爭淪陷區史料拾零〉,《歷史月刊》,第93期（1995.10）,頁22–25。

1995 "Documents from Wartime Shanghai, 1941–1945," *Newsletter of the Midwest Chinese Student & Alumni Services*, Winter, 1995, 1–3.

1995 〈袁同禮先生對國際文化交流之貢獻〉,《袁同禮先生百齡冥誕紀念專輯》（臺北,1995）,頁10–14;《傳記文學》,第68卷第2期（1996.12）,頁91–95。

1996 《書於竹帛—中國古代書史》新增訂本,臺北：漢美圖書公司,1996。xxvi,246頁,圖版28幅。

1997 〈悼念美國漢學大師顧立雅教授〉,《歷史月刊》,第112期(1997.1);《文獻》,1997年第3期,頁243–48。

1997 〈戰國策〉,劉學順譯,見李學勤主編,《中國古籍導讀》,瀋陽遼寧出版社,1997。

1998 〈書評〉,饒宗頤著,《符號、初文與字母—漢字樹》《漢學研究》15卷第2期（1998年12月）,頁413–6;《明報月刊》1998年10月號,頁92–93;《文獻》,1999年第2期,頁258–62。

1998 《中美書緣》,臺北：文華圖書館管理資訊股份有限公司,1998。xi,284頁,附圖表。

2000 〈懷念我在淮東中學的時代〉,《泰州中學建校100周年特刊》2000年。

2001 〈北京圖書館善本古籍流浪六十年〉,《傳記文學》,第79卷第6期（2001年12月）,頁15–18。

2002 〈懷念顧起潛先生〉,《我與上海圖書館》（上海,2002）,頁34–37;《北京圖書館學刊》,2002年第4期,頁75–77。

2002 《中國古代書籍、紙墨及印刷術》（增訂本）, 北京：北京圖書館出版社,2002。xii,361頁,插圖70幅。

2002 〈紙的起源新證—試論戰國秦簡中的「紙」字〉,《文獻》,2002年第1期,頁1–11。

2002 〈精寫本《江村書畫目》題記〉,《文獻》,2002年第3期,頁4–11。

2002 《書於竹帛》第四次增訂本,上海書店出版社,2002;〈世紀文庫〉本,上海世紀出版集團、上海書店出版社, 2004。26+212頁, 插圖28幅。

2003 〈中美圖書館代表團首次互訪記略（1973–1979）〉,《北京圖書館學刊》,2003年,第4期,頁74–77。

2003 〈《裘開明圖書館學論文選集》序言〉,桂林：廣西師範大學出版社,2003,頁1–3;《中國圖書館學報》,2003年第6期,頁70,91。

2004 *Written on Bamboo and Silk: The Beginnings of Chinese Books and Inscriptions*. 2nd revised edition with Afterword by Edward L. Shaughnessy. Chicago: University of Chicago Press, 2004. xxiv, 323 pp., 30 plates, tables.

2004 《中國紙和印刷文化史》,鄭如斯編訂,桂林：廣西師範大學出版社,2004,12+442頁,插圖174。

2004 〈中國印刷史書目〉,張樹棟增補,2004,見《中國紙和印刷文化史》附錄。

2005 〈吳光清博士生平概要〉,《國家圖書館學刊》,2005年第4期;《中國圖書館學會會報》,第74期,2005年6月。

2005 〈金大憶舊：我的青年時代〉,南京大學《思文》,2005年6月。

2005 〈金大憶舊：懷念校友吳光清〉,南京大學《思文》,2005年6月。

2005 〈吳光清博士生平概要〉,《中華民國圖書館學會會報》,第136/137期,2005年6月。

2006 〈留美雜憶〉,《傳記文學》,第89卷第1–4期（2006年7–10月）;《萬象》,2007年4–10月。

2006 〈芝加哥大學遠東圖書館建館札記〉,《中華民國圖書館學會會報》,第42/143 期,2006 年12月。

2007 「回憶在芝加哥大學工讀的歲月〉,《圖書館雜誌》, 2007年1月;《新華文摘》,2007年8月。

2007 《中国の紙と印刷の文化史》,久米康生譯,東京:法政大學出版社,2007。xiii,420頁。

2007 《留美雜憶:六十年來美國生活的回顧》,台北:傳記文學出版社,2007年,14+300頁,彩色插圖6頁;合肥:黃山出版社,2008年。10+321頁,彩色插圖6頁。

2008 《중국 종이와인쇄 문화사》사계절출판사 (Sakyejul Publishing Co.), 2008.

2008 《東西文化交流論叢》,北京:商務印書館,2008。

2010 《回顧集:錢存訓先生著述選集》,桂林:廣西師範大學出版社,2010年。

2011 *Collected Writings on Chinese Culture.* Hong Kong: The Chinese University Press, 2011.

T. H. TSIEN AT THE UNIVERSITY OF CHICAGO (1996)

INTERNATIONAL REVIEWS
OF PUBLICATIONS

Bie Liqian

In the academic world, a scholar's contribution to his/her related field is gauged by both the number of publications and the quality of the research methods and writing. Universities and other institutions regularly make decisions on hiring, levels of support, and promotion based on a value system that measures the merits of one's academic output. In other words, a scholar cannot establish status in the academic world without publishing. And, for appraisal purposes, a scholar's research ability, academic standing, and contribution to scholarship are manifested by their publications in academic journals, especially international journals.

Academic standards cannot be advanced without scholarly interchange, and it is only through favorable reviews on publications by fellow scholars that academics gradually achieve respect. Remarks made in international journals, often in the form of book reviews, form a basis of scholarly appraisal. They also represent objective evaluations of the achievement and influence of specific research.

Chinese scholars often publish the results of their research only in Chinese-language forums, which means that besides the Chinese readers, and a handful of China scholars in Western countries who are versatile enough to read Chinese, there is no international readership for these publications. Western-language publications are in a better position to attract attention from international academic circles. When a publication attempts to fill a certain gap of Western scholarship on China, there is no way to reach the goal of international circulation and interchange without publishing in Western languages.

Tsuen-Hsuin Tsien is one of a very few international scholars who are esteemed for voluminous academic output, and who receive wide recognition for disseminating Eastern culture by writing in Western languages.

Written on Bamboo and Silk

A brief survey reveals that over thirty reviews have been written by international and Chinese scholars on *Written on Bamboo and Silk*. The earliest review was published the same year that the first edition appeared in English in 1962. This review by Hyman Kublin, published in *Library Journal*, stated,

> Tsien's study is a triumph of modern sinology. His objective, achieved with admirable success, has been to trace the evolution of Chinese writing over the course of 3,000 years. In the painstaking and meticulous work, he has combed through the vast corps of source materials, archaeological, artistic, and literary, as well as the tremendous store of highly specialized research papers. Few, if any, of the purposes, techniques, usages, instruments, and materials of Chinese writing have escaped his attention. The result is a volume which is as definitive as extant research data will permit. To learn how Chinese writing developed and how it was used from the most ancient times to the emergence of the age of printing, this book is indispensable for all serious students of China and of early civilizations.

Thereafter, favorable comments on the work continued to appear, thanks to the lasting value of the material. It covers a range of topics previously unexplored by Western Sinologists and book historians. Because of the originality of the topic and the definitiveness of the contents, based on copious amounts of credible data, this innovative book assumed an inherited significance as soon as it was published. The review written by Arthur Hummel in the *American Historical Review* said:

> The author's talent for leading us into attractive byways without losing his way is one of the delights of this book. Another is his use, in every point, of the latest archaeological discoveries in Xhina since 1950, to supplement older information. Written in a simple and direct style, for the layman as well as for the scholar, it will find a hospitable place on many shelves.

Joseph Needham wrote a review of this book in 1964 in the *Journal of Asian Studies* and praised it as a companion volume to Thomas F. Carter's classic *The Invention of Printing in China and Its Spread Westward*, saying "we may say at once that it need not fear any comparison with that wonderful book," and "the text is a model of clarity and brevity in good Cartesian style."

Other reviews further affirm the academic standing of *Written on Bamboo and Silk*, citing its role of filling a gap in the history of the Chinese book. Tsien in the Foreword of the book discloses his intention of writing:

> The present study is intended to reconstruct from available evidences a general picture of the Chinese written records from about 1400 B.C., when the earliest known Chinese writing is found to have been recorded, to about A.D. 700, when printing is believed to have been in process of initiation. This period of more than two thousand years prior to the invention of printing marks the early stage in Chinese book history, when the materials, contents, forms of writing and its arrangement, and certain characteristics of format gradually took the shapes which became traditional for Chinese books and culture during the following stage when printing was applied. While printing is used as a landmark of book history, it merely changed the method and thus increased the quantity of production, without changing the general substance and format of the records.

Because Western scholarship on the early history of the Chinese book had been nearly non-existent before Tsien, his book was acclaimed as a companion volume, to Thomas Carter's *The Invention of Printing in China and Its Spread Westward* and Paul Pelliot's *The Origin of Chinese Printing*.

Besides introducing to Western scholars a wealth of information on the history of the Chinese book, *Written on Bamboo and Silk* also provides ample records on Chinese paleography and early instruments and materials of Chinese writing. Hsu Choyun wrote: "This book is the only systematic work in the English language on the history of Chinese writing before the invention of printing. Almost all of Ancient China's written records are included in this book, every last stroke . . . To use the invention of printing as a demarcation of the history of the book was a remarkable decision by the author."

Another Chinese scholar, Li Yan, reviewed the book's merits from a number of angles. "The content of this book is extensive, its viewpoint excellent, rich in original sources, and its construction is solid. Each chapter is a self-contained entity. Reading individual chapters separately will satisfy any specialist; or, read as a whole, it is a smoothly organized organic composition."

The second edition of *Written on Bamboo and Silk*, published in 2004, contains a lengthy Afterword by Edward L. Shaughnessy, Professor of Ancient Chinese History at the University of Chicago. From an archaeological perspective, Shaughnessy points out that the first edition of the book synthesized the discoveries on Chinese paleography in the first half of the 20th century, while the second edition substantially expands the scope of the archaeological findings of the latter half of that century. He also noted: "Although Tsuen-Hsuin Tsien had no way of knowing it when he was writing his now classic *Written on Bamboo and Silk*, his timing was as masterful as his scholarship."

Paper and Printing

Another Tsien monograph, *Paper and Printing*, is a comprehensive treatise that covers paper, ink, and printing; their role, contributions, and influences on the history of Chinese and world civilizations. There have been over twenty international reviews of *Paper and Printing*, which testifies to the academic interest that the book has received since its first printing in 1985.

Paper and Printing was the first book in Joseph Needham's monumental series to be written by a single, independent Chinese scholar. In the *Times Literary Supplement* in London, David Helliwell wrote, "the work has already become standard; indeed, the first printing sold out on publication."

A series of reviews on *Paper and Printing* confirm its place as an encyclopedic work and standard reference volume. Another review in

China Quarterly notes, "Tsien's is an encyclopedia on the subject." Still another, in *Printing Historical Society Bulletin*, "No short review can do justice to so notable a book about so remarkable a chapter of history, providing so great a display of historic detail."

Reviewers of *Paper and Printing* generally agree that the book is the most updated, most detailed, and most authoritative investigation of the topic in any language, and an excellent companion volume to *Written on Bamboo and Silk*.

Other Publications

There are many reviews of Tsien's other works. For example, *China: An Annotated Bibliography of Bibliographies* is an important reference book co-authored with James K. M. Cheng. The book incorporates 2,500 bibliography of bibliographies on China published before 1978 in English, Chinese, Japanese, French, German, Russian, and other European languages. A review appearing in an academic journal in Hong Kong noted, "It is an important reference work with annotations on all fields of China studies, which includes all bibliographies in different languages, arranged by subject classification, filling all the gaps of earlier lists."

The numerous reviews of his collected works in Chinese will not be mentioned here, including one volume on Chinese books, paper, and printing, published in Hong Kong in 1992 and in Beijing in 2002; and another book on Chinese-American cultural relations, published in Taipei in 1998. A considerable amount of commentary in Chinese exists for these titles, but this essay focuses exclusively on international reviews published in Western languages.

Consensus of the Reviewers

Besides discussing the content and value of Tsien's publications, certain reviewers also focus their observations on Tsien's research methodology, writing style, and even his scholarly temperament. Among the many aspects noted about Tsien's scholarship, there is a general consensus among reviewers that he has always employed rigorous scholarship. While others focus on the fact that Tsien's writing delivers substantial information and keen insight; synthesizes large amounts of documentary evidence and archaeological findings in light of modern scholarly perspectives; expertly investigates various issues on a macro scale; and boldly unveils the fallacies of past discussions.

Paper and Printing reviewers unanimously agreed that Tsien expertly cites large amounts of original sources, comprehensively describes the existing knowledge in a condensed manner, discusses related issues of import, analyzes differing opinions, and raises new directions for research. His narration is typified by an integrity of content, structure, and organization, which conveys a strength of persuasion, and personifies Tsien's research profile. Readers always feel that he is being scrupulous about every detail.

His writings are accompanied by lavish illustrations, ramifying footnotes, and substantial bibliographies that contain citations to publications in both the Eastern and Western scholarly worlds. Compared with other scholarly works in Western languages, Tsien's publications contain many more original Chinese sources. As a result of such documentation, Tsien outweighs other authorities in the details.

Conclusion

Having assembled almost one hundred reviews of Tsien's works, the widespread influence of his scholarship is obvious from the fact that these reviews were written and published in a range of languages and countries that include China, America, UK, France, Germany, and Italy.

In spite of a few minor comments on occasional errors in romanization and statistics, the overall success of Tsien's works are unanimously accepted. Words of admiration, such as "authority," "classic," "encyclopedic," and "model for posterity" appear frequently in these reviews.

The universal accord of favorable reviews is the result of Tsien's own high demands for his scholarly work. In his preface to Ming-Sun Poon's collection *Essays of the Flowerless Studio*, Tsien writes, "Writing short creative essays and scholarly articles are two contrastingly dissimilar pursuits. For the former, the merits are lightness and liveliness, flexibility and unpredictability, humor and sarcasm; authors create these essays at will, aiming at a large audience. In the case of the latter, the virtue is the tolerance of boredom and tedium; a virtue that can hardly attract more than a handful of scholarly readers. This is the divide between literary creation and academic research. The two are markedly different due to dissimilarities in motive, condition, method, and purpose." From this vivid description of the unlikeness of the boundaries and characteristics that distinguishes these two forms of writing, we feel acutely what Tsien has achieved and sacrificed in his dedication to academic research.

Published in Chinese in Nanshan lunxuej *(Beijing, 2006)*
and translated by Ming-Sun Poon.

Illustrations

(for the sections *Ancient Documents and Artifacts* and *Paper, Ink, and Printing*)

All other images in this volume courtesy of Tsuen-Hsuin Tsien

BIBLIOGRAPHY

ABBREVIATIONS USED IN THE NOTES AND BIBLIOGRAPHY

BIHP   *Guoli zhongyang yanjiuyuan lishi yuyan yanjiusuo jikan* 國立中央研究院歷史語言研究所集刊 (Bulletin of the Institute of History and Philology, Academia Sinica), Nanjing and Taibei.

CSJC   *Congshu jicheng* 叢書集成 (Collection of Collectanea). Taibei reprint, 1964.

CYPLWJ   *Qingzhu Cai Yuanpei xiansheng liushiwu sui lunwenji* 慶祝蔡元培先生六十五歲論文集 (Studies Presented to Cai Yuanpei on His Sixty-fifth Birthday). Shanghai: Commerical Press, 1932; Beijing: Academia Sinica Institute of History and Philology, [1933–1935].

DLZZ   *Dalu zazhi* 大陸雜誌 (The Continent Magazine). Taibei.

ECT   *Early Chinese Texts: A Bibliographical Guide.* Ed. by Michael Loewe. Berkeley: Society for the Study of Early China, Institute of Asian Studies, University of California, Berkeley, 1993.

ESSS   *Ershisi shi* (Twenty-Four Dynastic Histories). Shanghai: Tongwen shuju, 1886.

FEQ   *Far Eastern Quarterly.* Ann Arbor, MI. 1941–1956. Continued by *Journal of Asian Studies.*

GXJB   *Guoxue jiben congshu* 國學基本叢書 (Basic Sinological Series). Shanghai: Commercial Press.

HJAS   *Harvard Journal of Asiatic Studies,* Cambridge, Mass.

JAS   *Journal of Asian Studies,* Ann Arbor, Michigan.

MS   *Monumenta Serica: Journal of Oriental Studies* 華裔學誌, Tokyo, etc.

SBBY   *Sibu beiyao* 四部備要 (Essential Writings in Four Divisions). Shanghai: Zhonghua shuju, 1920s–1930s.

SBCK   *Sibu congkan* 四部叢刊 (Collected Works in Four Divisions). Shanghai: Commercial Press, 1929.

SSJZS   *Shisanjing zhushu* 十三經注疏 (Commentaries on Thirteen Classics). Nanjing: n.p, [1875–1908].

TPYL   *Taiping yulan* 太平御覽 (An Imperial Encyclopedia compiled during the Taiping Reign of the Song Dynasty). Comp. by Li Fang 李昉 (926–996) *et. al.* In *SBCK.*

WW   *Wenwu* 文物 (Cultural Relics). Beijing, since 1959. Originally published as *Wenwu cankao ziliao* 文物參考資料 (Materials for the Study of Cultural Relics), Beijing, 1950–1958.

ZBZZ   *Zhibuzuzhai congshu* (Collectanea of the Studio of Insufficient Knowledge). Ed. by Bao Tingbo 鮑廷博 (1728–1814). 240 vols. [China]: Gushu liutongchu, 1921.

ZGTS   *Zhongguo tushu wenshi lunji* 中國圖書文史論集 (Collected Essays on Chinese Bibliography, Literature and History: A Festschrift in Honor of the Eightieth Birthday of Professor Tsuen-hsuin Tsien). Ed. by Ma Tailai 馬泰來 *et al.* Taibei: Zhengzhong shuju, 1991; Beijing: Xiandai chubanshe, 1992.

A Ying. *Wan Qing xiaoshuo shi* 晚清小說史 (History of Late Qing Fiction). Shanghai: Commercial Press, 1937.

----. *Minjian chuanghua* 民間窗花 (Folk Paper Cuts). Beijing: Meishu chubanshe, 1954.

Ackerman, Phyllis. *Wallpaper: Its History, Design, and Use*. New York, Frederick A. Stokes Company, 1923.

Aleni, Giulio (Julius) 艾儒略 (Ai Rulue 1582–1649). *Xixue fan* 西學凡 (Summary of Western Learning). Fuzhou: Qinyitang 欽一堂, 1623.

----. *Zhifang waiji* 職方外紀 (Geography of the World; companion to Matteo Ricci's world map) 1623.

Alger, William R. *The Poetry of the Orient*. Boston: Roberts Brothers, 1865. Originally published as *The Poetry of the East*. Boston: Whittemore, Niles, and Hall, 1856.

Alibaux, Henri. "L'Invention du papier." *Gutenberg-Jahrbuch* (1939): 9–30.

Allen, David O. *India, Ancient and Modern, Geographical, Historical, Political, Social, and Religious*. Boston: J. P. Jewett and company; New York: Sheldon, Lamport and Blakeman, 1856.

An Zhimin 安志敏 and Chen Gongrou 陳公柔. "Changsha Zhanguo zengshu ji qi youguan wenti 長沙戰國繒書及其有關問題, (Problems Concerning the Silk Document of the Warring States Period found in Changsha)." *WW* 9 (1963): 48–60.

Ancient China: Studies in Early Civilization. Ed. by David T. Roy and Tsuen-hsuin Tsien. Hong Kong: Chinese University Press, 1978.

Bai Juyi 白居易 and Kong Zhuan 孔傳. *Bai Kong liutie* 白孔六帖 (Bai's Classified Encyclopedia Enlarged by Kong). 32 ce. Ming Jiajing (1522–1566) edition.

Baichuan xuehai 百川學海 (The Sea of Learning). Comp. by Zuo Gui 左圭 (13th century). Shanghai: Boguzhai, 1921.

Ban Gu 班固 (32–92). [*Qian*] *Han shu* [前]漢書 (History of the [Former] Han Dynasty). In *ESSS*. Trans. by Homer Dubs, *The History of the Former Han Dynasty*. Vols. I–III. Baltimore: Waverly Press, 1938–1956.

Baopuzi 抱朴子內外篇 (Book of the Preservation-of-Solidarity Master). Ed. by Ge Hong 葛洪 (284–364). In *SBCK*.

Barnard, Noel. *The Ch'u Silk Manuscript—Translation and Commentary*. Canberra: Dept. of Far Eastern History, Australian National University, 1973.

----. "A Preliminary Study of the Ch'u Silk Manuscript: A New Reconstruction of the Text." *MS* 17 (1958): 1–11.

Beihu lu 北戶錄 (Northern Family Records). Ed. by Duan Gonglu 段公路 (fl. 850). In *Hubei xianzheng yishu* 湖北先正遺書. [China]: Mianyang Lu shi Shenshiji zhai, 1923.

Beitang shuchao 北堂書鈔 (An Encyclopedia of the Tang Dynasty). Ed. by Yu Shinan 虞世南 (558–638). 20 ce. 1888.

Bencao gangmu 本草綱目 (The Great Pharmacopoeia). Ed. by Li Shizhen 李时珍 (1518–1593). Beijing: Renmin weisheng chubanshe, 1975.

Bernard, Henri. "Les adaptations chinoises d'ouvrages européens, 1514–1688." *MS* 10 (1945): 1–57, 309–388.

----, *Matteo Ricci's Scientific Contributions to China*. Trans. by Chalmers Werner. Peiping: Henri Vetch, 1935.

Bi Shutang 畢樹棠. *Catalogo di opere in cinese tradotte dall'italiano o riguardanti l'Italia*. Beijing: Zhongyi wenhua xiehui—Centro Culturale Italiano, 1942.

Bie Liqian 別立謙. "Lun Qian Cunxun dui Zhongguo shushi yanjiu de gongxian 論錢存訓對 中國書史研究的貢獻 (On T. H. Tsien's Contributions to the Study of Chinese Book

History)." M.A. Thesis, Peking University, 1998.

----. "Qian Cunxun xiansheng zhushu de guoji pinglun 錢存訓先生著述的國際評論 (International Review of T. H. Tsien's Writings)." In *Nanshan lunxueji*, 157–162.

Biggerstaff, Knight. "The T'ung Wen Kuan." *Chinese Social and Political Science Review* 18 (1934): 307–340.

Bliss, Douglas. P. *A History of Wood Engraving*. 2nd ed. London: Spring Books, 1964.

Blum, André. *On the Origin of Paper*. Trans. by Harry Miller Lydenberg. New York: R. R. Bowker Co., 1934.

Bluntschli, Johann Caspar. *Le droit international codifié*. Paris: Guillaumin et cie, 1870.

Bodde, Derk, *see* Fuchadunchong.

Breasted, James H. "The Physical Processes of Writing in the Early Orient and Their Relation to the Origin of the Alphabet." *American Journal of Semitic Languages and Literatures* 32 (1916): 230–249.

Bretschneider, E.V.E. *Botanicon Sinicum: Notes on Chinese Botany from Native and Western Sources*. 3 vols. London: Trübner, 1882–1895.

----. *History of European Botanical Discoveries in China*. London: Sampson Low, Marston; Leipzig: KF Koehler's Antiquarium, 1935.

----. "Oracle-bone Color Pigments." *HJAS* 2:1 (1937): 1–3. With a report on microchemical analysis of pigments by Professor A. A. Benedetti Pichler.

Bridgman, Elijah C. *A Chinese Chrestomathy in the Canton Dialect*. Macao: S.W. Williams, 1841.

Butler, Pierce. *The Origin of Printing in Europe*. Chicago: University of Chicago Press, 1940.

Cai Jixiang 蔡季襄. *Wan Zhou zengshu kaozheng* 晚周繒書考證 (A Study of the Silk Documents of the Late Zhou Dynasty). Shanghai, 1946; Taibei: Yiwen Publishing Co., 1972.

Cai Yong 蔡邕 (132–192). *Cai Zhonglang ji* 蔡中郎集 (Collected Writings of Cai Yong). *SBBY* edition. Shanghai: Zhonghua shuju, n.d.

Cambridge Factfinder, The. Ed. by David Crystal. Cambridge: Cambridge University Press, 1998.

Cao Xuequan 曹學佺 (1574–1647). *Shuzhong guangji* 蜀中廣記 (Treatise on Sichuan). *Sikuquanshu zhenben* 四庫全書珍本. Shanghai: Commercial Press, 1934.

Cao Zhi 曹植 (192–232). *Cao ji quan ping* 曹集詮評. Ed. by Ding Yan 丁晏 (1794–1875). In *GXJB*.

Carter, Thomas Francis. *The Invention of Printing in China and Its Spread Westward*. New York: Columbia University Press, 1925; 2nd ed. rev. by L. C. Goodrich. New York: Ronald Press, 1955.

Chalfant, Frank Herring. *Early Chinese Writing*. Pittsburgh: Carnegie Institute, 1906.

Chang Bide 昌彼得. "Guanyu Beiping tushuguan jicun Meiguo de shanbenshu 關於北平圖書館寄存美國的善本書 (Regarding the Sending of the Beiping Library Rare Books to the United States)." *Shumu jikan* 書目集刊. 4: 2 (1969.12): 3–11.

Chang Hsi-t'ung, *see* Zhang Xitong.

Chatto, William A. and John Jackson. *A Treatise on Wood Engraving, Historical and Practical*. 2nd ed., London: H. G. Bohn, 1861; Detroit: Gale Research, 1969.

Chavannes, Édouard. *Les documents chinois decouverts par Aurel Stein dans les sables du Turkestan Oriental*. Oxford: Imprimerie de l'Universite, 1913.

----. "Les livres chinois avant l'invention du papier." *Journal Asiatique*, series 10, 5 (1905): 5–75.

Chen Jiaren 陳家仁, *see* Lily Kecskes.

Chen Pan 陳槃. "Xian Qin liang Han boshu kao 先秦兩漢帛書考 (A Study of the Silk Documents of the Pre-Han and Han Dynasties)." *BIHP* 24 (1953): 185–196. With an appendix on the silk document from Changsha "Changsha gumu juanzhi caihui zhaopian xiao ji 長沙古墓絹質彩繪照片小記 (Notes on the Photo-copy of the Silk Document from the Ancient Tomb of Changsha)." 193–196.

Chen You 陳櫎 (fl. 1190–1219). *Fuxuan yelu* 負暄野錄 (Miscellaneous Notes by the Rustic while

Warming Himself under the Sun). In *ZBZZ*, series 26.

Chen Yuan 陳垣. "Jingyang Wang Zheng zhuan 涇陽王徵傳 (Biography of Wang Zheng of Jingyang)." *Bulletin of the National Library of Peiping*, 8:6 (1934): 12–15.

Cheng Dayue 程大約 (fl. 1541–1616). *Chengshi moyuan* 程氏墨苑 (Cheng's Collection of Inkcake Designs). 1606 edition.

Chiang Fu-tsung 蔣復璁, *see* Jiang Fucong.

Ch'ien, C. S. (Qian Zhongshu 錢鍾書). "An Early Chinese Version of Longfellow's 'Psalm of Life.'" *Philobiblon* 2:2 (March 1948): 10–17.

Chiera, Edward. *They Wrote on Clay: The Babylonian Tablets Speak Today*. Chicago: University of Chicago Press, 1938; Phoenix Books 1956.

Chinese Repository, The. Ed. by Elijah C. Bridgman and Samuel Wells Williams. Guangzhou (Canton), 1832–1851.

Ch'iu, A. Kaiming (Qiu Kaiming) 裘開明. "The Harvard-Yenching Institute Library." *FQ* 14 (1954): 147–152.

Chongwen zongmu 崇文總目 (General Catalogue of Noble Writings). Ed. by Wang Yaochen 王堯臣 (1001–1056). *GXJB* edition. Shanghai: Commercial Press, 1939.

Chouban yiwu shimo 籌辦夷務始末 (Chinese Diplomatic Relations). Comp. by Wenqing 文慶 (1796–1856) *et. al.* Beijing: Palace Museum, 1929–1931.

Chu, Raymond W. H. and Shuzo Uyenaka. "East Asian Library Collection in the University of Toronto." *Pacific Affairs* 46:4 (Winter 1973–1974): 548–556.

Church, Alfred Madison. "The Study of China and Japan in American Secondary Schools: What Is Worth Teaching and What Is Being Taught?" Ed.D thesis, Harvard University Graduate School of Education, 1939.

Cihai 辭海 (The Chinese Encyclopedic Dictionary). 3 vols. Shanghai: Shanghai cishu chubanshe, 1999.

Clapperton, Robert Henderson. *Paper: An Historical Account of Its Making by Hand from the Earliest Times Down to the Present Day*. Oxford: Shakespeare Head Press, 1934.

Code Napoléon. Limoges: Martial Ardant frères, 1800.

Cooper Union Museum for the Arts of Decoration. *Plane Geometry and Fancy Figures: An Exhibition of the Art and Technique of Paper Folding*. Introduction by Edward Kallop. New York: 1959.

Cordier, Henri. *Bibliotheca Sinica. Dictionnaire bibliographique des ouvrages relatifs à l'Empire chinois*. 2nd ed., rev. and enl. Paris: E. Guilmoto, 1904–1908.

Creel, Herrlee Glessner. *The Birth of China: A Study of the Formative Period of Chinese Civilization*. London: Jonathan Cape, 1936; New York: John Day, 1937.

----. *Chinese Thought: From Confucius to Mao Tse-tung*. New York: New American Library, 1953.

----. *Confucius: the Man and the Myth*. New York: John Day, 1949; London: Routledge & Kegan, 1951; Tokyo: Iwanami Shoten, 1961.

----. *The Origins of Statecraft of China, vol. I: The Western Chou Empire*. Chicago: University of Chicago Press, 1970.

----. *Shen Pu-hai: A Chinese Political Philosopher of the Fourth Century B.C.* Chicago and London: University of Chicago Press, 1974.

----. *Sinism: A Study of the Evolution of the Chinese World View*. Chicago: Open Court, 1929.

----. *Studies in Early Chinese Culture, first series*. Baltimore: Waverly Press, 1937.

----. *What Is Taoism? And Other Studies of Chinese Cultural History*. Chicago: University of Chicago Press, 1970.

----, ed. *Chinese civilization in liberal education; proceedings of a conference, held at the University of Chicago November 28, 29, 1958*. Chicago: University of Chicago Press, 1958.

Creel, Herlee Glessner, Chang Tsung-Ch'ien and Richard C. Rudolph, eds. *Literary Chinese by the*

Inductive Method. Chicago, University of Chicago Press, 1938–1952.

Crump, J.L., Jr. *Intrigues: Studies of the Chan-kuo-ts'e*. Ann Arbor, MI: University of Michigan Press, 1964. Review by T. H. Tsien, *JAS* 25:2 (1966): 328–329.

Da Dai liji 大戴禮記 (Collected Ritual of Dai the Elder). Comp. by Dai De 戴德. In *SBCK*.

Da Tang liudian 大唐六典, see *Tang liudian*.

De Martens, Charles [Karl von Martens]. *Guide Diplomatique*. Leipzig: F. A. Brockhaus, 1832.

De Ursis, Sabbathin 熊三拔 (Xiong Sanba 1575–1620). *Taixi shuifa* 泰西水法 (Hydraulic Machinery of the West). 1612.

----. *Yuelu shuo* 藥露說 (On Distilling Medicines). Orig. chapter 4 of *Taixi shuifa*. 1617.

Deng Zhicheng 鄧之誠. *Gudong suoji; xuji; sanji* 骨董瑣記；續集；三記. (Notes on Antiques and Cultural Objects, ser. 1–3). Beijing: n.p., 1933.

Ding Fubao 丁福保. *Shuowen jiezi gulin* 說文解字詁林 (Collected Commentaries on the Old Lexicon). 66 ce. Shanghai: Medical Bookstore, 1930.

Diringer, David. *The Hand-produced Book*. New York: Philosophical Library, 1953.

Dobberstein, Robert K. "Treatment of the Far East in Nineteenth-Century Textbooks." M.A. Thesis, University of Chicago, 1959.

Dong Zuobin 董作賓. "Jiaguwen duandai yanjiu li 甲骨文斷代研究例 (On the Dating of Shell and Bone Inscriptions)." *CYPLWJ* 1: 323–418.

----, "Lun Changsha chutu zhi zengshu 論長沙出土之繒書 (On the Silk Documents Unearthed at Changsha)." *DLZZ* 10: 6 (1955), 173–176.

----. *Qingming heshang tu* 清明河上圖 (Spring Festival at the River). Painted by Zhang Zeduan 張擇端 (fl. 1111–1120?). Taibei: Yiwen, 1953.

Dongguan Han ji 東觀漢記. (An Official History of the Latter Han Dynasty). Ed. by Liu Zhen 劉珍 (fl. 107–125). *SBBY* edition. Shanghai: Zhonghua shuju, 1933.

Du Dingyou 杜定友. *Du shi congzhu shumu* 杜氏叢著書目 (Du's Collected Writings. Orig. English title: *Mr. Ding U Doo: a bio-bibliography*). Ed. by Tsien Tsuen-Hsuin. n.p, 1936.

Du Ponceau, Peter S. *A Dissertation on the Nature and Character of the Chinese System of Writing*. Transactions of the Historical & Literary Committee of the American Philosophical Society, vol. 2. Philadelphia: Abraham Small, 1838.

Dye, D. S. (Daniel Sheets). *A Grammar of Chinese Lattice*. 2 vols. Cambridge, Mass., Harvard University Press, 1937.

East Asian Libraries: Problems and Prospects: A Report and Recommendations, prepared by the Steering Committee for a Study of the Problems of East Asian Libraries. New York: American Council of Learned Societies, 1977.

Eisen, Gustavus A. *Ancient Oriental Cylinder and Other Seals with a Description of the Collection of Mrs. William H. Moore*. The University of Chicago Oriental Institute publications, vol. 47. Chicago: The University of Chicago Press, 1940.

Elisséeff, Serge. "The Chinese-Japanese Library of the Harvard-Yenching Institute." *Harvard Library Bulletin* 10:1 (Winter 1956): 73–93.

Entwisle, E. A. *The Book of Wallpaper: A History and an Appreciation*. London, A. Barker [1954].

----. *A Literary History of Wallpaper*. London: Batsford, 1960.

Ershiwu shi bubian 二十五史補編 (Supplement to the Twenty-five Dynastic Histories). Shanghai: Kaiming shudian, 1936–1937.

Erya zhushu 爾雅注疏 (Commentaries on the Literary Expositor). Annotated by Guo Pu 郭璞 (276–324) and Xing Bing 邢昺(932–1010). *SSJZS* edition. Nanjing, 1887.

Fan Shi 范適. *Mingji xiyang chuanru zhi yixue* 明季西洋傳入之醫學 (Western Medicine Introduced to China at the End of the Ming Dynasty). Shanghai: Society of Chinese Medical History, 1943.

Fang Hao 方豪. *Xu Guangqi* 徐光啓 (Biography of Xu Guangqi). Chongqing: Victory Press, 1944.

Fang Junshi 方濬師 (1830–1889). *Jiaoxuan suilu* 蕉軒隨錄 (Records of the Banana-Grove Pavilion). Yangcheng [Guangzhou]: Tuiyibuzhai, 1872.

Fang Yulu 方于魯 (fl. 1580). *Fangshi mopu* 方氏墨譜 (Fang Catalogue of Inkstones). Meiyin tang 美蔭堂, 1588.

"Far Eastern Collections in the Hoover Library, Stanford University." *FQ* 14 (February 1956): 446–447.

Fawcett, Henry. *Manual of Political Economy*. London: Macmillan and Co., 1863.

Feng Guifen 馮桂芬 (1809–1874). *Xianzhitang gao* 顯志堂稿 (Collected Works of Feng Guifen). 1876.

Ferguson, John C. *Lidai zhulu jijin mu* 歷代著錄吉金目 (Catalogue of the Recorded Bronzes of Successive Dynasties). Shanghai: Commercial Press, 1939.

Franke, Herbert. *Kulturgeschichtliches über die chinesiche Tusche*. Munchen: Verlag der Bayerischen Akademie der Wissenschaften, 1962.

Franke, Wolfgang and Dschang Schau-dien 張紹典 (Zhang Shaodian). *Titelverzeichnis chinesischer Übersetzungen deutscher Werke*. Beijing: Deutschland-Institut, 1942.

Frankfort, Henry. *Cylinder Seals: A Documentary Essay on the Art and Religion of the Ancient Near East*. London: Macmillan, 1939.

Fryer, John. "An Account of the Department for the Translation of Foreign Books at the Kiangnan Arsenal." *North-China Herald*, 24 (January 29, 1880); also published in Chinese in *Gezhi huibian* 格致彙編 (Chinese Scientific and Industrial Magazine), third year, nos. 5–8 (1880).

Fu Xuan 傅玄 (217–278). *Fu Chungu ji* 傅鶉觚集 (Collected Writings of Fu Xuan). 2 ce. 1876.

Fuchs, Walter. *Der Jesuiten-Atlas der Kanghsi Zeit: seine Entstehungsgeschichte nebst Namensindices für die Karten der Mandjurei, Mongolei, Ostturkestan und Tibet, mit Wiedergabe der Jesuiten-Karten in Original Grösse*. Beijing: Fu-Jen-Universität, 1943.

Fuchadunchong 富察敦崇. *Yanjing suishi ji* [Yen-ching Sui-shih-chi] 燕京歲時記 (Record of Festivals in Yanjing). Beijing: n.p., [1906]. See translation by Derk Bodde, *Annual Customs and Festivals in Peking: As Recorded in the Yen-ching Sui-Shih-Chi*. Beijing: Henry Vetch, 1936.

Fujiwara Sukeyo 藤原佐世 (d. 898). *Nihonkoku genzaisho mokuroku* 日本國見在書目録 (Catalogue of Chinese Books Held in Japan after 875). Tōkyō: Koten Hozonkai Jimusho, 1925.

Fukui Junzō 福井準造. *Kinsei shakai shugi* 近世社会主義 (Contemporary Socialism). Orig. pub. Tokyo: Yūhikaku, 1899. Chinese translation by Zhao Bizhen 趙必振. Shanghai: Guangzhi shuju, 1903.

Fung, Margaret C. "Safekeeping of the National Peiping Library's Rare Chinese Books at the Library of Congress, 1941–1965." *Journal of Library History* 19:3 (1984): 359–372.

Furtado, Francois (Francisco) 傅汎際 (Fu Fanji 1589–1653). *Mingli tan* 名理探 (Exploration of Names and Principles. Trans. of *In libros Ethicorum Aristotelis ad Nicomacbum*). 1631.

Gaiyu congkao 陔餘叢考 (Collection of Miscellaneous Studies). 1750.

Gallagher, Louis J., trans. *China in the Sixteenth Century: The Journals of Matteo Ricci, 1583–1610*. New York: Random House, 1953.

Garnier, Albert J. *A Maker of Modern China*. London: Carey Press, 1945.

Gezhi jingyuan 格致鏡原 (Mirror of Science and Technological Origins). Ed. by Chen Yuanlong 陳元龍 (1652–1736). 24 ce. 1735.

Gelb, Ignace. J. *A Study of Writing*. Rev. ed., Chicago: University of Chicago Press, 1963.

Gongchandang xuanyan 共產黨宣言 (The Communist Manifesto). Trans. by Chen Wangdao 陳望道. Shanghai: Shehuizhuyi yanjiushe, 1920.

Goodrich, Chauncey. *A Pocket Dictionary (Chinese-English) and Pekingnese Syllabary*. Beijing: Pe-t'ang (Beitang) Press, 1891.

Goodrich, L. Carrington. "Printing: Preliminary Report on a New Discovery." *Technology and Culture* 8:3 (1967): 376–378.

Goodrich, L. Carrington and Chaoying Fang. *Dictionary of Ming Biography, 1368–1644.* New York: Columbia University Press, 1976.

Gray, William Scott. *The Teaching of Reading and Writing: An International Survey.* [Paris]: UNESCO, 1956.

Griffis, William Elliot. *The Mikado's Empire.* New York: Harper, 1876.

----. *Corea, the Hermit Nation.* New York: Scribner, 1882.

Guanzi 管子 (The Book of Master Guan). Annotated by Fang Xuanling 房玄齡 (578–648). In *SBCK.*

Gugong zhoukan 故宮周刊 (Weekly Bulletin of the Palace Museum, Beiping). No. 339 (1934).

Gujin shiwu kao 古今事物考 (Research into Things Ancient and Modern). Ed. by Wang Sanpin 王三聘 (fl. 1541). *CSJC* edition.

Gujin tushu jicheng 古今圖書集成 (An Imperial Encyclopedia). Ed. by Jiang Tingxi 蔣廷錫 (1669–1732) *et al.* 101 vols. Reprint ed. Taibei: Wen xing shu dian, 1964.

Guoli bianyiguan gongzuo gaikuang 國立編譯館工作概況 (Report of the National Institute of Compilation and Translation). Nanjing, 1946.

Guoli Zhongyang tushuguan 'diancang' guoli Beiping tushuguan shanben shumu 國立中央圖書館典藏國立北平圖書館善本書目. Taibei: National Central Library, 1969.

Guoyu 國語 (Discourses of the States). Annotated by Wei Zhao 韋昭 (197–278). In *SBCK.*

Haichao yin 海潮音 (Voice from the Sea Tide). Ed. by Qian Weizhen 錢慰貞. Nanjing: Haichao yinshe, 1920–1949; Taibei: Haichaoyin zazhishe, 1949–.

Han shu 漢書, *see* Ban Gu.

Hanfeizi 韓非子 (The Book of Master Han Fei). In *SBCK.* See partial translation by W. K. Liao, *The Complete Works of Han Fei Tzû: A Chinese Classic of Political Science.* 2 vols. London: Probsthain, 1939–1959.

Hanlin zhi 翰林志 (On the Hanlin Academy). Ed. by Li Zhao 李肇 (fl. 806–820). In *Baichuan xuehai.*

Hanshi waizhuan 韓詩外傳 (Discourses on the Han Text of the *Book of Poetry*). Ed. by Han Ying 韓嬰 (2nd cent. B.C.). In *SBCK.*

He Bingyou (Ho Peng-Yoke) 何丙郁. *He Bingyou Zhongguo kejishi lunji* 何丙郁中國科技史論集 (Science and Culture in Ancient China: Selected Works of Ho Peng-Yoke). Liaoning: Liaoning Education Press, 2002.

He Yanzhi 何延之 (fl. 713–742). *Lanting ji* 蘭亭集 (Records of Lanting). In *ZBZZ*, 10.

Hebei Diyi Bowuyuan banyuekan 河北第一博物院半月刊 (Fortnightly of the First Hebei Museum). No. 35, 1933.

Hepburn, James Curtis. *Japanese-English and English-Japanese Dictionary.* Orig. published as *A Japanese and English Dictionary; with an English and Japanese Index.* Shanghai: American Presbyterian Mission Press, 1867.

Hiraoka Takeo 平岡武夫. "Chikusatsu to Shina kodai no kiroku 竹冊と支那古代の記録 (Bamboo Tablets as Records of Ancient China)," *Tōhō gakuhō* (Kyoto) 13 (1943): 163–188.

"History of the Smithsonian Exchanges." *Annual Report of the Smithsonian Institution, 1881.* Washington: Government Printing Office, 1883, 746–748.

Ho Peng-Yoke 何丙郁, *see* He Bingyou.

Hoernle, A. F. Rudolph. "Who Was the Inventor of Rag-paper?" *Journal of the Royal Asiatic Society* (1903): 663–684.

Hoisington, Henry Richard. *The Oriental Astronomer.* Translation of Uḷḷamuḍaiyān's Tamil version of the Sanskrit *Parahitam.* Jaffna: American Mission Press, 1848.

----. *Tattuva-kattalei, Siva-Gnâna-Pôtham, and Siva-Pirakâsam: treatises on Hindu Philosophy. Trans. from the Tamil, with introduction and notes.* New Haven: Hamlen, 1854.

Hong Guang 洪光 and Huang Tianyou 黃天右. *Zhongguo zaozhi fazhan shilue* 中國造紙發展史略 (A Brief History of the Development of Papermaking in China). Beijing: Qinggongye chubanshe, 1957.

Hong Ye (William Hung) 洪業. *Du shi yinde* 杜詩引得 (A Concordance to the Poems of Tu Fu). Beijing: Harvard-Yenching Institute, 1940.

Hong Youfeng 洪有豐 and Yuan Tongli 袁同禮. *Qingdai cangshujia kao* 清代藏書家考 (Research on Qing Book Collectors). Reprint ed. Hong Kong: Zhongshan tushu, 1972.

Hou Han shu 後漢書 (History of the Later Han Dynasty). Ed. by Fan Ye 范曄 (398–445). In *ESSS*.

Howard, Richard C. "The Wason Collection on China and the Chinese." *Cornell University Library Bulletin* 193 (January 1975): 36–43.

Hu Shih [Shi] 胡適. "The Gest Oriental Library at Princeton University." *Princeton University Library Chronicle* 15 (Spring 1954): 113–141.

Hu Zhengyan 胡正言 (ca. 1582–ca. 1672). *Shizhuzhai shuhua pu* 十竹齋書畫譜 (A Manual of Calligraphy and Painting from the Ten Bamboo Studio) (1645?). Facsimile reprint. Beijing: Rongbaozhai (Peking Society of Woodcuts), 1935. See translation into German by Jan Tschichold, *Die Bildersammlung der Zehnbambushalle*. Basel: Holbein Verlag 1953; and into English (from the German) by Katherine Watson, *Chinese Colour Prints from the Ten Bamboo Studio*. London: Lund Humphries, 1972.

Huainanzi 淮南子 (The Book of [the Prince of] Huainan [Compendium of Natural Philosophy]). Attributed to Liu An 劉安. In *SBCK*.

Huang Jun 黃濬. *Hengzhai jinshi shixiaolu* 衡齋金石識小錄 (Inscriptions on Gold and Stone from Hengzhai). Beijing: Zunguzhai, 1935.

Huang Wenbi 黃文弼. *Luobuzhuo'er kaogu ji* 羅布淖爾考古記 (Archeology of Lopnor). Beijing: Guoli Beiping yanjiuyuan Zhongguo xibei kexue kaochatuan lishihui, 1948.

----. *Tulufan kaogu ji* 吐魯番考古記 (Archeology of Turfan). Beijing: National Academy of Sciences, 1954.

Huff, Elizabeth. "Far Eastern Collections in the East Asiatic Library of the University of California." *FQ* 14 (1955): 443–446.

Hulbert, Homer B. *History of Korea*. Seoul: The Methodist Publishing House, 1905.

Hulme, Edward Wynham. *Statistical Bibliography in Relation to the Growth of Modern Civilization*. London: Grafton, 1923.

Hummel, Arthur W. "The Growth of the Orientalia Collections." *The Library of Congress Quarterly Journal of Current Acquisitions* 11.2 (February 1954): 69–87.

----. "Review of *Written on Bamboo and Silk. The Beginnings of Chinese Books and Inscriptions*." In *American Historical Review* 68: 3 (April 1963): 812–813.

----, ed. *Eminent Chinese of the Ch'ing Period, 1644–1912*. 2 vols. Washington, D.C.: Government Printing Office, 1944.

Humphreys, Henry N. *A History of the Art of Printing from Its Invention to Its Wide-spread Development in the Middle of the Sixteenth Century*. London: B. Quaritch, 1867.

Hunter, Dard. *Chinese Ceremonial Paper*. Chillicothe, Ohio: Mountain House Press, 1937.

----. *Paper-making: The History and Technique of an Ancient Craft*. 2nd ed., rev. and enl. New York: Alfred A. Knopf, 1957.

Hunter, William C. *Bits of Old China*. London: K. Paul, Trench, & Co., 1885.

----. *The 'Fan Kwae' at Canton Before Treaty Days, 1825–1844, by an Old Resident*. London: K. Paul, Trench & co., 1882.

Irwin, Richard G. "John Fryer's Legacy of Chinese Writings." Unpublished paper.

Jao, Tsung-I 饒宗頤. *See* Rao Zongyi.

Jia Sixie 賈思勰 (5th century). *Qimin yaoshu* 齊民要術 (Important Arts for the People's Welfare). 4 ce. In *SBCK*. See also Shi Shenghan.

Jiang Fucong 蔣復璁 (Chiang Fu-tsung). "Yungui Guoli Beiping tushuguan cun Mei shanben gaishu 運歸國立北平圖書館存美善本概述 (A Brief Account of the Return of the National Beiping Library Rare Books Sent to the United States for Safe-keeping)." *Zhongmei yuekan* 中美月刊 11: 3 (1966): 5–7.

Jiang Guangci 蔣光慈. *Yixiang yu guguo* 異鄉與故國 (Strange Lands and Mother Country: Collected Essays). Shanghai: Xiandai Book Company, 1930.

Jiang Shaoshu 姜紹書. *Yunshizhai bitan* 韻石齋筆談 (Miscellaneous Notes from the Yunshi Studio), In *ZBZZ*, first series.

Jiang Xuanyi 蔣玄佁. *Changsha: Chu minzu ji qi yishu* 長沙：楚民族及其藝術 (Changsha: The Chu Tribe and Its Art). 2 vols. Shanghai: Kunst-archaeological Society, 1950.

Jiangcun shuhua mu 江村書畫目 (Catalog of Paintings and Calligraphy in the Collection of Gao Shiqi [高士奇 (1644–1703)]. 1705.

Jiatai Kuaiji zhi 嘉泰會稽志 (Gazetteer of Kuaiji from the Jiatai Reign Period [1201–1204]). 1926.

Jin Jian 金簡 (d. 1795). *Wuyingdian juzhenban chengshi* 武英殿聚珍版程式 (Rare Works in the Wuying Palace). 1776. See translation by Richard C. Rudolph, *A Chinese Printing Manual, 1776*. Los Angeles: Printed by The Ward Ritchie Press for members of The Typophiles, 1954.

Jin shu 晉書 (History of the Jin Dynasty). Ed. by Fang Xuanling 房玄齡 (578–648). In *ESSS*.

Jin Xiangheng 金祥恒. *Xu jiaguwen bian* 續甲骨文編 (Supplement to Sun's Dictionary of Bone and Shell Inscriptions). 4 ce. Taibei: Zhongguo Dong Ya xueshu yanjiu jihua weiyuanhui, 1959.

Jindai bishu 津逮秘書. Comp. by Mao Jin 毛晉 (1599–1659). Shanghai: Bogu zhai, 1923.

Jingzhou diqu bowoguan 荊州地區博物館. "Jiangling Zhangjiashan sanzuo Hanmu chutu dapi zhujian 江陵張家山三座漢墓出土大批竹簡 (A Large Number of Bamboo Tablets Unearthed in Three Han Dynasty Tombs at Zhangjiashan, Jiangling, Hubei). *WW* 1 (1985): 1–8.

Jiu Tang shu 舊唐書 (Old History of the Tang Dynasty, 618–906). Ed. by Liu Xu 劉昫 (887–946) *et. al.* In *ESSS*.

Kecskes, Lily (Chen Jiaren 陳家仁). "Chinese Ink and Inkmaking." *Printing History* 8 (1986): 3–12.

----. "Jinnianlai kaogu faxian de shuxie gongju" 近年來考古發現的書寫工具 (Recent Discoveries of Ancient Writing Implements). In *ZGTS*, Taibei, 91–100; Beijing, 119–32.

----. "A Study of Chinese Ink-making: Historical, Technical, and Aesthetic." Master's Thesis, University of Chicago, 1981.

Koizumi Akio 小泉顯夫 and Hamada Kōsaku 濱田耕作. *Rakurō saikyōzuka*. 樂浪彩篋冢 (The Tomb of Painted Basket and other Two Tombs of Lelang). Seoul: Society of the Study of Korean Antiquities, 1934.

Korea Review. Ed. by Homer B. Hulbert. Seoul: Printed at the Methodist Publishing House, 1901–1906.

Korean Repository, The. Ed. by Homer B. Hulbert. Seoul: Trilingual Press, 1892–1898.

Kudo, Motoo 工藤元男. "Maotai shutsudo "Sengoku juoka sho" to "Shiki" 馬王堆出土『戦国縦横家書』と『史記』 (The 'Zhanguo zongheng jiashu' and 'Shiji' Excavated at Mawangdui). *Chūgoku seishi no kisoteki kenkyū* 中国正史の基礎的研究 (Studies of Chinese History). Tokyo: Waseda University, 1984, 1–26.

Labarre, Émile J. *Dictionary of Paper and Paper-making Terms*. Amsterdam: Swets & Zeitlinger, 1937.

Lamelle, Edmund. "La propaganda du P. Nicolas Trigault en faveur des missions de Chine (1616)." *Archivum Historicum Societatis Iesu*, 9 (1940): 49–120.

Lao Gan 勞榦. "Lun Zhongguo zaozhishu zhi yuanshi 論中國造紙術之原始 (The Invention of Paper in China)." *BIHP* 19 (1948), 489–498.

Latourette, Kenneth Scott. *The Chinese: Their History and Culture*. 3rd ed., rev. New York: Macmillan, 1946.

----. *A History of Christian Missions in China*. New York: Macmillan, 1929.

Lau, D. [im]C.[heuk] 劉殿爵 (Liu Dianjue) and Chen Fangzheng 陳方正, eds. *Zhanguo ce zhuzi suoyin* 戰國策逐字索引. *A Concordance to the Zhanguoce*. Hong Kong: Commercial Press, 1992.

Laufer, Berthold. *Descriptive Account of the Collection of Chinese, Tibetan, Mongol, and Japanese Books in the Newberry Library*. Chicago: Newberry Library, 1913.

----. *Sino-Iranica: Chinese Contributions to the History of Civilization in Ancient Iran*. Chicago: Field Museum of Natural History, 1919.

Lee, Leo Ou-fan 李歐梵 (Li Oufan). *Wo de Hafo suiyue* 我的哈佛歲月 (*My Years at Harvard*). Taibei: Erya wenhua, 2005.

Legge, James, trans. *The Ch'un Ts'ew, with the Tso Chuen*. 2 vols. London: Trubner, 1871.

----. *The Li Ki*. Oxford: Clarendon Press, 1885.

----. *The Life and works of Mencius*. London: Trubner, 1875.

----. *The She King*. 2 vols. London: Trubner, 1871.

----. *The Shoo King; or The Book of Historical Documents*. London: 2 vols. Trubner, 1865.

Legman, G. "Bibliography of Paperfolding." *Journal of Occasional Bibliography*, Privately published. Malvern, Eng. 1952.

Lew, Timothy Tingfang 劉廷芳. *China in American School Textbooks: A Problem of Education in International Understanding and Worldwide Brotherhood*. Special supplement of the *Chinese Social and Political Science Review* (July 1923). Beijing: Chinese Social and Political Science Association, 1923.

Li Shuhua 李書華. "Zhi wei faming yiqian Zhongguo wenzi liuchuan gongju 紙未發明以前中國文字流傳工具 (Materials and Tools of Chinese Writing before the Invention of Paper)." *DLZZ* 1 (1955): 1–6; 2 (1955): 53–60.

Li Xueqin 李學勤. "Shilun Changsha Zidanku Chu boshu canpian 試論長沙子彈庫楚帛書殘片 (On Some Problems of the Fragments of the Chu Silk Documents Found at Zidanku, Changsha)." *WW* 11 (1992): 36–39.

Liang Qichao 梁啟超. "Jinhualun gemingzhe Jiede zhi xueshuo 進化論革命者頡德之學說 (The Theory of Benjamin Kidd, Revolutionizer of Evolution)." *Xinmin congbao* 新民叢報 (New Citizen Journal) 18 (1902).

----. *Lun yishu* 論譯書 (On Translation). In *Yinbingshi heji* 飲冰室合集 (Collected Works of Liang Qichao). 1, 64–76.

----. "Xiaoshuo yu qunzhi zhi guanxi 小說與群治之關係 (Fiction and Democracy.)" In *Yinbingshi heji* 飲冰室合集 (Collected Works of Liang Qichao). 4, 6–9.

----. *Xixue shumu biao* 西學書目表 (Bibliography and Critical Notes on Western Studies). Shanghai: Shiwu baoguan, 1896.

----. *Yinbingshi heji* 飲冰室合集 (Collected Works of Liang Qichao). Ed. by Lin Zhijun 林志鈞. Shanghai: Zhonghua shuju, 1936.

----. "Yiyin zhengzhi xiaoshuo xu 譯印政治小說序 (On Translation and Publication of Political Fiction)." In *Yinbingshi heji* 飲冰室合集 (Collected Works of Liang Qichao). 2, 34–39.

Liang Siyong 梁思永. "Xiaotun Longshan yu Yangshao 小屯龍山與仰韶 (Xiaotun, Longshan, and Yangshao)." In *CYPLWJ* 2, 555–568.

Library Quarterly. Ed. by University of Chicago, Graduate Library School. Chicago: University of Chicago Press, 1931–.

Ling Chunsheng 凌純聲. *Bark Cloth, Impressed Pottery, and the Invention of Paper and Printing* 樹皮布、印文陶與造紙印刷術發明. Taibei: Institute of Ethnography, Academia Sinica, 1963.

----. "Zhongguo gudai de shupibu wenhua yu zaozhi faming 中國古代的樹皮布文化與造
　　紙術發明 (Bark Cloth Culture and the Invention of Paper-making in Ancient China)."
　　Zhongyang yanjiuyuan lishi yuyan yanjiusuo jikan 中央研究院民族學研究所集刊
　　(*Bulletin of the Institute of Ethnology, Academic Sinica*) 11 (1961): 1–50.

Liu Dianjue 劉殿爵, *see* Lau, D. C.

Loewe, Michael, ed. *Early Chinese Texts: A Bibliographical Guide.* Berkeley: Society for the Study of
　　Ancient China, 1993. Chinese translation by Li Xueqin 李學勤 *et al. Zhongguo gudai dianji
　　daodu* 中國古代典籍導讀. Shenyang: Liaoning Education Press, 1997.

Longobardi, Nicholas (Nicolo) 龍華民 (Long Huamin 1566–1654). *Dizhen jie* 地震解 (An
　　Explanation of Earthquakes). 1626.

Loomis, Elias. *An Introduction to Practical Astronomy.* New York: Harper, 1855.

Lu Ji 陸璣 (261–303). *Maoshi caomu niaoshou chongyu shu* 毛詩草木鳥獸蟲魚疏 (On the Various
　　Plants, Birds, Animals, Insects, and Fishes Mentioned in the Book of Odes). Shanghai:
　　Commercial Press, 1936.

Lu Qian 盧前. "Shulin biehua 書林別話 (Comments on the World of Books)." 1947. Reprinted
　　in *Zhongguo jindai chuban shiliao* 中國近代出版史料 (Historical Materials on Modern
　　Publishing in China). Ed. by Zhang Jinglu 張靜廬. Beijing: Zhonghua shuju, 1957.

Lu Rong 陸容 (1436–1494). *Shuyuan zaji* 菽園雜記 (The Bean Garden Miscellany). In *CSJC.*

Lu Xun 魯迅. *Na han* 吶喊 (Cheers on the Sidelines). Shanghai: Beixin shuju, 1926.

Lu You 陸友 (14th century). *Mo shi* 墨史 (History of Ink). In *ZBZZ.*

Lu Yu 陸羽 (d. 804). *Chajing* 茶經 (Classic of Tea). In *Baichuan xuehai.*

----. *Chajing* 茶經 (Classic of Tea). In *Xuejin taoyuan* 學津討原. Shanghai: Hanfenlou, 1922.

Lun Heng 論衡, *see* Wang Chong.

Luo Changpei 羅常培. "Yesu huishi zai yinyunxue shang de gongxian 耶穌會士在音韻學上的貢獻
　　(Jesuit Contribution to Chinese Phonology)." *BIHP* 1 (1930): 3.

Luo Genze 羅根澤. "Zhanguo qian wu sijia zhuzuo shuo 戰國前無私家著作說 (Absence of
　　Books by Individual Writers before the Warring States Period)." *Gushi bian* 古史辨 4
　　(1933): 9–14, 29–61.

Luo Ji 羅濟. *Zhulei zaozhixue* 竹類造紙學 (Studies in the Making of Bamboo Paper). 1935.

Luo Zhenyu 羅振玉. *Zhensongtang jigu yiwen* 貞松堂集古遺文 (Miscellaneous Inscriptions in
　　the Luo Collection). 8 ce. 1931.

Ma Ang 馬昂 (fl. 1832). *Huobu wenzi kao* 貨布文字考 (A Study of Numismatic Inscriptions). 2 ce.
　　1924.

Ma Heng 馬衡. "Ji Han Juyan bi 記漢居延筆 (On the Brush-pen from Juyan)." *Guoxue jikan* 國
　　學季刊 (Sinological Quarterly of the National University of Peking) 3:1 (1932): 67–72.

----. "Zhongguo shuji zhidu bianqian zhi yanjiu 中國書籍制度變遷之研究 (A Brief Sketch of
　　the Evolution of the Chinese Book)." *Tushuguanxue jikan* 圖書館學季刊 (Library Science
　　Quarterly [Beiping]) 1:2 (1926): 199–213.

Malaguti, Faustino Giovita Mariano. *Leçons élémentaires de chimie.* Paris: Dezobry and E.
　　Magdeleine, 1853.

Marshman, Joshua and John Lassar 拉沙, trans. *Shengjing* 聖經 (Holy Bible). Serampore:
　　Serampore Mission, 1822.

Martin, William A. P. *The Awakening of China.* New York: Doubleday, Page & Company, 1907.

----. *A Cycle of Cathay; or, China, South and North.* New York and Chicago: F. H. Revell Co., 1896.

----. *The Siege in Peking; China Against the World.* Edinburgh, Oliphant, Anderson & Ferrier, 1900.

Martinique, Edward. "The Binding and Preservation of Chinese Double-leaved Books," *Library
　　Quarterly* 43 (1973): 227–236.

----. *Chinese Traditional Book-binding: A Survey of Its Evolution and Techniques.* Asian Library
　　Series, No. 19. San Francisco: Chinese Materials Center, 1983.

Marx, Karl. *The Communist Manifesto*. See *Gongchandang xuanyan*.

Mateer, Calvin W. *A Course of Mandarin Lessons* 官話類編 (Guanhua leibian). Shanghai: American Presbyterian Mission Press, 1892.

Mawangdui Han mu boshu 馬王堆漢墓帛書 (Silk Documents from the Han Tomb at Mawangdui, Changsha). Ed. by Mawangdui Han mu boshu zhengli xiaozu. Vol. 1–6. Beijing: Wenwu chubanshe, 1974–.

Mawangdui Han mu boshu gu ditu 馬王堆漢墓帛書古地圖 (Ancient Map on Silk Found at Mawangdui, Changsha). Ed. by Mawangdui Han mu boshu zhengli xiaozu. Beijing: Wenwu, 1977.

Mawangdui Hanmu boshu Zhanguo zonghengjia shu 馬王堆漢墓帛書戰國縱橫家書 (Silk Documents from the Han Tomb at Mawangdui, Changsha). Ed. by Mawangdui Han mu boshu zhengli xiaozu. Vol. 1–6. Beijing: Wenwu, 1976.

McCoy, William John. "Some Principles of Evolution in Form as Found in the Bronze Inscriptions of the Zhou Dynasty." M.A. Thesis, University of Chicago, 1948.

McIntosh, Gilbert. *The Mission Press in China*. Shanghai: American Presbyterian Mission Press, 1895.

Medhurst, Walter Henry 麥都思 (Mai Dousi). *Dongxi shiji hehe* 東西史記和合 (Comparative Chronology). Batavia, 1829.

Mei Yi-pao (Mei Yibao) 梅貽寶, trans. *The Ethical and Political Works of Motse*. London: Probsthain, 1929.

Mi Fu 米芾 (ca. 1100). *Shu shi* 書史 (History of Calligraphy). In *CSJC*.

Midwest Chinese Students and Alumni Services (CSAS) Newsletter 美中通訊 (Meizhong tongxun). Chicago: Midwest Chinese Students and Alumni Services, 1953–.

Miller, Constance R. "An Inquiry into the Technical and Cultural Prerequisites for the Invention of Printing in China and the West." M.A. Thesis, University of Chicago, 1975.

Milne, William. *A Retrospect of the First Ten Years of the Protestant Mission to China*. Malacca: Anglo-Chinese Press, 1820.

Min xiaoji 閩小紀 (Notes on Fujian). Ed. by Zhou Lianggong 周亮工 (1612–1672). In *CSJC*.

Ming shi 明史 (The History of the Ming Dynasty). Ed. by Zhang Tingyu 張廷玉 (1672–1755). 112 vols. In *ESSS*.

Minguo xuzuan Taizhou zhi 民國續纂泰州志 (Continuation of the *Taizhou Gazette*, Republican Period). Ed. by Zheng Fudong 鄭輔東 and Wang Yimou 王貽牟. 1930.

Morrison, Robert 馬禮遜 (Ma Lixun 1782–1834) and William Milne 米憐 (Mi Lian 1785–1822), trans. *Shentian shengshu* 神天聖書 (Holy Bible). Malacca, 1823.

Moule, A. C. "Review of *The Invention of Printing in China and Its Spread Westward* by Thomas Francis Carter." *Journal of the Royal Asiatic Society* 1 (Jan. 1926): 140–148.

Mutianzi zhuan 穆天子傳 (Account of the the Travels of King Mu). Annotated by Guo Pu 郭璞 (276–324). In *SBCK*.

Nanhua zhenjing 南華真經, *see Zhuangzi*.

Nanqi shu 南齊書 (History of the Southern Qi Dynasty, 479–502). Ed. by Xiao Zixian 蕭子顯 (489–537). In *ESSS*.

Newberry, Percy E. *Scarabs: An Introduction to the Study of Egyptian Seals and Signet Rings*. London: Archibald Constable, 1908.

Ni Wenzhenggong nianpu 倪文正公年譜 (Annalistic Biography of Ni Wengong (Ni Yuanlu). Ed. by Ni Huiding 倪會鼎 (1620–1706). In *CSJC*.

Nordstrand, Ove K. "Chinese Double-leaved Books and Their Restoration." *Libri* 17: 2 (1967): 104–130.

Nunn, G. Raymond. "Far Eastern Collections in the General Library of the University of Michigan." *FQ* 12 (May 1954): 381–382.

Nunn, G. Raymond and T. H. Tsien. "Far Eastern Resources in American Libraries." *The Library*

Quarterly 24:1 (January 1959): 27–42.

Oba Tsunekichi 小場恒吉 and Kayamoto Kamejirō 榧本龜次郎. *Rakurō Ō Kō bo* 樂浪王光墓 (The Tomb of Wang Guang at Lelang, Korea). Seoul: Society of the Study of Korean Antiquities, 1935.

Pan Jixing 潘吉星. "Dunhuang shishi xiejing zhi de yanjiu 敦煌石室寫經紙的研究 (Studies of Dunhuang Paper for Buddhist sutras)." *WW* 3 (1966): 39–47.

----. "Shijieshang zuizaodi zhiwu xianwei zhi 世界上最早的植物纖維紙 (The World's Earliest Plant Fiber Paper)." *WW* 11 (1964): 48–49.

----. "Xinjiang chutu guzhi yanjiu 新疆出土古紙研究 (Studies of Ancient Paper Specimens Unearthed in Xinjiang)." *WW* 10 (1973): 52–60.

----. *Zhongguo zaozhi jishu shigao* 中國造紙技術史稿 (History of Chinese Papermaking Technology). Beijing: Wenwu chubanshe, 1979.

Pan Mingshen 潘銘燊, *see* Poon Ming-sun.

Pelliot, Paul. "Les bronzes de la collection Eumorfopoulos publiés par M. W. P. Yetts, I et II." *T'oung Pao* 27:4/5 (1930): 359–406.

Peng Xinwei 彭信威. *Zhongguo huobi shi* [A History of Chinese Currency]. Shanghai: Renmin chubanshe, 1954. Trans. by Edward H. Kaplan as *A Monetary History of China*. Bellingham, WA: Western Washington, 1993.

Pfister, Louis. *Notices Biographiques et Bibliographiques sur les Jésuites de l'Ancienne Mission de Chine, 1552–1773*. 2 vols. Shanghai: Imprimerie de la Mission Catholique, 1932–1934. Issued originally as No. 59–60 of *Variétés sinologiques*.

Poon Ming-sun 潘銘燊 (Pan Mingshen). "Books and Printing in Sung China, 960–1279." Ph.D. dissertation, University of Chicago, 1979.

----. "Qian Cunxun jiaoshu zhushu biannian 錢存訓教授著述編年 (Bibliography (by chronology) of Professor T. H.Tsien's Writings)." In *Nanshan lunxueji*, 147–156.

----. "Qian Cunxun jiaoshou zhushu mulu 錢存訓教授著述目錄 (Bibliography (by classification) of Professor T. H.Tsien's Writings)." In *Zhong Mei shuyuan* 中美書緣 (Sino-American Cultural Relations). Taibei: Wenhua tushuguan guanli zixun, 1998, 295–298.

----, ed. *Nanshan lunxueji* 南山論學集 (Collection of Essays for Advanced Age). Beijing: Beijing Library, 2006.

Qian Cunxun 錢存訓, *see* Tsien, Tsuen-hsuin.

Qian Guisen 錢桂森. *Duan zhu Shuowen kao* 段注說文考 (Critical Study on the *Annotations of the First Dictionary*). n.p., n.d.

----. *Yisongxuan shigao* 一松軒詩稿 (Collected Poems of Qian Guisen). n.p., n.d.

Qian Han shu 前漢書, *see* Ban Gu.

Qian Shuoyou 潛說友. *Xianchun Lin'an zhi* 咸淳臨安志 (Gazetteer of Lin'an from the Xianchun period (1265–1274)). Qiantang: Wang shi zhenqi tang, 1830.

Qian Zhongshu 錢鍾書, *see* Ch'ien, C. S.

Qiu Kaiming 裘開明, *see* Ch'iu, A. Kaiming.

Quarterly Bulletin of Chinese Bibliography. Ed. by the National Library of Peiping. Shanghai: Chinese National Committee on Intellectual Cooperation, March 1934–. Imprint varies. New series March 1940–. See also Chinese version with different content *Tushu jikan* 圖書季刊.

Rao Zongyi 饒宗頤. "Changsha Chumu shizhanshenwu tujuan kaoshi 長沙楚墓時占神物圖卷考釋 (A Study of an Astrological Picture from a Changsha Tomb of the Warring States Period)." *Journal of Oriental Studies* 東方文化 (Hong Kong) 1 (January 1954): 69–84.

----. *Changsha chutu Zhanguo zengshu xinshi* 長沙出土戰國繒書新釋 (A Study of the Chu Silk Document with a New Reconstruction of the Text). Hong Kong: Yiyou changji yinwu gongsi, 1958.

----. "Changsha Zidanku Chuguo can boshu wenzi xiaoji 長沙子彈庫楚國殘帛書文字小記 (A Brief Note on the Text of the Fragments of Chu State Silk Documents Found at Zidanku, Changsha)." *WW* 11 (1992): 34–35.

----. "Chu zengshu shuzheng 楚繒書疏證 (A Brief Account of the Silk Documents of the Chu State)." *BIHP* 40 (1968): 1–32.

----. "Chu zengshu zhi moben ji tuxiang 楚繒書之摹本及圖像 (Copies and Images of the Chu State Silk Documents)." *Gugong jikan (Quarterly Bulletin of the National Palace Museum, Taipei)*. 3:2 (1968): 1–26.

Rao Zongyi 饒宗頤 and Zeng Xiantong 曾憲通. *Chu boshu* 楚帛書 (Silk Documents of the Chu State). Hong Kong: Zhonghua shuju, 1985.

Reischauer, Edwin O., trans. *Ennin's Diary: The Record of a Pilgrimage to China in Search of the Law*. New York: Ronald Press, 1955.

Renker, Armin. *Papier und Druck im Fernen Osten*. Mainz: Gutenberg-Gesellschaft, 1936.

Ricci, Matteo 利瑪竇 (Li Madou 1552–1610). *Jihe yuanben* 幾何原本 (Translation of Clavius' *Euclidis Elementorum*). 1607.

----. *Kunyu wanguo quantu* 坤輿萬國全圖 (*Il mappamondo cinese* Map of the World). Based on Ortelius' *Theatrum Orbis Terrarum*. 1584.

----. *Tianxue shiyi* 天學實義 (True Meaning of the Study of Heaven). 1596. Title later changed to *Tianzhu shiyi* 天主實義 (True Meaning of the Lord of Heaven).

----. *Xiguo jifa* 西國記法 (Arts of Memory Used Among the Western Countries). 1595.

Ritual and Reverence: Chinese Art at the University of Chicago: Catalogue. Ed. by Robert J. Poor, Edward L. Shaughnessy, Harrie A. Vanderstappen, Richard A. Born, and Sue Taylor. Chicago: David and Arthur Smart Gallery, University of Chicago Press, 1989.

Roy, David T. and Tsuen-hsuin Tsien, eds. *Ancient China: Studies in Early Civilization*. Hong Kong: The Chinese University Press, 1978.

Ruan Yuan 阮元. *Jiguzhai zhongding yiqi kuanshi* 積古齋鐘鼎彝器欵識 (Inscriptions on Bronzes in the Ruan Collection). 4 ce. 1804.

Rudolph, Richard C. "Chinese Movable Type Printing in the Eighteenth Century." In *Silver Jubilee Volume of the Zinbunkagaku Kenkyūsyo, Kyoto University*. Kyōto: Kyōto Daigaku Jinbun Kagaku Kenkyūjo, 1954, 317–335.

Ruggieri, Michel 羅明堅 (1543–1607). *Tianzhu shengjiao shilu* 天主聖教實錄 (A True Account of the Lord and Christianity). Guangzhou, 1884.

Sanborn, Kate. *Old Time Wall Papers: An Account of the Pictorial Papers on Our Forefathers' Walls, with a Study of the Historical Development of Wall Paper Making and Decoration*. Greenwich, Conn.; New York: The Literary Collector Press, 1905.

Sancai tuhui 三才圖會 (Universal Encyclopedia). Comp. by Wang Qi 王圻 (fl. 1565). 1609 edition.

Sanetō Keishū 實藤惠秀. *Nihon bunka no Shina e no eikyō* 日本文化の支那への影響 (Cultural Influence of Japan on China). Tokyo: Keisetsu Shoin, 1940.

Schall von Bell, Johann Adam 湯若望 (Tang Ruowang 1592–1666). *Huogong qieyao* 火攻挈要 (Treatise on Firearms). 1643.

----. *Kunyu gezhi* 坤輿格致 (Trans. of Agricola's *De re Metallica*). Presented to throne 1640.

----. *Yuanjing shuo* 遠鏡說 (On the Telescope; trans. of Girolamo Sirturi's *Telescopio*). ca. 1626.

Schyns, Joseph. *1500 Modern Chinese Novels and Plays*. Beijing: Catholic University Press, 1948.

Shang Chengzuo 商承祚. *Changsha guwu wenjianji* 長沙古物聞見記 (An Account of the Antique Objects Discovered at Changsha). 2 ce. Chengdu: Nanjing (Jinling) University, 1939.

----. "Zhanguo Chu boshu shulue 戰國楚帛書述略 (A Brief Account of the Chu Silk Documents of the Warring States Period)." *WW* 9 (1964): 8–20.

Shang Zhitan 商志醰. "Ji Shang Chengzuo jiaoshou cang Changsha Zidanku Chuguo can boshu 記商承祚教授藏長沙子彈庫楚國殘帛書 (The Fragmentary Silk Writings of the State of

Chu Unearthed from Zidangku in Changsha Collected by Professor Shang Chengzuo),"
WW 11 (1992): 32–33, 35.

Shaughnessy, Edward L. "1960 nian yilai Zhongguo guwenzixue de fazhan 1960 年以來中國古
文字學的發展 (Developments in Early China Paleography Since 1960), Wenxian 文獻
2005:4–2006:1; Zhongguo tushuguan xuehui huibao 中國圖書館學會會報 (Bulletin of the
Library Association of China) 74 (June 2005): 51–68. Orig. published as "Afterword" to
Written on Bamboo and Silk, 2nd edition, 2004. Trans. by Chester Wang 王正義.

----. "Zhijiage daxue suocang Shangdai jiagu 芝加哥大學所藏商代甲骨 (Inscribed Shang Oracle
Bones at the University of Chicago)." In ZGTS, Taibei, 197–208; Beijing, 231–243.

Shen Kuo 沈括 (1031–1095). Mengxi bitan 夢溪筆談 (Miscellaneous Jottings). In SBCK.

Shen, Philip 沈宣仁. "Introducing Chinese Paper-folding." Midwest Chinese Students and Alumni
Services (CSAS) Newsletter 美中通訊 (Meizhong tongxun) n.s., 2 (1958): 1.

Shi Hongbao 施鴻保 (1804–1871). Min zaji 閩雜記 (Miscellaneous Records of Fujian). Taibei: Min
Yue shuju, 1968.

Shi ming 釋名 (Explanation of Names). Comp. by Liu Xi 劉熙 (fl. 200). In SBCK.

Shi Shenghan 石聲漢. Qimin yaoshu jinshi 齊民要術今釋 (New Commentaries on the Qimin
yaoshu). 4 vols. Beijing: Science Press, 1957–1958. See also Jia Sixie.

Shiji 史記 (The Records of the Grand Historiographer). Ed. by Sima Qian 司馬遷 (ca. 145–86 B.C.).
In ESSS. Partially translated by Édouard Chavannes, Les Mémoires historiques de Se-ma Ts'ien.
5 vols. Paris, E. Leroux, 1900; Burton Watson, Records of the Grand Historian of China. 2 vols.
New York: Columbia University Press, 1961.

Shu Xincheng 舒新城. Jindai Zhongguo liuxue shi 近代中國留學史 (History of Chinese Students
Studying Abroad in Modern Times). Shanghai: Zhonghua shuju, 1933.

Shu Yuanyu 舒元輿 (d. 835). "Bei Shanxi guteng wen 悲剡溪古藤文 (The Lament of the Old
Rattan of Shanqi)." In Quan Tang wen 全唐文, 727/20a–21b. 1818.

Shuihudi Qin mu zhu jian 睡虎地秦墓竹簡 (Bamboo Tablets Found in the Qin Tomb at Shuihudi
in Yunmeng, Hubei. Ed. by Shuihudi Qin mu zhu jian zhengli xiaozu. 7 ce. Beijing: Wenwu
chubanshe. Large-character ed., 1977; paperback ed., 1978; rev. ed., 1990.

Shuijing zhu 水經注 (Commentary on the Waterways Classic). Annotated by Li Daoyuan 酈道元
(d. 527). In SBCK.

Shuofang beicheng 朔方備乘 (Complete Historical Record of the North). Comp. by He Qiutao 何
秋濤 (1824–1862). 24 vols. 1881.

Shuofu 說郛 (A Collection of Miscellaneous Writings). Comp. by Tao Zongyi 陶宗儀 (ca. 1320–
1399). 160 ce. 1647: 40 ce. 100 juan ed., 1927.

Shuowen jiezi 說文解字 (Analytical Dictionary of Characters). Comp. by Xu Shen 許慎 (ca. 58–
147). In SBCK.

Shuyuan zaji 菽園雜記, see Lu Rong.

Siegenthaler, Fred. "Tapa." In Handmade Papers of the World. Tokyo, Japan: Takeo Co., 1979.

Siku quanshu zongmu 四庫全書總目 (Annotated Bibliography of the Complete Library of the Four
Treasures). Comp. by Ji Yun 紀昀 (1724–1805). Wuyingdian, 1781.

Sima Guang 司馬光 (1019–1086). Zizhi tongjian 資治通鑑 (Comprehensive Mirror to Aid in
Government). 10 vols. Beijing: Guji chubanshe, 1956.

Sitwell, Sacheverell. British Architects and Craftsmen: A Survey of Taste, Design and Style During
Three Centuries, 1600 to 1830. London: Batsford, 1945; rev. ed. London: Pan Books, 1960.

Smogolenski, Jean-Nicholas (Smogulecki, Nikolaus) 穆尼閣 (Mu Nige 1611–1656). Tianbu
zhenyuan 天步真原 (Treatise on the Calculation of Eclipses). ca. 1656.

Sogabe Shizuo 曾我部靜雄. Shihei hattatsu shi 紙幣発達史 (The Development of Paper Money).
Tokyo: Insatsuchō, 1951.

Song shi 宋史 (Standard History of the Song Dynasty). Ed. by Tuotuo 脫脫 and Ouyang Xuan 歐

陽玄. In *ESSS*.

Song Yingxing 宋應星 (fl.1600). *Tiangong kaiwu* 天工開物 (Exploitation of Works of Nature). Shanghai: Commercial Press, 1937. *GXJB* edition. Translation by E-tu Zen Sun and Shiou-chuan Sun, *T'ien-kung k'ai-wu: Chinese Technology in the Seventeenth Century*. University Park, PA.: Pennsylvania State University Press, 1966.

Stein, Marc Aurel. *Ancient Khotan: Detailed Report of Archeological Exploration in Chinese Turkestan*. 2 vols. Oxford: Clarendon Press, 1907.

----. *Innermost Asia*. 4 vols. Oxford: The Clarendon Press, 1928.

----. *Serindia: Detailed Report of Explorations in Central Asia and Westernmost China*. 4 vols. Oxford: Clarendon Press, 1921.

Su Shi 蘇軾 (1037–1101). *Dongpo zhi lin* 東坡志林 ([Su] Dongpo's Forest of Anecdotes). In *CSJC*.

Su Yijian 蘇易簡 (953–996). *Wenfang sipu* 文房四譜 (Collected Studies of the Four Articles for Writing in a Scholar's Studio). In *CSJC*.

Sui shu 隋書 (History of the Sui Dynasty). Ed. by Wei Zheng 魏徵 (580–643) *et. al*. In *ESSS*.

Sun Haibo 孫海波. *Jiaguwen bian* 甲骨文編 (A Dictionary of Shell and Bone Inscriptions). 5 ce. Beiping: Harvard-Yenching Institute, 1934; rev. ed. Beijing: Zhonghua shuju, 1965.

Sun Yirang 孫詒讓 (1848–1908). *Zhouli zhengyi* 周禮正義 (Commentary on the *Rituals of the Zhou*). *SBBY* edition. Shanghai: Zhonghua shuju, 1934.

Taiping yulan 太平御覽 (An Imperial Encyclopedia Compiled During the Taiping Reign of the Song Dynasty). Comp. by Li Fang 李昉 (926–996) *et. al*. In *SBCK*.

Taizhou zhi 泰州志 (*Taizhou Gazette*). Ed. by Wang Youqing 王有慶 and Chen Shirong 陳世. Qing Daoguang reign (1827). See also *Taizhou xinzhi kanmiu* 泰州新志刊謬 and *Minguo xuzuan Taizhou zhi* 民國續纂泰州志.

Taizhou xinzhi kanmiu 泰州新志刊謬 (The New, Corrected *Taizhou Gazette*). Ed. by Ren Yu 任鈺 and Gong Xizuo 宮錫. 1908.

Tang guoshi bu 唐國史補 (Supplements to the History of the Tang Dynasty). Comp. by Li Zhao 李肇 (fl. 806–820). In *Jindai bishu*.

Tang liudian 唐六典 (Codes and Regulations of the Six Boards of the Tang Dynasty). Edited under Imperial Auspices of Tang Xuanzong 唐玄宗 (685–762). 8 ce. Japanese ed.: *Tō rikuten*, 1836.

Tao Zongyi 陶宗儀 (ca. 1320–1399). *Chuogeng lu* 輟耕錄. In *Jindai bishu*.

Ter[r]entius [Schreck], Joannes (1576–1630). *Renshen shuogai* 人身說概 (Explanation of the Human Body; trans. of Kaspar Bauchin's *Theatrum Anatomicum*). 1625.

Ter[r]entius [Schreck], Joannes (1576–1630) and Wang Zheng 王徵 (1571–1644). *Yuanxi qiqi tushuo luzui* 遠西奇器圖說錄最 (Collected Diagrams and Explanations of the Wonderful Machines of the Far West). Beijing, 1627.

Thomas, James. "Biographical Sketch of Alexander Wylie." In *Chinese Researches*. Ed. by James Thomas and Henri Cordier. Shanghai: n.p., 1897.

Tianxue chuhan 天學初函 (First Collectanea of Heavenly Studies). Comp. by Li Zhizao 李之藻 (1565–1630). 1629.

T'ien-hsia Monthly. Ed. by Lin Yutang 林語堂. Shanghai: Kelly and Walsh, 1935–.

Tongsu bian 通俗編 (Thesaurus of Popular Terms, Ideas, and Customs). Ed. by Zhai Hao 翟灝 (1736–1788). Wu bu yi zhai, 1751. Beijing: Commercial Press, 1958; reprint ed. Taibei: Dahua shuju, 1979.

Trigault, Nicholas 金尼閣 (Jin Nige 1577–1628). *Kuangyi* 況義 (Analogy; translation of *Aesop's Fables*). 1625.

----. *Xiru ermu zi* 西儒耳目資 (An Aid to the Eye and Ear of Western Scholars). 3 vols. 1626.

Tschichold, Jan, *see* Hu Zhengyan.

Tsien, Tsuen-hsuin 錢存訓. "An Guo 安國" and "Hua Sui 華燧." In Goodrich and Fang, eds. *Dictionary of Ming Biography*, 9P 12, 64, 7–49.

----. "Beauty Contests in Imperial China." *Midwest Chinese Students and Alumni Services (CSAS) Newsletter* 美中通訊 (Meizhong tongxun). 1965.

----. "Beiping tushuguan shanben shuji yun Mei jingguo 北平圖書館善本書籍運美經過 (Shipping the Beiping Library Rare Books to the United States)." *Zhuanji wenxue* 傳記文學 10: 2 (February 1967): 55–57.

----. "Biographies of Qi Baishi 齊白石, Gao Jianfu 高劍父, Gao Qifeng 高奇峰 and Feng Chengjun 馮承鈞." In *Biographical Dictionary of Republican China*. Ed. by Howard L. Boorman. 5 vols. New York: Columbia University Press, 1967–1979.

----. "[Bronze Movable Type Printing of Ming China: Problems of Its Origin and Technology]." In *Qingzhu Jiang Fucong xiansheng qishisui lunwenji* 慶祝蔣復璁先生七十歲論文集 (Collected Essays in Honor of the 70th Birthday of Dr. Chiang Fu-ts'ung). Ed. by Guoli gugong bowuyuan gugong jikan bianji weiyuanhui 國立故宮博物院故宮季刊編輯委員會編輯. Taibei: National Palace Museum, 1968.

----. "Chan kuo ts'e (The Stratagems of Warring States)." In *ECT*, 1–11.

----. *China: An Annotated Bibliography of Bibliographies,* in collaboration with James K. M. Cheng. Boston: G. K. Hall, 1978.

----. "China: the Birthplace of Paper, Printing and Movable Type." *UNESCO Courier*, 1972.

----. "The Chinese Background of European Printing." Paper presented at the 3rd International Conference of the History of Chinese Science and Technology, sponsored by the Chinese Academy of Sciences. Beijing, 1984.

----. "Chinese Library Association." In *Encyclopedia of Library and Information Science*, vol. 4. Ed. by Allen Kent and Harold Lancour. New York; Basel: M. Dekker, 1970.

----. "Current Status of East Asian Collections in American Libraries, 1974/75." Washington, D.C.: Center for Chinese Research Materials, Association of Research Libraries, 1976.

----. "East Asian Collections in America." In Tsuen-hsuin Tsien and Howard W. Winger, eds., *Area Studies and the Library*. Chicago: University of Chicago Press, 1966.

----. "East Asian Library Resources in America: A New Survey." *Association for Asian Studies Newsletter* 16 (February 1971): 1–11.

----. "The Evolution of the Nine Classics and Three Commentaries." In *A Sung Bibliography*. Ed. by Yves Hervouet. Hong Kong: Chinese University Press, 1978.

----. "The Far Eastern Library of the University of Chicago, 1936–1956." *FQ* 15 (May 1956): 656–658.

----. "First Chinese-American Exchange of Publications." *HJAS* 25 (1964–1965): 19–30.

----. "Handai shudao kao 漢代書刀考 (A Study of the Book-knife of the Han Dynasty)." *BIHP*, Extra volume, 4 (1961): 997–1008; translated by John Winkleman, "A Study of the Book-knife of Han China." *Chinese Culture*, 12: 1 (March 1971), 87–101.

----. "A History of Bibliographical Classification in China." *Library Quarterly* 22 (1952): 307–324.

----. *Huigu ji* 回顧集 (*Looking Back*). Guilin: Guangxi Normal University Press, 2010.

----. *Liu Mei zayi* 留美雜憶 (A Memoir of Sixty Years in America). Taibei: Biographical Literature Publishing, 2007; Heifei: Huangshan shushe, 2008.

----. *Paper and Printing*. In *Science and Civilization in China*. Ed. by Joseph Needham. Vol. 5, pt. 1. Cambridge: Cambridge University Press, 1985; 3rd rev. printing, 1987. Chinese translation by Liu Zuwei 劉祖慰, *Zhi he yinshua* 紙和印刷 (Beijing: Science Press, 1990); by Liu Tuo 劉拓 and Wang Liu Cixin 汪劉次昕, *Zaozhi ji yinshua* 造紙及印刷. Taibei: Commercial Press, 1995).

----. "The Pre-printing Records of China: A Study of the Development of Early Chinese Inscriptions and Books." Ph.D. dissertation, University of Chicago, 1957. Later published as *Written on Bamboo and Silk*.

----. "Raw Materials for Old Papermaking in China." *Journal of the American Oriental Society* 93:4 (Oct.–Dec. 1973): 510–519.

----. "Shuji, wenfang, zhuangshi yongzhi kaolue 書籍，文房，裝飾用紙烤略 (Chinese Paper for Graphic and Decorative Arts)." *Journal of the Institute of Chinese Studies of the Chinese University of Hong Kong* 香港中文大學中國文化研究所學報 9 (1978).

----. "Terminology of the Chinese Book and Bibliography." Institute for Far Eastern Librarianship, Graduate Library School, University of Chicago, 1969.

----. "Tushuguan yu xueshu yanjiu 圖書館與學術研究 (Libraries and Scholarly Research)." Journal of the University of Nanking, Division of the Humanities, 1931.

----. "Western Impact on China through Translation: A Bibliographical Study." M.A. Thesis, University of Chicago, 1952. Abstract published in *FQ* 1954.

----. *Written on Bamboo and Silk: The Beginnings of Chinese Books and Inscriptions.* Chicago: University of Chicago Press, 1962, 1963, 1969; rev. ed. 2004. Chinese ed.: *Zhongguo gudai shushi* 中國古代書史. Hong Kong: Chinese University Press, 1975, 1978; *Yinshua faming qian de Zhongguo shu he wenzhi jilu* 印刷發明前的中國書和文字記錄. Beijing: Yinshua gongye chubanshe, 1987; *Shu yu zhubo* 書於竹帛. Taibei: Hanmei tushu gongsi, 1996; 4th rev. ed., Shanghai: Shanghai shudian, 2002. Japanese ed.: *Chūgoku kodai shoseki* 中国古代書籍史trans. by Utsugi Akira 宇都木章, Sawaya Harutsugu 沢谷昭次 *et al.* Tokyo: Hōsei University Press, 1980. Korean ed.: *Chungguk kodae sŏsa* 中國古代書史, trans. by Kim Yun-ja 金允子. Seoul: Dongmoonsun Publishing Co., 1990, 1999. Reviewed by Joseph Needham, *JAS* 23:4 (1964): 604–605.

----. *Zhong Mei shuyuan* 中美書緣. Taibei: Wenhua Co., 1998; rev. ed: *Dongxi wenhua jiaoliu luncong* 東西文化交流論叢 (East-West Cultural Exchange). Beijing: Commercial Press, 2009.

----. *Zhongguo shuji zhimo ji yinshushi lunwenji* 中國書籍紙墨及印刷史論文集 (Collected Studies on the History of the Chinese Book, Paper, Ink and Printing). Hong Kong: Chinese University Press, 1992; rev. ed. *Zhongguo gudai shuji zhimo ji yinshushu* 中國古代書籍紙墨及印刷術 (Ancient Chinese Book, Paper, Ink, and Printing). Beijing: Beijing Library, 2002.

----. *Zhongguo zhi he yinshua* 中國紙和印刷文化史 (Paper and Printing in China: A Cultural History). Japanese edition 2007, Korean edition 2008.

----, ed. *Catalogue of Books in Western Languages.* 5 vols. Shanghai: National Jiaotong University Library, 1930s.

Tsien Tsuen-hsuin and Howard W. Winger, eds., *Area Studies and the Library.* Chicago: University of Chicago Press, 1966.

Tung Tso-pin 董作賓, *see* Dong Zuobin.

Tushu jikan 圖書季刊 (Quarterly Bulletin of Chinese Bibliography, Chinese version). Ed. by National Library of Peiping. Shanghai: Shijie wenhua hezuo Zhongguo xiehui. Imprint varies. March 1934–. See also *Quarterly Bulletin of Chinese Bibliography.*

Tytler, Lord, *See* Woodhouselee, Alexander Fraser.

University of Chicago, Committee on Far Eastern Studies and Library. *Far East: An Exhibition of Resources in the University of Chicago Library [at] the Joseph Regenstein Library, March–June, 1973.* Chicago: n.p., 1973.

University of Chicago, Far Eastern Library. *Catalogs of the Far Eastern Library, University of Chicago, Chicago, Illinois.* 18 vols. with supplements. Boston: G. K. Hall, 1973, 1981.

----. *Chinese Local Histories* 中文地方志目錄 (Zhongwen difangzhi mulu). Chicago, distributed by the University of Chicago Bookstore, 1969.

----. *Daisaku Ikeda collection of Japanese religion and culture.* Chicago : University of Chicago, Far Eastern Library, 1977.

----. *Far Eastern Serials.* Chicago: University of Chicago, Far Eastern Library, 1977.

----. *Selective List of Monthly Acquisitions* 新書目錄 (Xinshu mulu). 16 vols. (Title varies). Chicago: University of Chicago, Far Eastern Library, 1953–.

----. *The University of Chicago Doctoral Dissertations and Masters' Theses on Asia, 1894–1962.*

Chicago: University of Chicago, Far Eastern Library, 1962.

Vacca, Giovanni. "Della piegatura della carta applicata alla Geometria." *Periodico di Matematiche* ser. 4, 10 (1930): 43.

Vagnoni, Alphonsus 高一志 (Gao Yizhi 1566–1640). *Kongji gezhi* 空際格致 (Translation of Coimbra's *In Libros Meteorum of Aristotle*). 1633.

----. *Xixue zhiping* 西學治平 (Western Politics). 1630.

Van Gulik, R. H. *Mi Fu on Ink-stones*. Beiping: Henri Vetch, 1938.

Verbiest, Ferdinand 南懷仁 (Nan Huairen 1623–1688). *Kunyu tushuo* 坤輿圖說 (Illustrated Explanation of the Entire World). 1672.

Verhaeren, Hubert. "The Ancient Library of Pei-t'ang." *Quarterly Bulletin of Chinese Bibliography*, new series 1 (1940).

----. "Wang Zheng suoyi '*Qiqi tushuo*' 王徵所譯《奇器》 (On the Translation of the 'Illustrated Description of Mechanical Contrivances' by Wang Zheng)." *Bulletin of the Institutum S. Thomae* 2:1 (1947): 26–36.

Wan Jinli 萬金麗. *Wenfang sibao jingpin jianshang yu jiazhi* 文房四寶精品鑑賞與價值 (Appreciation and Value of Four Fine Articles in a Scholar's Studio). Beijing: Zhongguo zhigong chubanshe, 1994.

Wang Chi-chen. "Notes on Chinese Ink." *Metropolitan Museum Studies* 3: pt. 1 (1930): 114–133.

Wang Chong 王充 (ca. 27–100). *Lun Heng* 論衡 (Discourses Weighed in the Balance). In *SBCK*.

Wang Fu 王黼 (1079–1126) *et al. Xuanhe bogu tulu* 宣和博古圖錄 (Catalogue of Antique Objects in the Imperial Collection of the Song Dynasty). 30 ce. 1752.

Wang Guowei 王國維. "Jiandu jianshu kao 簡牘檢署考 (A Study of the Bamboo and Wooden Documents and the System of Sealing)." In *Haining Wang Jing'an xiansheng yishu* 海寧王靜安先生遺書 (Collected Writings of Wang Guowei), ce 26. Shanghai: Haining Wang shi, 1936.

Wang Jia 王嘉 (4th century). *Shiyi ji* 拾遺記 (Memoirs of Neglected Matters). In *Han Wei congshu* 漢魏叢書 (Collectanea of the Han and Wei Dynasties), ce 32. Shanghai: Commercial Press, 1925.

Wang Ming 王明. "Sui Tang shidai di zaozhi 隋唐時代的造紙 (Paper Manufacture During the Sui and Tang Dynasties)." *Kaogu xuebao* 11 (1956): 115–126.

Wang Quchang 王蘧常. *Yan Jidao nianpu* 嚴幾道年譜 (An Annalistic Biography of Yan Fu). Shanghai: Commercial Press, 1936.

Wang Shiduo 汪士鐸 (1802–1889). "Shi bo 釋帛 (On the Terms for Silk Textiles)." In *Wang Meicun xiansheng ji* 汪梅村先生集, [S. l.]: Hefei Zhang shi Weiguzhai kan, 1881.

Wang Yi-t'ung (Yitong) 王伊同. "The P'u-pan Chinese Library at the University of British Columbia." *Pacific Affairs* 34:1 (Spring 1961): 101–111.

Wang Yuquan 王毓銓. *Early Chinese Coinage*. New York: American Numismatic Society, 1951.

Wangdu Han mu bihua 望都漢墓壁畫 (Wall Painting of a Han Tomb Discovered at Wangdu, Hebei). Beijing: Zhongguo gudian yishu chubanshe, 1955.

Ward, John. *The Sacred Beetle: A Popular Treatise on Egyptian Scarabs in Art and History*. London: J. Murray, 1902.

Watson, Katherine, *see* Hu Zhengyan.

Wei shu 魏書 (History of the Wei Dynasty). Ed. by Wei Shou 魏收 (506–572). In *ESSS*.

Wei Yungong 魏允恭. *Jiangnan zhizaoju zhi* 江南製造局記 (An Account of the Jiangnan Arsenal). Shanghai: Wenbao shuju, 1905.

Weng Tongwen 翁同文. "Yinshuashu duiyu shuji chengben de yingxiang 印刷術對於書籍成本的影響 (The Influence of Printing Technology on the Cost of Books)." *Tsinghua Journal of Chinese Studies* 清華學報 6:1/2: 35–43.

Wenxian tongkao 文獻通考 (An Encyclopedia of Institutions). Ed. by Ma Duanlin 馬端臨 (fl.

1254–1322). 2 vols. Shanghai: Commercial Press, 1936.

Wheaton, Henry. *Elements of International Law*. London: B. Fellowes, 1836.

Wiborg, Frank Bestow. *Printing Ink: A History with a Treatise on Modern Methods of Manufacture and Use*. New York and London: Harper & Bros., 1926.

Williams, Frederick W. *The Life and Letters of Samuel Wells Williams. L.L.D.: Missionary, Diplomatist, Sinologue*. New York: Putnam, 1889.

Williams, Samuel Wells. *The Middle Kingdom*. New York & London: Wiley & Putnam, 1848.

----. *A Syllabic Dictionary of the Chinese Language*. Shanghai, American Mission Press, 1874.

Williamson, Alexander. "Report of the Committee." *The Chinese Recorder*. July 15, 1878. 9 (1878): 307–309. Published in Shanghai by the American Presbyterian Mission Press.

Wiseman, Donald J. *Cylinder Seals of Western Asia*. London: Batchwork Press, 1958.

Woodhouselee, Alexander Fraser (Lord Tytler). *Universal History, from the Creation of the World to the Beginning of the Eighteenth Century*. London: J. Murray, 1834.

Woolsey, Theodore Dwight. *Introduction to the Study of International Law*. Boston and Cambridge: J. Munroe and company, 1860.

Wu K.[wang] T.[sing] (Guangqing) 吳光清. "The Development of Typography in China during the Nineteenth Century." *Library Quarterly* 22:3 (1952): 288–301.

----. "Libraries and Book-collecting in China before the Invention of Printing." *T'ien-hsia Monthly* 5 (1937): 237–260.

Wu Zimu 吳自牧. *Mengliang lu* 夢粱錄 (Dreaming of the Capital While Rice Is Cooking). 3 vols. In *CSJC*.

Wubei zhi 武備志 (Record of Military Equipment). Ed. by Mao Yuanyi 茅元儀 (1594–1640). 1621–1627.

Wuqiu Yan 吾邱衍 (1272?–1311). *Xue gu bian* 學古編 (Studies of Antiquities). In *Shuofu* 說郛, *juan* 97, 1927 edition.

Wylie, Alexander. *Memorials of Protestant Missionaries to the Chinese*. Shanghai: American Presbyterian Mission Press, 1867.

----. *Notes on Chinese Literature: with Introductory Remarks on the Progressive Advancement of the Art; and a List of Translations from the Chinese into Various European Languages*. Reprint. Shanghai: Presbyterian Missionary Press, 1922.

Xi'an Banpo: yuanshi shizu gongshe juluo yizhi 西安半坡：原始氏族公社聚落遺址 (The Neolithic Village at Pan P'o, Sian[*sic*]). Ed. by the Institute of Archaeology, Academia Sinica. Beijing: Wenwu chubanshe, 1963.

Xijing zaji 西京雜記 (Miscellaneous Records of the Western Capital). Attributed to Liu Xin 劉歆 (d. 23) and compiled by Ge Hong 葛洪 (284–364). Shanghai: Commercial Press, 1929. In *SBCK*.

Xin Tang shu 新唐書 (New History of the Tang Dynasty). Ed. by Ouyang Xiu 歐陽修 (1007–1072). In *ESSS*.

Xiong Zhengwen 熊正文. "Zhi zai Songdai de teshu yongtu 紙在宋代的特殊用途 (Special Uses of Paper in the Song Dynasty). *Shihuo banyuekan* 食貨半月刊 5: 12.

Xu Jian 徐堅 (659–729) *et. al. Chuxue ji* 初學記 (Entry into Learning [a T'ang Encyclopedia]). 12 ce. 1883.

Yan Yiping 嚴一萍. "Chu zengshu xinkao (shang, zhong, xia) 楚繒書新考（上, 中, 下）(A New Study of the Chu State Silk Documents: Parts 1, 2, 3)." *Zhongguo wenzi* 26–28 (1967–1968).

Yang Jialuo 楊家駱. *Tushu nianjian* 圖書年鑑 (Chinese Book Annual). Nanjing: Zhongguo tushu da cidian bianjiguan, 1933.

Yang Liansheng 楊聯陞. *Money and Credit in China: A Short History*. Cambridge, Mass.: Harvard University Press, 1952.

Yang Shouqing 楊壽清. *Zhongguo chuban jie jianshi* (A Short History of the Chinese Press).

Shanghai: Yongxiang Press, 1946.

Yang Zhongxi 楊鍾羲. *Xueqiao shihua: xuji* 雪橋詩話續集 (Sequel to Snow Bridge Poetry Talks). In *Qiushuzhai congshu* 求恕齋叢書. 1917.

Yanzi chunqiu 晏子春秋 (Spring and Autumn Annals of Master Yan). Attributed to Yan Ying 晏嬰 (6th century B.C.). In *SBCK*.

Ye Dehui 葉德輝. *Shulin qinghua* 書林清話 (Plain Talks on Books). Reprint ed. Taibei: Shijie shuju, 1961.

Yetts, W. Perceval. *The George Eumorfopoulos Collection: Catalogue of the Chinese and Corean Bronze, Sculpture, Jade, Jewelery, and Miscellaneous Objects.* 3 vols. London: Ernest Benn, 1929.

Yexi yuanqi 葉戲原起 (Origins of the Leaf Game). Ed. by Wang Shihan 汪師韓 (fl. 1771–1773). In *Congmu Wang shi yishu* 叢睦汪氏遺書. Changsha, 1886.

Yili zhushu 儀禮注疏 (Commentaries on the *Book of Etiquette and Ceremonial*). Annotated by Zheng Xuan 鄭玄 (127–200) and Jia Gongyan 賈公彥 (fl. 650). Nanchang, 1887. *SSJZS* edition. See translation by John Steele, *The I-li: or, Book of Etiquette and Ceremonial.* London: Probsthain, 1917.

Ying Shao 應劭 (ca. 140–206). *Fengsu tongyi* 風俗通義 (Popular Traditions and Customs). 2 vols. Beijing: Centre franco-chinois des sinologiques, 1943. Text with index.

Yishu gonghui bao 譯書公會報 (Weekly Edition of Translation Society). Shanghai, 1897–1898.

Yixueguan kaiban zhangcheng 譯學館開辦章程 (Announcement of the Translation School). Beijing, 1903.

"Youguan Beitu cun Mei shanben yun Tai dang'an 有關北圖存美善本運台檔案 (Archival Materials Relating to the Shipping to Taiwan of the Beiping Library Rare Books Stored in the United States)." *Guoli zhongyang tushuguan guankan* 國立中央圖書館, 16:1 (1964).

Yu Chenghong 喻誠鴻 and Li Yun 李澐. *Zhongguo zaozhi yong zhiwu xianwei tupu* 中國造紙用植物纖維圖譜 (Map of Plant Fibers Used in Papermaking in China). Beijing: Science Press, 1955.

Yuan Tung-li (Tongli) 袁同禮. *Bibliography of Chinese Mathematics, 1918–1960.* Washington, D.C.: n.p, 1963.

----. *China in Western Literature 1921–1958: A Continuation of Cordier's 'Bibliotecha Sinica.'* New Haven: Far Eastern Publications, Yale University, 1958.

----. *Doctoral Dissertations by Chinese Students in Great Britain and Northern Ireland, 1916–1961.* Washington, D.C.: n.p., 1963. Reprinted from *Chinese Culture* 中國文化季刊 4:4 (March 1963).

----. *Economic and Social Development of Modern China: A Bibliographical Guide.* New Haven: Human Relations Area Files, 1956.

----. *A Guide to Doctoral Dissertations by Chinese Students in America, 1905–1960.* Washington, D.C.: n.p., 1961.

----. *A Guide to Doctoral Dissertations by Chinese Students in Continental Europe, 1907–1962.* Washington, D.C.: n.p., 1964. Reprinted from *Chinese Culture* 中國文化季刊 5:3,4; 6:1.

----. "Mingdai sijia cangshu gailue 明代私家藏術概略 (A Brief Discussion of Private Book Collectors in the Ming Dynasty)." In Hong and Yuan, *Qingdai cangshujia kao.*

----. "Qingdai sijia cangshu gailue 清代私家藏術概略 (A Brief Discussion of Private Book Collectors in the Qing Dynasty)." In Hong and Yuan, *Qingdai cangshujia kao.*

----. *Russian Works on China, 1918–1960, in American Libraries.* New Haven: Far Eastern Publications, Yale University, 1961.

----. "Sinological Literature in German, 1939–1944." *Quarterly Bulletin of Chinese Bibliography.* New series 9 (March-December 1947): 21–64.

----. "Songdai sijia cangshu gailue 宋代私家藏術概略 (A Brief Discussion of Private Book

Collectors in the Song Dynasty)." In Hong and Yuan, *Qingdai cangshujia kao*.

----. *The T. L. Yuan Bibliography of Western Writings on Chinese Art and Archaeology*. Ed. by Harrie Vanderstappen with an introduction by T. H. Tsien. London: Mansell, 1975.

----. *Yongle da dian xiancun juan mubiao* 永樂大典現存卷目表 (Table of Extant Volumes of the *Yongle da dian*). [1929].

----, ed. *Xinjiang yanjiu congkan* 新疆研究叢刊 (Collectanea of Materials on Xinjiang). Taibei: Taiwan Commercial Press, 1963–.

Yuanhe junxianzhi 元和郡縣志 (Yuanhe Gazette). Ed. by Li Jifu 李吉甫 (758–814). In *CSJC*.

Yuejue shu 越絕書 (Lost Records of the State of Yue). Ed. by Yuan Kang 袁康 (fl. 40). In *SBCK*.

Yufu zhi 輿服志 (Monograph on Ceremonies). Ed. by Dong Ba 董巴 (3rd century). Quoted in *TPYL*, 605/7a.

Yule, Henry. *The Book of Ser Marco Polo, the Venetian*. 2 vols. 3rd ed. Rev. London: J. Murray, 1903.

Yunmeng Shuihudi Qin mu 雲夢睡虎地秦墓 (The Excavation of the Qin Tomb at Shuihudi in Yunmeng, Hubei). Beijing: Wenwu chubanshe, 1981.

Zeng Ming 曾鳴. "Guanyu boshu 'Zhanguo ce' zhong Su Qin shuxin ruogan niandai wenti di shangque 關於帛書《戰國策》中蘇秦書信若干年代問題的商榷 (Some Questions of Dating the 'Su Qin shuxin' in the Silk Manuscript of the *Zhanguo ce*)." *WW* 8 (1975): 23–30.

Zhang Wenguan 張文爟. *Zhanguo ce tanzou* 戰國策譚撮. 1587.

Zhang Xitong [Chang Hsi-t'ung]. "The Earliest Phase of the Introduction of Western Political Science into China." *Yenching Journal of Social Studies* 5 (1950): 1417–1444.

Zhang Xiumin 張秀民. "Mingdai de tonghuozi 明代的銅活字 (On Bronze Movable Type of the Ming Dynasty)." *Tushuguan* 圖書館 4 (1961): 55.

----. "Qingdai de tonghuozi 清代的銅活字 (Copper Type in the Qing Dynasty)." *WW* 1 (1962): 49.

----. "Qingdai Jingxian Zhai shi de nihuozi yinben 清代涇縣翟氏的泥活字印本 (On the Books Printed with Clay Movable Type by the Zhai Family of Jing County, Anhui, in the Qing Dynasty)." *WW* 1 (1962): 30.

----. "Yuan Ming liangdai de muhuozi 元明兩代的木活字 (On Movable Wooden Type of the Yuan and Ming Dynasties)." *Tushuguan* 圖書館 1 (1962): 56.

Zhang Yanchang 張燕昌 (1738–1814). *Jinsujian shuo* 金粟箋說 (On the Paper from the Jinsu Monastery). In *CSJC*.

Zhang Yanyuan 張彥遠 (9th cent). *Lidai minghua ji* 歷代名畫記 (Catalogue of Famous Paintings). In *Jindai bishu*.

Zhang Zhidong 張之洞. *Zhang Wenxiang gong quanji* 張文襄公全集 (Collected Works of Zhang Zhidong). Ed. by Wang Shunan 王樹枏. Beijing: Wenhuazhai, 1928.

Zhang Zhongyi 張仲一. *Huizhou Mingdai zhuzhai* 徽州明代住宅 (Ming Dynasty Dwelling Houses in Huizhou). Beijing: Architectural Engineering Press, 1957.

Zhangjiashan Hanmu Hanjian zhujian zhengli xiaozu 張家山漢墓漢簡竹簡整理小組. "Jiangling Zhangjiashan Han jian gaishu 江陵張家山漢簡概述 (Han Tablets found in Zhangjiashan, Jiangling, Hubei)." *WW* 1 (1985): 9–15.

Zhanguo ce 戰國策 (Strategies of Warring States). Annotated by Gao You 高誘 (ca. 168–212) and Yao Hong 姚宏 (ca. 1100–1146). 6 ce. *SBBY* edition. Shanghai: Zhonghua shuju, 1927. See translation by J. I. Crump, Jr., *Chan-kuo ts'e*. Oxford: Clarendon Press, 1970; article by T. H. Tsien, "Chan kuo ts'e," in *ECT*, 1–11.

Zhanguo ce 戰國策 (Strategies of Warring States). Ed. by Wang Tingxiang 王廷相 (1474–1544). 1522.

Zhanguo ce 戰國策 (Strategies of Warring States). Ed. by Ge Zi 葛鼐. 1523.

Zhanguo ce 戰國策 (Strategies of Warring States). Ed. by Gong Lei 龔雷. Wu men Gong Lei 吳門龔雷, 1528.

Zhanguo ce 戰國策 (Strategies of Warring States). Ed. by Du Shi 杜詩. 1552.

Zhanguo ce 戰國策 (Strategies of Warring States). Three-color edition by Wucheng Min Qiji 烏程 閔齊伋, 1619.

Zhanguo ce (Strategies of Warring States). Ed. by Kong Guangsen 孔廣森. 3-color edition (see Min Qiji). ca. 1780.

Zhanguo ce (Strategies of Warring States). Ed. by Li Xiling 李錫齡. 3-color edition (see Min Qiji). Hongdao shuyuan 宏道書院, ca. 1850.

Zhao Weixi 趙惟熙. *Xixue shumu dawen* 西學書目答問 (Answers about Bibliography of Western Studies). China: Guiyang xueshu, 1901.

Zhao Xigu 趙希鵠 (fl. 1225–1264). *Dongtian qinglu* 洞天清錄 (Clarification of Strange Things). In *Shuofu* 說郛 (1647).

Zhejiang sheng zhengfu 浙江省政府, ed. *Zhejiang zhi zhiye* 浙江之紙業 (The Zhejiang Paper Industry). Hangzhou, 1930.

Zheng Liangshu 鄭良樹. *Zhanguo ce yanjiu* 戰國策研究 (Research on the *Zhanguo ce*). Singapore: Youlian, 1972; Taipei: Xuesheng shudian, 1972.

Zhonghua nianjian 中華年鑑 (Chinese Yearbook). Nanjing: Zhonghua nianjianshe, 1948.

Zhou Changshou 周昌壽. "Yikan kexue shuji kaolue 譯刊科學書籍考略 (A History of Translation of Scientific Works)." In *Zhang Jusheng xiansheng qishi shengri jinian lunwenji* 張菊生先生七十生日紀念論文集 (Essays Dedicated to Zhang Jusheng on His Seventieth Birthday). Ed. by Hu Shi 胡適, Cai Yuanpei 蔡元培, and Wang Yunwu 王雲五. Shanghai: Commercial Press, 1937: 425–428.

Zhou Mi 周密 (1232–1308). *Guixin zashi* 癸辛雜識 (Miscellaneous Information from Guixin Street [in Hangzhou]). In *Xuejin taoyuan* 學津討原. Shanghai: Hanfenlou, 1922.

Zhouli zhushu 周禮注疏 (Commentaries on the Rituals of Zhou). Annotated by Zheng Xuan 鄭玄 (127–200), Lu Deming 陸德明 (fl. 620), and Jia Gongyan 賈公彥 (fl. 650) with critical notes by Ruan Yuan 阮元 (1764–1849). [China]: Nanjiing shuyuan, 1887.

Zhuangzi 莊子 or *Nanhua zhenjing* 南華真經 (The Book of Master Zhuang). Annotated by Guo Xiang 郭象 (fl. 300) and Lu Deming 陸德明 (fl. 620). In *SBCK*.

Zhushu jinian 竹書紀年 (The Bambook Books [Annals]). In *Han Wei congshu* 漢魏叢書 (Collectanea of the Han and Wei Dynasties). Shanghai: Commercial Press, 1925.

Zizhi tongjian 資治通鑑, *see* Sima Guang.

INDEX

Asia: Asian studies, 193–200; impact on
America, 201–4
Asia Library (Hawai'i), 318
Asia Library (Michigan), 229
Asia Minor, 151
Asian Studies and State Universities, 203
Association for Asian Studies, 343, 378; annual
conferences, 245, 269, 327, 343, 356; grants,
199, 224
Association of American Research Libraries,
328
astronomy: books on, 165, 171, 194; cultural
exchange through, 164, 168, 169, 172
Aurel Stein Expeditions. *See also* Turkestan:
1900-1901 discoveries, 57, 123; 1908
discoveries, 28

B
Babylonia, 151, 193
Bacon, Francis, 5, 183, 371–72
Bai Juyi, 57
bai tie (visiting card), 95
Baiguan gongqing biao, 47–48
bamboo *(zhu):* influence on writing style, 5,
14; in paper, 72, 73, 75, 77, 80–83, 131–32;
products, 104, 109; as writing material,
17–18, 20–21, 149
bamboo holders, 53, 54–55
bamboo stylus, 56–57, 60
bamboo tablets, 10–11, 12, 31, 60; on ink,
116–17; official documents on, 18, 20; *Shiji*
on, 15; size and form, 21–24
Ban Gu, 65
Bank of China, 277, 289, 293
Banpo excavations, 58, 149
Bao Biao, 39–40, 41, 44
Bao Yun, 207
baobei zhuang (wrapped-back binding), 142
Baopuzi, 151n24
Baoshan Chu tomb, 54–55, 56
baptism, 299
bark cloth *(tapa),* 79, 101, 148, 148n9
Barnard, Noel, 29n24
Bartlett, Hazel, 270, 271
Bates, M.S., 279, 361
Bauchin, Kaspar: on anatomy, 168
Beal, Edwin G., 211n24, 238, 238n4, 239
'Beauty Contests in Imperial China' (Tsien,
T.H.), 328

bedding: paper in, 79, 87, 101
beichao zhi (type of paper), 131–32
Beijing collection: paper manuscripts, 75
Beijing Women's Daily, 308
Belgium, 157n46
Bencao zongmu (General view of Plants, an
herbal of Medical Plants), 212
Bergman, Folke, 56
Berkeley, Reginald, 183
Bernard, Henri, 165
bi (brush), 53, 65–67. *See also* brush *(bi)*
Bi Sheng, 136
Bian Que, 35
Bible, 4; impact on printing development, 157;
movable type printing of, 174; translations
of, 170, 220
bibliographic control. *See also* classification
systems: Far Eastern Library, 353, 354, 365;
system development for, 224
Bibliographic Literature, 266
bibliographies. *See also* individual titles and
publications: compiled by M.S. Poon,
331, 345; compiled by T.H. Tsien, 324, 325,
359, 360, 369; compiled by T.L. Yuan,
264–66; as historical records, 5, 9, 20, 92;
importance of, 371, 373–74; national, 306,
352–53, 362; of T.H. Tsien's publications,
380–92; of translated works, 163, 166; on
Zhanguoce, 34, 37–39
bibliography (studies). *See* Chinese
bibliography
Bibliography of the Song Dynasty, 38–39
*Bibliography of Western Writings on Chinese
Art and Archaeology* (Yuan, T.L.), 265
bibliology, 375
Bibliotheca Sinica (Cordier, Henri), 265
Bibliothèque Nationale de France, 342
Bicun Han tomb discoveries, 122
Bie Liqian, 331
binding techniques: bamboo and wooden
tablets, 23–24, 24–25; chinese books,
139–41, 141–43
Bingxin, 281–82
Biographical Dictionary of Republican China,
327
Biographical Literature Co., 312
Birth of China (Creel, H.G.), 242, 245
block printing. *See* woodblock printing
Bloomfield, Maurice, 194–95

East-West cultural relations: study of, 359, 378
Eastern Han dynasty: book knives, 68; historical records on, 50; ink in, 52, 61, 122; paper in, 91, 92, 117; paper production in, 73, 83; paper products in, 101; writing material in, 20; writing tools in, 52
Eastern Western Monthly Magazine, 173
Economic and Social Development of Modern China: A Bibliographical Guide, 1918-1960 (Yuan, T.L.), 265
Eddin, Ahmed Sibab, 80n29
Edkins, Joseph, 172
education: Chinese postwar, 228; civil service examination, 156, 157, 276, 324, 375; impact on printing, 157; impact on writing, 15; influence of early literature on, 4
effigies, 94, 99
Egypt, 17, 150, 151, 152, 372
Eisler, Robert: on European banking system, 98n11
Elliot, Jeanette: and T.H. Tsien Book Fund, 333
Emerson, Ralph Waldo, 203
Emperor Frederick II, 149n15
Emperor Jiaqing, 127
Emperor Jing (Liu Qi), 48
Emperor Kangxi, 338
Emperor Tongzhi, 205n4, 328, 331; first Sino-American publications exchange, 205, 208, 219
Emperor Wu (Liu Yu), 27
Emperor Wu (Liu Zhi), 49, 64
Emperor Yongle, 212
Encyclopedia of Library and Information Science, 327
Endere ruins discoveries, 123
Engels, Friedrich, 179
engraving techniques: for movable type, 138, 154n32; printing developed from, 150; for printing woodblocks, 130, 133–34; on stone tablets, 152, 154
Ennin, 156n40
erasers. See book knife *(shudao)*
Eroshenko, Vasili, 183
Erya Zhushu: on paper, 146n6; on writing brush, 53
Euclid, 164; on algebra, 172
Europe: Chinese exchange students in, 265–66; Chinese paper products in, 103,

107, 109; paper and printing in, 145, 145n1, 149, 150; paper ban, 149n15; paper cost, 149n14; paper currency, 98; paper making in, 75, 87, 95, 149; printing in, 156n35, 157–58; research trips to, 341–42; scholarly exchanges, 262–63; typography, 157n46
European scholarship on Asia, 193–94
evacuation of Americans in China, 238–39
'ever-normal granary,' 202
'Evolution of the Nine Classics and Three Commentaries' (Tsien, T.H.), 327
exchange students, 265–66, 291, 297–98, 311–12
Exhibition of Far Eastern Library Resources, 47
Explorations in the History of Science and Technology in China, 162

F
Fadeev, Alexander, 183
Fahua jing, 156n38
Fairbank, John K., 261
family life, 294–300
family reunion, 258, 293–94
Fan Ning, 76
Fan Qin, 64
Fan Xuanzi, 59
Fan Ye, 60
Fang Chaoying, 327
Fang Junshi, 206n7
Fang Xuanling, 60
Fang Yi, 338
Fang Yulu: *Fangshi mopu*, 127
Fanmatan tomb ink slabs, 55
fans, paper, 109
Fanyi guan (Translation Bureau), 177
Far East Quarterly, 371
Far Eastern Association, 199, 224
Far Eastern Library, 226, 229, 232; Asian book collection, 200; book fund, 333; collection development, 261–62, 304–6, 308–10; establishment, 242, 245; rare book collection, 306–8; services and facilities, 312–13, 364–66; staff and further collection expansion, 310–12; T.H. Tsien's career at, 289, 348, 353, 363
Far Eastern Quarterly, 303, 327, 378
Far Eastern Resources in American Libraries (Nunn, R. and Tsien, T.H.), 205n1
fascicles, 142–43

Lee, Hwa-wei, 350
Lee Ou-fan, Leo, 312
Legaist School, 243
Legge, James, 250
Lelang (Korea) excavations: ink slab
    discoveries, 64
Lew, Timothy T., 191–92
lexicons, 22, 67, 177, 180. See also *Erya zhushu*;
    Shuowen jiezi
Li Bo, 100
Li Daoyuan, 62
Li Fangfu, 262
Li Hongzao, 307
Li Kejia, 40
Li Shanlan, 172
Li Shaozhang, 199
Li Tinggui, 59
Li Xiling, 40–41
Li Xueqin, 29n24
Li Yan: reviewing T.H. Tsien, 396
Li You, 67
Li Yuan, 67n100
Li Zhao, 81
Li Zhizao: *Tianxue chuhan*, 166
Li Zongtong, 232
Li Zongtong collection, 307
Liang Dingfen, 307
Liang Qichao, 179, 179n41/189n41
Liang Shiqiu, 183
Lianhua jing, 308
liansi (fourfold), 132
Liberal Arts Education and Chinese Culture,
    244
libraries. *See also* individual libraries
'Libraries and Book-collecting in China Before
    the Invention of Printing' (Wu, K.T.), 270
Library and Research (Tsien, T.H.), 280
Library Journal: reviews on T.H. Tsien's work,
    358, 394
Library of Congress: Beiping National
    Library and, 227, 261, 262; Chinese rare
    books preservation initiative, 237–39,
    238n3, 264, 285, 341, 344, 353, 362–63; first
    publications exchange with China, 200,
    201, 329; John Crerar Library, 222, 305;
    and K.T. Wu, 267–68; Orientalia Division
    collection, 205–15, 205n2, 211n24, 214n27,
    219–20, 231, 359–60; rare book collection
    of, 306–7

Library of Congress Quarterly Journal, 271
Library Quarterly, 271, 303, 377
library sciences, 267–68, 360; at Graduate
    Library School, 301–3; studies taken by
    T.H. Tsien, 279–80, 361
lime, 82
Lin Shu, 182, 182n47
Lin Yu-tang, 268
Lin Zexu, 175
Lindley, John: *Botany*, 172
linen, 72, 87, 146
Ling Chun-sheng, 148n11/159n11
Ling Shun-sheng, 79n23, 79n24
Lishi yanjiu, 246
'List of Books on Music in Chinese and
    Japanese' (Wu, K.T. and Sakanishi, S.), 271
*List of Doctoral Dissertations on East and
    South Asia*, 312
List of Far Eastern periodicals, 312
Literary Chinese by Inductive Method (Creel,
    H.G.), 243, 315
literature. *See also Zhanguo ce*: Chinese
    impact on Western, 203; classification
    of, 5; Meiji collection, 232; quality and
    quantity of Chinese classical, 4–5; role
    in invention of printing, 156; role of
    Western, 179, 186–87; transmission of
    ancient, 9
lithography: development in, 174; early books,
    170
Liu Gongquan, 141
Liu Guojun, 352, 364
Liu Jie, 241
Liu Linsheng, 269
Liu Mei zayi (Tsien, T.H.), 360, 379
Liu Xi, 67
Liu Xiang: comment on *Zhanguo ce*, 33–34;
    compilation of *Zhanguo ce*, 34–38, 39, 43
Liujiaqu tomb ink cakes, 122
Liuqiu, 4, 195
Loewe, Michael, 46, 327, 364
London Mission Press, 173
London Times, 250
Longfellow, Henry W.: *Psalm of Life*, 206
Longmen Bookstore, 281
Longobardi, Nicholas: on earthquakes, 168
Loomis, Elias: on calculus and geometry, 172
Lopnor paper fragments, 74
Lord of Chu (Liu Wu), 48

Russell, Bertrand: publication of, 279, 361, 377
Russia, 313; book exchange with China, 208–9, 210; paper money, 98n10; relations with China, 184–85
Russian Works on China (Yuan, T.L.), 265
Ruying (Anhui province), 49
Ryder, Arthur W., 195

S

Sakanishi, S., 271
Salisbury, Edward Elbridge, 194
sandalwood *(tanpi)*, 72, 83, 109, 118
Sanskrit studies, 193, 194–95
Sawaya, Harutsugu, 335, 358
scarab beetle stamps, 151, 152
Schall von Bell, J. Adam, 168, 169
Schiffer, Jacob C., 149n13
scholarly exchanges. *See also* exchange students: arranged by T.L. Yuan, 262–63
'Scholarship, Book Production and Libraries in China, 678-1944' (Wu, K.T.), 268, 270
Schynes, Joseph, 183n49
Science and Civilisation in China (Needham, J.), 247, 250, 251–52, 359. *See also Paper and Printing*
Science and Culture in Ancient China: Selected Works of Ho Peng-Yoke, 288
sciences: exchange publications, 214; impact, 179, 186; translated works, 165–69, 171, 172, 175, 180, 185
Scientific Book Depot *(Gezhi shushi)*, 178
screens, paper, 79, 101, 104
scribes, 157
seal inscriptions, 312
seal style, 12–13, 23
sealing boards, 25–26
sealing clays: East Asian Collection, 47–51, 307
sealing technique, 25–26
seals, 12. *See also* sealing clays; printing developed from, 150–52, 150n20, 151n24, 154, 157; use as mechanical duplication method, 3
seaweed, 72, 73, 81, 85
seeds and grains exchange, 220
Seikadō Library, 335
Seward, William H., 206n8
Shakespeare, William, 181, 183
Shang Chengzuo, 29n24

Shang dynasty. *See also* bone inscriptions; stone inscriptions: books of, 18; ink in, 58; seals of, 150–51; vocabulary use during, 13; writing brushes, 53
Shang Zhitan, 29n24
Shanghai, 262; missionary presses at, 173; publishing center, 178; rare books shipment to U.S., 236–39
Shanghai Customs, 362; rare books shipment to U.S., 237
Shanghai Shuhuashe, 129n1
Shanteng paper, 76
Shanxi University, 178
Shaughnessy, Edward L., 245, 321; comment on T.H. Tsien's work, 368, 396
sheat, 53, 54, 55, 56
shell-and-bone style, 12–13, 257
shell inscriptions, 9, 293
Shen, 107n33
Shen Jin, 306
Shen Kuo, 59
Shen Pu-hai: A Chinese Political Philosopher of the Fourth Century B.C. (Creel, H.G.), 243
Sheng Hongzhi, 62
Shenghuo quanguo zongshumu, 180
Sherra, Jess H., 364
Shiji (Records of the Grand Historian), 15; course material, 243; part of study material, 243; on tapa, 148n10; and *Zhanguo ce*, 35, 38, 43
Shiming, 62
shimo (stone ink), 61–62
Shiyu (topical discourses), 35–36
Shu yu zhubo (Tsien, T.H.), 379
Shu Yuanyu, 77
shudao (book knife), 12, 65–68
Shuihudi tomb discoveries, 54, 62, 112, 116–17, 122
Shuowen jiezi (Dictionary of Characters), 146; on ink, 61; on ink slabs, 62; on paper, 146, 146n2, 146n5; on writing brush, 53
Sibubeiyao, 41, 44
Sibucongkan, 41, 44
sichao (silk note), 98
Sicily, 149n15
Siegenthaler, Fred, 148n8
Sienkiewicz, Henryk, 182
Siku, 40
Siku Quanshu, 357